CAT

INTERACTIVE TEXT

Level C Paper 6

Managing People

This Interactive Text

BPP is the **official provider** of training materials for the ACCA's CAT qualification. This Interactive Text forms part of a suite of learning tools which also includes CD-ROMs for tuition and computer based assessment, and the innovative, internet-based 'virtual campus'.

In this June 2002 edition

- Updated in the light of the examiner's review of the previous edition of this Interactive Text

- Plenty of activities, examples and quizzes to demonstrate and practise techniques

- Latest syllabus and teaching guide cross-referenced to the Text

- Updated for technical developments and recent articles

- Mind Map summaries of key syllabus topics

- Pilot Paper for Paper C6 Managing People. Full suggested solutions have been prepared by BPP Publishing

- List of key terms and full index

FOR DECEMBER 2002 AND 2003 EXAMS

BPP Publishing
June 2002

First edition 1998
Fifth edition June 2002

ISBN 0 7517 5809 4 (Previous ISBN 0 7517 0399 0)

British Library Cataloguing-in-Publication Data
A catalogue record for this book
is available from the British Library

Published by

BPP Publishing Limited
Aldine House, Aldine Place
London W12 8AW

www.bpp.com

Printed in Great Britain by WM Print
Frederick Street
Walsall
West Midlands
WS2 9NE

We are grateful to the Association of Chartered Certified Accountants for
permission to reproduce the syllabus, teaching guide and Pilot Paper Question
Bank of which the Association holds the copyright. The Pilot Paper Answer Bank
has been prepared by BPP Publishing Limited.

We are grateful to Claire Wright for the preparation of the Mind Maps
reproduced in this text.

BPP
PUBLISHING

HOW TO USE THIS INTERACTIVE TEXT

Aim of this Interactive Text

> To provide the knowledge and practice to help you succeed in the examination for C6
> *Managing People*

To pass the examination you need a thorough understanding in all areas covered by the syllabus and teaching guide.

Recommended approach

- To pass you need to be able to answer questions on **everything** specified by the syllabus and teaching guide. Read the text very carefully and do not skip any of it.

- Learning is an **active** process. Do **all** the activities as you work through the text so you can be sure you really understand what you have read.

- After you have covered the material in the Interactive Text, work through the **Pilot Paper Question Bank**, checking your answers carefully against the **Answer Bank**.

- Before you take the exam, check that you still remember the material using the following quick revision plan.

   - Read through the **chapter learning objectives**. Are there any gaps in your knowledge? If so, study the section again.

   - Read and learn the **key terms**.

   - Look at the **exam alerts**. These show the sorts of thing that are likely to come up.

   - Read and learn the **key learning points**, which are a summary of each chapter.

   - Do the **quick quizzes** again. If you know what you're doing, they shouldn't take long.

This approach is only a suggestion. You or your college may well adapt it to suit your needs.

Remember this is a **practical** course.

- Try to relate the material to your experience in the workplace or any other work experience you may have had.

- Try to make as many links as you can to the other papers at Level C.

A note on the mind map summaries

Mind maps are simply a way of plotting key points and ideas, and the relationships between them, in a visual and creative way.

- **Reviewing** mind maps is helpful for people who process information visually: the shapes and illustrations may act as an aide memoir for your revision.

- **Creating** your own mind maps is a powerful process which consolidates learning and recall by reflecting the way in which **your** brain interprets and structures information.

We have included mind map summaries in order to provide the **visual review** element, and to suggest ways in which you might begin to **create your own** mind maps, if you do not already use this powerful technique. Like everything else in this text, mind maps will work best for your learning and revision if you use them ACTIVELY.

BPP PUBLISHING

SYLLABUS

MANAGING PEOPLE

AIM

To develop knowledge and understanding of the techniques, processes and procedures which are required to ensure the efficient and effective use and deployment of human resources.

OBJECTIVES

At the completion of this module candidates should be able to:

1   describe future personnel requirements
2   describe recruitment and selection procedures
3   examine the role and process of employee development
4   explain the principles of successful team performance
5   plan, monitor and evaluate team based work activities
6   describe the principles of motivation
7   describe the elements of disciplinary and grievance procedures
8   explain the principles of effective counselling

CONTENT

(a)   Recruitment and selection process and procedures: determining requirements, job analysis, description and specification, recruitment planning, interviewing and selection.

(b)   Training and development: staff appraisal, assessing competence, learning and skills development.

(c)   Work organisation: teams and team based work organisation, objective setting, defining and allocating authority and responsibility, direction, supervision and delegation, resource allocation, project planning (outline only), establishing work standards, performance measurement.

(d)   Motivation: basic concepts and models of motivation, individual and group behaviour, effective leadership and supervision.

(e)   Working with people: effective interpersonal relationships, informing and consulting, counselling approaches and techniques, handling disagreement and conflict, grievance and disciplinary procedures.

TEACHING GUIDE

For **December 2002** exams. Look on the ACCA's website for any changes relating to June 2003 and December 2003. If there are changes, they will be reflected in the Practice & Revision Kit.

**Covered
in chapter**

Session 1
The organisation of work

1,2,3

- explain the role of the manager in the organisation of work
- identify and explain the contribution made by modern writers on management
- identify the differences between classical and modern theories of management
- identify the difference between individual and group contribution to work performance
- list the management tasks involved in organising the work of others
- outline areas of management authority and responsibility
- describe the way management can assess the work of others
- list the systems of performance reward for individual and group contribution

Session 2
The role of the supervisor

3

- examine the role of the supervisor in relation to delegation, resource allocation and project planning
- list the responsibilities of the supervisor
- explain the role of assessing staff
- illustrate ways of rewarding staff

Session 3
Team management

4,11

- define the purpose of a team
- outline the composition of successful teams
- explain the development of a team
- list team building tools
- examine ways of rewarding a team
- identify methods to evaluate team performance

Session 4
Objective setting

6

- explain the importance of objective setting
- explain the behavioural theories of objective setting
- explain the importance of understanding ethics and social responsibility
- compare and contrast the difference between corporate objectives and personal objectives
- illustrate the difference between quantitative and qualitative target setting
- outline the management role in identifying performance standards and accountability
- identify methods to measure achievement of objectives

Session 5
Authority and responsibility

1,5

- describe, recognise and understand the importance of organisational structure
- define the terms authority and responsibility
- explain the term legitimised power
- describe the process of determining authority and responsibility
- examine the case of responsibility without authority

Teaching guide

BPP
PUBLISHING

**Covered
in chapter**

Session 18
Conducting the appraisal interview

10

- identify the management skills involved in the process
- describe the process of preparation of an appraisal interview, including location of interview, pre interview correspondence
- identify the key communication skills required to conduct an effective appraisal interview
- explain the importance of feedback from the appraisal interview

Session 19
Individual development

10

- explain the link between the appraisal process and effective employee development
- describe the role of the appraisee in the process
- suggest ways in which self-development can be part of the process

Session 20
The learning process

9

- explain the process of learning in the workplace
- describe the ways in which individuals learn
- explain the effect on learning of individual differences
- outline the barriers to learning
- describe the role of management in the learning process
- suggest ways in which the organisation can motivate individuals to learn

Session 21
Skills development

9

- describe the role of the manager in work based skills development
- identify the methods used to develop skills
- outline how to plan a skills development programme
- explain the role of mentoring in the process of skills development

Session 22
Motivation, concepts and models

11

- outline the key theories on motivation
- outline the difference between content and process theories of motivation
- describe ways in which management can motivate staff
- explain the importance of the reward system in the process of motivation
- outline the importance of feedback

Session 23
Individual and group behaviour

2,11

- explain the concept of organisational culture and its limitations
- discuss the differences between individual and group behaviour
- outline the contribution of individuals and teams to organisational success
- identify work that benefits from either an individual or team approach
- compare and contrast negative and positive behaviour

BPP PUBLISHING

**Covered
in chapter**

Session 30
Grievance and discipline

14

- outline a suitable framework (both internal and external to the organisation) for dealing with grievance and disciplinary matters
- explain the need for effective organisational procedures
- explain the role of management in respect of disciplinary matters
- suggest ways in which the outcome of the disciplinary process should be communicated to the individual concerned
- outline the features of an appeals procedure

Session 31
Revision

- work organisation
- recruitment and selection

Session 32
Revision

- training and development
- motivation
- working with people

THE EXAMINATION PAPER

Assessment methods and format of the paper

Questions based on demonstrating that the candidates have acquired the above skills.

	Number of marks
Answer any four questions from a choice of five (25 marks each)	100

Time allowed: 3 hours

Prerequisite knowledge

Knowledge of Office Practice and Procedure (A2) and successful completion of Level B.

Development of Paper C6

Paper C6 provides a broad introduction to managing people. This paper provides the foundation for continuing professional development at Parts 2 and 3 of ACCA examinations.

Analysis of past papers

The analysis below shows the topics which have been examined under the current syllabus, including the CAT Pilot paper.

Marks

December 2001

1	Managerial roles: Mintzberg	25
2	Personal Development Plans	25
3	Employment references in selection	25
4	Motivation: 'content' and 'process' theories	25
5	Assertiveness and aggression	25

June 2001

1	Power, authority and delegation	25
2	Selection interviews	25
3	Training: typcs and cvaluation	25
4	Motivation: job design and financial rewards	25
5	Conflict	25

December 2000

1	Team development	25
2	Recruitment consultants	25
3	The learning organisation	25
4	Action-centred leadership	25
5	Effective communication	25

The examination paper

BPP PUBLISHING

Part A
The organisational context

Chapter 1   Organisation structure

Chapter topic list

1 The organisation
2 Organisation structures
3 Tall and flat organisations
4 Departmentation
5 Centralisation and decentralisation
6 Organisation charts
7 The organic organisation

Learning objectives

On completion of this chapter you will be able to:

Syllabus reference

- describe, recognise and understand the importance of organisation structure

c

BPP PUBLISHING

1   THE ORGANISATION

1.1   Here are some examples of organisations.

- A multinational car manufacturer (eg Ford)
- An accountancy firm (eg Ernst and Young)
- A charity (eg Oxfam)
- A local authority
- A trade union (eg Unison)
- An army

What organisations have in common

1.2   The definition below states what all organisations have in common.

KEY TERM

An **organisation** is: 'a *social arrangement* which pursues collective *goals*, which *controls* its own performance and which has a *boundary* separating it from its environment'.

1.3   Here is how this definition applies to two of the organisations listed in paragraph 1.1.

Characteristic	Car manufacturer (eg Ford)	Army
Social arrangement: individuals gathered together for a purpose	People work in different divisions, making different cars	Soldiers are in different regiments, and there is a chain of command from the top to the bottom
Collective goals: the organisation has goals over and above the goals of the people within it	Sell cars, make money	Defend the country, defeat the enemy, international peace keeping
Controls performance: performance is monitored against the goals and adjusted if necessary to ensure the goals are accomplished	Costs and quality are reviewed and controlled. Standards are constantly improved	Strict disciplinary procedures, training
Boundary: the organisation is distinct from its environment	Physical: factory gates Social: employment status	Physical: barracks Social: different rules than for civilians

(a)   Organisations are preoccupied with **performance**, and meeting or improving their standards.

(b)   Organisations contain formal, documented **systems and procedures** which enable them to control what they do.

(c)   Different people do different things, or **specialise** in one activity.

(d)   Organisations pursue a **variety of objectives** and goals.

(e)   Most organisations obtain **inputs** (eg materials), and **process** them into **outputs** (eg for others to buy).

Why do organisations exist?

1.4   Organisations achieve results which individuals cannot achieve by themselves. Organisations:

(a)   **Overcome people's individual limitations,** whether physical or intellectual.

(b)   **Enable people to specialise** in what they do best.

(c)   **Save time**, because people can work together or do two aspects of a different task at the same time.

(d)   **Accumulate** and share **knowledge** (eg about how best to build cars).

(e)   Enable people to **pool their expertise**.

(f)   Enable **synergy**: by bringing together two individuals their combined output will exceed their output if they continued working separately.

In brief, organisations enable people to be **more productive**.

How organisations differ

1.5   The enormous variety of organisations was suggested in paragraph 1.1, and organisations differ in many ways. Here are some possible differences.

Factor	Example
Ownership (public vs private)	Private sector: owned by private owners/shareholders. Public sector: owned by the government
Control	By the owners themselves, by people working on their behalf, or indirectly by government-sponsored regulators
Activity (ie what they do)	Manufacturing, healthcare
Profit or non-profit **orientation**	Business exists to make a profit. The army, on the other hand, is not profit orientated
Legal status size	Limited company or partnership
Sources of **finance**	Borrowing, government funding, share issues
Technology	High use of technology (eg computer firms) vs low use (eg corner shop)

Two key differences in the list above are what the organisation does and whether or not it is profit orientated.

1.6   **Within** a typical organisation, there are many different types of activity being carried out.

*   **Purchasing materials** and components
*   Carrying out **operations** on purchased materials and components
*   **Accounting and record keeping**, eg keeping track of costs
*   **Research and development** of new products or technologies
*   Taking **orders** from customers
*   **Planning** and implementing marketing strategies to obtain new customers.
*   **Employing** people and paying them
*   **Co-ordinating** all the above to ensure the organisation reaches its goals

BPP PUBLISHING

2 ORGANISATION STRUCTURES

KEY TERM

Organisation structure is the grouping of people into departments or section and the allocation of responsibility and authority.

2.1 Organisation structure implies a framework intended to:

(a) **Link individuals** in an established network of relationships so that authority, responsibility and communications can be controlled.

(b) **Allocate the tasks** required to fulfil the objective of the organisation to suitable individual or groups.

(c) Give each individual or group the **authority** required to perform the allocated tasks, while controlling their behaviour and use of resources in the interests of the organisation as a whole.

(d) **Co-ordinate** the objectives and activities of separate units, so that overall aims are achieved without gaps or overlaps in the flow of work.

(e) Facilitate the **flow of work**, information and other resources through the organisation.

The structure of the organisation is absolutely critical as it has a central role as the communications system of the organisation.

2.2 Organisation chart

An organisation chart illustrates the framework within which the entity operates. Among other things it includes

(a) The control system
(b) The command structure and the power structure
(c) The pattern of communications
(d) The linking mechanisms between the roles
(e) How authority is allocated
(f) How formal, specific responsibilities are allocated
(g) How tasks are allocated
(h) The flow of work (in a large and complex organisation)
(i) The inter-relationships between departments, tasks and people

2.3 Types of organisation structure

An organisation can be structured in different ways. Examples include

- by geography
- by function
- by product/brand

These are discussed later in this chapter.

2.4 Hybrid structure

One category of structure is referred to as the **hybrid** structure, which is a mixture of some or all of the other types. For example the sales department may be organised by geography, but the purchasing department by product type.

Principles of organisation

2.5 Henry **Fayol** (1841-1925), an early management theorist, suggested that all organisations should follow the guiding principles outlined in the table below.

Principle	Comment
Division of work ie specialisation	The object of specialisation is to produce more and obtain better results.
Authority and responsibility	The holder of an office should have enough authority to carry out all the responsibilities assigned to him.
Discipline	A fair disciplinary system can be a strength of an organisation.
Unity of command	For any action, a subordinate should receive orders from one boss only. Fayol saw dual command as a disease, whether it is caused by imperfect demarcation between departments, or by a superior S2 giving orders to an employee, E, without going via the intermediate superior, S1.
Unity of direction	There should be one head and one plan for each activity. Unity of direction relates to the organisation itself, whereas unity of command relates to the personnel in the organisation.
Subordination of individual interests	The interest of one employee or group of employees should not prevail over that of the general interest of the organisation.
Remuneration	It should be 'fair', satisfying both employer and employee alike.
Scalar chain	The scalar chain is the term used to describe the chain of superiors from lowest to highest rank. (This is discussed in section 3 below.)

2.6 Henry Mintzberg took a slightly different approach, and said that an organisation can co-ordinate itself by various methods.

Method of co-ordination	Description
Mutual adjustment	Informal communication between people doing the work.
Direct supervision	One person supervises everybody and tells everybody what to do.
Standardisation of **work** processes	There is a uniform procedure for each task which is always adopted. For example, bank reconciliations in an accounts department must be done every week, no matter who does the work.
Standardisation of **outputs**	The results of work are specified, the means are not.
Standardisation of skills and knowledge	For example, all teachers have to be trained before being let loose in the classroom.

Other 'classical' theorists

2.7   The German writer Max Weber was inclined to regard **bureaucracy** as the ideal form of organisation, because it is impersonal and rational, based on a set pattern of behaviour and work allocation, and not allowing personality conflicts to get in the way of achieving goals.

2.8   Weber regarded an organisation as an **authority structure**. He was interested in why individuals obeyed commands, and he identified three grounds on which **legitimate authority** could exist.

(a)   **Charismatic leadership**: the leader is regarded as having some special power or attribute.

(b)   **Traditional, or patriarchal leadership**: authority is bestowed by tradition or hereditary entitlement, as in the family firm. Decisions and actions are bound by precedent.

(c)   **Bureaucracy**: authority is bestowed by dividing an organisation into jurisdictional areas (production, marketing, sales and so on) each with specified duties. Authority to carry them out is given to the **officials in charge**, and rules and regulations are established in order to ensure their achievement. Leadership is therefore of a '**rational-legal**' nature: managers get things done because **their orders are accepted as legitimate and justified.**

KEY TERMS

A **bureaucracy** is 'a continuous organisation of official functions bound by rules' (Weber).

*   **Authority structure**. In a bureaucracy people obey instructions because their superiors have authority that is legitimate and rational.

*   **Continuous organisation**. The organisation does not disappear if people leave: new people will fill their shoes.

*   **Official functions**. The organisation is divided into areas (eg production, marketing) with specified duties. Authority to carry them out is given to the officials in charge.

*   **Rules**. A rule defines and specifies a course of action that must be taken under given circumstances.

Characteristics of bureaucracy

2.9

Characteristic	Description
Hierarchy	An organisation exists even before it is filled with people. Each lower office is under the control and supervision of a higher one.
Specialisation and training	There is a high degree of specialisation of labour. Employment is based on ability, not personal loyalty.
Professional nature of employment	Officials are full-time employees; promotion is according to seniority and achievement; pay scales are prescribed according to the position or office held in the organisation structure.

Characteristic	Description
Impersonal nature	Employees work full time within the impersonal rules and regulations and act according to formal, impersonal procedures.
Rationality	The jurisdictional areas of the organisation are determined rationally. The hierarchy of authority and office structure is clearly defined. Duties are established and measures of performance set.
Uniformity in the performance of tasks	Procedures ensure that, regardless of who carried out the tasks, tasks should be executed in the same way.
Technical competence	All officials are technically competent. Their competence within the area of their expertise is rarely questioned.
Stability	The organisation changes rarely.

2.10 **Benefits of bureaucracy**

(a) Bureaucracies are **ideal for standardised, routine tasks**. For example, processing driving licence applications is fairly routine, requiring systematic work.

(b) Bureaucracies can be very efficient.

(c) **Rigid adherence to procedures is necessary** for **fairness**, adherence to the **law, safety** and **security** (eg procedures over computer use).

(d) **Some people like** the structured, predictable environment.

2.11 **Problems with bureaucracy**

(a) It results in **slow decision-making**, because of the complexity of the organisation.

(b) Uniformity creates **conformity**.

(c) Bureaucracies can **inhibit people's personal growth**.

(d) Bureaucracies are **bad at innovation**: they can repress creativity and initiative.

(e) Bureaucracies find it **hard to learn from their mistakes**.

(f) Bureaucracies are **slow to change**. *Crozier* stated that 'a system of organisation whose main characteristic is its rigidity will not adjust easily to change and will tend to resist change as much as possible'.

(g) **Communication is restricted** to the established structures, and important information may avoid detection.

(h) Bureaucracies find it hard to deal with change in their environment.

Modern theories of management

2.12 Modern management theorists have moved away from 'classical' organisational principles such as those outlined by Fayol. They instead emphasise values such as the following.

(a) **Multi-skilling.** Contrary to the idea of specialisation, multi-skilled teams enable tasks to be performed more flexibly, using labour more efficiently.

(b) **Flexibility.** This is perhaps the major value of modern management theory. Arising from the competitive need to respond swiftly (and without organisational trauma) to rapidly-changing customer demands and technological changes, organisations and processes are being re-engineered. This has created the following.

(i) Smaller, multi skilled, temporary structures, such as project or task-force teams.

(ii) Multi-functional units, facilitating communication and co-ordination across departmental boundaries. This is called **matrix organisation**, and it blurs the principle of 'unity of command', since an employee may report both to his department superior **and** to a project or product manager whose job is to manage all areas of activity related to the product or project.

(iii) Flexible deployment of the labour resource, for example through part-time and temporary working, contracting out tasks, flexitime, annual (rather than daily) hours contracts and so on.

(c) **Empowerment**. An article in *Personnel Management* (11/93) included definitions of empowerment from a number of leading figures in business.

(i) 'The purpose of empowerment is to free someone from rigorous control by instructions and orders, and give them freedom to take responsibility for their ideas and actions, to release hidden resources, which would otherwise remain inaccessible.'

(ii) 'It means people using their own judgement in the interests of the organisation and the customer, within a disciplined context.'

(iii) 'What [companies] mean by empowerment varies dramatically. ... Many of them are really talking about firing middle management. But companies which are really serious are talking about the orderly distribution of power and authority.'

2.13 We will consider the structural implications of these modern theories below.

Activity 1.1

Jason, Mark, Gary and Robbie set up in business together as repairers of musical instruments - specialising in guitars and drums. They are a bit uncertain as to how they should run the business, but when they discuss it in the pub, they decide that attention needs to be paid to three major areas: taking orders from customers, doing the repairs (of course) and checking the quality of the repairs before notifying the customers.

Suggest three ways in which they could structure their business.

---

3 TALL AND FLAT ORGANISATIONS

Span of control

KEY TERM

The **span of control** refers to the number of subordinates immediately reporting to a superior official.

3.1 Span of control or 'span of management', refers to the number of subordinates responsible to a superior. In other words, if a manager has five subordinates, the span of control is five.

3.2 Various classical theorists such as Urwick and Graicunas suggest the following.

(a) There are physical and mental **limitations** to any given manager's ability to control people, relationships and activities.

(b) There needs to be **tight managerial control** from the top of an organisation downward. The span of control should therefore, they argued, be **restricted**, to allow maximum control consistent with the manager's capabilities: usually between three and six. If the span of control is too wide, too much of the manager's time will be taken up with **routine problems and supervision**, leaving less time for planning. Even so, subordinates may not get the supervision, control and communication that they require.

3.3 On the other hand, if the span is too **narrow**, the manager may fail to delegate, keeping too much routine work to himself and depriving subordinates of decision-making **authority** and **responsibility**. There may be a tendency to interfere in or over-supervise the work that is delegated to subordinates - and the relative costs of supervision will thus be unnecessarily high. Subordinates tend to be dissatisfied in such situations, having too little challenge and responsibility and perhaps feeling that the superior does not trust them.

3.4 **Influences on span of control**

(a) A manager's **capabilities** limit the span of control. These are the physical and mental limitations to any single manager's ability to control people and activities.

(b) The **nature of the manager's work load**

The more non-supervisory work in a manager's workload:

- The narrower the span of control
- The greater the delegation of authority to subordinates

(c) The **geographical dispersion** of subordinates.

(d) **Subordinates' work:** if all subordinates do similar tasks a wide span is possible

(e) The **nature of problems** that a supervisor might have to help subordinates with. Time consuming problems suggest a narrow span of control.

(f) The degree of **interaction between subordinates**. If subordinates can help each other, a wide span is possible.

(g) If **close group cohesion** is desirable, a narrow span of control might be needed.

(h) The amount of **help that supervisors receive** from other parts of the organisation.

Tall and flat organisations

3.5 The span of control concept and the scalar chain concept have implications for the 'shape' of an organisation.

> **KEY TERMS**
>
> A **tall organisation** is one which, in relation to its size, has a large number of levels of management hierarchy. This implies a **narrow** span of control.
>
> A **flat organisation** is one which, in relation to its size, has a small number of hierarchical levels. This implies a **wide** span of control.
>
> **Delayering** is the reduction of the number of management levels from bottom to top.

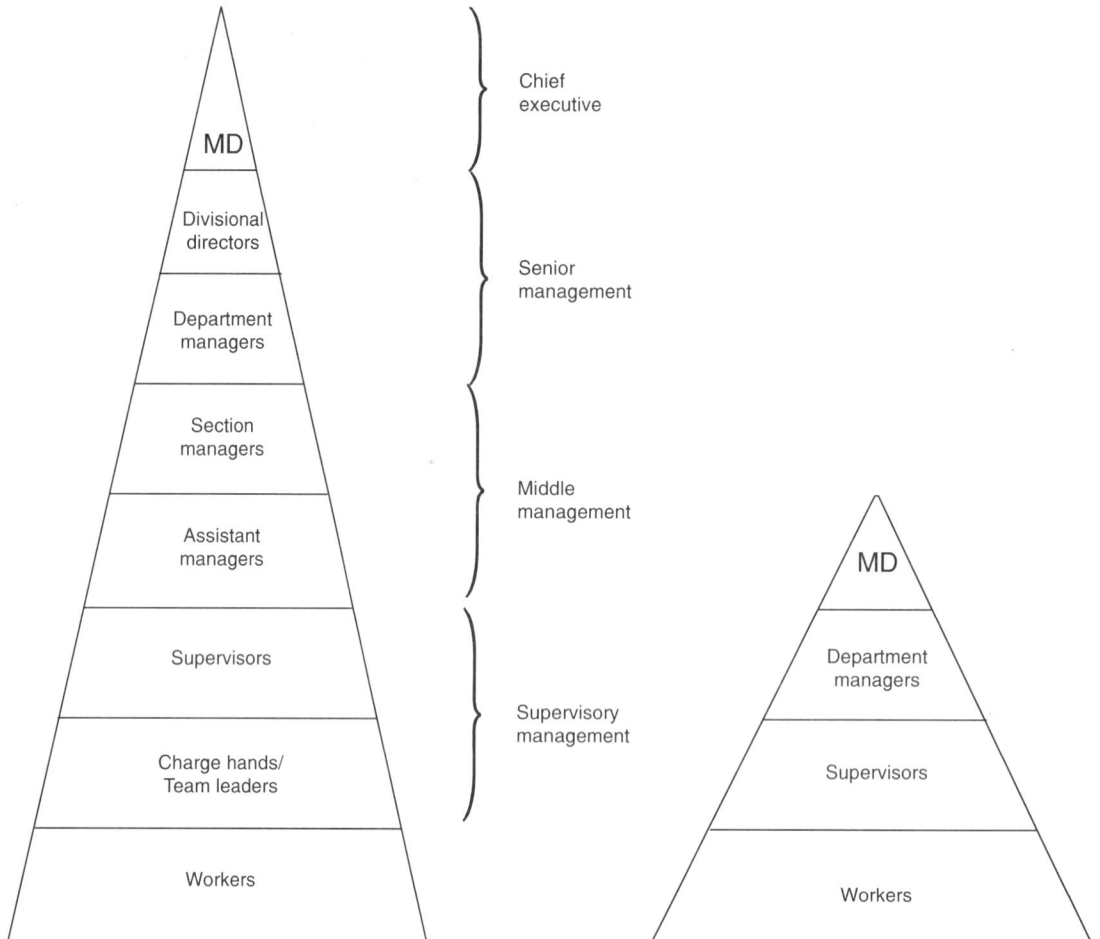

Tall organisation

For	Against
Narrow control spans	Inhibits delegation
Small groups enable team members to participate in decisions	Rigid supervision can be imposed, blocking initiative
A large number of steps on the promotional ladders - assists management training	The same work passes through too many hands
	Increases administration and overhead costs
	Extra communication problems, as the strategic apex is further away

Flat organisation

For	Against
More opportunity for delegation	Implies that jobs **can** be delegated. Managers may only get a superficial idea of what goes on. If they are overworked they are more likely to be involved in crisis management
Relatively cheap	Sacrifices control
In theory, speeds up communication between strategic apex and operating core	Middle managers are often necessary to convert the grand vision of the strategic apex into operational terms

3.6 Many organisations are delayering. Middle line jobs are vanishing. Organisations are increasing the average span of control, are reducing management levels and are becoming flatter. Why?

(a) **Information technology** reduces the need for middle managers to process information.

(b) **Empowerment.** Many organisations, especially service businesses, are keen to delegate authority down the line to the lowest possible level. Front-line workers in the operating core are allowed to take decisions. This is because it is often the best way to satisfy customers. This perhaps removes the needs for some middle management jobs.

(c) **Fashion.** Delayering is fashionable, so if senior managers believe that tall structures are inherently inflexible they might cut the numbers of management levels.

4 DEPARTMENTATION

4.1 In most organisations, tasks and people are grouped together in some rational way: on the basis of specialisation, say, or shared technology or customer base. This is known as **departmentation**. Different patterns of departmentation are possible, and the pattern selected will depend on the individual circumstances of the organisation.

Geographic departmentation

4.2 **Geographic area**. Some authority is retained at Head Office but day to day operations are handled on a territorial basis (eg Southern region, Western region). (Within many sales departments, the sales staff are organised territorially.)

(a) **Advantages**

(i) There is **local decision-making** at the point of contact between the organisation (eg a salesperson) and its customers suppliers or other stakeholders.

(ii) It may be **cheaper sometimes** to establish area factories/offices than to service markets from one location (eg costs of transportation and travelling may be reduced).

(b) **Disadvantages**

(i) **Duplication** and possible loss of economies of scale might arise. For example, a national organisation divided into ten regions might have a customer liaison department in each regional office. If the organisation did all customer liaison work from head office it might need fewer managerial staff.

(ii) **Inconsistency in standards** is likely to develop, ie there might be different standards adopted in different areas.

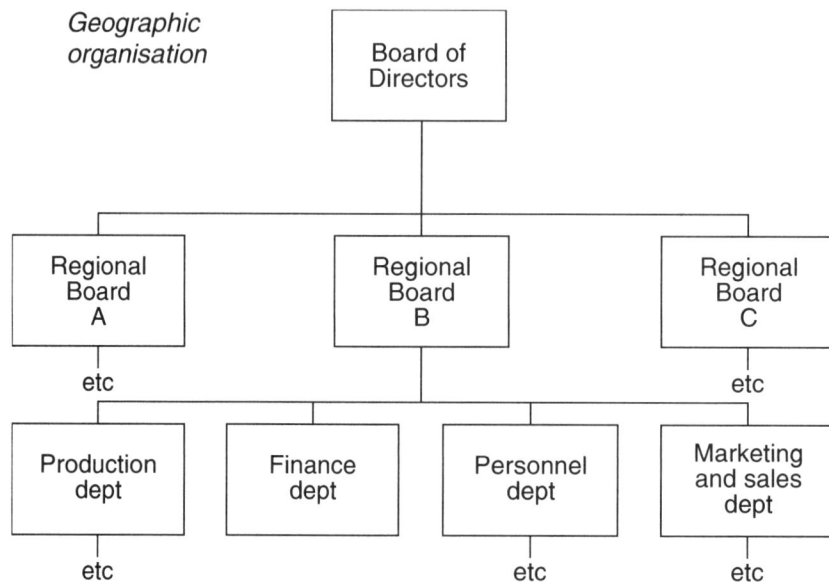

Geographic organisation

```
                        ┌─────────────┐
                        │  Board of   │
                        │  Directors  │
                        └─────────────┘
                               │
        ┌──────────────────────┼──────────────────────┐
 ┌─────────────┐        ┌─────────────┐        ┌─────────────┐
 │  Regional   │        │  Regional   │        │  Regional   │
 │   Board     │        │   Board     │        │   Board     │
 │     A       │        │     B       │        │     C       │
 └─────────────┘        └─────────────┘        └─────────────┘
      etc                      │                    etc
        ┌──────────────┬───────┴───────┬──────────────┐
 ┌─────────────┐ ┌─────────────┐ ┌─────────────┐ ┌─────────────┐
 │ Production  │ │  Finance    │ │ Personnel   │ │ Marketing   │
 │   dept      │ │   dept      │ │   dept      │ │ and sales   │
 │             │ │             │ │             │ │   dept      │
 └─────────────┘ └─────────────┘ └─────────────┘ └─────────────┘
      etc                              etc             etc
```

Function

4.3 **Functional organisation** involves setting up departments for people who do similar jobs. Primary functions in a manufacturing company might be production, sales, finance, and general administration. Sub-departments of marketing might be selling, distribution and warehousing.

(a) **Advantages**

(i) **Expertise is pooled** thanks to the division of work into specialist areas.

(ii) It **avoids duplication** (eg one management accounts department rather than several) and helps ensure economies of scale.

(ii) It makes **easier** the **recruitment**, training, and motivation of professional specialists.

(iv) It suits **centralised** businesses.

(b) **Disadvantages**

(i) It is organisation by **internal work**, rather than by **customer or product**, which are what ultimately drive a business. The customer is only interested in the product, and functional structure may not be the best at satisfying the customer.

(ii) **Communication problems** may arise between different functions, who each have their own jargon.

(iii) **Poor co-ordination**, especially if rooted in a **tall** organisation structure. Decisions by one function/department involving another might have to be referred upwards, and dealt with at a high level, thereby increasing the burdens on senior management.

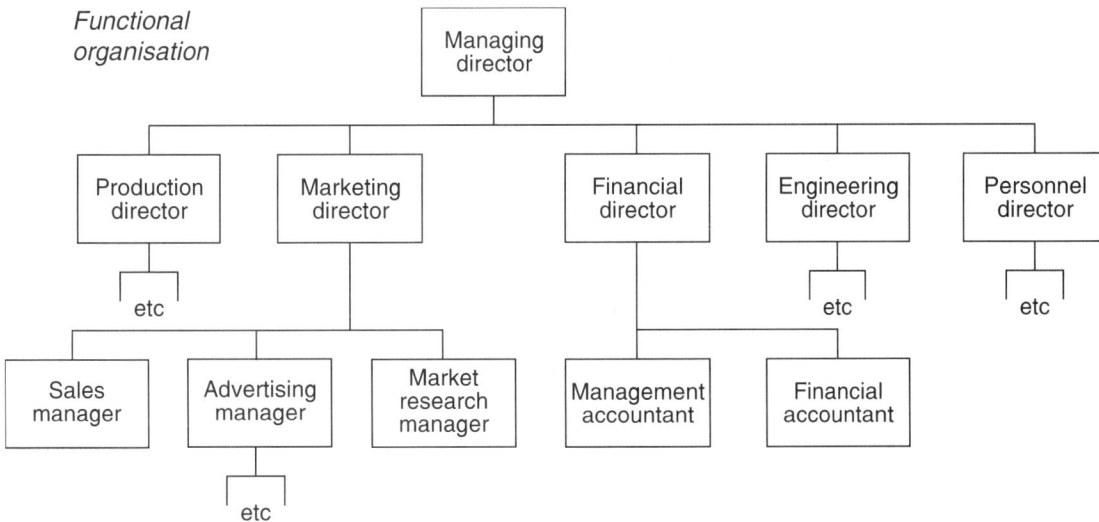

Functional organisation

Product/brand departmentation

4.4 Some organisations group activities on the basis of **products** or product lines. Some functional departmentation remains (eg manufacturing, distribution, marketing and sales) but a divisional manager is given responsibility for the product or product line, with authority over personnel of different functions.

(a) **Advantages**

(i) **Accountability**. Individual managers can be held **accountable** for the **profitability** of individual products.

(ii) **Specialisation**. For example, some salespeople will be trained to sell a specific product in which they may develop technical expertise and thereby offer a better sales service to customers.

(iii) **Co-ordination**. The different functional activities and efforts required to make and sell each product can be co-ordinated and integrated by the divisional/product manager.

(b) **Disadvantages**

(i) It **increases the overhead costs** and managerial complexity of the organisation.

(ii) Different product divisions may **fail to share resources** and customers.

4.5 **By brand**. A brand is the name (eg 'Persil') or design which identifies the products or services of a manufacturer or provider and distinguishes them from those of competitors. (Large organisations may produce a number of different brands of the same basic product, such as washing powder or toothpaste.) Branding brings the product to the attention of buyers and creates **brand loyalty** - often the customers do not realise that two 'rival' brands are in fact produced by the same manufacturer.

(a) Because **each brand is promoted and sold in its own way** it becomes necessary to have brand departmentation. As with product departmentation, some functional departmentation remains but brand managers have responsibility for the brand's marketing and this can affect every function.

(b) Brand departmentation has similar advantages and disadvantages to product departmentation.

BPP PUBLISHING

Product/brand organisation

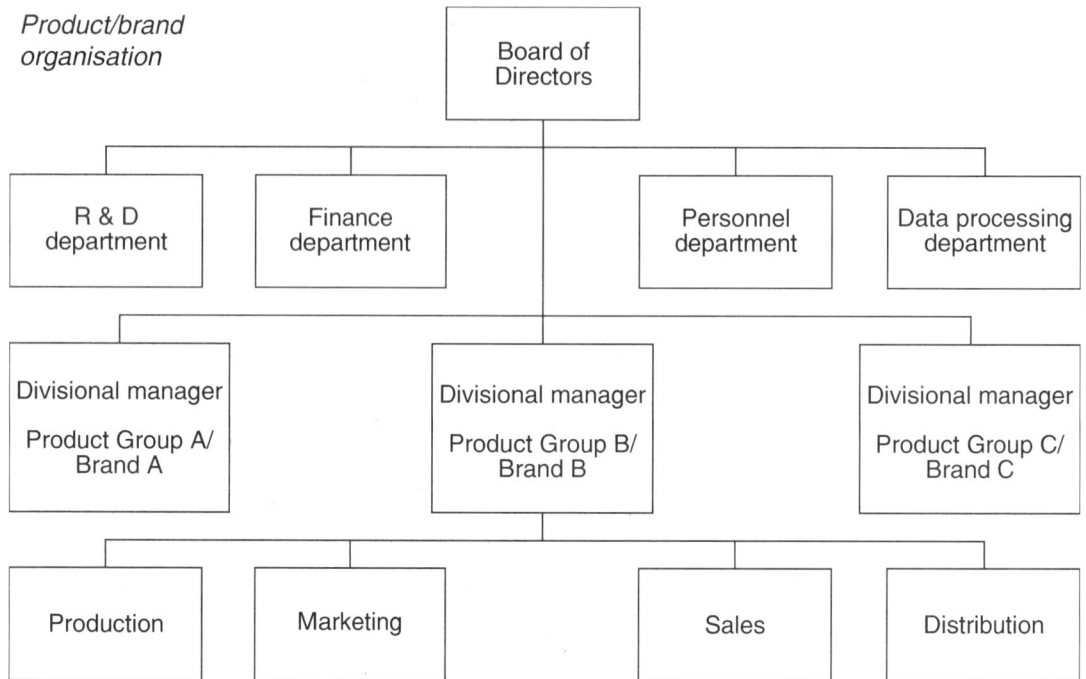

Customer departmentation

4.6 An organisation may organise its activities on the basis of types of customer, or market segment.

(a) Departmentation by customer is commonly associated with **sales departments** and selling effort, but it might also be used by a jobbing or contracting firm where a team of managers may be given the responsibility of liaising with major customers (eg discussing specifications and completion dates, quality of work, progress chasing etc).

(b) Many businesses distinguish between **business** and **household** customers.

Divisionalisation

KEY TERM

Divisionalisation is the division of a business into **autonomous** regions or product businesses, each with its own revenues, expenditures and capital asset purchase programmes, and therefore each with its own profit and loss responsibility.

4.7 Each division of the organisation might be:

- Subsidiary companies under the holding company
- Profit centres or investment centres within a single company

4.8 **Successful divisionalisation**

(a) Each division must have **properly delegated authority**, but must be held properly accountable to head office (eg for profits earned).

(b) Each unit must be **large enough** to support the quantity and quality of management it needs.

(c) It **must not rely on head office** for excessive management support.

(d) Each unit must have a **potential for growth** in its own area of operations.

(e) There should be scope and **challenge in the job for the management** of each unit.

(f) If units deal with each other, it should be as an **'arm's length' transaction**. There should be no insistence on preferential treatment to be given to a 'fellow unit' by another unit of the overall organisation.

4.9 **Advantages**

(a) It **focuses the attention of management** below 'top level' on business performance.

(b) It **reduces the likelihood of unprofitable products** and activities being continued.

(c) It encourages a **greater attention to efficiency**, lower costs and higher profits.

(d) **Knowledge.** The manager of the unit knows better than anyone else how he is doing, and needs no one to tell him. Senior managers need only set broad targets for achievement.

(e) It gives **more authority to junior managers**, and therefore provides them with work which grooms them for more senior positions in the future.

(f) It provides an organisation structure which **reduces the number of levels** of management. The top executives in each division should be able to report directly to the chief executive of the holding company.

4.10 **Disadvantages**

(a) It is **not always practical**. In some businesses, it is impossible to identify completely independent products or markets for which separate divisions can be set up.

(b) Divisionalisation is only possible at a fairly senior management level, because there is a **limit** to how much **independence** in the division of work can be arranged. For example, every product needs a manufacturing function and a selling function.

(c) There may be more **resource problems**. Many divisions get their resources from head office which chooses between other divisions. If it were an independent company, the division might find it easier to raise money.

Activity 1.2

Why do you think a diversified conglomerate might have a relatively small head office, despite the large number of businesses in the group?

Matrix and project organisation

Matrix

4.11 As discussed earlier, matrix organisation 'crosses' **functional** and **product/customer/project** organisation.

BPP PUBLISHING

		Production Dept	Sales Dept	Finance Dept	Distribution Dept	R & D Dept	Marketing Dept
Area Manager A*							
Area Manager B*							
Area Manager C*							

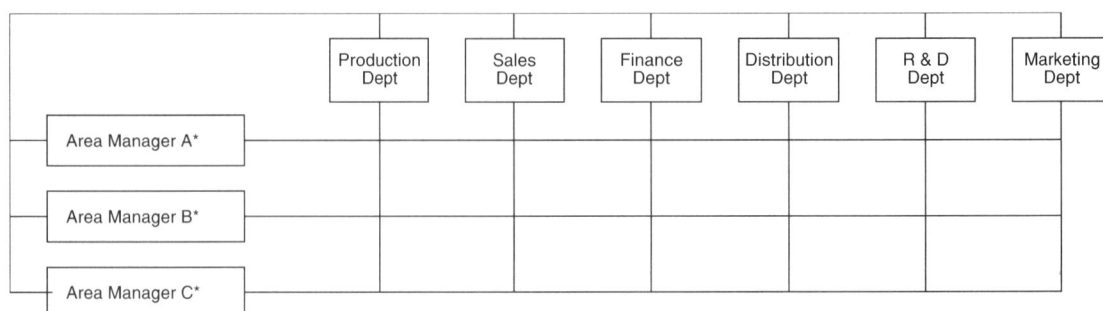

4.12 Advantages

(a) Greater **flexibility**

    (i) **People**. Employees develop an attitude geared to accepting change, and departmental monopolies are broken down.

    (ii) **Tasks and structure**. The matrix structure may be readily amended.

(c) **Better inter-disciplinary co-operation** and a mixing of skills and expertise.

(d) **Motivation by providing employees** with greater participation in planning and control decisions.

4.13 Disadvantages

(a) Dual authority threatens a **conflict** between functional managers and product/ project area managers.

(b) An individual with two or more bosses is more likely to suffer **stress** at work.

(c) Matrix management can be **more costly** - product management posts are added, meetings have to be held, and so on.

(d) **Slower decision making.**

The new organisation

4.14 Some recent trends and ideas on organisation structure include the following.

(a) **Flat structures.** The flattening of hierarchies does away with levels of organisation which lengthened lines of communication and decision-making and encouraged ever-increasing specialisation. Flat structures are more responsive, because there is a more direct relationship between the organisation's strategic centre and the operational units serving the customer.

(b) **'Horizontal structures'.** What Tom Peters (*Liberation Management*) calls 'going horizontal' is a recognition that functional versatility (through multi-functional project teams and multi-skilling, for example) is the key to flexibility. In the words (quoted by Peters) of a Motorola executive: 'The traditional job descriptions were barriers. We needed an organisation soft enough between the organisational disciplines so that ... people would run freely across functional barriers or organisational barriers with the common goal of getting the job done, rather than just making certain that their specific part of the job was completed.'

(c) **'Chunked' and 'unglued' structures.** So far, this has meant teamworking and decentralisation, or empowerment, creating smaller and more flexible units within the overall structure. Charles Handy's 'shamrock organisation' (with its three-leafed structured of core, subcontractor and flexible part-time labour) is gaining ground as a workable model for a leaner and more flexible workforce, within a controlled framework.

(d) **Output-focused structures**. The key to all the above trends is the focus on results, and on the customer, instead of internal processes and functions for their own sake. A **project management** orientation and structure, for example, is being applied to the supply of services within the organisation (to internal customers) as well as to the external market, in order to facilitate listening and responding to customer demands.

(e) **'Jobless' structures.** Meanwhile, the employee becomes not a job-holder but the vendor of a portfolio of demonstrated outputs and competencies. However daunting, this is a concrete expression of the concept of **employability**, which says that a person needs to have a portfolio of skills which are valuable on the open labour market: employees need to be mobile, moving beween organisations rather than settling in to a particular job.

5 CENTRALISATION AND DECENTRALISATION

5.1 A centralised organisation is one in which authority is concentrated in one place. For example, if you meet a sales person who always says 'Sorry, I'll have to refer that to head office', this implies that the organisation is centralised.

5.2 We can look at centralisation in two ways.

(a) **Geography**. It used to be the case in Russia that trivial decisions in the province had to be referred thousands of miles away to a Ministry in Moscow. In some firms decision might have to be constantly referred to head office.

(b) **Authority**. Centralisation also refers to the extent to which people have to refer decisions upwards to their superiors.

5.3 The table on the next page summarises some of the key issues.

Arguments in favour of centralisation and decentralisation

Pro centralisation	*Pro decentralisation/delegation*
1 Decisions are made at one point and so are easier to co-ordinate.	1 Avoids overburdening top managers, in terms of workload and stress.
2 Senior managers in an organisation can take a wider view of problems and consequences.	2 Improves motivation of more junior managers who are given responsibility-important since job challenge and cntrcprcncurial skills arc highly valued in today's work environment.
3 Senior management can keep a proper balance between different departments or functions - eg by deciding on the resources to allocate to each.	3 Greater awareness of local problems by decision makers. Geographically dispersed organisations should often be decentralised on a regional/area basis.
4 Quality of decisions is (theoretically) higher due to senior managers' skills and experience.	4 Greater speed of decision making, and response to changing events, since no need to refer decisions upwards. This is particularly important in rapidly changing markets.
5 Possibly cheaper, by reducing number of mangers needed and so lower costs of overheads.	5 Helps junior managers to develop and helps the process of transition from functional to general management.
6 Crisis decisions are taken more quickly at the centre, without need to refer back, get authority etc.	6 Separate spheres of responsibility can be identified: controls, performance measurement and accountability are better.
7 Policies, procedures and documentation can be standardised organisation-wide.	7 Communication technology allows decisions to be made locally, with information and input from head office if required.

---

6   ORGANISATION CHARTS

6.1   Organisation charts, such as those used to illustrate Section 4 above, are a traditional way of setting out in diagrammatic form:

(a)   The **units** (departments etc) into which the organisation is divided and how they relate to each other

(b)   The formal **communication** and reporting **channels** of the organisation

(c)   The **structure** of **authority, responsibility and delegation** in the organisation including, for example, the extent of decentralisation and matrix authority relationships

(d)   Any **problems** in the above: insufficient delegation, long lines of communication or unclear authority relationships.

6.2   So far we have seen the most common **vertical organisation chart**. There are alternatives.

(a)   The **horizontal chart**. This may suggest a less hierarchical, more horizontal organisation style of culture, in which the superior-subordinate nature of relationships is played down.

Horizontal

```
                ┌ Sales        ┌ Financial
                │   director   │   accountant
                │              │
                │ Finance      │ Management
   MD ──────────┼   director   ┼   accountant
                │              │
                │ Production   │
                └   director   └ Treasurer
```

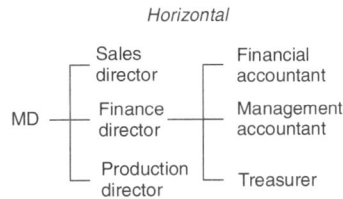

(b) **The concentric chart,** in which levels of the hierarchy are shown in circles spreading outwards from the centre.

(c) **Matrix charts,** as shown in paragraph 4.11, which use both vertical and horizontal elements to show dual authority.

(d) '**Metaphors**', such as Charles Handy's 'cloverleaf' or 'shamrock' organisation structure, pyramids, network spider-webs – or any illustration the organisation finds helpful.

Exam alert

In December 1999, a question was set on the ways an organisation might be structured, and their advantages and disadvantages (see Section 4 of this chapter). It also asked you to define what an organisation chart demonstrates. Remember to think carefully about what this, and any other management 'tool', is really able to accomplish.

6.3 Note that organisation charts only give an **impression** of the structure and self-image of the organisation. They can aid managerial thinking and communication, but have limitations.

(a) They are a **static** model, while organisations are **dynamic**, constantly changing. It must be realised that charts are like snapshots of the organisation frozen in time. They go swiftly **out of date**.

(b) They show only the **formal structure** of authority and communication. As we see in Chapter 2, there is a lot of **informal** influence and communication going on in an organisation that the average chart does not show.

BPP PUBLISHING

(c) They describe the **structure** of the organisation – **not** the organisation itself, its **mission** and **values**, its people and activities.

Activity 1.3

Get hold of a copy of your organisation's chart. (Check the Office Manual, or ask the Personnel Department.) What does it tell you about the organisation, the role of the Accounts Department, and your position within it? If no chart is available, try drawing one!

---

7 THE ORGANIC ORGANISATION

7.1 A radical departure from the bureaucracy is the **organic organisation**. The term was coined by Burns and Stalker, who contrasted organic organisations with **mechanistic** organisations. 'Mechanistic organisation' is really another term for bureaucracy, as we discussed in paragraph 2.7 above in the context of Weber's work.

7.2 **Mechanistic and organic organisations**

Item	Mechanistic	Organic
The job	Tasks are specialised and broken down into subtasks	Specialist knowledge and expertise is **understood** to contribute to the common task of the concern
How the job fits in	People are concerned with completing the task **efficiently**, but are not concerned with how the task can be made to improve organisational **effectiveness**.	Each task is seen and understood to be set by the **total situation** of the firm: people are concerned with the task insofar as it contributes to **organisational effectiveness**
Co-ordination	**Managers** are responsible for co-ordinating tasks	People adjust and redefine their tasks through interaction with others. This is rather like co-ordination by **mutual adjustment**
Job description	There are **precise** job descriptions and delineations of responsibility	Job descriptions are **less precise**: it is harder to pass the buck
Commitment	**Doing the job** takes priority over serving the interests of the organisation	**Commitment to the organisation** concern spreads beyond any technical definition
Legal contract vs common interest	**Hierarchic** structure of control. An individual's performance assessment derives from a **contractual relationship** with an impersonal organisation	**Network structure** of control. An individual's job performance and conduct derive from a supposed **community of interest** between the individual and the organisation, and the individual's colleagues. (Loyalty to the team is an important control mechanism)
Decisions	Decisions are taken by senior managers who are assumed to know everything	Relevant technical and commercial knowledge can be located anywhere. 'Omniscience is no longer imputed to the head of the concern.'

Communication patterns	Communication is mainly **vertical** (up and down the scalar chain), and takes the form of **commands** and obedience.	Communication is **lateral** (eg along gangplanks) and communication between people of different rank represents **consultation**, rather than command
Content of communications	Operations and working behaviour are governed by **instructions** issued by superiors	Communication consists of **information and advice** rather than instructions and decisions
Mission	Insistence on **loyalty** to the concern and **obedience** to superiors.	Commitment to the organisation's **mission** is more highly valued than loyalty as such
Internal vs external expertise	**Internal knowledge** (eg of the organisation's specific activities) is more highly valued than general knowledge	'Importance and prestige attach to **affiliations and expertise valid** in the industrial, technical and commercial milieus **external to the firm**'

7.3 Organic organisations have their own structures and control mechanisms.

Feature	Description
Status	Although organic systems are not hierarchical in the way that bureaucracies are, there are **differences of status**, determined by people's greater expertise, experience and so forth.
Commitment	The degree of **commitment** employees have to the firm is more **extensive** in organic than in mechanistic systems. This is similar to the idea that an organisation's mission should motivate and inspire employees.
Shared values and culture	The reduced importance of hierarchy is replaced by 'the development of **shared beliefs and values**'. In other words, corporate **cultures** becomes very powerful.

7.4 The organic and mechanistic approaches represent **two ends of the spectrum**: there are intermediate stages between bureaucratic and organic organisations. Different departments of a business may be run on different lines.

BPP PUBLISHING

Key learning points

- An organisation is a **social arrangement** which pursues **collective goals**.

- Many organisations are based on the principle of **hierarchy**. There is a line of decision making power from the top of the organisation to the bottom. In general, no employee reports to two bosses, whereas the boss may manage a number of different employees. This **scalar chain** is intimately connected to the concept of **span of control**, which is the number of individuals under the direct supervision of any one person.

- Recent trends have been towards **delayering** organisations of levels of management. In other words, **tall organisations** (with many management levels, and narrow spans of control) are turning into **flat organisations** (with fewer management levels, wider spans of control) as a result of technological changes and the granting of more decision making power to front line employees.

- Organisations can be **departmentalised** on a **functional** basis (with separate departments for production, marketing, finance etc), a **geographical** basis (by region, or country), a **product** basis (eg world wide divisions for product X, Y etc), a **brand** basis, or a **matrix** basis (eg someone selling product X in country A would report to both a product X manager and a country A manager). Some organisations might feature a variety of these types.

- In a **divisional structure** some activities are **decentralised** to business units or regions. **Centralisation** offers control, but sacrifices local knowledge and flexibility.

- Modern management theory stresses **flexibility** as a key value, and organisational measures such as matrix and horizontal structures, multi-skilling, empowerment and flexible labour deployment are currently being explored.

- *See the Part A mind map summary on page 38.*

Quick quiz

1 List the principles of organisation.

2 List methods of co-ordination.

3 What is span of control?

4 What is delayering?

5 What is functional organisation?

6 What is a matrix organisation?

Answers to quick quiz

1 Division of work; authority and responsibility; discipline; unity of command; unity of direction; subordination of individual interests; remuneration; scalar chain.

2 Mutual adjustment, direct supervision; standardisation (of work process, outputs, skills and knowledge).

3 The number of subordinates immediately reporting to a given official.

4 The reduction in the number of management levels.

5 People are grouped together as they do similar work.

6 A matrix organisation crosses functional boundaries and involves overlapping chains of command.

Answers to activities

Answer 1.1

The group has identified three major functions of their business (sales, repairs and quality control) and to main product areas (guitars and drums). They might decide to structure the business in the following ways.

(a)   Have one 'general manager' (whose responsibilities may include quality control) and three 'operatives' who share the sales and repair tasks.

(b)   Divide tasks by function: have one person in change of sales, one quality controller and two repairers (perhaps one for drums and one for guitars).

(c)   Divide tasks by product: have a two-man drums team (who share sales/repair/control tasks between them) and a similar guitar team.

Since there are only four individuals, each (we assume) capable of performing any of the functions for either of the products, they may decide to have a looser social arrangement. They may prefer to discuss who is going to do what, as and when jobs come in. A larger organisation would not have this luxury.

Answer 1.2

Here are a couple of possibilities.

(a)   The various businesses are so different that there are few scale economies that can be made by integrating functions.

(b)   Head office management might be committed to delegation: they might prefer to let the business managers get on with the job of managing providing they come up with the results at the end of the year.

Chapter 2   Organisation culture

Chapter topic list

1   Organisation culture

2   Excellence

3   The informal organisation

⊕ **Learning objectives**

On completion of this chapter you will be able to:

Syllabus reference

- explain the concept of organisation culture and its limitations   d

BPP PUBLISHING

1   ORGANISATION CULTURE

KEY TERM

An **organisation culture** contains 'assumptions about the basis of power and influence, about what motivates people, how they think and learn, how things can be changed. These assumptions result in quite different styles of management structures, procedures and reward systems'. (*Handy*)

Schwartz and Davies describe organisational culture as 'the collection of traditions, values, policies, beliefs and attitudes that constitute a pervasive context for everything we do and think in an organisation'.

A widely accepted simple and informal description of culture is 'The way we do things around here'. If you think of the concept of organisational culture within your own organisation, you may appreciate that this is a very cogent definition

Exam alert

This topic is specifically mentioned in the Teaching Guide. The examiner has said that 'this session must encourage an understanding of that which is meant by organisational culture and its effect upon the organisational structure, operations and management'.

1.1   Elements of organisation culture

Item	Example
Beliefs and values, which are often unquestioned	'The customer always prefers good quality to a cheaper price'
Customs: acceptable ways of behaviour, sometimes enforced by rules	Few organisations have a dress code as explicit as BT's. In the City of London, standard business dress is taken for granted.
Artefacts: tools, buildings office layout	**Microsoft** encourages communication between employees by setting aside spaces for the purpose
Rituals: formal, repeated behaviour	In some firms, sales people compete with each other, and there is a reward, given at a ceremony, for the salesperson who docs best in any period
Symbols: signs which stand in for other signs	**Corporate logos.** British Airways has recently decided to internationalise its image from being formal, aloof and too 'British', to being more culturally diverse, reflecting the fact that most of its customers are not British

KEY TERM

Culture embraces the norms, values and standards of an organisation.

- **Norms** are visible elements, status symbols and rules
- **Values** are connected to moral codes such as honesty
- **Standards** tell employees how to think, feel and perceive

BPP PUBLISHING

1.2 **Manifestations of culture**

An organisation culture takes shape in:

- How formal the organisation **structure** is
- **Communication:** are managers approachable?
- Attitudes to **quality**
- Office **layout**
- The type of **people** employed
- **Symbols, legends,** corporate **myths**

- **Management** style
- **Freedom** for subordinates to show initiative
- Attitudes to **risk**
- Attitudes to the **customer**
- Attitudes to **technology**

Activity 2.1

What do you think would differentiate the culture of

- A regiment in the army

- An advertising agency?

1.3 **Characteristics of culture**

Characteristic	Comment
Exclusive	Organisation culture reinforces a sense of identity, but can suppress important information inconsistent with the culture
Group	A culture is shared: it sets criteria by which people are judged
Coherent	The assumptions of a culture should reinforce each other
Consistent over time	A culture gives its participants a sense of continuity
Consequences	The group's or the individual's actions follows on from the culture
Supportive	Some activities are justified if they are consistent with the culture
Pattern	The way a member of staff treats a customer might reflect the way a member of staff is treated by his or her superior
Offers solutions to dilemmas	A culture helps people act on persistent problems (eg cost vs quality)
Cultures can learn	Cultures can change over time

Some different organisation cultures

1.4 Charles Handy (in *Gods of Management*) believes that organisation cultures (and in fact structures) can be grouped into four different 'ideal' types. To each type, Handy attached the name of a Greek deity. In Ancient Greece people followed a particular god, not out of contempt for all the others, but accepting that each god represented a particular **trait or set of values** (Mars for soldiers etc). Handy holds that this is true of organisations which do different things.

Zeus

1.5   **Zeus** is the god representing the **power culture** or **club culture**

Characteristic	Comment
Based on personalities	Zeus is a dynamic entrepreneur who rules with snap decisions. Power and influence stem from a central source, perhaps the owner-directors or the founder of the business. Important decisions are made by key people. Employees will try to second guess what the boss thinks.
Adaptable and informal	The organisation is not rigidly structured, and is capable of adapting quickly to meet change. However, success in adapting will depend on the luck or judgement of the key individuals who make the rapid decisions.
Small size	Personal influence decreases as the size of an organisation gets bigger. The power culture is therefore best suited to smaller entrepreneurial organisations, where the leaders have direct communications with all employees.
Good personal relations	People have to get on well with each other for this culture to work. Staff have to empathise with each other. These organisations are like clubs of 'like-minded people ... working on empathetic initiative with personal contact rather than formal liaison.'

This may be expressed as a **web**. The boss sits in the centre, surrounded by ever widening circles of intimates and influence. The diagonal lines represent **business functions** (eg finance, marketing) but these are less important than the concentric circles.

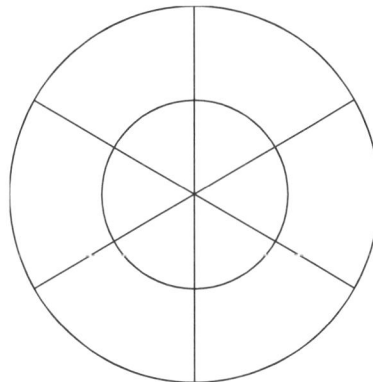

Apollo

1.6   Apollo is the god of the **role culture** proper place. There is a presumption of logic and rationality, or **bureaucracy.** Everything and everybody are in their proper place.

Characteristic	Comment
Formal structure, rules and procedures	Job descriptions establish definite tasks for each person's job and procedures are established for many work routines, communication between individuals and departments, and the settlement of disputes and appeals.
Process orientated	Individuals are required to perform their job to the full, but not to overstep the boundaries of their authority.

Characteristic	Comment
Roles, not personalities	The organisation structure defines the authority and responsibility of individual managers, who enact the **role** expected of their position. As many people are capable of doing the same job, the efficiency of this organisation depends on the structuring of jobs and the design of communications and formal relationships, rather than on individual personalities.
Not entrepreneurial	Individuals who work for such organisations tend to learn an expertise without experiencing risk; many do their job adequately, but are not over-ambitious.
Stability	The bureaucratic style can be very efficient in a stable environment when the organisation is large, where the work is predictable.
Slow to change	Unfortunately, bureaucracies are very slow to adapt to change and respond to change by doing more of the same (eg by generating cross functional liaison teams and a bureaucracy to support them).

This may be expressed as a Greek temple. A series of job boxes make up the functions (the pillars) which are then co-ordinated through the pediment at the top.

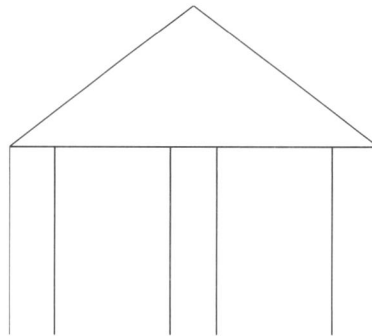

Athena

1.7 **Athena** is the goddess of the **task culture**. Management is seen as completing a succession of **projects** or **solving problems,** often as **part of a team**.

Characteristic	Comment
Team based	The task culture is reflected in a matrix organisation or else in project teams and task forces. In such organisations, there is no dominant or clear leader
Get the job done	The principal concern in a task culture is to get the job done
Expertise	The individuals who are important are the experts with the ability to accomplish a particular aspect of the task. Each individual in the team considers he has more influence than he would have if the work were organised on a formal 'role culture' basis. Expertise and talent are more important than length of service.
Results-orientated	Performance is judged by results. Such organisations are flexible and constantly changing. For example, project teams are disbanded as soon as their task has been completed

Characteristic	Comment
Costly, because of variety	Task cultures are expensive. Experts demand a market price. Task cultures also depend on variety. To tap creativity requires a tolerance of perhaps costly mistakes. They are ideal when funds are available. Where cost is a worry, controls are necessary.
Job satisfaction	Job satisfaction tends to be high owing to the degree of individual participation and group identity. But this type of structure might only be successful if the nature of the work is suited to matrix project organisation or project work, and the employees of the organisation want the work organised in this way

A net which can pull its cords this way and that and can regroup at will illustrates this culture. This also means that resources are easy obtained from all parts of the organisation. These cultures are suited to organisations who are concerned with problem solving and short-term one-off exercises. Young, energetic people are attracted to this type of organisation.

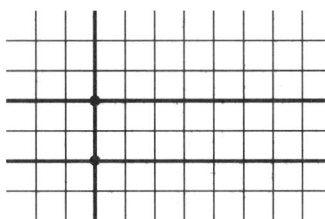

Dionysus

1.8 Dionysus is the god of the **existential culture**. In the three cultures so far, the individual is subordinate to the organisation or task. An existential culture is found in an organisation whose purpose is to **serve the interests of the individuals within it**. These organisations are rare.

Case examples

(a) Studio artists look on their job as a means of expressing themselves artistically.

(b) University lecturers might use their official position as a springboard from which to launch a wider career.

(c) Doctors come together to provide a practice.

(d) Barristers (in the UK) work through chambers. The clerk co-ordinates their work and hands out briefs, but does not control them.

1.9 The organisation depends on the talent of the individuals - a set of stars that operate independently. They may be pulled into clusters more like the task culture or collegial model. The difference is that management is derived from the consent of the managed, rather than the delegated authority of the owners. Management in these organisations are often lower in status than the professionals and are labelled secretaries, administrators, bursars, registrars and chief clerk.

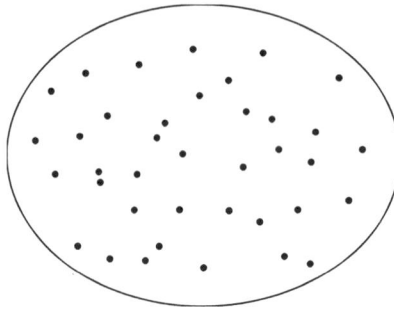

1.10 The descriptions above interrelate four different strands:

- The **individual**
- The type of **work** the organisation does
- The **culture** of the organisation
- The **environment**

1.11 Organisational effectiveness perhaps depends on an **appropriate fit** of all of them.

Case example

Handy cites a pharmaceutical company which at one time had all its manufacturing subcontracted, until the turnover and cost considerations justified a factory of its own. The company hired nine talented individuals to design and run the factory. Result:

(a) The **design team** ran on a task culture, with a democratic/consultative leadership style, using project teams for certain problems. This was successful while the factory was being built.

(b) After its opening, the factory, staffed by 400, was run on similar lines. There were numerous problems. Every problem was treated as a project, and the workforce resented being asked to help sort out 'management' problems. In the end, the factory was run in a slightly more autocratic way. Handy states that this is a classic case of an **Athenian** culture to create a factory being superseded by an **Apollonian** culture to run it. Different cultures suit different businesses.

Activity 2.2

Review the following statements. Ascribe each of them to one of Handy's four corporate cultures.

People are controlled and influenced by:

(a) The personal exercise of rewards, punishments or charisma

(b) Impersonal exercise of economic and political power to enforce procedures and standards of performance

(c) Communication and discussion of task requirements leading to appropriate action motivated by personal commitment to goal achievement

(d) Intrinsic interest and enjoyment in the activities to be done, and/or concern and caring for the needs of the other people involved

---

1.12 Organisations, says Handy, have a tendency to develop Apollonian cultures because of **comparability** and **consistency**.

(a) **Consistency** in behaviour enables better planning and greater cost-effectiveness.

(b) **Comparability** is necessary so that effort can be directed at the most needy areas. Operational efficiency in different locations can be compared.

1.13 **Large size and consistency** are desirable from the control standpoint. However, 'Size ... brings formality, impersonality and rules and procedures in its train... Similarly, consistency implies budgets, norms, standardised methods, fixed reporting periods, common documents and the whole barrage of bureaucracy.' Handy believes that there are three 'strands of resistance' to Apollo.

(a) As an organisation gets larger, it becomes internally more complex and unmanageable.

(b) Apollonian cultures put the role above the individual. Individuals resent it.

(c) **Changes in society**. 'There is in other words a growing clash in Western Society between organisation logic and the feelings of the individual'. Handy goes on to say that this is encouraged by an education system that values self-expression and team work as opposed to rote learning.

Changing culture

1.14 A rigidified culture can lead directly to bankruptcy. Baker warned that: 'changing the distinctive culture of a large, old organisation is enormously difficult and may take years'. Most research suggests between three and eight years.

1.15 Kilmann suggests the following steps for closing 'culture gaps'.

Step 1. Find out about what 'norms' of behaviour are currently present. In other words, find out about attitudes toward performance/excellence, teamwork, communication, leadership, profitability, staff relations, customer relations, honesty and security, training and innovation.

Step 2. Decide the ways in which norms need to be changed

Step 3. Establish new norms. This needs:

- Top management commitment
- Leadership by example
- Support for positive behaviour and confrontation of negative behaviour
- Consistency between reward system and positive behaviour
- Communication of desired norms
- Recruitment and selection of the 'right' people
- Induction programmes for new employees on the desired norms
- Training and skills development

Step 4. Identify culture gaps between the norms

Step 5. Close culture gaps

2 EXCELLENCE

2.1 Excellent companies, according to Peters and Waterman, are good at:

- Producing commercially viable **new products**
- Responding to **changes in their environment**

2.2 Peters and Waterman noted that **excellent companies share certain characteristics**.

1	A bias for action and experimentation, for 'getting on with it'.
2	Closeness to the customer - quality, service and reliability. Many get their best ideas from customers.
3	Autonomy and entrepreneurship.
4	Productivity through people; at Texas Instruments, every worker is 'seen as a source of ideas, not just a pair of hands'.
5	Hands-on management, driven by value: managers walking factory floors to find out what is going on.
6	'Stick to the knitting' - stick with what you know and can run.
7	Simple structures, small numbers of top-level staff. Matrix structures are unpopular; most are very simple, often with many relatively small autonomous divisions.
8	Simultaneous loose-tight properties - they are at once centralised and decentralised. Autonomy is allowed on the shop-floor and in project teams but all parts of the organisation must adhere to core values.

2.3   For many years, Peters believed the central theme of Western thinking on management was that managers make decisions in a rational way. Complex logical and mathematical methods were developed for the process: decision trees, critical path analysis etc. In other words, the dominant culture was Apollonian.

2.4   However, behaviour in organisations is also about creativity, emotion, hunches, gut reactions, politics, enthusiasm and other unquantifiable human qualities that do not fit well into the rational model.

Generating an 'excellent' culture

2.5   Peters and Waterman argue that employees can be 'switched on' to extraordinary loyalty and effort in the following cases.

(a)   **Mission.** The cause is perceived to be in some sense great. Commitment comes from believing that a task is inherently worthwhile. Devotion to the **customer,** and the customer's needs and wants, is an important motivator in this way.

(b)   **Positive reinforcement.** People are treated as winners. Success should be recognised and rewarded. 'Label a man a loser and he'll start acting like one.' Repressive control systems and negative reinforcement break down the employee's self-image. Positive reinforcement can satisfy people's dual need to be:

  •   A conforming, secure part of a successful team
  •   Stars in their own right

(c)   **Loose-tight management** means applying control (through firm central direction, and shared values and beliefs) but also allowing maximum individual autonomy (at least, the illusion of control) and even competition between individual or groups within the organisation. Culture, peer pressure, a focus on action, customer-orientation etc are 'non-aversive' ways of exercising control over employees.

2.6   **The trouble with 'excellence'**

(a)   **'One best way'.** Handy's approach was that different jobs and different people need different cultures. Excellence does not seem to welcome this diversity.

(b)   **Not international.** 'Excellence', MBWA and so forth might reflect specifically **American** business culture.

(c) **Excellent companies can fail.** Many of the sample of 'excellent' companies faltered in their performance since Peters and Waterman's work was first outlined, such as Wang Laboratories and IBM, which faced massive changes in the computer industries.

(d) **Tom Peters has rejected 'excellence'.** Peters declared in *Thriving on Chaos* that 'there are no excellent companies' and proposed flexibility instead. Key issues are the 'usual suspects':

- Flexibility
- Very loose 'organic' structures
- Delayering

Activity 2.3

You are the consultant to a large airline. As you walk through its offices, you notice that people's job titles are on their office doors, not their names. Late one evening as you leave you encounter one of the senior directors overlooking the airport. 'They're all here', he says, 'the whole fleet, apart from one which is due back from Switzerland in half an hour.' 'What if you wish to fly to Switzerland **tonight?**' you ask. 'Go by Helvetic Airways. None of this lot are leaving until tomorrow morning', he says.

What does the above tell you about the culture of the airline?

Section summary

2.7 (a) Culture embodies values and beliefs in an organisation. It influences how people understand the world, what behaviour is rewarded, and how people act in particular circumstances.

(b) A strong culture can enable an organisation to work better, as suggested by excellence theories, but can inhibit change. Culture cannot substitute for strategy.

(c) Culture and structure are linked together.

3 THE INFORMAL ORGANISATION

The informal organisation

3.1 An **informal organisation** exists side by side with the formal one. When people work together, they establish social relationships and customary ways of doing things:

(a) Social **groups,** or cliques (sometimes acting against one another).

(b) **Informal ways of getting things done** - ie norms and rules which are different in character from the rules which are **imposed** by the formal organisation.

3.2 The informal organisation can improve communications and facilitate the co-ordination of various individuals or departments. Informal methods may be more flexible and adaptable to required changes than the formal ways of doing things.

3.3 Certain **individuals can have an important informal influence** in an organisation. To take an illustrative example, the managing director of XY Company is a very remote individual and the production and sales directors have difficulty in communicating and working with him effectively. The financial director, however, has a remarkably good personal understanding with the managing director and can approach him readily in all matters at work. The sales and production directors therefore often ask the financial director to put their views informally to the managing director and to sound out his opinion before they approach him formally.

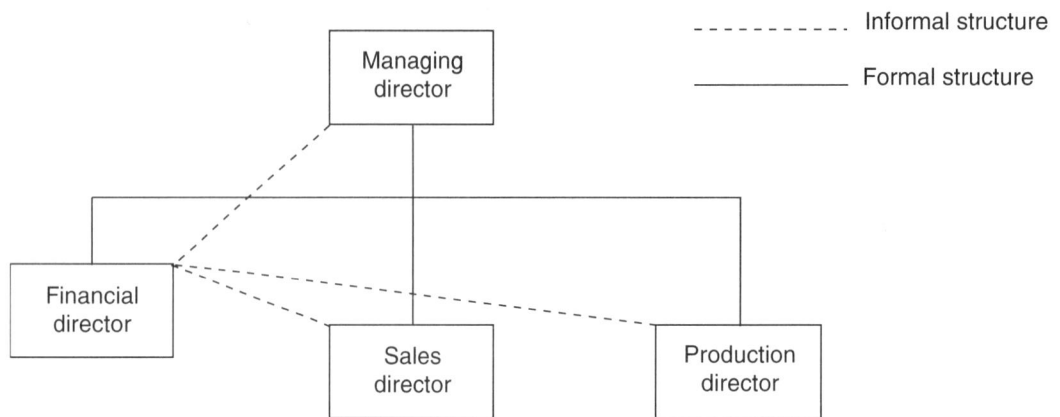

3.4 The **informal structure supplements the formal structure** which improves the way in which top management sets about its job. The informal structure of a company may 'take over' from the formal organisation when the formal structure is slow to adapt to change.

3.5 An **informal organisation** is **loosely structured, flexible and spontaneous**. Membership is gained consciously or unconsciously and it is often hard to determine the time when a person becomes a member.

Key learning points

- Culture in an organisation is found in the formalisation of its structure, how decisions are taken, the degree to which authority and responsibility are delegated, and the degree to which initiative is allowed.

- Charles Handy notes four **cultures**, to which he gives the names of Greek deities. The **club/power culture (Zeus)** is run by one individual, who makes snap decisions, with people who share his or her outlook and values. The **role culture (Apollo)** describes a rule-driven specialised bureaucracy. A **task culture (Athena)** is one in which people group and regroup into teams to accomplish specific projects. An **existential culture (Dionysus)** is one in which management serves employees who are professionals or experts. Some companies or tasks require more than one of these cultures.

- The importance of corporate culture for organisation success has been highlighted by **excellence** theories. However, while culture can help success it can be disadvantageous, as it **resists change**.

- In most organisations, there is an **informal structure**, derived out of a network of personal relations. The formal structure of authority might be subverted by the informal structure.

- *See the Part A mind map summary on page 38.*

Quick quiz

1 What are the elements of culture?

2 What characterises a 'power' culture?

3 What do Handy's descriptions integrate?

4 What are excellent companies good at?

5 What is the informal organisation?

Answers to quick quiz_____

1 Beliefs and values, customs, artefacts, rituals, symbols.

2 Based on personalities; adaptable and informal; small businesses.

3   The individual, the work, the organisation, the environment.

4   Innovation; responding to change.

5   A network of personal relationships in which individuals have more or less influence than would be suggested by their function in the organisation hierarchy.

Answers to activities

Answer 2.1

Here are some hints. The army is very disciplined. Decision-making is made by officers; behaviour between ranks (eg saluting) is sometimes very formal. Each regiment has its own history, of battles fought and honours won, and new recruits are expected to feel a continuity with the past.

An advertising agency, with a different mission, is more fluid. Individual creativity, within the commercial needs of the firm, is expected. .

Answer 2.2

(a)   Zeus
(b)   Apollo
(c)   Athena
(d)   Dionysus

Answer 2.3

This is not so much a commercial airline, but a military airforce. Hence, the concentration on rank, and the 'I counted them all out, and I've counted them in' mentality. A corporate culture which delighted in, or was relieved by, assets not used and more importantly, potential customers not served, is hardly a **business** operation at all. (**Note.** This exercise was drawn from a case history described by Charles Hampden-Turner.)

BPP PUBLISHING

PART A   MIND MAP SUMMARY

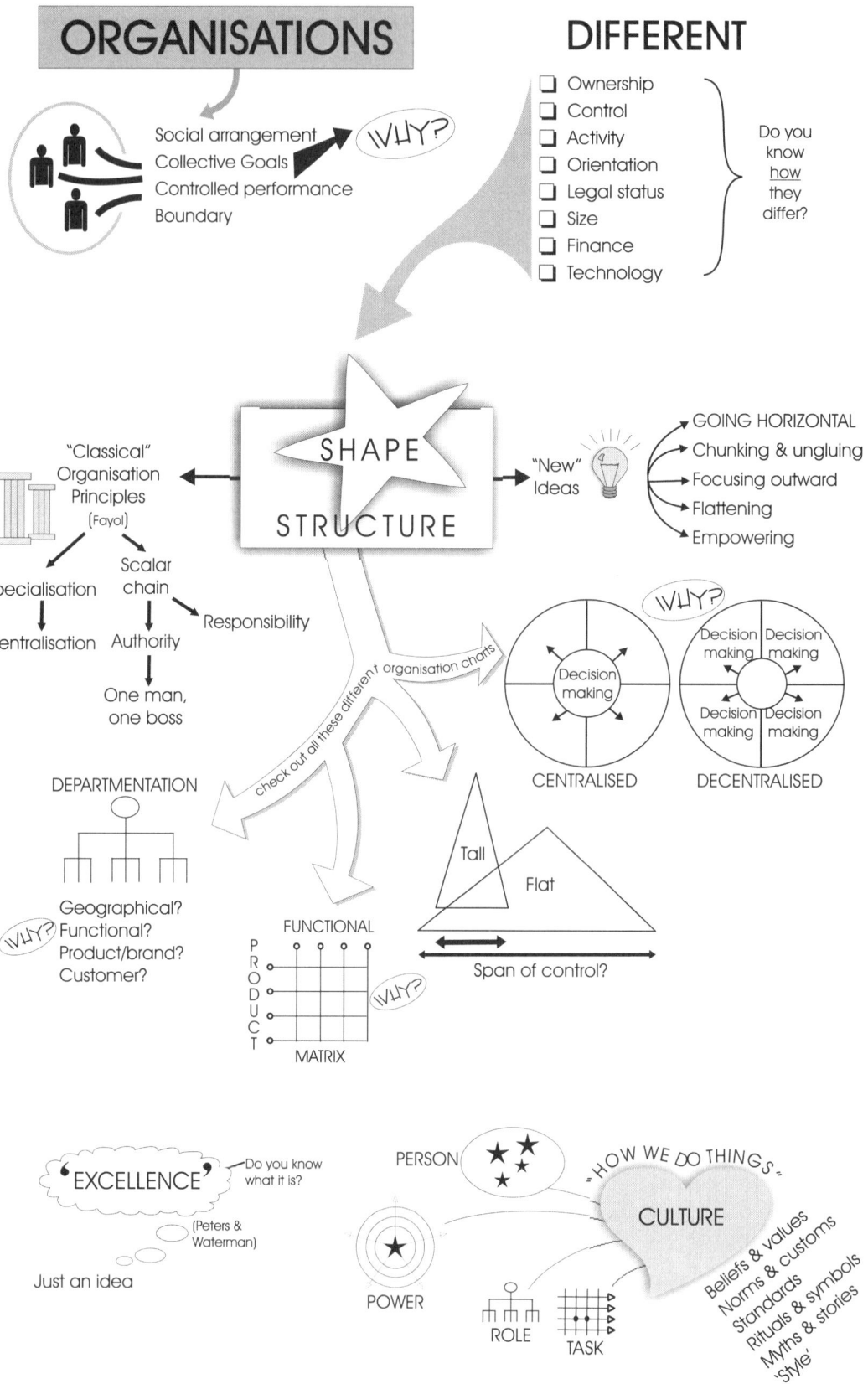

ORGANISATIONS

Social arrangement
Collective Goals
Controlled performance
Boundary

WHY?

DIFFERENT

- ❑ Ownership
- ❑ Control
- ❑ Activity
- ❑ Orientation
- ❑ Legal status
- ❑ Size
- ❑ Finance
- ❑ Technology

Do you
know
how
they
differ?

SHAPE
STRUCTURE

"Classical"
Organisation
Principles
(Fayol)

Specialisation

Centralisation

Scalar
chain

Authority

One man,
one boss

Responsibility

"New"
Ideas

GOING HORIZONTAL
Chunking & ungluing
Focusing outward
Flattening
Empowering

check out all these different organisation charts

WHY?

CENTRALISED

Decision
making

Decision making | Decision making
Decision making | Decision making

DECENTRALISED

DEPARTMENTATION

WHY? Geographical?
Functional?
Product/brand?
Customer?

FUNCTIONAL

P
R
O
D
U
C
T

MATRIX

WHY?

Tall

Flat

Span of control?

'EXCELLENCE'

Do you know
what it is?

(Peters &
Waterman)

Just an idea

PERSON

POWER

ROLE

TASK

"HOW WE DO THINGS"

CULTURE

Beliefs & values
Norms & customs
Standards
Rituals & symbols
Myths & stories
'Style'

Part B
Organising tasks and people

Chapter 3 Management and supervision

Learning objectives

On completion of this chapter you will be able to:

	Syllabus reference
• explain the role of the manager in the organisation of work	c
• examine the role of the supervisor in relation to delegation, resource allocation and project planning	c
• list the responsibilities of the supervisor	c
• explain the role of assessing staff	c
• list the management tasks involved in organising the work of others	c
• outline areas of management authority and responsibility	c
• identify and explain the contribution made by modern writers on management	c
• identify the differences beween classical and modern theories of management	c

BPP
PUBLISHING

1 THE MANAGER

KEY TERM

Management can be defined as: 'getting things done through other people'.

1.1 A supervisor is a type of manager.

Managerial elements

1.2 **Henri Fayol**, who represents the **classical school** of organisation theory, listed the elements of **management**.

Element	Comment
Planning for the future	Selecting objectives and the strategies, policies, programmes and procedures for achieving them.
Organising the work	Establishing a **structure of tasks** to be performed to achieve the goals, **grouping these tasks into jobs** for individuals, creating **groups of jobs** within departments, **delegating authority** to carry out the jobs, providing **systems of information,** and co-ordinating activities.
Commanding	Giving instructions to subordinates to carry out tasks over which the manager has authority for decisions and responsibility for performance.
Co-ordinating	**Harmonising** the activities of individuals and groups within the organisation, reconciling differences of resources.
Controlling	**Measuring** the activities of individuals and groups, to ensure that their performance is in accordance with plans. Deviations from plan are identified and corrected.

Activity 3.1

Using Fayol's elements of management, indicate under which of the five headings the activities below fall.

1 Ensuring that the sales department does not exceed its budget.
2 Deciding which products will form the main thrust of advertising during the next financial year.
3 Ensuring that new working practices are communicated to the workforce.
4 Ensuring that the sales department liaises with production on delivery dates.
5 Changing work schedules to reduce idle time.

Fayol's management principles

1.3 As well as listing the five elements of management, Fayol also devised 14 management principles. These are:

(1) **Division of labour.** The more people specialise the more efficiently they can perform their work. This principle is epitomised by the modern assembly line.

(2) **Authority.** Managers must give orders so that they can get things done. While their *formal* authority gives them the right to command, managers will not always compel obedience unless they have *personal* authority (such as relevant expertise) as well.

(3) **Discipline.** Members in an organisation need to respect the rules and agreements that govern the organisation. To Fayol, discipline results from good leadership at all levels of the organisation, fair agreements such as provisions for rewarding superior performance), and judiciously enforced penalties for infractions.

(4) **Unity of command.** Each employee must receive instructions from only one person. Fayol believed that when an employee reported to more than one manager, conflicts in instructions and confusion of authority would result.

(5) **Unity of direction.** Those operations within the organisation that have the same objective should be directed by only one manager using one plan. For example, the personnel department in a company should not have two directors, each with a different hiring policy.

(6) **Subordination of Individual Interest to the Common Good.** In any undertaking, the interests of employees should not take precedence over the interests of the organisation as a whole.

(7) **Remuneration.** Compensation for work done should be fair to both employees and employers.

(8) **Centralization.** Decreasing the role of subordinates in decision making is centralization; increasing their role is decentralisation. Fayol believed that managers should retain final responsibility, but should at the same time give their subordinates enough authority to do their job properly. The problem is to find the proper degree of centralisation in every case.

(9) **The Hierarchy.** The line of authority in an organisation – often represented today by the neat boxes and lines of the organisation chart – runs in order of rank from top management to the lowest level of the enterprise.

(10) **Order.** Materials and people should be in the right place at the right time. People, in particular, should be in the jobs or positions they are most suited to.

(11) **Equity**: Managers should be both friendly and fair to their subordinates.

(12) **Stability of Staff.** A high employee turnover rate undermines the efficient functioning of an organisation.

(13) **Initiative.** Subordinates should be given the freedom to conceive and carry out their plans, even though some mistakes may result.

(14) **Esprit de Corps.** Promoting team spirit will give the organisation a sense of unity. To Fayol, even small factors could help to develop the spirit. He suggested, for example, the use of verbal communication instead of formal, written communication whenever possible.

Managerial roles: Modern theories

1.4 Managerial **functions** are those activities necessary for the **organisation** to be managed. As we saw in the activity above, however, a manager will do a number of **tasks** in each day. Henry Mintzberg suggests that in their daily working lives, managers fulfil three **types** of managerial role.

Role category	Role	Comment
Interpersonal, from formal authority and position	**Figurehead** (or ceremonial)	Representing the company at dinners, conferences etc
	Leader	Hiring, firing and training staff, motivating employees, and reconciling individual needs with the requirements of the organisation
	Liaison	Making contacts with people in other departments
Informational Managers have: • Access to all their staff • Many external contracts	**Monitor**	The manager *monitors* the environment, and receives information from subordinates, superiors and peers in other departments. It might be gossip or speculation.
	Spokesperson	The manager provides information to interested parties either within or outside the organisation
	Disseminator	The manager *disseminates* this information to subordinates
Decisional The manager's formal authority and access to information mean that no one else is in a position to take decisions relating to the work of the department as a whole.	**Entrepreneur**	A manager initiates projects, a number of which may be on the go at any one time.
	Disturbance handler	A manager has to respond to pressures over which the department has no control, taking decisions in unusual or unexpected situations.
	Resource allocator	A manager takes decisions relating to the allocation of scarce resources. The manager determines the department's direction and authorises decisions taken by subordinates.
	Negotiator	Both inside and outside the organisation takes up a great deal of management time.

1.5 **Debunking myths about management work**

(a) Managers are **not reflective, systematic planners.**

(b) **Managerial work is disjointed** and discontinuous.

(c) Managers **do** have **routine** duties to perform, especially of a ceremonial nature (receiving important guests) or related to authority (signing cheques as a signatory).

(d) Managers **prefer verbal** (and informal) information to the formal output of management information systems. Verbal information is 'hotter' and probably easier to grasp.

1.6 Mintzberg states that general management is, in practice, a matter of **judgement and intuition**, gained from **experience** in **particular situations** rather than from abstract principles. 'Fragmentation and verbal communication' characterise the manager's work.

Exam alert

A specific question on Mintzberg was set in June 1999 and again in December 2001. These questions required you to describe Mintzberg's roles (factual knowledge), to state your *opinion* on whether management is the same as 'planning and organising' or whether it is something else, and to *distinguish* Mintzberg's view of the process of management from those of classical writers such as Fayol. Be ready to think about the implications of a given theory and how it confirms or undermines other theories.

1.7 A manager will play some roles more than others: senior officials, for example, are more likely to be called upon to at as figureheads than team leaders, who will be more concerned with resource allocation and disturbance handling.

Activity 3.2

The *Telegraph Magazine* asked a cinema manager: 'What do you actually do? The answer was as follows.

'Everything, apart from being the projectionist and cleaning the lavatories. My office is also the ticket office. If there is a big queue at the confectionery kiosk, I'll help serve and I'll usher people to their seat if we're really busy. Sometimes I go into the cinema before a show and tell the audience about any special events, such as a director coming to give a talk.

'I get in around lunchtime, deal with messages and ensure that the lights and heating are working. I write orders for posters and publicity pictures, popcorn and ice creams and cope with the correspondence for the 2,000 members on our mailing list. I'll brief the projectionist, ushers and kiosk staff and at about 1.45pm the first matinee customers arrive. Our afternoon audience is mainly elderly people and they take some time to settle, so I'll help them to their seats and only start the film when everyone is comfortable. In the evening, more ushers and bar staff arrive and I'll brief them about the programme, seating and timing. While the film is on, I'm selling tickets for the other screen, counting the takings and planning tomorrow. If I get a moment I try to grab something to eat.'

Which of Mintzberg's roles does this manager take on in his 'average' day?

Managers and leaders

1.8 The terms **management** and **leadership** are often used interchangeably, and it will not matter much whether you refer to 'management style' or 'leadership style', for example. However, it is worth noting that it is possible to distinguish between the two ideas.

(a) The functions of management, as discussed above, include planning, organising, co-ordination and controlling. Management is primarily concerned with logic, structure and control. If done well, it produces predictable results, on time.

(b) Leadership, properly considered, involves a different kind of function. It involves essentially people-centred activities, with effects potentially beyond the scope of controlled performance. A leader's special function is to:

(i) **Create a vision** of something different to the current status quo

(ii) **Communicate the vision**. This will be particularly powerful if it meets the needs of other people, and if the leader can give it credibility in their eyes

(iii) **Energise, inspire and motivate** others to translate the vision into achievement

(iv) **Create the culture** that will support the achievement, through shared language, rituals, myths and beliefs

1.9 In other words, while management have authority by virtue of their position in the organisation to secure the obedience or compliance of their subordinates, leaders direct the efforts of others through vision, inspiration and motivation - forms of **influence**

> **KEY TERM**
>
> **Influence** is the process by which an individual or group exercises power to determine or modify the behaviour of others.

1.10 For routine work, mere **compliance** with directives may be sufficient for the organisation's needs. However, if it wishes to secure **extra input** from its employees – in terms of co-operation, effort and creativity – it may strive for the inspirational quality of leadership, over and above efficient management.

2 THE SUPERVISOR

2.1 There are different levels of management in most organisations. A **finance department** in an organisation might be headed by the **finance director** (A) supported by a chief **financial accountant** (B) and chief **management accountant** (C). Lower down in the hierarchy assistant accountants might report to (B) and (C).

2.2 The supervisor is the lowest level of management.

> **KEY TERM**
>
> 'A **supervisor** is a person selected by middle management to take charge of a group of people, or special task, to ensure that work is carried out satisfactorily ... the job is largely reactive dealing with situations as they arise, allocating and reporting back to higher management.' (Savedra and Hawthorn).

2.3 Features of supervision

(a) A supervisor is usually a 'front-line' manager, dealing with the levels of the organisation where the bread-and-butter work is done. The supervisor's **subordinates are non-managerial employees**.

(b) A supervisor does not spend all his or her time on the managerial aspects of his job. Much of the time will be spent doing **technical/operational work** himself.

(c) A supervisor is a '**gatekeeper**' or filter for communication in the organisation.

(d) The supervisor monitors and controls work by means of **day-to-day, frequent and detailed information**: higher levels of management plan and control using longer-term, less frequent and less detailed information, which must be 'edited' or selected and reported by the supervisor.

(e) The **managerial aspects and responsibilities of a supervisor's job are often ill-defined**, and given no precise targets to achievement.

What do supervisors do?

2.4 As a supervisor's job is a junior management job, the tasks of supervision can then be listed under similar headings to the tasks of management.

2.5 **Planning**
- Planning **work** so as to **meet work targets** or schedules set by more senior management
- Planning the **work for each employee;** making estimates of overtime required
- Planning the total **resources** required by the section to meet the total work-load
- Planning work **methods and procedures**
- Attending departmental planning **meetings**
- Preparing **budgets** for the section
- Planning **staff training** and staff development
- Planning the **induction** of new staff
- Planning **improvements** in the work

2.6 **Organising and overseeing the work of others**
- **Ordering** materials and equipment from internal stores or external suppliers
- **Authorising spending** by others on materials, sundry supplies or equipment
- **Interviewing** and selecting staff
- Authorising overtime
- **Allocating work** to staff
- **Allocating equipment** to staff
- Reorganising work (for example when urgent jobs come in)
- Establishing **performance standards** for staff
- Organising transport
- Deciding **job priorities**
- General 'housekeeping' duties
- Maintaining **liaison** with more senior management

Activity 3.3

Bert Close has decided to delegate the task of identifying the reasons for machine 'down' time (when machines are not working) over the past three months to Brenda Cartwright. This will involve her in talking to operators, foremen and supervisors and also liaising with other departments to establish the effects of this down time. What will Bert need to do to delegate this task effectively? List at least four items he will need to cover with Brenda.

2.7 **Controlling: making sure the work is done properly**
- Keeping records of total time worked on the section
- Deciding when sub-standard work must be re-done
- Attending progress control meetings
- Dealing with trade union representatives
- Dealing with personal problems of staff
- Disciplining staff (for late arrival at work and so on)

BPP PUBLISHING

- Counselling staff
- Ensuring that work procedures are followed
- Ensuring that the quality of work is sustained to the required levels
- Ensuring that safety standards are maintained
- Checking the progress of new staff/staff training, on-the-job training
- Co-ordinating the work of the section with the work of other sections
- Ensuring that work targets are achieved, and explaining the cause to senior management of any failure to achieve these targets

2.8 Motivating employees, and dealing with others: appraisal

- Dealing with staff problems
- Dealing with people in other sections
- Reporting to a senior manager
- Dealing with customers
- Motivating staff to improve work performance
- Applying disciplinary measures to subordinates who act unreasonably or work badly
- Helping staff to understand the organisation's goals and targets
- Training staff, and identifying the need for more training

2.9 Communicating

- Telling employees about plans, targets and work schedules
- Telling managers about the work that has been done
- Filling in reports (for example absentee reports for the personnel department)
- Writing memos, notes and reports
- Passing information between employees and managers, and between sections
- Collecting information and distributing it to the other persons interested in it.
- Keeping up-to-date with developments

2.10 'Doing'

- Doing operations work
- Standing in for a senior manager when he or she is on holiday or otherwise absent
- Giving advice to others to help solve problems

Activity 3.4

Look at the job of the supervisor (or similar position) in your office (your own job, if you are in such a position).

(a) Identify the (i) managerial and (ii) technical aspects of the job, and list as many as you can. Think of the duties they entail.

(b) Get hold of a copy of the **job description** of a supervisory job (or have a look at one in the organisation manual). Does it bear any relation to the list you compiled yourself? Is it a realistic description of the actual work of the supervisor? Is the 'supervisory' part of the job well-defined (as compared with the technical part)? Are there targets or standards, and training requirements?

(c) Consider your own experience of promotion to a supervisory post (or ask your supervisor). What preparation, training, coaching, and/or advice was given by the manager for this first step into managerial work - was it 'sink or swim'?

3 WORK PLANNING

The resources at the supervisor's disposal

3.1 A supervisor is asked to get a piece of work done, or organise other people to get the work done. A supervisor has resources, as follows.

(a) **Human resources**. A supervisor can deploy his or her staff to do different tasks at different times.

(b) **Material resources**, for example. Some discretion over the use of machinery.

(c) **Financial resources**, within budget guideline.

Work planning

3.2 **Work planning** is the establishment of work methods and practices to ensure that predetermined objectives are efficiently met at all levels.

(a) **Task sequencing or prioritisation** (ie considering tasks in order of importance for the objective concerned.

(b) **Scheduling or timetabling tasks**, and allocating them to different individuals within appropriate time scales.

(c) **Establishing checks and controls** to ensure that:

(i) Priority deadlines are being met and work is not 'falling behind'.
(ii) Routine tasks are achieving their objectives.

(d) **Contingency plans:** arrangements for what should be done if a major upset were to occur, eg if the company's main computer were to break down.

(e) **Co-ordinating the efforts of individuals.**

(f) **Reviewing and controlling performance.**

3.3 Some jobs (eg assembly line worker), are entirely routine, and can be performed one step at a time, but for most people, some kind of planning and judgement will be required.

Assessing where resources are most usefully allocated

3.4 A manager or supervisor is responsible for allocating resources between:

(a) **Different ways** to achieve the same objective (eg to increase total profits, sell more, or cut costs etc).

(b) **Competing areas,** where total resources are limited.

3.5 **ABC analysis (Pareto analysis)** suggests that only a small proportion of items will be significant. For example a business might have 99 customers who each spend £10 per month and 1 customer who spends £100,000 per month. Pareto's Law assumes that, for sales, approximately 80% of sales volume is accounted for by 20% of the customers. This means that the manager will:

(a) Concentrate scarce resources on the crucial 20%.

(b) Devise policies and procedures for the remaining 80%, or delegate.

3.6 A piece of work will be **high priority** in the following cases.

• **If it has to be completed by a certain time** (ie a deadline)

- **If other tasks depend on it**
- **If other people depend on it**

3.7 **Routine priorities** or regular peak times (eg tax returns etc) can be **planned ahead of time**, and other tasks planned around them.

3.8 **Non-routine priorities** occur when **unexpected demands** are made. Thus planning of work should cover routine scheduled peaks and contingency plans for unscheduled peaks and emergencies.

Methodical working

3.9 **Efficiency** requires working systematically or methodically.

(a) Ensure that **resources** are available, in sufficient supply and good condition

(b) Organise work in **batches** to save time spent in turning from one job to another

(c) Work to **plans**, schedules, checklists etc

(d) Taking advantage of work **patterns**

(e) Follow up tasks:
- Check on the progress of an operation
- Checking the task is completed when the deadline is reached
- Check payments are made when they fall due
- Retrieve files relevant to future discussions, meetings, correspondence

---

Activity 3.5

Choose a task or event that needs planning.

(a) Make a checklist
(b) Re-arrange items in order of priority and time sequence
(c) Estimate the time for each activity and schedule it, working back from a deadline
(d) Prepare an action sheet
(e) Draw a chart with columns for time units, and rows for activities
(f) Decide what items may have to be 'brought forward' later and how

---

Scheduling

3.10 **Scheduling** is where priorities and deadlines are planned and controlled. A schedule establishes a timetable for a logical sequence of tasks, leading up to completion date.

(a) All involved in a task must be given adequate **notice** of work schedules.

(b) The schedules themselves should allow a **realistic time allocation** for each task.

(c) Allowance will have to be made for **unexpected events**.

(d) A **deadline** is the *end* of the longest span of time which may be allotted to a task, ie the last acceptable date for completion. Failure to meet them has a 'knock-on' effect on other parts of the organisation, and on other tasks within an individual's duties. Diary entries may be made on appropriate days (eg: - 'Production completed?' 'Payment received?' 'Bring forward file x' 'One week left for revision').

3.11 A number of activities may have to be undertaken in sequence, with some depending on, or taking priority over others.

(a) **Activity scheduling** provides a list of necessary activities in the order in which they must be completed. You might use this to plan each day's work.

(b) **Time scheduling** adds to this the time scale for each activity, and is useful for setting deadlines for tasks. The time for each step is estimated; the total time for the task can then be calculated, allowing for some steps which may be undertaken simultaneously by different people or departments.

Work programmes and other aids to planning

3.12 From activity and time schedules, detailed **work programmes** can be designed for jobs which are carried out over a period of time. Some tasks will have to be started well before the deadline, others may be commenced immediately before, others will be done on the day itself. **Organising a meeting**, for example, may include:

Step 1. Booking accommodation two months before

Step 2. Retrieving relevant files one week before

Step 3. Preparing and circulating an agenda 2-3 days before

Step 4. Checking conference room layout the day before

Step 5. Taking minutes on the day

The same applies to stock ordering in advance of production (based on a schedule of known delivery times), preparing correspondence in advance of posting etc.

3.13 Once time scales are known and final deadlines set, it is possible to produce **job cards, route cards** and **action sheets**.

	Activity	Days before	Date	Begun	Completed
1	Request file	6	3.9		
2	Draft report	5	4.9		
3	Type report	3	6.9		
4	Approve report	1	8.9		
5	Signature	1	8.9		
6	Internal messenger	same day	9.9		

3.14 Longer-term schedules may be shown conveniently on charts, pegboards or year planners, holiday planners etc. These can be used to show lengths of time and the relationships between various tasks or timetabled events.

Work allocation

3.15 Managers and supervisors divide duties and allocate them to available staff and machinery. Here are all the considerations.

(a) **General tasks.** Some tasks (eg filing, photo-copying) may not have the attention of a dedicated employee. Who will do the work, and will it interfere with their other duties?

(b) **Peak periods** in some tasks may necessitate re-distribution of staff to cope with the work load.

(c) **Status and staff attitudes** must be considered. Flexibility in reassigning people from one job to another or varying the work they do may be hampered by an employee's perception of his or her own status.

(d) Individual **temperaments** and abilities may differ.

(e) Planning should allow for **flexibility** in the event of an employee proving unfit for a task, or more able than his present tasks indicate.

(f) Efforts will have to be **co-ordinated** so that all those involved in a process (eg sales orders) work together as a team or a number of groups.

Projects

> **KEY TERM**
>
> A **project** is 'an undertaking that has a beginning and an end and is carried out to meet established goals within cost, schedule and quality objectives' (Haynes, *Project Management*).

3.16 The difference between project planning and other parts of planning is that a **project is not a repetitive activity**.

Characteristics of projects

- Specific start and end points
- Well-defined objectives
- The project endeavour is to a degree unique and not repetitious
- The project usually contains costs and time schedules
- A project cuts across many organisational and functional boundaries

3.17 **Examples of projects**

Project	Comment
Building and construction	Any building project, such as the construction of 'Cyberjaya', a new high-tech city in Malaysia.
Management	Development of an information system.
Supervision	Installing new machinery

3.18 The job of **project management** is to foresee as many dangers as possible, and to plan, organise and control activities so that they are avoided.

The role of the project manager or supervisor

3.19 Projects have to be co-ordinated. A project manager's duties are outlined below.

Duty	Comment
Outline project planning	• Developing project targets such as overall costs or timescale (eg project should take 20 weeks).
	• Dividing the project into activities (eg analysis, programming, testing), and placing these activities into the right sequence, often a complicated task if overlapping.
	• Developing the procedures and structures, manage the project (eg plan weekly team meetings, performance reviews etc).

Duty	Comment
Detailed planning	Identifying the tasks, resource requirements, network analysis for scheduling.
Teambuilding	The project manager has to meld the various people into an effective team.
Communication	The project manager must let superiors know what is going on, and ensure that members of the project team are properly briefed.
Co-ordinating project activities	Between the project team and users, and other external parties (eg suppliers of hardware and software).
Monitoring and control	The project manager should estimate the causes for each departure from the standard, and take corrective measures.
Problem-resolution	Unforeseen problems may arise, and it falls upon the project manager to sort them out, or to delegate the responsibility for so doing to a subordinate.
Quality control	There is often a short-sighted trade-off between getting the project out on time and the project's quality.

Exam alert

The pilot paper asked a question about a **multi-function project team**. 'Project team' in this context means that the team will not be working together permanently, and you should understand by now that 'multi-function' means that the team's members are drawn from different functional departments in the business.

4 A BRIEF HISTORY OF MANAGEMENT

The classical school

4.1 Henri Fayol (1841-1925) was a French industrialist who put forward and popularised the concept of the '**universality of management principles**': in other words, the idea that all organisations could be structured and managed according to certain rational principles. Fayol himself recognised that applying such principles in practice was not simple: 'Seldom do we have to apply the same principles twice in identical conditions; allowance must be made for different changing circumstances.'

Fayol's 14 principles of management are set out in paragraph 1.3.

Activity 3.6

A quick test of how much you recall from Chapter 1! Borderline Computers use project teams to carry out research, deal with customer needs and to introduce new systems. Identify which of Fayol's principles would clash with this method of working.

F W Taylor and scientific management

4.2 Frederick W Taylor pioneered the **scientific management** movement in the USA. He argued that management should be based on 'well-recognised, clearly defined and fixed principles, instead of depending on more or less hazy ideas.' Taylor was a very skilled engineer and he took an engineering efficiency approach to management.

4.3 **Principles of scientific management**

(a) **The development of a true science of work.** 'All knowledge which had hitherto been kept in the heads of workmen should be gathered and recorded by **management**. Every single subject, large and small, becomes the question for scientific investigation, for reduction to law.'

(b) **The scientific selection and progressive development of workers:** workers should be carefully trained and given jobs to which they are best suited.

(c) **The bringing together of the science and the scientifically selected and trained men.** The application of techniques to decide what should be done and how, using workers who are both properly trained and willing to maximise output, should result in maximum productivity.

(d) **The constant and intimate co-operation between management and workers:** 'the relations between employers and men form without question the most important part of this art.'

4.4 **Scientific management in practice**

(a) **Work study techniques** were used to analyse tasks and establish the most efficient methods to use, No variation was permitted in the way work was done, since the aim was to use the 'one best way'.

(b) **Planning the work and doing the work were separated.** It was assumed that the persons who were intellectually equipped to do a particular type of work were probably unlikely to be able to plan it to the best advantage. With a working population that had minimal education and included a high proportion of immigrants from non-anglophone countries, this was probably a reasonable approach.

(c) **Workers were paid incentives** on the basis of acceptance of the new methods and output norms; the new methods greatly increased productivity and profits. Pay was assumed to be the only important motivating force.

4.5 Scientific management as practised by Taylor and contemporaries such as Gilbreth and Gantt was very much about **manual work**. However, the rational, efficiency oriented engineering approach of these pioneers is conceptually very close to the organisational ideas of Weber and Fayol discussed in Chapter 1.

4.6 Scientific management is still practised today, whenever there is a concern for productivity and efficiency.

Mayo: reaction to scientific management

4.7 It is clear to us today that treating work people as though they are machines is not a recipe for either harmony in the workplace or for high quality work. In the 1920s research began to show that managers needed to consider the complexity of **human behaviour.**

4.8 In the 1930s, there developed a renewed understanding that organisations are made up of **people** – not just functions. By robbing the worker of any sense of **contribution** to the total product or task, the organisation was losing out on an important source of energy and creativity. A new approach set out to redress the balance.

Human relations

4.9 The 'human relations' approach emphasised the importance of human attitudes, values and relationships for the efficient and effective functioning of work organisations. Its pioneer, **Elton Mayo** (1880-1949) wrote: 'We have thought that first-class technical training was sufficient in a modern and mechanical age. As a consequence we are **technically competent** as no other age in history has been, and we combine this with **utter social incompetence**.'

4.10 Early work focused on the idea that people need companionship and belonging, and seek satisfaction in the **social relationships** they form at work. This emphasis resulted from a famous set of experiments (the **Hawthorne Studies**) carried out by Mayo and his colleagues for the Western Electric Company in the USA. The company was using a group of girls as 'guinea pigs' to assess the affect of lighting on productivity: they were astonished to find that productivity shot up, whatever they did with the lighting. Their conclusion was that: 'Management, by **consultation** with the girl workers, by clear **explanation** of the proposed experiments and the reasons for them, by accepting the workers' verdict in several instances, unwittingly scored a success in two most important human matters – the girls became a self-governing team, and a team that **co-operated** wholeheartedly with management.'

4.11 Mayo's ideas were followed by various social psychologists (like **Maslow** and **Herzberg** whom we will meet later in this text), who shifted attention towards human beings' 'higher' **psychological needs** for growth, challenge, responsibility and self-fulfilment. Herzberg suggested that only these things could positively encourage or motivate employees to improved work performance. This has had a profound effect on the way management is perceived – as we will see when we look at fashionable concepts such as empowerment.

4.12 As we have seen, early theorists saw the organisation primarily as a structure of **tasks and authority** which could be drawn in an organisation chart. But that is like a snapshot of an organisation, showing what it looks like frozen at a particular moment in time. In fact, organisations are neither self-contained nor static: they are **open systems**.

The organisation as a system

4.13 There is no universally accepted definition of a **system**, but it can be described as 'an entity which consists of interdependent parts'. Every system has a **boundary** which defines what it is: what is inside and what is outside the system. Anything outside the system is said to be its **environment**.

In **systems theory**, it is possible to have a **closed system**, which is shut off from the environment and independent of it. An **open system**, however, is one which is connected to and interacts with its environment. It takes in influences from the environment and itself influences the environment by its activities.

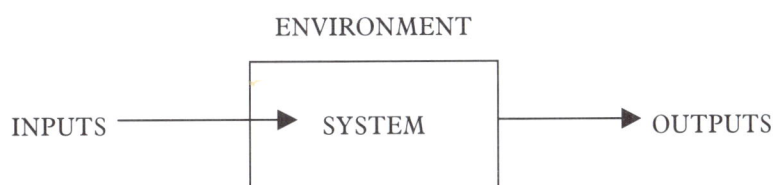

ENVIRONMENT

INPUTS ⟶ SYSTEM ⟶ OUTPUTS

4.14 Organisations are open social systems. Why? They are **social systems** because they are comprised of people. They are **open systems** because those people participate in other social systems in the environment (such as the family or class system) and bring with them all sorts of influences from the environment: advertising messages, family pressures, government demands (eg for tax), social attitudes and so on. In addition, the organisation itself takes in a wide variety of inputs, or resources, from the environment, and generates outputs to it as a result of its activities.

Activity 3.7

Suggest four inputs and five outputs of an organisational system.

4.15 The systems approach also emphasises the existence of **sub-systems**, or parts of a bigger system. An organisation is a 'structured socio-technical system', consisting of at least three sub-systems.

(a) **A structure,** (division of labour, authority relationships and communication channels)

(b) **A technological system** (the work to be done, and the techniques and tools used to do it)

(c) **A social system** (the people within the organisation, the ways they think and interact with each other)

4.16 Looking at the organisation as a system helps managers to remember that:

(a) The organisation is not a static structure as conventional organisation charts suggest. It is continuously reacting to internal and external changes.

(b) Sub-systems of the organisation each have potentially conflicting goals which must be integrated, often with some compromise.

(c) An awareness of the environment of the organisation (including competitor activity, technological change and customer needs) is vital if the organisation is to survive.

Activity 3.8

Below are a number of statements. Indicate whether they apply to the systems approach. Mark alongside T for true or F for false.

(a) The organisation is static.

(b) People, technology, organisation structure and environment are equally important in the systems approach.

(c) All sub-systems are in complete agreement.

(d) It is important that all employees are happy in their work.

(e) The organisation is aware of change affecting business.

(f) There is interdependence beween all aspects of the organisation

4.17 Once you see the organisation as a system, it becomes clear that there can be no 'one best way' to design and manage such dynamic and varied processes. This is where **contingency theory** comes in.

The contingency approach

4.18 The contingency approach to organisation developed as a reaction to the idea that there are universal principles for designing organisations, motivating staff and so on. Newer research indicated that different forms of organisational structure could be equally successful, that there was no inevitable link between classical organisation structures and effectiveness, and that there were a number of **variables** to be considered in the **design** of organisations and their style of management. Essentially, it all depends on the **total picture** of internal factors and external environment of each organisation. Managers have to find a 'best fit' between varying demands.

- The tasks
- The people
- The environment

4.19 We will note contingency approaches to various aspects of management as we proceed through this text.

Activity 3.9

Cobble and Carter is an accountancy practice. The partners now find that their present, highly bureaucratic methods of organisation are unsatisfactory. Customer needs are wide and varied, decision making is too slow and the staff are becoming demotivated. The partners now have to consider changing their methods to overcome the present difficulties and have decided to use a new approach. This would involve partners being responsible for various companies and they would be assisted by small teams.

(a) Give three advantages if they adopt this approach.
(b) identify three areas they would need to consider and investigate before making a final decision.

---

5 TECHNOLOGY AND STRUCTURE

5.1 Two important research programmes took place in England in the 1950s. These programmes were concerned with the influence of production technology on the way work is organised.

Woodward: types of production system

5.2 Joan Woodward investigated specific features of organisation structure, such as size of span of control and the extent of division of functions among specialists. She discovered considerable differences between firms in these matters and established that the differences were related to the type of production technology in use.

(a) Production systems may be divided into three main categories, ranging from least to most complex.

- Unit and small batch
- Large batch and mass production
- Process production

These three categories were further subdivided into 9 sub-categories.

(b) The main point of difference was the **degree of control possible over the output of the system**. In the case of one-off production to customers' requirements, it is very difficult to predict the results of development work, while in continuous flow production of chemicals, the equipment can be set for a given result.

5.3 Some aspects of the organisation vary directly as the technology varies. For instance, the length of the scalar chain increases as complexity increases. However, other variables, such as span of control, do not vary linearly. Woodward found that span of control was greatest in mass production systems, while small work groups with more personal relationships with their supervisors were typical of both unit and process systems.

Socio-technical systems: Trist and Bamforth

5.4   Trist and Bamforth studied the effect of the introduction of new technology in coal mining.

Case example

The traditional method was based upon a small, integrated work group consisting of a skilled man, his mate and one or two labourers. There was a high degree of autonomy at the work group level and close working relationships. It was usual for the group to be paid for its work as a group. The work was hard, the conditions unpleasant and there was often conflict, and even violence between work groups. However, 'The system as a whole contained its bad in a way that did not destroy its good'.

The introduction of large-scale coal-cutting machinery created a need for larger, more specialised groups. A single cycle of mechanised production might extend over three 7 ½ shifts, each performing a separate process and made up of 10 to 20 men. The members of each shift would be spread over about 200 yards of coal face tunnel, which was typically 3 feet high and 6 feet wide. This physical dispersion and the spread of the work over three shifts destroyed the previous close working relationships. Many symptoms of social stress appeared, including scapegoating across shifts, formation of cliques and absenteeism.

Trist studied the new technology and found that it was possible to organise its use in such a way that some of the **social** characteristics of the traditional method were preserved. The use of this new method led to greater productivity, lower cost, considerably less absenteeism and accidents, and greater work satisfaction, since it was a **socio-technical system** which was better geared to the workers' social and psychological needs for job autonomy and close working relationships.

---

6   MODERN WRITERS ON MANAGEMENT

6.1   In the second half of the twentieth century, writing on management became more diverse.

(a)   The early emphasis on the organisation of work and work people has been continued in the field of **supervisory studies** and the development of specific management techniques such as **project management.** The search for efficiency continues in the field of **work study** and **industrial engineering.**

(b)   Human relations theory has been enhanced by developments in the study of motivation, group and individual behaviour, leadership and other aspects of industrial psychology.

(c)   There was much new writing on the nature of the **manager's task**: what it is to be a manager and what managers do.

6.2   This sector deals with the contributions of some more recent writers on the general nature of management.

Peter Drucker: the management process

6.3   Peter Drucker worked in the 1940s and 1950s as a business adviser to a number of US corporations. He was also a prolific writer on management.

6.4   Drucker argued that the manager of a business has a basic function - **economic performance.** In this respect, the business manager is different from the manager of any other type of organisation. Management can only justify its existence and its authority by the economic results it produces, even though as a consequence of its actions, significant non-economic results occur as well.

6.5 He then described the jobs of management within this basic function of economic performance as follows.

(a) **Managing a business**. The purposes of the business are:

- To create a customer
- Innovation

(b) **Managing managers**. The requirements here are:

- Management by objectives
- Proper structure of managers' jobs
- Creating the right spirit in the organisation
- Making a provision for the managers of tomorrow
- Arriving at sound principles of organisation structure

(c) **Managing worker and work**.

6.6 A manager's performance in all areas of management, including management of the business, can be enhanced by a study of the principles of management, the acquisition of 'organised knowledge' (eg management techniques) and the systematic self-assessment.

6.7 Later Drucker grouped the work of the manager into five categories.

(a) **Setting objectives for the organisation**. Managers decide what the objectives of the organisation should be and quantify the targets of achievement for each objective. They must then communicate these targets to other people in the organisation.

(b) **Organising the work**. The work to be done in the organisation must be divided into manageable activities and manageable jobs. The jobs must be integrated into a formal organisation structure, and people must be selected to do the jobs.

(c) **Motivating** employees and communicating information to them to enable them to do their work.

(d) **The job of measurement**. Management must:

(i) Establish **objectives** or yardsticks of performance for every person in the organisation

(ii) Analyse **actual performance**, appraise it against the objectives or yardsticks which have been set, and analyse the comparison

(iii) Communicate the findings and explain their significance both to subordinate employees and also to superiors

(e) **Developing people**. The manager 'brings out what is in them or he stifles them. He strengthens their integrity or he corrupts them'.

6.8 Every manager performs all five functions listed above, no matter how good or bad a manager he is. However a bad manager performs these functions badly, whereas a good manager performs them well. Drucker emphasised the importance of communication in the functions of management, which should be evident in items (a), (c) and (d) above.

BPP PUBLISHING

Ouchi: Theory Z

6.9 McGregor labelled two typical American approaches to management 'Theory X' and 'Theory Y' (covered in chapter 11 of this book). When the Japanese economy was performing well, a generation ago, it became fashionable to study Japanese management methods and promote them as a solution to the West's then seemingly intractable industrial problems. Ouchi called these methods 'Theory Z'.

6.10 The characteristics of a Theory Z organisation offer some interesting contrasts with the Western way of doing things.

   (a) Long term, often lifetime employment with one company, with a high value placed on mutual loyalty.

   (b) Relatively slow promotion.

   (c) Fairly specialised career paths for managers and the development of company-specific skills.

   (d) Implicit, informal control systems supported by explicit measures of performance.

   (e) Decision by consensus but ultimate individual responsibility.

   (f) Attention to the welfare of subordinates.

   (g) Informal relationships.

6.11 Theory Z was welcomed as a more human and therefore more effective way of managing people. It has had no lasting effect on Western management practice, unlike Japanese engineering and the JIT phenomenon.

Key learning points

- Organisations typically employ managers to direct them. The classic functions of managers were: **planning**, **organising**, **commanding**, **co-ordinating** and **controlling** (Fayol). In businesses, we can add the need to achieve **economic results.**

- A manager's job is not clear-cut and systematic in practice. More recent descriptions of the manager's role (Mintzberg) describe **interpersonal** roles (figurehead, leader, liaison), **informational** roles (monitor, disseminator, spokesperson) and **decisional** roles (entrepreneur, disturbance-handler, resource allocator, negotiator).

- The **supervisor** is at the first level of management, being closest to operational work. A supervisor is a person normally selected to take charge of a group of people or special task to ensure that work is carried out satisfactorily, as well as fulfilling his or her own tasks.

- Supervisors often have to plan the use of **resources** in their section and **schedule** activities to ensure that work is done on time, to standard and to budget. Supervisors might act as project managers: a **project** is a defined task with a beginning and an end point.

- **Classical** organisation and management theories emphasise issues of:

   ° **hierarchy and structure** of authority
   ° **control** by managers and technical specialists over workers and work
   ° principles of 'good' **organisation**

- **Human relations** approaches reacted against the impersonal rationality of classical theories and emphasised the importance of people, their relationships and attitudes at work.

- Later theories emphasised the organisation's openness to **environmental influences**, and its **internal complexity**. The organisation could be viewed as an open socio-technical system. Given this dynamic, complex nature, there could be no 'one best way to manage': the **contingency approach** basically says, 'It all depends...'

- *See the Part B mind map summaries on pages 105 and 106.*

Quick quiz

1 What do you understand by the phrase 'organisations offer the advantage of synergy'?

2 List some of the different activities within an organisation.

3 List the traditional management functions.

4 List three categories of managerial roles.

5 What is span of control?

6 'A supervisor's job is like any other manager's.' Do you agree?

7 List some aids to planning work.

8 What is unusual about project management?

9 What did the Human Relations School recognise?

10 Why is the contingency approach useful?

Answers to quick quiz

1 By bringing together two individuals, their combined output would exceed their total output if they continued to work together separately: the whole is greater than the sum of the parts

2 Buying, selling, accounting, research and development, employing people, making/providing goods and services

3 The functions of management are: planning, organising, co-ordinating, controlling and commanding.

4 Interpersonal, informational, decisional

5 The number of subordinates immediately reporting to a superior

6 No - a supervisor is in charge of non-managerial employees, whereas a manager might be in charge of other managers in the levels below; a supervisor's job often contains a technical aspect.

7 Scheduling, deadlines, contingency plans, job cards.

8 A project has specific start and end points, whereas other activities might be continuous.

9 The importance of people and their needs in motivated work performance.

10 It encourages managerial flexibility.

Answers to activities

Answer 3.1

Fayol's functions would define the activities: 1 = controlling; 2 = planning; 3 = commanding; 4 = co-ordinating; 5 = organising.

Answer 3.2

Your answer may well be that the cinema manager takes on all of Mintzberg's roles, although **figurehead** and **negotiator** play a very minor part in his day.

Answer 3.3

Your answer should include some of the following.

To delegate, Bert must identify the objectives of the task; explain the limits within which Brenda will work, such as liaising with the sales department but not contacting customers; establish deadlines; indicate in what format the results should be made (oral report, written report, memo); and agree how progress will be monitored (brief weekly meetings, weekly memo or informal chats).

Answer 3.6

Borderline Computers' methods would conflict with Fayol's principles of specialisation, the scalar chain of command, and unity of command. Sticking to those principles would prevent rapid decision-making and communication and reduce the efficiency of the teams' performance.

Answer 3.7

Inputs to an organisational system include:

- Materials, components
- Labour (ie employees)
- Money
- Information and ideas

Outputs include:

- Goods and/or services
- Trained and/or experienced labour
- Money (dividends to shareholders, wages to employees)
- Information
- Environmental consequences of its activities (such as pollution or traffic)
- Social consequences of its activities (fashion trends, sensible or dangerous behaviour).

Answer 3.8

Systems approach methods, applied to the given statements (True or False), are as follows. (a) F; (b) T; (c) F; (d) F; (e) T; (f) T.

Answer 3.9

Your answer concerning Cobble and Carter's proposed change from the classical approach, should have included some of the following.

(a)   The advantage of the new approach is that they would be able to respond to different companies in relevant and effective ways. Decision making would be quicker. The smaller teams would feel more responsible for their work, thus increasing motivation. With the improved efficiency, cost savings would be increased.

(b)   They would need to consider staffing levels and redeployment, a logical division of customers, the specialist knowledge required, limits of authority and costs.

Chapter 4   Teams

Chapter topic list

1   Individuals, groups and teams

2   Membership of the team

3   Development of the team

4   Building the team

5   Effective teams

Learning objectives

On completion of this chapter you will be able to:

Syllabus reference

- identify methods to evaluate team performance   c

- define the purpose of a team   c

- outline the composition of successful teams   c

- explain the development of a team   c

- list team building tools   c

1 INDIVIDUALS, GROUPS AND TEAMS

1.1 As an employee your relationship with the organisation is as an individual: after all, the employment contract is with you as an individual, and you are recruited as an individual. In your working life, though, you will generally find yourself working as part of a group or **team**. If you are a supervisor or a manager, you may direct a team.

Groups

> ### KEY TERM
> A **group** is 'any collection of people who perceive themselves to be a group'.

1.2 Groups have certain attributes that a random 'crowd' does not possess.

(a) **A sense of identity**. There are acknowledged boundaries to the group which define who is 'in' and who is 'out', who is 'us' and who is 'them'.

(b) **Loyalty to the group,** and acceptance within the group. This generally expresses itself as conformity or the acceptance of the 'norms' of behaviour and attitudes that bind the group together and exclude others from it.

(c) **Purpose and leadership.** Most groups have an express purpose, whatever field they are in: most will, spontaneously or formally, choose individuals or sub-groups to lead them towards the fulfilment of those goals.

1.3 Any organisation is composed of many groups, with such attributes of their own. People in organisations will be drawn together into groups by:

- A **preference for small groups**, where closer relationships can develop
- The **need to belong** and to make a contribution that will be noticed and appreciated
- **Familiarity:** a shared office or canteen
- **Common** rank, specialisms, objectives and interests
- The attractiveness of a particular group **activity** (joining an interesting club, say)
- **Resources** offered to groups (for example sports facilities)
- **'Power'** greater than the individuals could muster (trade union, pressure group)
- **Formal** directives

1.4 **Informal** groups will invariably be present in any organisation. Informal groups include workplace 'cliques', and networks of people who regularly get together to exchange information, groups of 'mates' who socialise outside work and so on. They have a constantly fluctuating membership and structure.

1.5 **Formal** groups will be consciously organised by the organisation, for a task which they are held responsible - they are task oriented, and become **teams**. Although many people enjoy working in teams, their popularity in the work place arises because of their effectiveness in fulfilling the organisation's work.

Activity 4.1

What primary groups are you a member of in your study or work environment(s)? How big are these groups? How does the size of your class, study group, work-team - or whatever- affect your ability to come up with questions or ideas and give you the help and support to do something you couldn't do alone?

Teams

1.6 Roles of teams

Type of role	Comments
Work organisation	Combine skills of different individuals.
	Avoids complex communication between different business functions.
Control	Fear of letting down the team can be a powerful motivator - teams can be used to control the performance and behaviour of individuals.
	Teams can be used to resolve conflict
Knowledge generation	Teams can generate ideas.
Decision-making	Decisions can be evaluated from more than one viewpoint.
	Teams can be set up to investigate new developments.

Teamworking

1.7 The basic work units of organisations have traditionally been specialised functional departments. In more recent times, organisations are adopting small, flexible teams. Teamworking allows work to be shared among a number of individuals, so it gets done faster than by individuals working alone. Individuals working alone may achieve less.

- They lose sight of their 'whole' tasks
- They have to co-ordinate their efforts through lengthy channels of communication

1.8 A team may be called together temporarily, to achieve specific task objectives (**project team**), or may be more or less permanent, with responsibilities for a particular product, product group or stage of the production process (a **product or process team**).

There are two basic approaches to the organisation of team work: multi-skilled teams and multi-disciplinary teams.

Multi-disciplinary teams

1.9 **Multi-disciplinary teams** bring together individuals with **different skills and specialisms**, so that their skills, experience and knowledge can be **pooled** or exchanged.

1.10 Multi-disciplinary teams:

(a) Increase workers' **awareness of their overall objectives** and targets.

(b) **Aid co-ordination** between different areas of the business.

(c) **Help to generate solutions to problems**, and suggestions for improvements, since a multi-disciplinary team has access to more 'pieces of the jigsaw'.

Multi skilled teams

1.11 A multi-skilled team brings together a number of individuals who can **perform *any* of the** group's tasks. These tasks can then be shared out in a more flexible way between group members, according to who is available and best placed to do a given job at the time it is required.

1.12 The recognition that greater autonomy can - and perhaps should - be given to work teams is reflected clearly in the comparatively recent concept of **empowerment**, which is discussed in the next chapter.

1.13 Teams and teamworking are very much in fashion, but there are potential drawbacks.

(a) Teamworking is **not suitable for all jobs** - some managers do not like to admit this.

(b) Teamwork should be introduced because it leads to better performance, not because people feel better or more secure.

(c) The teams can delay good decision-making. The team might produce the compromise decision, not the right decision.

(d) Social relationships might be maintained at the expense of other aspects of performance.

(e) **Group norms** may **restrict individual personality** and flair.

(f) **Group think**. The cosy consensus prevents consideration of alternatives or constructive criticism.

(g) Personality clashes and political behaviour can get in the way of decision making.

Activity 4.2

Identify some differences between your contribution as an individual to your organisation and your contribution as a team member.

Activity 4.3

Before reading on, list five 'types' of people that you would want to have on a project team, involved (say) in organising an end-of-term party.

---

2   MEMBERSHIP OF THE TEAM

Who should belong?

2.1 Team members should be good at getting things done and establishing good working relationships. Here is what determines membership.

(a) The technical specialist **skills needed**. A team might exist to combine expertise from different departments.

(b) **Power** in the wider organisation. Team members may have influence.

(c) Access to **resources**.

(d) The **personalities** and goals of the individual **members** of the team will help to determine the group's and goals.

(e) The **blend** of the individual skills and abilities of its members.

2.2 **Belbin** drew up a list of the most effective character-mix in a team. This involves eight necessary roles which should ideally be **balanced** and evenly 'spread' in the team.

Member	Role
Co-ordinator	Presides and co-ordinates; balanced, disciplined, good at working through others.
Shaper	Highly strung, dominant, extrovert, passionate about the task itself, a spur to action.
Plant	Introverted, but intellectually dominant and imaginative; source of ideas and proposals but with disadvantages of introversion.
Monitor-evaluator	Analytically (rather than creatively) intelligent; dissects ideas, spots flaws; possibly aloof, tactless - but necessary.
Resource-investigator	Popular, sociable, extrovert, relaxed; source of new contacts, but not an originator; needs to be made use of.
Implementer	Practical organiser, turning ideas into tasks; scheduling, planning and so on; trustworthy and efficient, but not excited; not a leader, but an administrator.
Team worker	Most concerned with team maintenance – supportive, understanding, diplomatic; popular but uncompetitive - contribution noticed only in absence.
Finisher	Chivvies the team to meet deadlines, attend to details; urgency and follow-through important, though not always popular.

The **specialist** joins the team to offer expert advice when needed.

> **Exam alert**
>
> In this his article in the November/December 2000 ACCA *Technician Bulletin*, the examiner noted: 'Students often confuse Tuckman's interesting ideas on teams with those of Belbin. The difference is quite clear: Tuckman deals with the process of formation, while Belbin describes the roles undertaken once the team has formed and is working.' Bear this in mind as you read on to the work of Tuckman – and indeed any management theory. It is helpful to cite theories in your exam answers – but only if you cite them correctly!

How do people contribute?

2.3 **Analysing the functioning of a team**

(a) Assess who (if anybody) is performing each of Belbin's **team roles**. Who is the team's plant? co-ordinator? monitor-evaluator? and so on.

(b) Analyse the **frequency and type** of individual members' contributions to group discussions and interactions.

    (i) Identify which members of the team habitually make the most contributions, and which the least. (You could do this by taking a count of contributions from each member, during a sample 10-15 minutes of group discussion.)

(ii)   If the same people tend to dominate discussion **whatever** is discussed, the team has a problem.

2.4   Neil Rackham and Terry Morgan have developed a helpful categorisation of the types of contribution people can make to team discussion and decision-making.

Category	Behaviour	Example
Proposing	Putting forward suggestions, new concepts or courses of action	'Why don't we look at a flexi-time system?'
Building	Extending or developing someone else's proposal.	'Yes. We could have a daily or weekly hours allowance, apart from a core period in the middle of the day.'
Supporting	Supporting another person or his/her proposal.	'Yes, I agree, flexi-time would be worth looking at.'
Seeking information	Asking for more facts, opinions or clarification.	'What exactly do you mean by "flexi-time"?'
Giving information	Offering facts, opinions or clarification.	'There's a helpful outline of flexi-time in this article.'
Disagreeing	Offering criticism or alternative factors or opinions which contradict a person's proposals or opinions.	'I don't think we can take the risk of not having any staff here at certain periods of the day.'
Attacking	Attempting to undermine another person or their position: more emotive than disagreeing.	'In fact, I don't think you've thought this through at all.'
Defending	Arguing for one's own point of view.	'Actually, I've given this a lot of thought, and I think it makes sense.'
Blocking/ difficulty stating	Putting obstacles in the way of a proposal, without offering any alternatives.	'What if the other teams get jealous? It would only cause conflict.'
Open behaviour	Risking ridicule and loss of status by being honest about feelings and opinions.	'I thing some of us are afraid that flexi-time will show up how little work they really do in a day.'
Shutting-out behaviour	Interrupting or overriding others; taking over.	'Nonsense. Let's move onto something else - we've had enough of this discussion.
Bringing-in behaviour	Involving another member; encouraging contribution.	'Actually, I'd like to hear what Fred has to say. Go on, Fred.'
Testing understanding	Checking whether points have been understood.	'So flexi-time could work over a day or a week; have I got that right?'
Summarising	Drawing together or summing up previous discussion.	'We've now heard two sides to the flexi-time issue: on the one hand, flexibility; on the other side possible risk. Now … '

2.5 Each type of behaviour may be appropriate in the right situation at the right time. A team may be low on some types of contribution - and it may be up to the team leader to encourage, or deliberately adopt, desirable behaviours (such as bringing-in, supporting or seeking information) in order to provide balance.

3 DEVELOPMENT OF THE TEAM

Exam alert

The pilot paper and the December 2000 exam both asked a practical question about team development and team-building, the subject of this section and the next. Much of it might seem common sense but remember to apply the models we give you. Tuckman and Woodcock featured in the December 2000 exam.

3.1 You probably have had experience of being put into a group of people you do not know. Many teams are set up this way and it takes some time for the team to become effective.

3.2 Four stages in this development were identified by Tuckman. We have added a fifth at the end.

FORMATION . of Teams

Step 1. **Forming**

The team is just coming together. Each member wishes to impress his or her **personality** on the group. The individuals will be trying to find out about each other, and about the aims and norms of the team. There will at this stage probably be a **wariness about introducing new ideas**. The **objectives** being pursued may as yet be **unclear** and a leader may not yet have emerged. This period is essential, but may be time wasting: the team as a unit will not be used to being autonomous, and will probably not be an efficient agent in the planning of its activities or the activities of others.

Step 2. **Storming**

This frequently involves more or less open **conflict** between team members. There may be **changes** agreed in the original objectives, procedures and norms established for the group. If the team is developing successfully this may be a fruitful phase as more realistic targets are set and **trust** between the group members increases.

Step 3. **Norming**

A period of **settling down**: there will be agreements about work sharing, individual requirements and expectations of output. Norms and procedures may evolve which enable methodical working to be introduced and maintained.

Step 4. **Performing**

The team sets to work to execute its task. The difficulties of growth and development no longer hinder the group's objectives.

Step 5. **Dorming**

Often, after a team has been performing effectively for a while it becomes complacent. The team goes into a semi-automatic mode of operation, with no fresh energy or attention focused on the task - even if it changes - and with efforts devoted primarily to the maintenance of the team itself.

BPP PUBLISHING

Activity 4.4

Read the following statements and decide to which category they belong (forming, storming, norming, performing, dorming).

(a) Two of the group arguing as to whose idea is best.
(b) Progress becomes static.
(c) Desired outputs being achieved.
(d) Shy member of group not participating.
(e) Activities being allocated.

3.3 Another model was developed by Woodcock, who classified teams into four categories.

Category	Comment
Undeveloped	The team-leader takes most decisions. People are not quite sure what the objectives should be. Personal interaction is based on hiding feelings.
Experimenting	The group turns in on itself, with people raising and facing key issues.
Consolidating	The task and its objectives become clear, people begin to get along with each other on a personal level, and people begin to agree on procedures.
Mature	Working methods are methodical, people are open with their feelings 'leadership style is contributory and the group recognises its responsibilities to the rest of the organisation'.

4 BUILDING THE TEAM

4.1 In Section 3, we suggested that teams have a natural evolutionary life cycle, and that four stages can be identified. Not all teams develop into mature teams, and might be stuck, stagnating, in any one of the stages.

4.2 So, it often falls to the supervisor or manager to build the team. There are three main issues involved in team building.

Issues	Comments
Team identity	Get people to see themselves as part of this group
Team solidarity	Encourage loyalty so that members put in extra effort for the sake of the team
Shared objectives	Encourage the team to commit itself to shared work objectives and to co-operate willingly and effectively in achieving them.

4.3 Teambuilding exercises should seek to achieve these objectives. However, with the best will in the world, problems can develop. Woodcock refers to blockages and building blocks in the team building process. Adapted, these are as follows.

Issue	Blockage	Building block
Leadership	Inappropriate	The leader can adopt a suitable leadership style. See Chapter 10
Membership	Insufficient mix of skills and personalities	Ensure team members are suitably qualified; if necessary, get them to adopt another role (see Para 2.2) than what they would normally
Climate	Unconstructive	Strive to achieve an atmosphere of co-operation
Objectives	Not clear	The team has been brought together for some organisational purpose, so this can be clarified and developed into sub-objectives which are agreed
Achievement	Poor achievement	Performance is improved in a climate of trust and learning
Work methods	Ineffective	Develop sensible procedures for carrying out the team's business
Communications	Not open; people are afraid to challenge or confront key issues	Develop a climate in which people can speak their minds, constructively
Individuals	Development needs not attended to	Individuals are given opportunities to grow or develop within the team; easier in multi-skilled teams
Creativity	Low	Techniques such as brainstorming can enhance creativity, but a lot depends on how new ideas are treated
Interpersonal relations	Poor and unconstructive	Some people will never get on or have much in common, but they can still work together effectively. Exercises might be needed to break the ice
Review and control	Non-existent	The performance of the team can be reviewed at regular intervals

4.4 We can now discuss some of the techniques for building team identity, team solidarity and the commitment to shared-objectives. But first try the Activity below.

Activity 4.5

Why might the following be effective as team-building exercises?

(a) Sending a project team (involved in the design of electronic systems for racing cars) on a recreational day out 'karting'.

(b) Sending two sales teams on a day out playing 'War Games', each being an opposing combat team trying to capture the other's flag, armed with paint guns.

(c) Sending a project team on a conference at a venue away from work, with a brief to review the past year and come up with a 'vision' for the next year.

BPP PUBLISHING

These are actually commonly-used techniques. If you are interested, you might locate an activity centre or company near you which offers outdoor pursuits, war games or corporate entertainment and ask them about team-building exercises and the effect they have on people

4.5 A manager might seek to reinforce the sense of identity of the group. Arguably this is in part the creation of boundaries, identifying who is in the team and who is not.

(a) **Name**. Staff at McDonald's restaurants are known as the Crew. In other cases, the name would be more official describing what the team actually does (eg Systems Implementation Task Force)

(b) **Badge or uniform**. This often applies to service industries, but it is unlikely that it would be applied within an organisation

(c) Expressing the team's **self-image:** teams often develop their own jargon, especially for new projects

(d) Building a team **mythology** - in other words, stories from the past ('classic mistakes' as well as successes.)

(e) **A separate space**: it might help if team members work together in the same or adjacent offices, but this is not always possible.

Activity 4.6

Consider the group of people you are studying with. Do you feel you are a team? Appoint a leader - someone you think is a 'co-ordinator' type, who will keep the discussion on track and under control - and try another brainstorming session. This time you are going to organise the end of term party.

4.6 **Team solidarity** implies cohesion and loyalty inside the team. A team leader might be interested in:

(a) Expressing solidarity

(b) Encouraging interpersonal relationships - although the purpose of these is to ensure that work does get done.

(c) Dealing with conflict by getting it out into the open; disagreements should be expressed and then resolved

(d) Controlling competition. The team leader needs to treat each member of the team fairly and to be seen to do so; favouritism undermines solidarity.

(e) Encouraging some competition with other groups if appropriate. For example, sales teams might be offered a prize for the highest monthly orders; London Underground runs best-kept station competitions.

Activity 4.7

Can you see any dangers in creating a very close-knit group? Think of the effect of strong team cohesion:

(a) what the group spends its energies and attention on;
(b) how the group regards outsiders, and any information or feedback they supply;
(c) how the group makes decisions.

What could be done about these dangerous effects?

4.7 Getting commitment to the team's objectives

- Clearly set out the objectives of the team
- Allowing the team to participate in setting objectives
- Regular feedback on progress and results with constructive criticism
- Get the team involved in providing feedback
- Positive reinforcement (praise etc) can encourage the team
- Where appropriate, champion the success of the team within the organisation

5 EFFECTIVE TEAMS

5.1 Some teams work more effectively than others, for a variety of reasons, and we can identify ways of evaluating whether a team is effective.

Quantifiable factors		
Factor	**Effective team**	**Ineffective team**
Labour turnover	Low	High
Accident rate	Low	High
Absenteeism	Low	High
Output and productivity	High	Low
Quality of output	High	Low
Individual targets	Achieved	Not achieved
Stoppages and interruptions to the work flow	Low	High (eg because of misunderstandings, disagreements)

Qualitative factors		
Factor	**Effective team**	**Ineffective team**
Commitment to targets and organisational goals	High	Low
Understanding of team's work and why it exists	High	Low
Understanding of individual roles	High	Low
Communication between team members	Free and open	Mistrust
Ideas	Shared for the team's benefit	'Owned' (and hidden) by individuals for their own benefit
Feedback	Constructive criticism	Point scoring, undermining
Problem-solving	Addresses causes	Only looks at symptoms
Interest in work decisions	Active	Passive acceptance
Opinions	Consensus	Imposed solutions
Job satisfaction	High	Low
Motivation in leader's absence	High	'When the cat's away...'

Activity 4.8

Try to interview somebody who manages a work team, who would be willing to talk to you for just 10 or 15 minutes. Run through the checklist of factors given above, asking your interviewee to give a 'Yes' or 'No' to each of the statements. Put a question mark (?) where is was difficult for the respondent to answer, because the factor was not easy to define or measure. You might want to reconsider some of our factors, or the way they are phrased in the light of the answers you get. What conclusions can you draw from your survey?

5.2   Handy takes a contingency approach to the problem of group effectiveness, which, he argues, depends on:

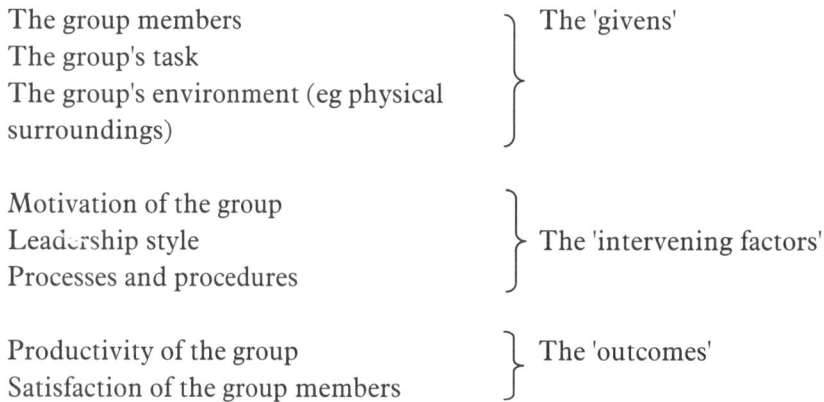

The group members
The group's task
The group's environment (eg physical surroundings)
} The 'givens'

Motivation of the group
Leadership style
Processes and procedures
} The 'intervening factors'

Productivity of the group
Satisfaction of the group members
} The 'outcomes'

Case example

(Adapted from *People Management* October 1997)

The annual staff survey at *Nationwide Building Society* usually places its customer service teams for mortgages and insurance at mid-table in terms of employee satisfaction. This year the teams are at the top. At the same time their productivity has increased by half, sickness absence has fallen by 75 percent and overtime is down to zero.

In the early 1990s Nationwide began to abandon traditional management hierarchies in the non-retail part of its business. In customer service, they were looking for an approach that would further develop multi-skilling while supporting a flatter structure. Self managed teamworking seemed the obvious answer, as it also addressed issues such as morale and job satisfaction.

They work on the premise that the people who know how best to carry out and improve their own work are the teams themselves. Members have shared authority and responsibility to plan, implement and control how their targets are achieved.

In 1995 the Nationwide began a project in the Northampton administrative centre, revolutionising the basis under which the 12 teams in the mortgage and insurance customer service department operated. They increased the level of training and worked on their decision-making, conflict management and team-building skills. Each team had between nine and 18 members, including a leader, but he or she had a coaching, rather than directing, role.

When work comes in, the team decides who is the most appropriate person to take it on, depending on skills and existing workloads. While teams are encouraged to share recourses with each other when necessary, there is also a competitive element. But this is never allowed to detract from the performance of the department - you are only as good as your worst-performing team.

The results of each team are charted, allowing comparative league tables to be created. Initially, one team finished consistently at the foot of the productivity table. Its members consulted colleagues in the more successful teams and altered their work processes accordingly.

Members compared their sickness and overtime figures with those of other teams, and then took responsibility for controlling these elements. Often this was done using a sense of ownership and pride which, could with peer pressure, reduce the need for managerial intervention.

Key learning points

- A **group** is a collection of individuals who perceive themselves as a group. It thus has a sense of **identity**.

- A **team** is more than a group. It has an **objective**, and may be set up by the organisation under the supervision or coaching of a team leader, although (as we saw in the Nationwide example at the end of the chapter) **self-managed teams** are growing in popularity.

- Teamworking has four main roles: **organising** work; **controlling** activities; **generating** knowledge; **decision-making**.

- **Multidisciplinary** teams contain people from different departments, pooling the skills of specialists.

- **Multi-skilled** teams contain people who themselves have more than one skill.

- Problems with teams include **conflict** on the one hand, and **group think** on the other.

- Ideally teams should have a **mix** of personalities and roles. **Belbin** suggests: co-ordinator, shaper, plant, monitor-evaluator, resource-investigator, implementer, team-worker, finisher and, occasionally, specialist.

- Team members make different types of **contribution** (eg proposing, defending, blocking)

- A team develops in **stages**: forming, storming, norming, performing and dorming. (Alternatively, try undeveloped team, experimenting team, consolidating team, mature team.) These processes can be enhanced by active **team building** measures to support team identity, solidarity and commitment to objectives.

- A team can be evaluated on the basis of quantifiable and qualitative factors, covering its **operations** and its **output**.

- *See the Part B mind map summary on page 107.*

Quick quiz

1 What is a team?

2 What are Belbin's eight roles for a well-rounded team?

3 Outline what happens in the 'storming' stage of the team development.

4 Describe a mature team.

5 List teambuilding issues.

6 Suggest five ways in which a manager can get a team 'behind' task objectives.

7 List six of Rackham and Morgan's categories of contribution to group discussion.

8 Suggest five quantifiable characteristics of effective teams and five qualitative characteristics of ineffective teams.

Answers to quick quiz

1 A small number of people with complementary skills who are committed to a common purpose, performance goals and approach for which they hold themselves basically accountable.

2 Co-ordinator, shaper, plant, monitor-evaluator, resource-investigator, implementer, teams worker, finisher.

3 Storming brings out members' own ideas and attitudes. There may be conflict as well as creativity.

4 Members work well together; objectives and procedures are clear.

5 Leaders, Members. Climate. Objectives. Achievement. Work methods. Communications. Individuals, Creativity. Interpersonal communications. Review and control.

6 Set clear objectives, get the team to set targets/standard, provide information and resources, give feedback, praise and reward, and champion the team in the organisation.

7 Proposing, building, supporting, seeking information, giving information, disagreeing.

8 Refer to Paragraph 5.1

Answers to activities

Answer 4.1

The primary groups are probably your tutor group or class. If at work, it would be the section in which you work. If the groups are large, you may feel reluctant to put forward ideas or ask questions, but even within a large group you should feel there is support and that help is at hand if you need it.

Answer 4.2

Individuals contribute	Groups contribute
• A set of skills	• A mix of skills
• Objectives set by manager	• Some teams can set their own objectives under the corporate framework
• A point of view	• A number of different points of view, enabling a swift overview of different ways of looking at a problem
• Creative ideas related to the individual's expertise	• Creative ideas arising from new combinations of expertise
• 'I can't be in two places at once'	• Flexibility as team members can be deployed in different ways
• Limited opportunity for self-criticism	• Opportunity for exercising control

Answer 4.3

For your ideal team, you might have listed: a person with originality and ideas; a 'get up and go' type, with energy and enthusiasm; a quite logical thinker who can be sensible about the ideas put forward; a plodder who will be happy to do the routine leg-work; and a team player who can organise the others and help them reach agreement on ideas.

Answer 4.4

Categorising the behaviour of group members in the situations described results in the following: (a) storming, (b) dorming, (c) performing, (d) forming, (e) norming.

Answer 4.5

(a) Recreation helps the team to build informal relationships: in this case, the chosen activity also reminds them of their tasks, and may make them feel special, as part of the motor racing industry, by giving them a taste of what the end user of their product does.

(b) A team challenge purses the group to consider its strengths and weaknesses, to find it natural leader, This exercise creates and 'us' and 'them ' challenge: perceiving the rival team as the enemy heightens the solidarity of the group.

(c) This exercise encourages the group the raise problems and conflicts freely, away from the normal environment of work and also encourages brainstorming and the expression of team members' dreams for what the team can achieve in the future.

Answer 4.7

Problems may arise in an ultra close-knit group because:

(a) The group's energies may be focused on its own maintenance and relationships, instead of on the task.

(b) The group may be suspicious or dismissive of outsiders, and may reject any contradictory information or criticism they supply; the group will be blinkered and stick to its own views, no matter what; cohesive groups thus often get the impression that they are infallible: they can't be wrong - and therefore can't learn from this mistake.

(c) The group may squash any dissent or opinions that might rock the boat. Close-knit groups tend to preserve a consensus - falsely if required - and to take risky decisions, because they have suppressed alternative facts and viewpoints.

This phenomenon is called '**groupthink**'. In order to limit its effect, the team must be encouraged:

(a) Actively to seek outside ideas and feedback;
(b) To welcome self-criticism within the group; and
(c) Consciously to evaluate conflicting evidence and opinions.

Answer 4.8

Hopefully, you found the checklist in Section 5 effective. If not, change the wording. From the answers you received you should be able to judge how effective the team/group is.

BPP PUBLISHING

Chapter 5   Authority, power and delegation

Chapter topic list

1   Power and authority

2   Responsibility and accountability

3   Delegation

4   Empowerment

Learning objectives

On completion of this chapter you will be able to:

	Syllabus reference
• define the terms authority and responsibility	c
• identify different types of power, including legitimised power	c
• examine the relationships between authority and responsibility	c
• explain the importance and benefits of delegation, including empowerment	c
• describe the skills and process of delegation	c

1   POWER AND AUTHORITY

1.1   Organisations feature a large number of different activities to be co-ordinated, and large numbers of people whose **co-operation and support** is necessary for the manager to get anything done. As you have probably noticed if you have worked for any length of time, organisations rarely run as clockwork, and all depend on the directed energy of those within them.

> **KEY TERM**
>
> **Power** is the **ability** to get things done.

1.2   A manager without power, of whatever kind, cannot do his/her job properly, and this applies to supervisors too. Power is not something a person has in isolation: it is exercised over other individuals or groups.

1.3   **Types of power**

Type of power	Description
Physical, coercive power	This is the power of physical force or punishment. Physical power is absent from most organisations, but organisations can sometimes use hidden forms of coercion to get what they want
Resource power	Access to or control over valued resources is a source of power. For example, managers have a resource of information or other contacts. The amount of resource power a person has depends on the scarcity of the resource, how much the resource is valued by others, and how far the resource is under the manager's control
Legitimate or position power	This is power associated with a particular job or position in the hierarchy. For example, your boss has the power to authorise certain expenses, or organise work. This is equivalent to authority
Expert power	A person may have power if his/her experience, qualifications or expertise are recognised. Typically, accountants have a type of expert power because of their knowledge of the tax system.
Personal power	A person may be powerful simply by force of personality, which can influence other people, inspire them etc.
Negative power	This is the power to disrupt operations, such as strike, refusal to communicate information

> **KEY TERM**
>
> **Authority** is the *right* of a person to ask someone else to do something and expect it to be done. Authority is thus another word for position power.

1.4   Managerial authority consists of:

(a)   **Making decisions within the scope of authority** given to the position. For example, a supervisor's authority is limited to his/her team and with certain limits. For items of expenditure more than a certain amount, the supervisor may have to go to someone else up the hierarchy.

(b) **Assigning tasks** to subordinates, and expecting satisfactory performance of these tasks.

Activity 5.1

What types of authority and power are being exercised in the following case?

Marcus is an accountant supervising a team of eight technicians. He has to submit bank reconciliation statements every week to the chief accountant. However, the company runs four different bank accounts and Marcus gets a team member, Dave, to do it for him. Marcus asks Isabella to deal with the purchase ledger - the company obtains supplies from all over the world, and Isabella, having worked once for an international bank, is familiar with letters of credit and other documentation involved with overseas trade. Isabella has recently told Marcus that Maphia Ltd, a supplier, should not be paid because of problems with the import documentation, even though Marcus has promised Maphia to pay them. Marcus is getting increasingly annoyed with Sandra who seems to be leaving Marcus's typing until last, although she says she has piles of other work to do. 'Like reading the newspaper,' thinks Marcus, who is considering pulling rank by giving her an oral warning.

KEY TERM

Line authority is the authority a manager has over a subordinate, arising from their respective positions in the organisation hierarchy. In other words, if you have line authority you an exercise position power over someone immediately below you.

1.5 There are other forms of authority which individuals (or departments) may exercise in the organisation.

KEY TERMS

Staff authority is the influence wielded when an expert gives specialist **advice** to another manager or department, even if there is no direct line authority. (An example might be the influence of legal advice from the legal department, or advice on budgetary constraints from the accounts department.)

Functional authority is staff authority which has been built into the structure and policies of the organisation, for example where a specialist department lays down *procedures* and *rules* for other departments to follow within the area of its expertise. (The Personnel department, for example, may impose certain recruitment and selection procedures on other departments.)

Exam alert

A detailed question was set in June 2001, covering the *distinction* between 'power' and 'authority', five different *types* of power, and the *need* for delegation. This shows that you need to give detailed attention to distinctions and categories – even if they appear in brief list form (as in paragraph 1.3 above). It also illustrates the need to pay attention to the *key words* in exam questions, so that you can gain marks in all parts by answering the *specific* topic areas and angles of the question.

2 RESPONSIBILITY AND ACCOUNTABILITY

> **KEY TERMS**
>
> **Responsibility** is the **obligation** a person has to fulfil a task, which (s)he has been given.
>
> **Accountability** is a person's liability to be called to account for the fulfilment of tasks they have been given.

2.1 You might be a bit confused by the various terms. They are related but they mean different things. But just keep in mind:

	Comment
You are **given authority** to do something	As a supervisor, you have the authority to plan command and control the work of your team, within certain limitations.
You are **responsible for** something	Your boss has left you in charge of the team. He says 'I'd like you to get a balance sheet and P & L prepared by 6pm tonight.' That is your responsibility. You are busy on other things, but you give the balance sheet to one team member and a P & L to the other.
You are **accountable to** someone.	You give the completed balance sheet and P & L to your boss who is annoyed that some of the figures don't agree. You are accountable to the boss: you cannot blame your subordinates; you were given the task, and the authority to make sure it was done. As head of the department you are accountable for what they do.

Activity 5.2

Can a person delegate responsibility, authority and accountability to a subordinate?

Responsibility without authority

2.2 In practice, matters are rarely as clear-cut, and in many organisations responsibility and authority are:

	Comments
Not clear	When the organisation is doing something new or in a different way, its existing rules and procedures may be out of date or unable to cope with the new development. Various people may try to 'empire build'. The managers may not have designed the organisation very well.
Shifting	In large organisations there may be real conflict between different departments; or the organisation may, as it adapts to its environment, need to change.

2.3 Don't skip this activity as the issues it covers are identified in the ACCA's Teaching Guide for this unit. Having completed the activity, you should have some idea of the subject matter of the next two sections.

Activity 5.3

You have just joined a small accounts department. The financial controller keeps a very close eye on expenditure and, being prudent, believes that nothing should be spent that is not strictly necessary. She has recently gone on a three week holiday to Venezuela. You have been told that you need to prepare management accounts, and for this you have to obtain information from the payroll department in two weeks time. This is standard procedure. However, there are two problems. One of the other people in your department has gone sick, and a temporary replacement will be needed very shortly. The personnel department say: 'We need a staff requisition from the Financial Controller before we can get in a temp. Sorry, you'll just have to cancel your weekend'. The payroll department is happy to give you the information you need - except directors' salaries, essential for the accounts to be truly accurate.

What is the underlying cause of the problem and what, in future, should you ask the Financial Controller to do to put it right?

3 DELEGATION

> **KEY TERM**
>
> **Delegation** of authority is when a superior gives to a subordinate part of his or her own authority to make decisions.

3.1 Note that delegation can only occur if the superior initially possesses the authority to delegate; a subordinate cannot be given organisational authority to make decisions unless it would otherwise be the superior's right to make those decisions personally.

3.2 Managers and supervisors must delegate some authority because:

(a) There are **physical and mental limitations** to the work load of any individual or group in authority.

(b) Managers and supervisors are free to **concentrate on the aspects of the work** (such as planning), which only they are competent (and paid) to do.

(c) The **increasing size and complexity** of some organisations calls for specialisation, both managerial and technical.

3.3 However, by delegating authority to assistants, the supervisor takes on the extra tasks of:
- **Monitoring their performance**
- **Co-ordinating** the efforts of different assistants.

3.4 **The process of delegation**

Step 1. **Specify the expected performance** levels of the assistant, keeping in mind the assistant's level of expertise.

Step 2. **Formally assign tasks** to the assistant, who should formally agree to do them.

Step 3. **Allocate resources and authority** to the assistant to enable him or her to carry out the delegated tasks at the expected level of performance.

Step 4. **Maintain contact** with the assistant to review the progress made and to make constructive criticism. **Feedback** is essential for control, and also as part of the learning process.

3.5 Remember that ultimate **accountability** for the task remains with the supervisor: if it is not well done it is at least partly the fault of poor delegation, and it is still the supervisor's responsibility to get it re-done.

Problems of delegation

3.6 Many managers and supervisors are **reluctant to delegate** and attempt to do many routine matters themselves in addition to their more important duties.

(a) **Low confidence and trust** in the abilities of their staff: the suspicion that 'if you want it done well, you have to do it yourself'.

(b) The burden of **accountability for the mistakes of subordinates**, aggravated by (a) above.

(c) A **desire to 'stay in touch'** with the department or team - both in terms of workload and staff - particularly if the manager does not feel 'at home' in a management role.

(d) **Feeling threatened.** An unwillingness to admit that assistants have developed to the extent that they could perform some of the supervisor's duties. The supervisor may feel threatened by this sense of 'redundancy'.

(e) **Poor control and communication systems** in the organisation, so that the manager feels he has to do everything himself, if he is to retain real control and responsibility for a task, and if he wants to know what is going on.

(f) An **organisational culture** that has failed to reward or recognise effective delegation, so that the manager may not realise that delegation is positively regarded (rather than as shirking responsibility).

(g) **Lack of understanding** of what delegation involves - not giving assistants total control, or making the manager himself redundant.

3.7 As an accountant, you might like the idea of a **trust-control dilemma** in a superior-subordinate relationship. The sum of trust and control is a constant amount:

$$T + C = Y$$

where $T =$ the trust the superior has in the subordinate, and the trust which the subordinate feels the superior has in him;

$C =$ the degree of control exercised by the superior over the subordinate;

$Y =$ a constant, unchanging value;

If there is any increase in C (if the superior retains more 'control' or authority), the subordinate will immediately recognise that he is being trusted less. If the superior wishes to show more trust in the subordinate, he can only do so by reducing C: by delegating more authority.

3.8 **Overcoming the reluctance of managers to delegate**

(a) **Train the subordinates** so that they are capable of handling delegated authority in a responsible way. If assistants are of the right 'quality', supervisors will be prepared to trust them more.

(b) Have a system of **open communications**, in which the supervisor and assistants freely interchange ideas and information. If the assistant is given all the information needed to do the job, and if the supervisor is aware of what the assistant is doing:

(i) The assistant will make better-informed decisions.

(ii) The supervisor will not panic because he does not know what is going on.

(c) **Ensure that a system of control is established**. If responsibility and accountability are monitored at all levels of the management hierarchy, the dangers of relinquishing authority and control to assistants are significantly lessened.

3.9 **When to delegate**

(a) Is the **acceptance** of staff affected required (for morale, relationships, ease of implementation of the decision etc)?

(b) Is the **quality** of the decision most important? Many technical financial decisions may be of this type, and should be retained by the supervisor if he or she alone has the knowledge and experience to make them.

(c) Is the **expertise or experience** of assistants relevant or **necessary** to the task, and will it enhance the quality of the decision?

(d) Can **trust** be placed in the competence and reliability of the assistants?

(e) Does the **decision** require tact and confidentiality, or, on the other hand, maximum exposure and assimilation by employees?

3.10 In instances where **reference upwards** to the manager's own superior may be necessary, the manager should consider:

(a) Whether the decision is **relevant** to the superior: will it have any impact on the boss's area of responsibility, such as strategy, staffing, or the departmental budget?

(b) Whether the superior has **authority** or **information** relevant to the decision that the manager does not possess: for example, authority over issues which affect other departments or interdepartmental relations, or information only available at senior levels.

(c) The **political climate** of the organisation: will the superior expect to be consulted, and resent any attempt to make the decision without his authority?

Activity 5.4

You are the manager of an accounts section of your organisation and have stopped to talk to one of the clerks in the office to see what progress he is making. He complains bitterly that he is not learning anything. He gets only routine work to do and it is the same routine. He has not even been given the chance to swap jobs with someone else. You have picked up the same message from others in the office. You discuss the situation with Jean Howe the recently appointed supervisor. She appears to be very busy and harassed. When confronted with your observations she says that she is fed up with the job. She is worked off her feet, comes early, goes late, takes work home and gets criticised behind her back by incompetent clerks.

What has gone wrong?

Exam alert

Delegation was covered comprehensively in June 1998. The question asked for definitions of responsibility, authority and delegation. Then you had to show how delegation could be effective and how problems could be overcome.

4 EMPOWERMENT

4.1 Empowerment and delegation are related.

> **KEY TERM**
>
> **Empowerment** is the current term for making workers (and particularly work teams) responsible for achieving, and even setting, work targets, with the freedom to make decisions about how they are to be achieved.

4.2 **Empowerment** goes in hand in hand with:

(a) **Delayering** or a cut in the number of levels (and managers) in the chain of command, since responsibility previously held by middle managers is, in effect, being given to operational workers.

(b) **Flexibility**, since giving responsibility to the people closest to the products and customer encourages responsiveness - and cutting out layers of communication, decision-making and reporting speeds up the process.

(c) **New technology**, since there are more 'knowledge workers'. Such people need less supervision, being better able to identify and control the means to clearly understood ends. Better information systems also remove the mystique and power of managers as possessors of knowledge and information in the organisation.

4.3 **Reasons for empowerment**

> 'The people lower down the organisation possess the knowledge of what is going wrong with a process but lack the authority to make changes. Those further up the structure have the authority to make changes, but lack the profound knowledge required to identify the right solutions. The only solution is to change the culture of the organisation so that everyone can become involved in the process of improvement and work together to make the changes.' (Max Hand)

The change in organisation structure and culture as a result of empowerment can be shown in the diagram below.

Traditional hierarchical structure: fulfilling management requirements

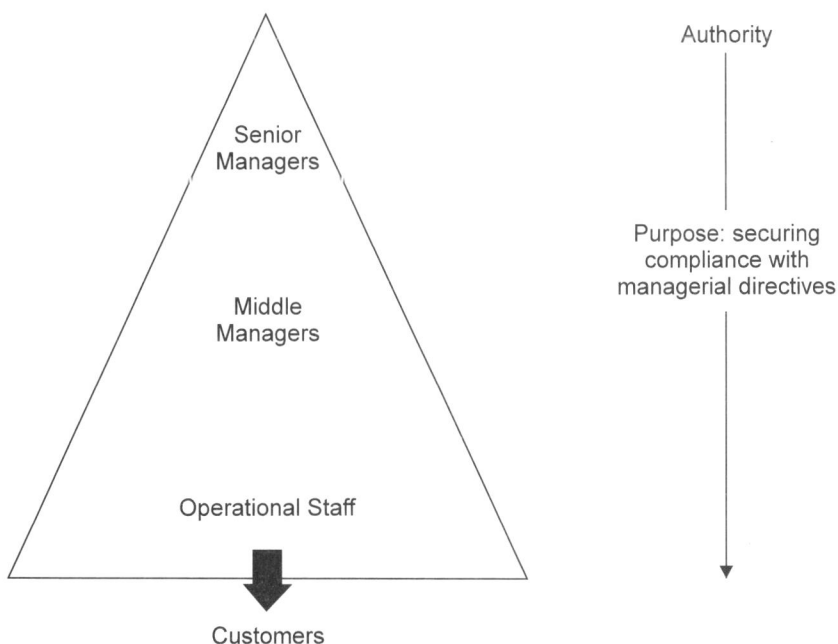

Empowerment structure: supporting workers in serving the customer

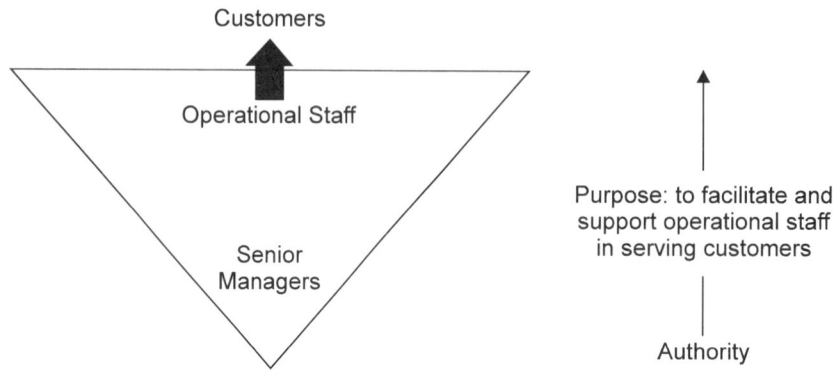

Customers

Operational Staff

Senior
Managers

Purpose: to facilitate and
support operational staff
in serving customers

Authority

4.4   The argument, in a nutshell, is that by empowering workers (or 'decentralising' control of business units, or devolving/delegating responsibility, or removing levels in hierarchies that restrict freedom), not only will the job be done more effectively but the people who do the job will get more out of it.

Case example

The validity of this view and its relevance to modern trends appears to be borne out by the approach to empowerment adopted by *Harvester Restaurants*, as described in *Personnel Management*. The management structure comprises a branch manager and a 'coach', while everyone else is a team member. Everyone within a team has one or more 'accountabilities' (these include recruitment, drawing up rotas, keeping track of sales targets and so on) which are shared out by the team members at their weekly team meetings. All the team members at different times act as 'co-ordinator' to the person responsible for taking the snap decisions that are frequently necessary in a busy restaurant. Apparently all of the staff involved agree that empowerment has made their jobs more interesting and has hugely increased their motivation and sense of involvement.

Exam alert

You can mention empowerment in the contexts of team-working, motivation and leadership.

Key learning points

- **Power** is the ability to get things done.

- There are many types of power in organisations: position or **legitimate power**, expert power, personal power, resource power and negative power are examples.

- **Authority** is related to position power. It is the right to take certain decisions within certain boundaries.

- A person with **responsibility** is given a task to get done. Such a person must have the necessary authority to command resources and staff to get the job. Responsibility without authority is stressful for the individual.

- Responsibility can be **delegated**, but the person delegating responsibility still remains accountable to his or her boss that the job has been done to the right standard. Accountability is not delegated.

- **Delegation** is necessary to get work distributed throughout the organisation. Successful delegation requires the resolution of the Trust-Control dilemma. Some managers and supervisors are reluctant to delegate.

- Successful delegation requires that people have the right skills and the authority to do the job, and are given feedback.

- **Empowerment** takes the process of delegation further. Its advantages are not simply that it releases managers to do more important things, but that front line staff are closest to customers are best able to take decisions concerning them.

- *See the Part B mind map summary on pages 105 and 106.*

Quick quiz

1 What is legitimate power?

2 Give an example of negative power

3 How can uncertainty give power to managers in one department as opposed to another?

4 Why might functional authority be a good thing for the organisation?

5 Why can't accountability be delegated?

6 Why are there problems in determining authority and responsibility?

7 List the stages in the process of delegation.

8 List some problems in delegation.

Answers to quick quiz

1 Legitimate power is power arising from formal position in the organisation hierarchy; authority, in other words

2 Going on strike; refusal to communicate; withhold information; delaying etc.

3 If the department reduces the level of uncertainty other departments face.

4 Because it is exercised impersonally, impartially and automatically.

5 Because the delegator has been given the task by his/her own boss.

6 Because the boundaries are often unclear and shifting.

7 Specify performance levels; formally assign task; allocate resources and authority; give feedback.

8 Low trust, low competence, fear, worry about accountability.

Answers to activities

Answer 5.1

Marcus exercises position power because he has the right, given to him by the chief accountant, to get his staff, such as Dave, to do bank reconciliations. Dave does not do bank recs because of Marcus's personality or expertise, but because of the simple fact that Marcus is his boss. Marcus also exercises position power by getting Isabella to do the purchase ledger. However, Isabella exercises expert power because she knows more about import/export documentation than Marcus. She does not have the authority to stop the payment to Maphia, and Marcus can ignore what she says, but that would be a bad decision. Sandra is exercising negative power as far as Marcus is concerned, although she is claiming, perhaps, to exercise resource power - her time is a scarce resource. No-one appears to be exercising physical power as such, although Marcus's use of the disciplinary procedures would be a type of coercive power.

Answer 5.2

Responsibility for a task can be delegated, simply by using your authority to give the job to someone else. But accountability cannot be delegated: you are still accountable for the work you have delegated to a junior. It is your job to ensure the job is done: you are accountable to your boss.

Answer 5.3

The immediate problem is that the Financial Controller should have considered these issues before she went to Venezuela. The underlying cause, as far as you are concerned, is that you have responsibility to do a task but without the authority - to obtain all the information you need and to hire a temp - to do the job. In future the Financial Controller should, when delegating the task, delegate the authority to do it.

Answer 5.4

The problem appears to be that the new supervisor is taking too much of the department's work on to herself. While she is overworked, her subordinates are apparently not being stretched and as a result motivation and morale amongst them are poor. The supervisor herself is unhappy with the position and there is a danger that declining job satisfaction will lead to inefficiencies and eventually staff resignations.

There could be a number of causes contributing to the problem.

(a) Jean Howe may have been badly selected, ie she may not have the ability required for a supervisory job.

(b) Alternatively she may just be unaware of what is involved in a supervisor's role. She may not have realised that much of the task consists of managing subordinates; she is not required to shoulder all the detailed technical work herself.

(c) There may be personality problems involved. Jean Howe regards her clerks as incompetent and this attitude may arise simply form an inability to get on with them socially. (Another possibility is that her staff actually are incompetent.)

(d) The supervisor does much of the department's work herself. This may be because she does not understand the kind of tasks which can be delegated and the way in which delegation of authority can improve the motivation and job satisfaction of subordinates.

As manager you have already gone some way towards identifying the actual causes of the problem You have spoken to some of the subordinates concerned and also to the supervisor. You could supplement this by a review of personnel records relating to Jean Howe to discover how her career has progressed so far and what training she had received (if any) in the duties of a supervisor. You may then be in a position to determine which of the possible causes of the problems are operating in this case.

Chapter 6 Performance, objectives and targets

Chapter topic list

1   Introducing 'control systems'

2   Organisational objectives and targets

3   Personal objectives and targets

4   Performance management: an introduction

Learning objectives

On completion of this chapter you will be able to:

Syllabus reference

- explain the importance of objective setting   c

- explain the behavioural theories of objective setting   c

- compare and contrast corporate and personal objectives   c

- illustrate quantitative and qualitative targets   c

- explain the importance of understanding ethics and social responsibility   c

- identify performance measures and work standards and how they can be established   c

- define performance management and indicate how it can be applied   c

1 INTRODUCING 'CONTROL SYSTEMS'

1.1 Go back to the definition of organisation in Chapter 1: **it is a social arrangement for the controlled performance of collective goals**. In this chapter we look at 'controlled performance' and various sorts of goal, in the context of the organisation and the individual within it.

Exam alert

A look at the wider context of the management function of control will help you to get a grasp of this topic, and to understand why it is important for organisations and individuals, and for your exam.

1.2 Because organisations have goals they want to satisfy, they need to direct their activities by:

- Deciding what they want to achieve
- Deciding how and when to do it and who is to do it
- Checking that they do achieve what they want, by monitoring what has been achieved and comparing it with the plan
- Taking action to correct any deviation

1.3 The overall framework for this is a system of **planning and control**. This is best demonstrated by means of a diagram.

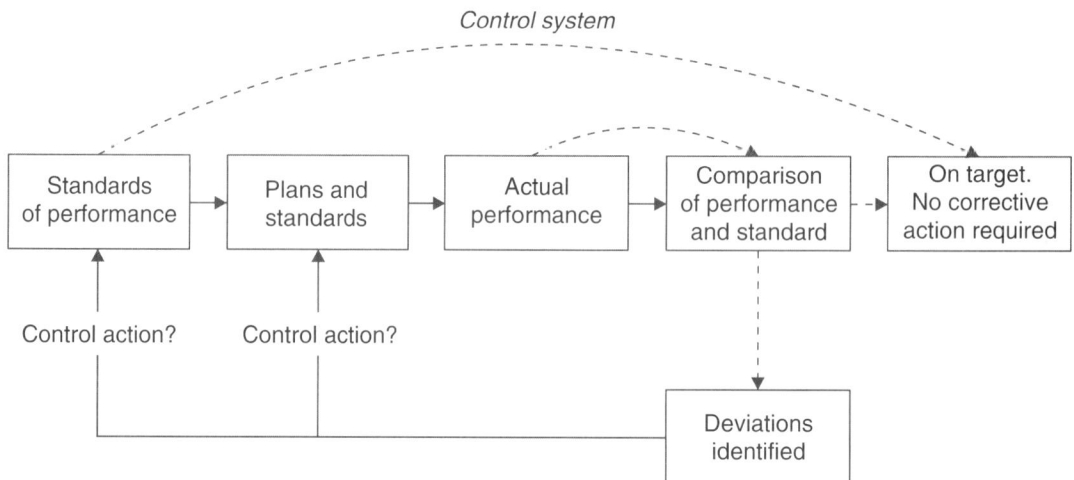

Control system

Where there is a deviation from standard, a decision has to be made as to whether to adjust the plans or the standard, or whether it is the performance itself that needs correction.

Case examples

The **need for control, monitoring and evaluation** is illustrated below.

(a) **Water utilities** are required to monitor the cleanliness of water provided for drinking. Such control is continuous. Any sudden deterioration in water quality must be dealt with.

(c) Most companies monitor which of their **products make money** and which do not. If a product's sales are falling, a firm might advertise it more heavily to increase sales. On the other hand, it might evaluate the market for the product and decide to cease production altogether.

2 ORGANISATIONAL OBJECTIVES AND TARGETS

Mission

2.1   Overall, the main direction of an organisation is set by its mission.

> **KEY TERM**
>
> **Mission** 'describes the organisation's basic function in society', ie why it exists (Mintzberg).

Case examples

The following statements were taken from annual reports of the organisations concerned. Are they 'mission statements'? If so, are they any good?

(a)   **Glaxo** 'is an integrated research-based group of companies whose corporate purpose is to create, discover, develop, manufacture and market throughout the world, safe, effective medicines of the highest quality which will bring benefit to patients through improved longevity and quality of life, and to society through economic value.'

(b)   **The British Film Institute.** 'The BFI is the UK national agency with responsibility for encouraging and conserving the arts of film and television. Our aim is to ensure that the many audiences in the UK are offered access to the widest possible choice of cinema and television, so that their enjoyment is enhanced through a deeper understanding of the history and potential of these vital and popular art forms.'

2.2   Mission has four elements.

Elements	Comments
Purpose	Why does the organisation exist and for whom (eg shareholders)
Strategy	What business are we in?
Policies and standards of behaviour	Mission should influence what people actually do and how they behave: the mission of a hospital is to save lives, and this affects how doctors and nurses interact with patients
Values	What people believe to be important, such as customer satisfaction: if this is critical to the mission this will influence issues such as the speed at which phones are answered etc.

2.3   Even though the mission can be very general, you can see it does have real implications for how individuals go about what they do.

Goals, aims and objectives

2.4   Many different writers use different terminology to describe the same thing. In this area you have to be especially careful.

> **KEY TERM**
>
> **Goals**: 'The intentions behind decision or actions' (Henry Mintzberg) or 'a desired end result' (Shorter Oxford English Dictionary)

2.5   There are two types of goal.

   •   Non-operational, **qualitative** goals (**aims**)
   •   Operational, **quantitative** goals (**objectives**)

2.6   **Aims** are qualitative goals. In other words they cannot be quantified. For example, a university's may be: 'to seek truth'. (You would not see: 'increase truth by 5%')

2.7   **Objectives** are operational goals. In other words they can be expressed in quantitative form.

Characteristics	Example
Objectives are SMART	• Operational goal: cut costs.
• Specific • Measurable • Attainable • Realistic • Time-bounded	• Objective: reduce budgeted expenditure on paper-clips by 5% by December 31 2004

2.8   In practice, people often use the words goals, aims and objectives interchangeably. But remember that some goals fulfil SMART criteria and others do not, even though they are still meaningful.

Activity 6.1

Most organisations establish closed or quantifiable objectives.

(a)   Give reasons why aims (non-operational goals) might still be important.
(b)   Give an example of when SMART targets might be essential.

The purpose of setting goals and objectives

2.9   'Objectives are needed in every area where performance and results directly and vitally affect the survival and prosperity of the business' (Drucker). Objectives in these key areas should enable management to:

   (a)   **Implement** the mission, by outlining what needs to be achieved.

   (b)   **Publicise** the direction of the organisation to managers and staff, so that they know where their efforts should be directed.

   (c)   **Appraise** the validity of decisions about **strategies** (by assessing whether these are sufficient to achieve the stated objectives).

   (d)   **Assess and control actual performance,** as objectives can be used as targets for achievement.

2.10   There is a **hierarchy of objectives/goals,** with one primary corporate objective (restricted by certain constraints on corporate activity) and a series of subordinate objectives/goals which should combine to ensure the achievement of the overall objective.

Primary objectives

2.11   People might disagree on the choice of the overall corporate objective, although for a **business** it must be a **financial objective,** such as profitability, return on capital employed or earnings per share.

Secondary objectives

2.12 Secondary or **subordinate** goals and objectives can be listed under the following broad headings. They support the primary goal.

(a) **Market position**
Total market share of each market, growth of sales, customers or potential customers, the need to avoid relying on a single customer for a large proportion of total sales, what markets should the company be in.

(b) **Product development**
Bring in new products, develop a product range, investment in research and development, provide products of a certain quality at a certain price level.

(c) **Technology**
Improve productivity, reduce the cost per unit of output, exploit appropriate technology.

(d) **Employees and management**
Train employees in certain skills, reduce labour turnover.

Activity 6.2

Review the list of goals and objectives above. How do you think of each of them relates to the financial objectives in 2.11? What conflicts are there?

Plans and standards

2.13 Plans state what should be done to achieve the objectives. Standards and targets specify a desired level of performance. Here are some examples.

(a) **Physical standards** eg units of raw material per unit produced.

(b) **Cost standards**. These convert physical standards into a money measurement by the application of standard prices. For example, the standard labour cost of making product X might be 4 hours at £5 per hour = £20.

(c) **Capital standards**. These establish some form of standard for capital invested (eg the ratio of current assets to current liabilities) or a desired share price.

(d) **Revenue standards**. These measure expected performance in terms of revenue earned (such as turnover per square metre of shelf space in a supermarket).

(e) **Deadlines for programme completion.** Performance might be measured in terms of actual completion dates for parts of a project compared against a budgeted programme duration.

(f) The **achievement of stated goals** (eg meeting profit objective).

(g) **Intangible standards**. Intangible standards might relate to employee motivation, quality of service, customer goodwill, corporate image, product image etc. It is possible to measure some of these by attitude surveys, market research etc.

2.14 Standards and targets are used in the **control system** to monitor whether performance is in fact proceeding according to plan.

BPP
PUBLISHING

Case example

We now relate the control system to a practical example, such as **monthly budgetary control variance reports**.

(a) Standard costs and a master budget are prepared for the year. Management organises the resources of the business (inputs) so as to achieve the budget targets.

(b) At the end of each month, actual results (output, sales, costs, revenues etc) are reported back to management. The reports are the measured output of the control system, and the process of sending them to the managers responsible provides the feedback loop.

(c) Managers compare actual results against the plan and where necessary, take corrective action to adjust the workings of the system, probably by amending the inputs to the system.

2.15 The American management writers Cyert and March suggest that traditional ideas on organisational objectives are too simplistic and do not recognise managerial and economic reality. Many business organisations have market power and therefore discretion as to objectives. They argue that:

(a) The firm is a **connection of groups.** There are therefore multiple goals, especially as this network changes over time.

(b) There is **unresolved conflict** because of the existence of this network.

(c) Objectives are rarely thought through and are often stated in **non-operational terms.** In practice, objectives tend to be stable because of:

- Limited bargaining time
- Control systems
- Departmentalisation
- Precedents becoming institutionalised as 'the way things are always done'.

(d) One reasons why firms fail to achieve optimal results is the development of **'organisational slack'.**

- Payment is based only on what is necessary
- Maximum efficiency is not known
- Because of limited market information it is not possible to maximise profit

(e) In general, Cyert and March identify the following goals for any organisation.

- Production
- Inventory
- Market and market share
- Profit

(f) They conclude that **'Organisations cannot have objectives, only people have objectives'.**

Ethics and social responsibility

2.16 In Chapter 3, we mentioned that organisations can be viewed as **open systems**, which influence and are influenced by their environment. Managers need to take into account the effect of organisational outputs into the market and the wider **social community**, for several reasons.

(a) The modern **marketing concept** says that in order to survive and succeed, organisations must satisfy the needs, wants and *values* of customers and potential customers. Communication and education have made people much more aware of issues such as the environment, the exploitation of workers, product safety and consumer rights. Therefore an organisation may have to be *seen* to be responsible in these areas in order to retain public support for its products.

(b) Despite high unemployment, there are skill shortages in the labour pool and employers must compete to attract and retain high quality employees. If the organisation gets a reputation as a **socially responsible** employer it will find it easier to do this, than if it has a poor 'employer brand'.

(c) Organisations **rely** on the society, and local community of which they are a part, for access to facilities, business relationships, media coverage, labour, supplies, customers and so on. Organisations which acknowledge their responsibilities as part of the community may find that many areas of their operation are facilitated.

(d) The law, regulations and Codes of Practice **impose** certain social responsibilities on organisations, in areas such as employment protection, equal opportunities, environmental care, health and safety, product labelling and consumer rights. There are financial and operational **penalties** for organisations which fail to comply.

2.17 The **social responsibilities of a business**, depending on the nature of its operations, may include:

(a) The impact of its operations on the **natural environment**

(b) Its treatment of **staff** and potential staff, for example, the hiring and promotion of people from minority groups, policies on sexual harassment, refusal to exploit cheap labour in developing countries

(c) Non-reliance on contracts with **military** or **political connotations.**

(d) **Charitable support** and activity in the local community or in areas related to the organisation's field of activity

(e) **Above-minimum** standards of product health, safety and labelling

---

Activity 6.3

See if you can come up with examples of socially responsible objectives, in line with (a) to (e) above.

KEY TERM

Ethics are the moral principles by which people act or do business.

2.18 **Business ethics** are the values underlying what an organisation understands by socially responsible behaviour. An organisation may have *values* to do with non-discrimination, fairness and integrity. It is very important that managers understand:

(a) The importance of **ethical behaviour** – as outlined above

(b) The differences in what is considered ethical behaviour in **different cultures**

2.19 Theorist **Elaine Sternberg** suggests that two **ethical values** are particularly pertinent for business, because without them business could not operate at all. There are:

(a) **Ordinary decency.** This includes respect for property rights, honesty, fairness and legality.

(b) **Distributive justice**. This means that organisational rewards should be proportional to the contributions people make to organisational ends. The supply and demand for labour will influence how much a person is actually paid, but if that person is worth employing and the job worth doing, then the contribution will justify the expense.

2.20 Business ethics in a **global market place**, are however, far from clear cut. If you are working outside the UK, you will need to develop – in line with whatever policies your organisation may have in place – a kind of 'situational' ethic to cover various issues.

(a) **Gifts** may be construed as bribes in Western business circles, but are indispensable in others

(b) Attitudes to **women** in business

(c) The 'exploitation' of **cheap labour** in very poor countries

(d) The expression and nature of **agreements**

2.21 A business may operate on principles which strive to be:

- Ethical and legal (eg The Body Shop)
- Unethical but legal (eg arms sales to brutal regimes)
- Ethical but illegal (eg publishing stolen documents on government mismanagement)
- Unethical and illegal (eg the drugs trade, employing child labour)

2.22 Assuming a firm wishes to act ethically, it can embed **social responsibility** in its decision processes in the following ways.

(a) Include it in the **corporate culture,** or codes of practice

(b) Ensure that **incentive systems** are designed to support ethical behaviour (eg safety)

(c) Identify social responsibility in the **mission statement**, as a public declaration of what the organisation stands for

3 PERSONAL OBJECTIVES AND TARGETS

Behavioural theories of objective setting

3.1 People are 'purposive': that is, they act in pursuit of particular goals or purposes. The goals or objectives of an individual influence:

(a) What (s)he **perceives**, since we filter out messages not relevant to our goals and objectives and select those which are relevant

(b) What (s)he **learns,** since learning is a process of selecting and analysing experience in order to take it into account in acting in future, so that our goals and objectives may be more effectively met

(c) What (s)he **does,** since people behave in such a way as to satisfy their goals. This is the basis of motivation, since organisations can **motivate** people to behave in desirable ways (effective work performance) by offering them the means to fulfil their goals.

3.2 In order for learning and motivation to be effective, it is essential that **people know exactly what their objectives are**. This enables them to do the following.

(a) **Plan and direct their effort** towards the objectives

(b) **Monitor their performance** against objectives and adjust (or **learn**) if required

(c) Experience the **reward of achievement** once the objectives have been reached

(d) Feel that their tasks have **meaning and purpose**, which is an important element in job satisfaction

(e) Experience the **motivation of a challenge**: the need to expend energy and effort in a particular direction in order to achieve something

(f) Avoid the **de-motivation** of impossible or inadequately rewarded tasks. As we will discuss in the chapter on motivation, there is a calculation involved in motivated performance. If objectives are vague, unrealistic or unattainable, there may be little incentive to pursue them: hence the importance of SMART objectives.

3.3 We will be discussing specific behavioural theories in relation to motivation and learning in later chapters.

The hierarchy of objectives

3.4 **Individual objectives must be directed towards, or 'dovetailed with' organisational goals.**

(a) **Direction**. Each job is directed towards the same organisational goals. Each managerial job must be focused on the success of the business as a whole, not just one part of it.

(b) **Target**. Each manager's targeted performance must be derived from targets of achievement for the organisation as a whole.

(c) **Performance measurement**. A manager's results must be measured in terms of his or her contribution to the business as a whole.

(d) **Each manager must know** what his or her targets of performance are.

3.5 The hierarchy of objectives which emerges is this.

STRATEGIC PLANS (LONGER-TERM)
|
TACTICAL PLANS
(Shorter-term, for product
market development,
resource development,
operations and organisation)
|
UNIT, OR
DEPARTMENTAL PLANS
|
INDIVIDUAL MANAGERS' OBJECTIVES

Types of objectives for individuals and teams

3.6 **Work objectives**

(a) At team level, they relate to the purpose of the team and the contribution it is expected to make to the goals of the department and the organisation.

(b) At individual level, they are related specifically to the job. They clarify what the individual is expected to do and they enable the performance of the individual to be measured.

3.7 **Standing aims and objectives**

(a) **Qualitative aims** cover issues such as promptness and courtesy when dealing with customer requests; they are always relevant.

(b) A **quantified target** for a sales team would be to ensure that all phone calls are picked up within three rings.

3.8 Output or improvement targets

These have most of the features of SMART objectives. A sales person may be given a target of increasing the number of sales made in a particular district in a certain time. Many firms have targets which involve reducing the number of defects in goods produced, or seek to find ways of working more efficiently.

3.9 Developmental goals

These deal with how an individual can improve his/her own performance and skills. These goals are often set at the appraisal interview and are part of the performance management system. In the control model outlined in Section 1, setting developmental goals would be an example of action taken to improve the individual's and the organisation's performance.

Integrating the organisation's and the individual's objectives: MBO

3.10 The diagram of the hierarchy of objectives in paragraph 3.5 shows a cascade of objectives from the organisation to the individual. This is not always easy to achieve. However, a method of doing so was suggested by proponents of **management by objectives**.

Setting unit objectives for departments: Steps 1 to 4

3.11 **Unit objectives** are required for all departments.

Step 1. They must be set first of all in terms of primary targets, for example relating to achievement of production schedules and delivery dates, the quality of output or efficiency in the use of resources (labour, productivity, material usage)services, or

Step 2. For each of these primary targets, secondary targets (or sub-targets) will be set.

Step 3. **Identify which individual managers** within the unit are in a position to influence the achievement of each of them.

Step 4. Top management will then make a **unit improvement plan** for each unit of the business, setting out specifically the objectives for improvement, the performance standards and the time scale. Each unit improvement plan must be approved by the senior manager with overall responsibility for the unit.

Setting key results: Steps 5 to 7

3.12 **Step 5.** The unit improvement plan is then broken down into a series of **key results** and **performance standards**. For example, the key results of an information systems manager might be as given below.

ITEM	KEY RESULT
Service to users	To ensure that users get regular software upgrades, with appropriate helplines and training.
Use of resources and efficiency levels	The time when users cannot use the network must not exceed 5%.
Costs	The cost per operating hour must not exceed £60.
Quality	Queries from users must be responded to within ten minutes.

Step 6. A personal **job improvement plan** should be agreed with each manager, which will make a quantifiable and measurable contribution to achievement of the plans for the department, branch or company as a whole, within specified time periods.

Step 7. A systematic **performance review** is also necessary.

- A performance review must be a formal and disciplined review of the results achieved by each manager, carried out regularly on pre-determined dates. Performance standards in key results areas provide the means of comparison for actual results achieved.

- Failure to achieve satisfactory results should initiate control action first by the manager, with prompting from his or her superior.

Performance measures for individuals: some guidelines and examples

3.13 The Key Results table above indicated some examples of how a unit's objectives could be tied in with what an individual (a manager in that case) is expected to achieve. But clearly, performance has to be measured properly for any changes to be effected.

3.14 Some principles for devising performance measures are these.

Principle	Comment
Job-related	They should be related to the actual job, and the key tasks outlined in the job description (see chapter 7)
Controllable	People should not be assessed according to factors which they cannot control
Objective and observable	This is contentious. Certain aspects of performance can be measured, such as volume sales, but matters such as courtesy or friendliness which are important to some businesses are harder to measure
Data must be available	There is no use identifying performance measures if the data cannot actually be collected

Activity 6.4

A senior sales executive has a job which involves: 'building the firm's sales' and maintaining 'a high degree of satisfaction with the company's products and services'. The firm buys sports equipment, running machines and so on, which it sells to gyms and individuals. The firm also charges fees to service the equipment. Service contracts are the sales executive's responsibility, and he has to manage that side of the business.

Here some possible performance indicators to assess the sales executive's performance in the role. What do you think of them? Are they any good?

(a) Number of new customers gained per period
(b) Value of revenue from existing customers per period
(c) Renewal of service contracts
(d) Record of customer complaints about poor quality products
(e) Regular customer satisfaction survey
(f) Market share related to competitors

3.15 In an ideal world, when setting objectives and planning the operations of the organisation, the manager will:

- Start from the facts of the situation
- Trace through all possible courses of action, and their consequences
- Choose the course of action with the greatest net benefits.

3.16 This ideal model cannot readily be realised. In practice, managers are limited by time, by the information they have and by their own skills, habits and reflexes.

3.17 **Simon** evolved a 'best practicable model' which would fit the problems of real life. This approach Simon characterised as **bounded rationality**.

(a) In this model the **manager does not optimise** (ie get the best possible solution).

(b) Instead the manager **satifices**. In other words, the manager carries on searching until he or she finds an option which appears tolerably satisfactory, and adopts it, even though it may be less than perfect.

4   PERFORMANCE MANAGEMENT: AN INTRODUCTION

KEY TERM

Performance management is: 'a means of getting better results...by understanding and managing performance within an agreed framework of planned goals, standards and competence requirements. It is a process to establish a shared understanding about what is to be achieved, and an approach to managing and developing people..[so that it]...will be achieved' (**Armstrong**, Handbook of Personnel Management Practice).

Exam alert

The definition is long, but it is worth learning, because the ability to define performance management is explicitly mentioned in the ACCA's Teaching Guide. Performance management was the subject of a very detailed question in the June 2000 exam.

4.1 Armstrong then describes some other features of performance management.

Aspect	Comment
Agreed framework of goals, standards and competence requirements	As in MBO, the manager and the employee agree about a standard of performance, goals and the skills needed.
Performance management is a process	Managing people's performance is an everyday issue to generate real results. It is not just a system of form filling.
Shared understanding	People need to understand the nature of high levels of performance so they can work towards them.
Approach to managing and developing people	(1) How managers work with their teams
	(2) How team members work with managers and each other.
	(3) Developing individuals to improve their performance.
Achievement	The aim is to enable people to realise their potential and maximise their contribution to the organisation's well being.

Aspect	Comment
Line management	A performance management system is primarily the concern, not of experts in the personnel/HRM department, but of the managers responsible for driving the business.
All staff	Everybody is involved in the success of the organisation, so managers must be included in the system.
Specific	As each organisation has unique issues to face, performance management systems cannot really be bought off the peg.
Future-based	Performance management is forward-looking, based on the organisation's future needs and what the individual must do to satisfy them

4.2 **The process of performance management** — PMA Perf Agreement.

Step 1. From the **business plan**, identify the requirements and competences required to carry it out.

Step 2. Draw up a **performance agreement**, defining the expectations of the individual or team, covering standards of performance, performance indicators and the skills and competences people need.

Step 3. Draw up a **performance and development plan** with the individual. These record the actions needed to improve performance, normally covering development in the current job. They are discussed with job holders and will cover, typically:
- The areas of performance the individual feels in need of development
- What the individual and manager agree is needed to enhance performance
- Development and training initiatives

Step 4. **Manage performance continually throughout the year,** not just at appraisal interviews done to satisfy the personnel department. Managers can review actual performance, with more informal interim reviews at various times of the year.

   (a) High performance is reinforced by praise, recognition, increasing responsibility. Low performance results in coaching or counselling

   (b) Work plans are updated as necessary.

   (c) Deal with performance problems, by identifying what they are, establish the reasons for the shortfall, take control action (with adequate resources) and provide feedback

Step 5. Performance review. At a defined period each year, success against the plan is reviewed, but the whole point is to assess what is going to happen in future.

Activity 6.5

What are the advantages to employees of introducing such a system.?

4.3 Organisations are introducing such systems for much the same reason as they pursued management by objectives, in other words, to:
- Tie in individual performance with the performance of the organisation
- Indicate where training and development may be necessary

BPP PUBLISHING

4.4 Many of the issues covered in this brief outline are explored in later chapters. The purpose of introducing it here is to show how the wider goals and expectations of the organisation depend on how individuals work together.

Key learning points

- Organisations have **goals**, which they aspire to achieve.

- Achieving these goals requires a system of **planning and control**: deciding what should be done (goals and objectives), how it is to be done (plans and standard-setting), reviewing what is actually done, comparing actual outcome with plans, and taking corrective action.

- The **mission** is the organisation's overall purpose and reason for existence. While it seems abstract and general it has implications for the commercial strategy, the values of the organisation, and policies and actual standards of behaviour of the people within it.

- **Goals** give flesh to the mission. They can be quantified (objectives) or not quantified (**aims**). Most organisations use a combination of both. Quantified or specific **objectives** have SMART characteristics.

- There is **hierarchy of objectives**. A primary objective of a business might be profit; secondary objectives relate to ways to achieve it.

- The organisation will only achieve its goals through the work of the individuals within it. Therefore, techniques have been suggested to break down the goals into **targets for departments and individuals**. Management by objectives was one such technique, although it perhaps has been superseded by the more modern approach of performance management.

- **Standards of performance** set for individuals should be **job related, controllable, observable**.

- **Performance management** suggests that people must agree performance standards, that the responsibility for performance management is principally that of line management, and that it is a conscious commitment to developing and managing people in organisations. It is a continuous process.

- *This chapter will be reviewed in the Part D mind map summaries in the context of performance review.*

Quick quiz

1 How can organisations direct their activities?

2 What are the elements of a control system?

3 What are four elements of mission?

4 What do you understand by SMART?

5 Why might an organisation wish to be 'socially responsible?

6 List four types of objectives for an individual.

7 How must objectives be interlocked?

8 Define performance management

9 List the steps in performance management

10 How can managers and staff become more committed to objectives, according to supporters of MBO and performance management?

Answers to quick quiz_____

1 By deciding what should be done, how it should be done, reviewing outcomes, and monitoring performance

2 Plans and standards; sensor to detect actual performance; comparator to compare performance with plans and standards; effector to take control action where necessary. Feedback is information about performance.

3 Purpose; business strategy; policies and standards of behaviour; values

4 Specific, measurable, attainable, realistic, time-bounded

5 To retain and attract customers and employees and community support. To comply with legal and policy provisions.

6 Work-based; standing; output or improvement; developmental

7 Vertically; horizontally (across departments); over time

8 Performance management is 'a means of getting better results...by understanding and managing performance within an agreed framework of planned goals, standards and competence requirements. It is a process to establish a shared understanding about what is to be achieved, and an approach to managing and developing people..[so that it]...will be achieved' (Armstrong, Handbook of Personnel Management Practice).

9 Steps in performance management

Step 1 From the business plan, identify the requirements and competences required to carry it out.

Step 2 Develop a performance agreement.

Step 3 Draw up a performance and development plan with the individual.

Step 4 Manage performance continually throughout the year,

Step 5 Performance review.

10 By participating in setting them.

Answers to activities

Answer 6.1

(a) Aims can be just as helpful: customer satisfaction is not something which is achieved just once. Some goals are hard to quantify, for example 'to retain technological leadership'. Quantified objectives are hard to change when circumstances change, as changing them looks like an admission of defeat. Not everything can be measured easily.

(b) An example of when a SMART, quantified target is essential was the need to repair many computer programs by the Year 2000, so that they did not crash. There was a definite deadline, and all relevant software had to be replaced or changed.

Answer 6.2

(a) Market position. Markets are customers. Customers are source of revenue. Markets are where organisations compete with each other. Gaining market share now helps future profitability - but this market share may be expensive in the short term.

(b) Product development is another way of competing, to make profits to satisfy the corporate objectives. This, too, is expensive.

(c) and (d) are to do with organising the production process. This means making operations efficient and effective.

Answer 6.3

Examples (our suggestions only) include:

(a) The Body Shop (among others) not using animal testing on ingredients, Shell (as a **negative** example) causing environmental devastation in Nigeria's river deltas, recyclable packaging

(b)   British Airways extension of married employees' benefits to homosexual partners, anti-ageist policies, the Body shop (again) building economic infrastructures in rural communities

(c)   Sanctions or boycotts of countries such as (in the past) South Africa or Iraq

(d)   Major supermarkets and retailers such as WH Smith often sponsor community facilities, charities and sporting events

(e)   Some organisations have very stringent quality standards

Answer 6.4

These measures do not all address some of the key issues of the job.

(a)   *Number of new customers.* This is helpful as far as it goes but omits two crucial issues: how much the customers actually spend and what the potential is. Demand for this service might be expanding rapidly, and the firm might be increasing sales revenue but losing market share.

(b)   *Revenue from existing customers* is useful – repeat business is generally cheaper than gaining new customers, and it implies customer satisfaction.

(c)   *Renewal of service contracts* is very relevant to the executive's role.

(d)   *Customer complaints about poor quality products.* As the company does not make its own products, this is not really under the control of the sales manager. Instead the purchasing manager should be more concerned. Complaints about the service contract are the sales executive's concern.

(e)   *Customer satisfaction survey.* This is a tool for the sales manager to use as well as a performance measure, but not everything is under the sales executive's control.

Answer 6.5

The key to performance management is that it is forward looking and constructive. Objective-setting gives employees the security in knowing exactly what is expected of them, and this is agreed at the outset with the manager, thus identifying unrealistic expectations. The employee at the outset can indicate the resources needed.

PART B   MINDMAP SUMMARY CHAPTERS 3 & 5

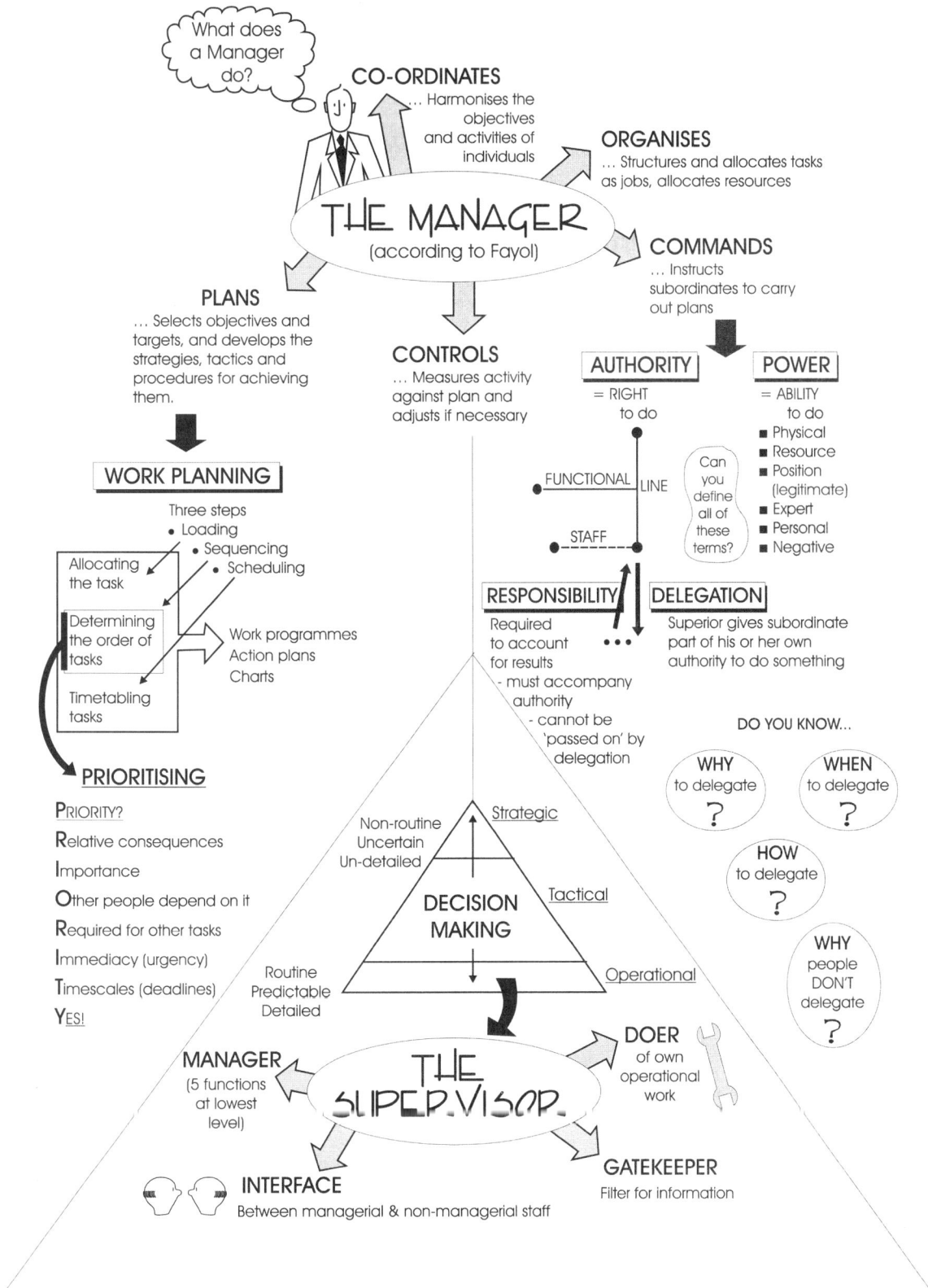

What does a Manager do?

CO-ORDINATES
... Harmonises the objectives and activities of individuals

ORGANISES
... Structures and allocates tasks as jobs, allocates resources

THE MANAGER
(according to Fayol)

COMMANDS
... Instructs subordinates to carry out plans

PLANS
... Selects objectives and targets, and develops the strategies, tactics and procedures for achieving them.

CONTROLS
... Measures activity against plan and adjusts if necessary

AUTHORITY
= RIGHT to do

POWER
= ABILITY to do
- Physical
- Resource
- Position (legitimate)
- Expert
- Personal
- Negative

Can you define all of these terms?

WORK PLANNING

Three steps
- Loading
- Sequencing
- Scheduling

FUNCTIONAL LINE

STAFF

Allocating the task

Determining the order of tasks

Work programmes
Action plans
Charts

RESPONSIBILITY
Required to account for results
- must accompany authority
- cannot be 'passed on' by delegation

DELEGATION
Superior gives subordinate part of his or her own authority to do something

Timetabling tasks

PRIORITISING

Priority?
Relative consequences
Importance
Other people depend on it
Required for other tasks
Immediacy (urgency)
Timescales (deadlines)
Yes!

DO YOU KNOW...

WHY to delegate ?
WHEN to delegate ?
HOW to delegate ?
WHY people DON'T delegate ?

Non-routine
Uncertain
Un-detailed

Strategic

DECISION MAKING

Tactical

Routine
Predictable
Detailed

Operational

MANAGER
(5 functions at lowest level)

THE SUPERVISOR

DOER
of own operational work

INTERFACE
Between managerial & non-managerial staff

GATEKEEPER
Filter for information

continued overleaf ...

BPP PUBLISHING

PART B   MIND MAP SUMMARY CHAPTERS 3 & 5 (contd)

BUT IS THE MANAGER'S JOB REALLY
SO (COMPARATIVELY) CLEAR CUT ?

FOR **1** THING...   MINTZBERG

"Managerial work is not systematic, continuous or routine. In practice it is verbal, intuitive and fragmented."

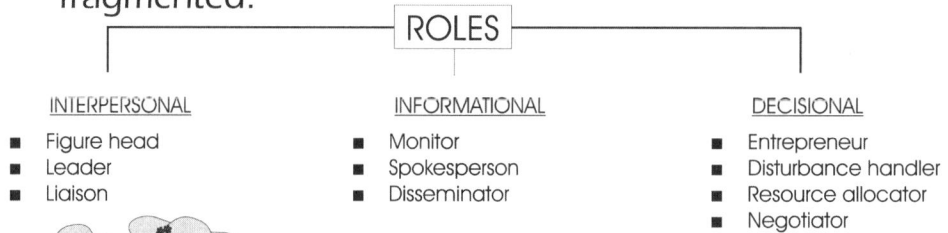

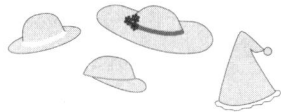

ROLES

INTERPERSONAL	INFORMATIONAL	DECISIONAL
■ Figure head	■ Monitor	■ Entrepreneur
■ Leader	■ Spokesperson	■ Disturbance handler
■ Liaison	■ Disseminator	■ Resource allocator
		■ Negotiator

Can you describe each of the (10) roles?

2...   DIFFERENT SCHOOLS OF THOUGHT

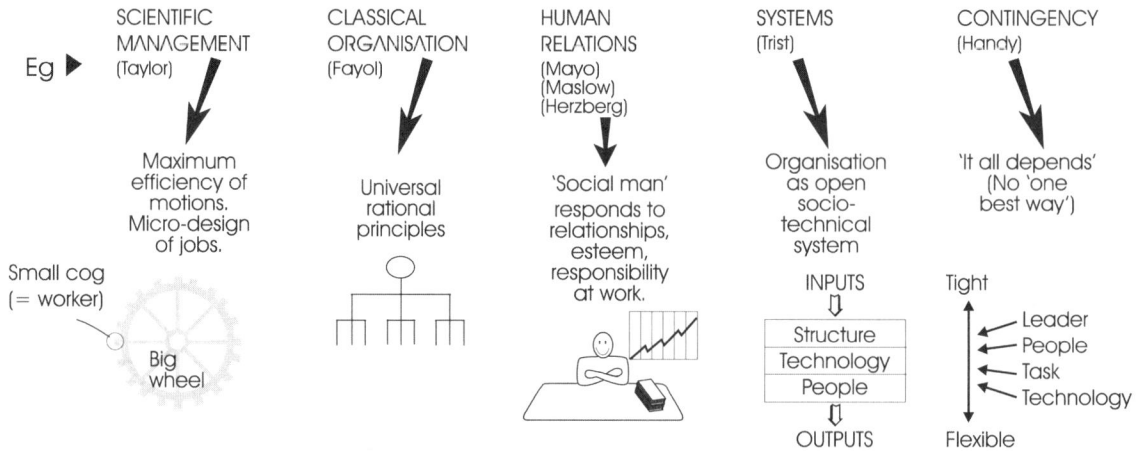

Eg ▶

SCIENTIFIC MANAGEMENT (Taylor)	CLASSICAL ORGANISATION (Fayol)	HUMAN RELATIONS (Mayo) (Maslow) (Herzberg)	SYSTEMS (Trist)	CONTINGENCY (Handy)
Maximum efficiency of motions. Micro-design of jobs.	Universal rational principles	'Social man' responds to relationships, esteem, responsibility at work.	Organisation as open socio-technical system	'It all depends' (No 'one best way')

Small cog (= worker)

Big wheel

INPUTS
⇩
Structure
Technology
People
⇩
OUTPUTS

Tight

Leader
People
Task
Technology

Flexible

3... EMPOWERMENT

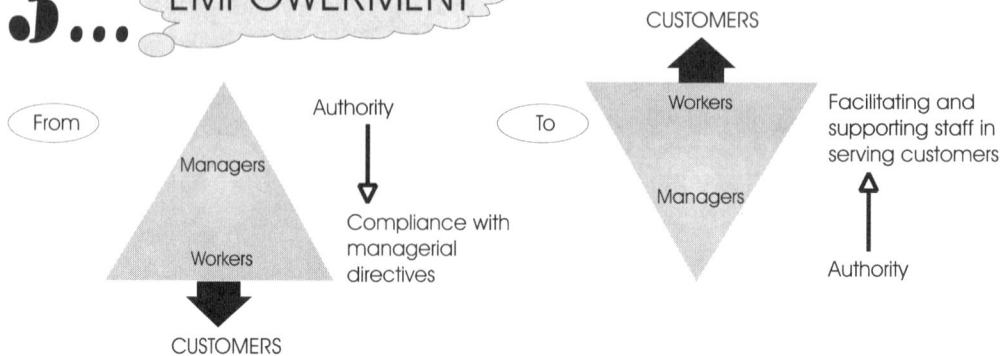

From

Managers

Workers

CUSTOMERS

Authority
⇩
Compliance with managerial directives

To

CUSTOMERS

Workers

Managers

Authority

Facilitating and supporting staff in serving customers

PART B   MIND MAP SUMMARY CHAPTER 4

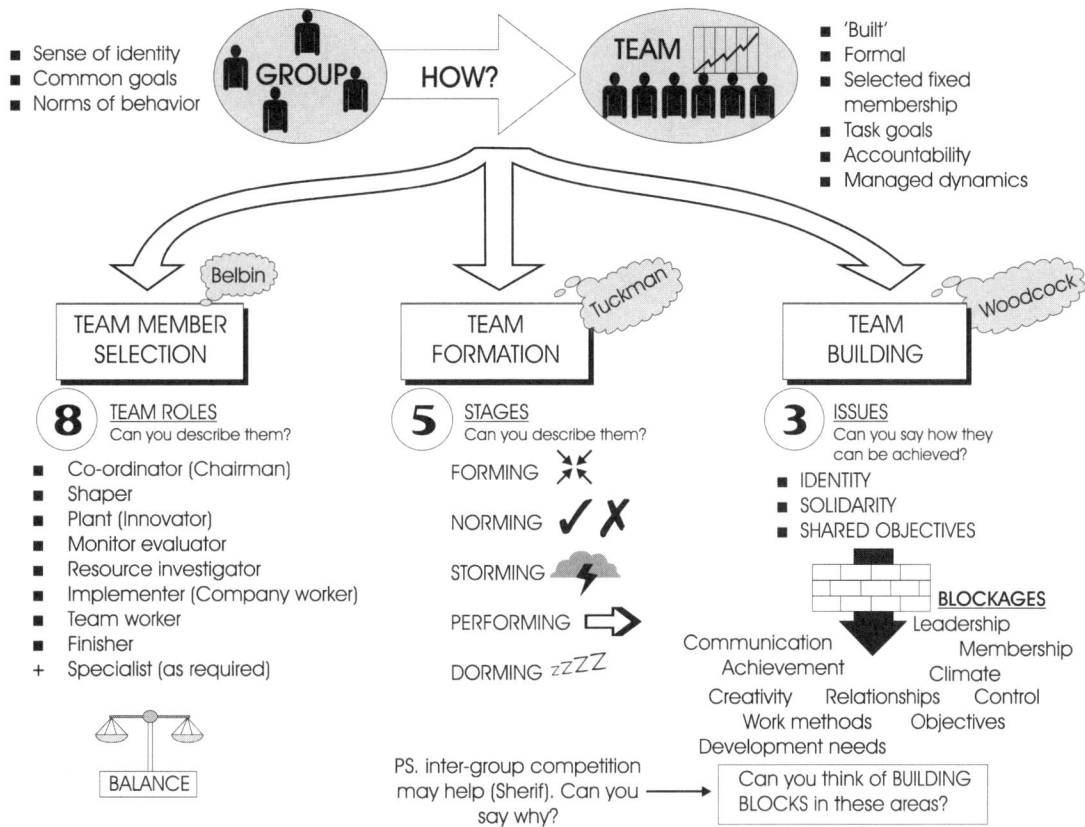

- Sense of identity
- Common goals
- Norms of behavior

GROUP HOW? → **TEAM**

- 'Built'
- Formal
- Selected fixed membership
- Task goals
- Accountability
- Managed dynamics

Belbin

TEAM MEMBER SELECTION

8 TEAM ROLES
Can you describe them?

- Co-ordinator (Chairman)
- Shaper
- Plant (Innovator)
- Monitor evaluator
- Resource investigator
- Implementer (Company worker)
- Team worker
- Finisher
- + Specialist (as required)

BALANCE

Tuckman

TEAM FORMATION

5 STAGES
Can you describe them?

FORMING
NORMING ✓ ✗
STORMING
PERFORMING ⇒
DORMING zzZZ

PS. inter-group competition may help (Sherif). Can you say why? →

Woodcock

TEAM BUILDING

3 ISSUES
Can you say how they can be achieved?

- IDENTITY
- SOLIDARITY
- SHARED OBJECTIVES

BLOCKAGES
Leadership
Membership
Communication
Achievement
Climate
Creativity   Relationships   Control
Work methods   Objectives
Development needs

Can you think of BUILDING BLOCKS in these areas?

EFECTIVE TEAMS?

1 What is an effective team?
- Commitment to goals
- Balance of roles
- Trust & communication
- Shared ideas
- Satisfying relationships
- Problem-solving
- Productivity and quality high
- Member satisfaction high
- Turnover/absence/accidents low

2 What do you use them for?
- Multi-skilling
- Pooling skills (multi-disciplinary)
- Brainstorming
- Quality circles
- Training groups
- Representative committees
- Panels
- Project teams

PS What is a project?

3 Why wouldn't you?
- Not suitable for all tasks
- Slower decision-making
- Group processes and maintenance may distract from task
- Danger of 'Groupthink'

EG Can you outline the advantages and disadvantages of committees?

Handy

IT ALL DEPENDS   CONTINGENCY APPROACH

INTERVENING FACTORS
- Group motivation
- Leadership
- Processes and procedures

GIVENS
- Group members
- Group task
- Environment

OUTCOMES
- Group productivity
- Group member satisfaction

Part C
Recruitment and selection

Chapter 7 Recruitment

Chapter topic list

1   The importance of recruitment and selection

2   Who is involved in recruitment and selection?

3   The recruitment process

4   Job analysis

5   Job description

6   Person specification

7   Advertising the position

Learning objectives

On completion of this chapter you will be able to:

Syllabus reference

- explain the importance of effective recruitment and selection to the organisation   a

- define the recruitment and selection process   a

- outline the roles and responsibilities of those involved in the process of recruitment and selection   a

- outline a plan for an effective recruitment process   a

- identify the stages in the recruitment process   a

- define the purpose of job analysis   a

- identify methods of job analysis   a

- outline the skills involved in carrying out a job analysis   a

- justify the use of job analysis   a

- outline the purpose and use of a job description and personnel specification   a

- explain how to revise a job description and personnel specification   a

- compare and contrast the purpose of the job description and the person specification   a

- compare and contrast the choice of media for job advertising   a

BPP
PUBLISHING

1 THE IMPORTANCE OF RECRUITMENT AND SELECTION

1.1 Look at the case example below.

Case example

London bus drivers

The pressures faced by recruiters is exemplified by recruiting for the bus industry, here as described in the *Financial Times* (20 August 1997).

'London bus drivers tend not to say in a job for more than a few months. The capital's bus companies are facing the highest levels of staff turnover since the 1950s. A combination of the reviving economy and the expanding London bus network means that some bus companies are having to replace up to 40 per cent of drivers a year.

Pay is one issue, shift work is another. A number of bus drivers, for instance, are skilled workers for whom the job was a welcome safety net during the recession of the early 1990s. But the pay, at £230 to £300 for a 40 hour week, is not enough to keep them now.

But the bus companies, competing in a deregulated market, are under pressure to match their services to commuter needs, rather than the body clocks of their drivers.

The squeeze on numbers of these semi-skilled workers - it takes six weeks to train a bus driver - is now so acute that some bus companies are looking outside London for staff. Go Ahead Group, which owns London General Transport with 1,400 drivers, has launched a scheme to recruit drivers from the provinces.

Some argue that what is really needed is a fundamental change of culture at London Transport. This is the authority that puts out to tender the coveted 400 London bus routes. The companies with the lowest cost base scoop the best routes as they require less public subsidy.

CentreWest, owed by FirstBus, believes that recruiting drivers from outside their local area spells trouble. Instead, it has broadened its recruitment policy to include significantly older and younger drivers, as well as more women.

Metroline hopes to keep its drivers by offering the prospect of "virtually a job for life and very high staff share ownership as well as good pension schemes".

Bus bosses agree that the work has got tougher, with congestion now blocking London's roads from 7am to midnight.'

1.2 The main belief of human resources management (HRM) approach is that **employees** are a 'scarce resource' to be used properly.

(a) Recruitment (and training) issues are central to the **business strategy,** as we have seen above.

(b) Organisations need to deploy **skills** in order to succeed. Although the labour market might seem a 'buyer's market', in practice there are:

- Skills shortages in key sectors (eg computing services) which drive up prices
- Mismatches between available supply and the skills demanded

(c) In most companies, recruitment is an on-going process, and so the composition of the labour force changes fairly slowly. Only rarely (as when Nissan built its first UK plant) will a firm recruit an entire labour force from scratch.

1.3 The **overall aim of the recruitment and selection process** in an organisation is to obtain the quantity and quality of employees required to fulfil the objectives of the organisation.

1.4 This process can be broken down into three main stages.

(a) Defining requirements, including the preparation of **job descriptions, job specifications and personnel specifications.**

(b) **Attracting potential employees**, including the evaluation and use of various methods of reaching sources of applicants.

(c) **Selecting** the appropriate people for the job or the appropriate job for the people.

KEY TERMS

Recruitment is the part of the process concerned with finding the applicants: it is a positive action by management, going into the labour market (internal and external), communicating opportunities and information, generating interest.

Selection is the part of the employee resourcing process which involves choosing between applicants for jobs: it is largely a 'negative' process, eliminating unsuitable applicants.

---

2 WHO IS INVOLVED IN RECRUITMENT AND SELECTION?

Activity 7.1

Think back to when you started work or when you obtained your current position. How many people did you have to see? Were you interviewed by your immediate boss or someone else?

2.1 Precisely who is involved in recruitment and selection varies from organisation to organisation.

Senior managers

2.2 **Senior managers' role**

(a) Senior managers/directors are obviously involved in recruiting people - from within or outside the organisation - for **senior positions.**

(b) However, for most positions they will **not be directly involved**: but they are responsible for **human resources planning** (see below), in other words identifying the overall needs of the organisation.

The personnel/human resources department

2.3 Some firms employ **specialists** to manage their recruitment and other activities relevant to human resources. They may be congregated in a personnel department or **human resources department.** Typical job titles you might come across are **personnel manager** or **human resources manager**.

2.4 The **role of the human resources (HR) department in recruitment and selection**

- Assessing needs for human resources
- Maintaining records of people employed
- Keeping in touch with trends in the labour market

- Advertising for new employees
- Ensuring the organisation complies with equal opportunities and other legislation
- Designing application forms
- Liaising with recruitment consultants
- Preliminary interviews and selection testing

The full extent of the involvement of the HR department will vary according to the circumstances of the organisation.

Line managers

2.5 In many cases the recruit's prospective boss will be involved in the recruitment.

(a) In a small business he/she might have sole responsibility for recruitment.

(b) In larger organisations, line managers may be responsible for:

    (i) Asking for more human resources

    (ii) Advising on requirements

    (iii) Having a final say on candidates presented in the personnel department, perhaps at a final interview.

Recruitment consultants

2.6 For some firms, help from **recruitment consultants** or agencies is useful. The tasks involved in this include:

(a) Analysing, or being informed of, the requirements - the demands of the post, the organisation's preferences for qualifications, personality and so on.

(b) Helping to draw up, or offering advice on, job descriptions, person specifications and other recruitment and selection aids.

(c) Designing job advertisements.

(d) Screening applications, so that those most obviously unsuitable are weeded out immediately.

(e) Helping with short-listing for interview.

(f) Advising on the constitution and procedures of the interview.

(g) Offering a list of suitable candidates with notes and recommendations.

Much will depend on whether the consultant is employed to perform the necessary tasks, or merely to **advise** and recommend.

2.7 The decision of **whether or not to use consultants** will depend on a number of factors.

(a) **Cost**.

(b) **The level of expertise** and specialist techniques or knowledge which **the consultant can bring** to the process.

(c) **The level of expertise**, and specialist knowledge available **within the organisation**.

(d) Whether there is a **need for impartiality** which can only be filled by an outsider trained in objective assessment. If fresh blood is desired in the organisation, it may be a mistake to have staff selecting clones of the common organisational type.

(e) Whether the import of an outside agent will be **regarded as helpful** by in-house staff.

(f) Whether the **structure and politics of the organisation** are conducive to allowing in-house staff to make decisions of this kind. Consultants are not tied by status or rank and can discuss problems freely at all levels. They are also not likely to fear the consequences of their recommendations for their jobs or career prospects.

(g) **Time**. Consultants will need to learn about the job, the organisation and the organisation's requirements. The client will not only have to pay fees for this period of acclimatisation: it may require a post to be filled more quickly than the process allows.

(h) **Supply of labour**. If there is a large and reasonably accessible pool of labour from which to fill a post, consultants will be less valuable. If the vacancy is a standard one, and there are ready channels for reaching labour (such as professional journals), the use of specialists may not be cost effective.

Exam alert

In December 2000, a specific question was set on the use of recruitment consultants. Don't underestimate the importance of what may seem 'minor' topic areas: you needed to find 25 marks' worth of detail for your answer!

---

3 THE RECRUITMENT PROCESS

3.1 The essential points in this chapter can be summarised in diagrammatic form on the next page.

(a) Detailed **human resource planning** defines what resources the organisation needs to meet its objectives.

(b) The **sources of labour** should be forecast. **Internal** and **external** sources, and media for reaching both, will be considered.

(c) **Job analysis,** so that for any given job there is:

    (i) A **job description**: a statement of the component tasks, duties, objectives and standards

    (ii) A **job specification**: a specification of the skills, knowledge and qualities required to perform the job

    (iii) A **person specification**: a reworking of the job specification in terms of the kind of person needed to perform the job.

(d) An identification of vacancies, from the requirements of the manpower plan or by a **job requisition** from a department, branch or office which has a vacancy.

(e) Preparation and publication of advertising **information**, which will.

    (i) Attract the attention and interest of potentially suitable candidates.

    (ii) Give a favourable (but accurate) impression of the job and the organisation.

    (iii) Equip those interested to make an attractive and relevant application (how and to whom to apply, desired skills, qualifications and so on).

(f) **Processing applications** and assessing candidates.

(g) **Notifying applicants** of the results of the selection process.

BPP
PUBLISHING

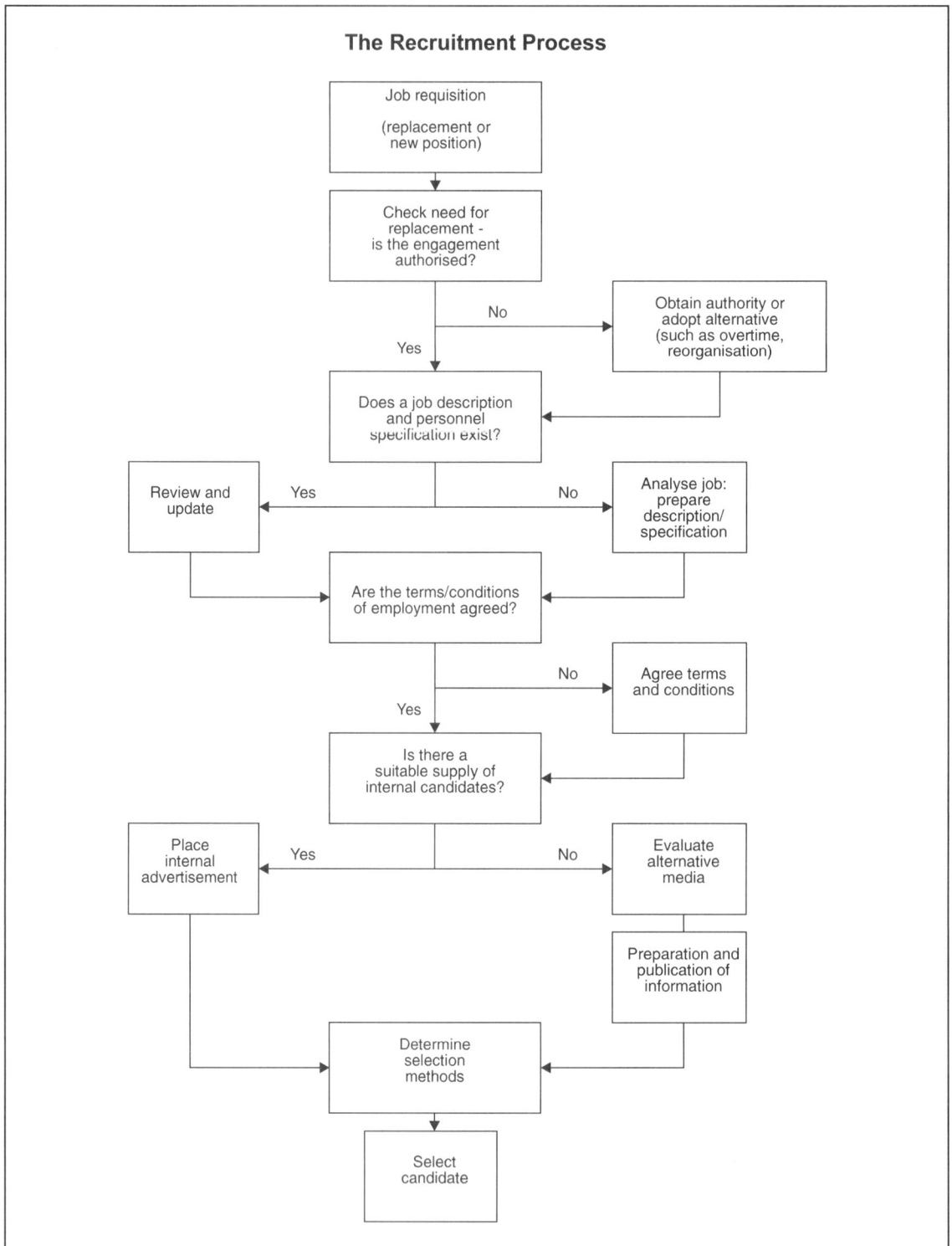

The Recruitment Process

```
                    ┌─────────────────────┐
                    │   Job requisition   │
                    │   (replacement or   │
                    │    new position)    │
                    └─────────────────────┘
                              │
                              ▼
                    ┌─────────────────────┐         ┌──────────────────────┐
                    │    Check need for   │   No    │  Obtain authority or  │
                    │    replacement -    │────────▶│   adopt alternative   │
                    │  is the engagement  │         │  (such as overtime,   │
                    │     authorised?     │         │    reorganisation)    │
                    └─────────────────────┘         └──────────────────────┘
                              │ Yes                             │
                              ▼                                 │
                    ┌─────────────────────┐                    │
   ┌───────────┐    │ Does a job description │ ◀────────────────┘
   │ Review and │◀──│    and personnel     │
   │   update   │Yes│  specification exist? │ No  ┌──────────────┐
   └───────────┘    └─────────────────────┘─────▶│ Analyse job: │
        │                                         │   prepare    │
        │                                         │ description/ │
        │                                         │specification │
        │                                         └──────────────┘
        │           ┌─────────────────────┐              │
        └──────────▶│ Are the terms/conditions │◀─────────┘
                    │  of employment agreed? │
                    └─────────────────────┘
                              │                  ┌──────────────┐
                              │        No        │ Agree terms  │
                              ├─────────────────▶│and conditions│
                              │ Yes              └──────────────┘
                              ▼                         │
                    ┌─────────────────────┐            │
                    │      Is there a     │◀───────────┘
                    │  suitable supply of │
                    │ internal candidates?│
                    └─────────────────────┘
   ┌───────────┐           │                   ┌──────────────┐
   │   Place   │◀──────────┤        No         │  Evaluate    │
   │ internal  │   Yes                         │ alternative  │
   │advertisement│ ─────────────────────────▶ │    media     │
   └───────────┘                               └──────────────┘
        │                                             │
        │                                      ┌──────────────┐
        │                                      │Preparation and│
        │                                      │ publication of │
        │                                      │  information   │
        │                                      └──────────────┘
        │           ┌─────────────────────┐          │
        └──────────▶│     Determine       │◀─────────┘
                    │     selection       │
                    │     methods         │
                    └─────────────────────┘
                              │
                              ▼
                    ┌─────────────────────┐
                    │       Select        │
                    │     candidate       │
                    └─────────────────────┘
```

Exam alert

The pilot paper asked a question about a firm which, although expanding, was finding it difficult to recruit 'good quality staff'. You were asked to design the recruitment process to ensure it was effective.

Recruitment policy

3.2 Detailed procedures for recruitment should only be devised and implemented within the context of a coherent **policy**, or code of conduct. A typical recruitment policy might deal with:

- **Internal advertisement** of vacancies

- Efficient and courteous **processing** of applications
- Fair and accurate provision of information to potential recruits
- Selection of candidates on the basis of suitability, without discrimination

3.3 The Chartered Institute of Personnel and Development has issued a Recruitment Code.

The CIPD Recruitment Code

1 Job advertisements should state clearly the form of reply desired, in particular whether this should be a formal application form or by curriculum vitae. Preferences should also be stated if handwritten replies are required.

2 An acknowledgement of reply should be made promptly to each applicant by the employing organisation or its agent. If it is likely to take some time before acknowledgements are made, this should be made clear in the advertisement.

3 Applicants should be informed of the progress of the selection procedures, what there will be (eg group selection, aptitude tests, etc), the steps and time involved and the policy regarding expenses.

4 Detailed personal information (eg religion, medical history, place of birth, family background, etc) should not be called for unless it is relevant to the selection process.

5 Before applying for references, potential employers must secure permission of the applicant.

6 Applications must be treated as confidential.

7 The code also recommends certain courtesies and obligations on the part of the applicants.

3.4 Detailed **procedures** should be devised in order to make recruitment activity systematic and consistent throughout the organisation (especially where it is decentralised in the hands of line managers). Apart from the manpower resourcing requirements which need to be effectively and efficiently met, there is a **marketing** aspect to recruitment, as one 'interface' between the organisation and the outside world: applicants who feel they have been unfairly treated, or recruits who leave because they feel they have been misled, do not enhance the organisation's reputation in the labour market or the world at large.

Activity 7.2

Find out, if you do not already know, what are the recruitment and selection procedures in your organisation, and who is responsible for each stage. The procedures manual should set this out, or you may need to ask someone in the personnel department.

Get hold of and examine some of the documentation your organisation uses. We show specimens in this chapter, but practice and terminology varies, so your own 'house style' will be invaluable. Compare your organisation's documentation with our example.

---

4 JOB ANALYSIS

4.1 The management of the organisation needs to analyse the sort of work needed to be done.

KEY TERM

Job analysis is:

'the process of collecting, analysing and setting out information about the content of jobs in order to provide the basis for a job description and data for recruitment, training, job evaluation and performance management. Job analysis concentrates on what job holders are expected to do.' (Armstrong)

4.2 The definition shows why job analysis is important - the firm has to know what people are doing in order to recruit effectively.

4.3 **Information that might be obtained from a job analysis.**

Information	Comments
Purpose of the job	This might seem obvious. As a technician, you will be expected to process or provide financial data. But this has to be set in the context of the organisation as a whole.
Content of the job	The tasks you are expected to do. If the purpose of the job is to ensure, for example, that people get paid on time, the tasks involve include many activities related to payroll.
Accountabilities	These are the results for which you are responsible. In practice they might be phrased in the same way as a description of a task.
Performance criteria	These are the criteria which measure how good you are at the job. For a payroll technician, performance criteria includes task-related matters such the timeliness and accuracy of your work - which are easily assessed.
Responsibility	This denotes the importance of the job. For example, a person running a department and taking decisions involving large amounts of money is more responsible that someone who only does what he or she is told. Similarly, someone might have a lot of discretion in determining what he or she will do or how he or she spends the day, whereas other people's tasks might be programmed in some detail according to a predictable routine.
Organisational factors	Who does the jobholder report to directly (line manager) or on grounds of functional authority?
Developmental factors	Relating to the job, such as likely promotion paths, if any, career prospects and so forth. Some jobs are 'dead-end' if they lead nowhere.
Environmental factors	Working conditions, security and safety issues, equipment etc.

Carrying out a job analysis

4.4 A job analysis has to be done systematically - that is why it is called an **analysis** - as the purpose is to obtain facts about the job. Therefore the job analysis involves the use of a number of different techniques to gather the data. The stages should be:

Step 1. **Obtain documentary information**, for main tasks etc

Step 2. Ask managers about more **general aspects** such as the job's purpose, the main activities, the responsibilities involved and the relationships with others.

Step 3. **Ask the job holders** similar questions about their jobs - perceptions might differ.

Step 4. **Watch** people at work - but they may not like it, and they may think you are engaged on a time and motion study.

Exam alert

A very detailed question on the various aspects of job analysis (all discussed in this section) was set in December 1999.

Techniques of job analysis

4.5 **Interviews** establish basic facts about the job, from the job holder's point of view. You'll need to get hold of two sorts of information.

(a) **Basic facts** about the job, such as the job title, the jobholder's manager or team leader, people reporting to the jobholder, the main tasks or duties, official targets or performance standards.

(b) More **subjective issues**, which are harder to test which are still important, such as:

- The amount of supervision a person receives
- How much freedom a person has to take decisions
- How hard the job is
- The skills/qualifications you need to carry out the job
- How the job fits in elsewhere with the company
- How work is allocated
- Decision-making authority

This information should always be checked for accuracy.

4.6 **Advantages and disadvantages of interviewing**

Advantages	Disadvantages
Flexibility	Time consuming
Interactive	Hard to analyse
Easy to organise and carry out	Interviewee might feel on the defensive and might not be entirely frank
New or follow-on questions can be asked in the light of information received	
Reveals other organisational problems	

4.7 **Questionnaires** are sometimes used in job analysis. Their success depends on the willingness of people to complete them accurately.

- They gather purely factual information
- They can cover large numbers of staff
- They provide a structure to the process of information gathering

4.8 **Checklists and inventories**. A checklist would contain a list of activities and the job holder would have to note down how important these are in the job.

Activity description	Time spent on activity	Importance of activity
Processes sales invoices	Less than 10%	Unimportant
	10% to 20%	Not very important
	20-30%	Important
	...and so on	Very important

4.9 **Observation**. People are watched doing the job. This is easy enough for jobs which can be easily observed or which are physical, but is harder for knowledge based work. But observation is quite common in assessing performance - trainee school teachers are observed in the classroom.

4.10 **Self description**. Jobholders are asked to prepare their own job descriptions and to analyse their own jobs. This is quite difficult to do, because people often find it hard to stand back from what they are doing.

4.11 **Diaries and logs** - people keep records of what they do over a period of time, and these can be used by the analyst to develop job descriptions. You may come across something like this in your working life, if, say, you have to keep a timesheet covering work for a particular client, or if it is part of your training record.

4.12 **Which method should you use?** It depends. Any job analysis exercise might involve a variety of methods: Questionnaires or checklists save time. Interviews give a better idea of the detail. Self-description to shows how people *perceive* their jobs, which may be very different from how managers perceive their jobs. Diaries and logs are useful for management jobs, in which a lot is going on.

4.13 It is not always easy to carry out a job analysis, especially for managers and supervisors. In part of this text, we identified the growth of the use of **teams** and **flexible working** in which people are expected to exercise initiative. The case example below shows how job analysis techniques can be adapted

---

Case example

People Management, 6 March 1997, described **workset**, a job analysis system developed by Belbin. Workset uses colour coding to classify work and working time into seven types.

1	Blue: tasks the job holder carries out in a prescribed manner to an approved standard
2	Yellow: individual responsibility to meet an objective (results, not means)
3	Green: tasks that vary according to the reactions and needs of others
4	Orange: shared rather than individual responsibility for meeting an objective
5	Grey: work incidental to the job, not relevant to the four core categories
6	White: new or creative undertaking outside normal duties
7	Pink: demands the presence of the job holder but leads to no useful results

The manager gives an outline of the proportion of time which the manager expects the jobholder to spend on each 'colour' of work. The job holder then briefs the manager on what has actually been done. This highlights differences: between managers' and job-holders' perceptions of jobs; between the perceptions of different jobholders in the same nominal position, who had widely different ideas as to what they were supposed to do.

Important issues arise when there is a gap in perception. Underperformance in different kinds of work can be identified, and people can be steered to the sort of work which suits them best.

Activity 7.3

Analyse your own working time according to the Workset classification above. Do the results surprise you?

Competences

4.14 A more recent approach to job design is the development and outlining of competences.

KEY TERM

A person's **competence** is 'a capacity that leads to behaviour that meets the job demands within the parameters of the organisational environment and that, in turn, brings about desired results', (Boyzatis). Some take this further and suggest that a competence embodies the ability to transfer skills and knowledge to new situations within the occupational area.

4.15 **Different sorts of competences**.

(a) **Behavioural/personal** competences: underlying personal characteristics people bring to work (eg interpersonal skills); personal characteristics and behaviour for successful performance, for example, 'ability to relate well to others'. Most jobs require people to be good communicators.

(b) **Work-based/occupational competences** refer to 'expectations of workplace performance and the outputs and standards people in specific roles are expected to obtain'. This approach is used in NVQ systems (see below). They cover what people have to do to achieve the results of the job. For example, a competence of a Certified Accountant includes 'produce financial and other statements and report to management'.

(c) **Generic competences** can apply to all people in an occupation.

4.16 Many lists of competences confuse the following.

- Areas of **work** at which people are competent
- Underlying aspects of behaviour

4.17 **Examples of competences for managers**.

Competence area	Competence
Intellectual	• Strategic perspective
	• Analytical judgement
	• Planning and organising
Interpersonal	• Managing staff
	• Persuasiveness
	• Assertiveness and decisiveness
	• Interpersonal sensitivity
	• Oral communication
Adaptability	
Results	• Initiative
	• Motivation to achievement
	• Business sense

These competences can be elaborated by identifying *positive* and *negative* indicators.

5   JOB DESCRIPTION

5.1   The job analysis is used to develop the job description.

> ### KEY TERM
>
> **Job description.** A job description sets out the purpose of a job, where it fits in the organisation structure, the context within which the job holder functions and the principal accountability of job holders and the main tasks they have to carry out.

5.2   **Purpose of job description**

Purpose	Comment
Organisational	The job description defines the job's place in the organisational structure
Recruitment	The job description provides information for identifying the sort of person needed (person specification)
Legal	The job description provides the basis for a contract of employment
Performance	Performance objectives can be set around the job description

5.3   **Contents of a job description**

(a) **Job title** (eg Assistant Financial Controller). This indicates the function/department in which the job is performed, and the level of job within that function.

(b) **Reporting to** (eg the Assistant Financial controller reports to the Financial Controller), in other words the person's immediate boss. (No other relationships are suggested here.)

(c) **Subordinates** directly reporting to the job holders.

(d) **Overall purpose** of the job, distinguishing it from other jobs.

(e) **Principal accountabilities or main tasks**

   (i)   Group the main activities into a number of broad areas.

   (ii) Define each activity as a statement of accountability: what the job holder is expected to achieve (eg **tests** new system to ensure they meet agreed systems specifications).

(f) The current fashion for multi-skilled teams means that **flexibility** is sometimes expected.

Examples of job descriptions are on the next page.

Activity 7.4

Studying has placed you in a role in which you have to perform a fairly consistent set of duties, in fairly consistent conditions, within a structure that requires you to interact with other people, both superiors and peers (and possibly subordinates). Draw up a job description for yourself.

JOB DESCRIPTION

1   *Job title:* Baking Furnace Labourer.

2   *Department:* 'B' Baking.

3   *Date:* 20 November 19X0.

4   *Prepared by:* H Crust, baking furnace manager.

5   *Responsible to:* baking furnace chargehand.

6   *Age range:* 20-40.

7   *Supervises work of:* N/A.

8   *Has regular co-operative contract with:* Slinger/Crane driver.

9   *Main duties/responsibilities:* Stacking formed electrodes in furnace, packing for stability. Subsequently unloads baked electrodes and prepares furnace for next load.

10 *Working conditions:* stacking is heavy work and requires some manipulation of 100lb (45kg) electrodes. Unloading is hot (35° - 40°C) and very dusty.

11 *Employment conditions:*

Wages £3.60 ph + group bonus (average earnings £219.46 pw).

Hours: Continuous rotating three-shift working days, 6 days on, 2 days off. NB must remain on shift until relieved.

Trade Union: National Union of Bread Bakers, optional.

MIDWEST BANK PLC

1   *Job title:*   Clerk (Grade 2).

2   *Branch:*   All branches and administrative offices.

3   *Job summary:*   To provide clerical support to activities within the bank.

4   *Job content:*   Typical duties will include:

(a)   Cashier's duties;
(b)   Processing of branch clearing;
(c)   processing of standing orders;
(d)   support to branch management.

5   *Reporting structure*

Administrative officer/assistant manager

Supervisor (Grade 3)

Clerk (Grade 2)

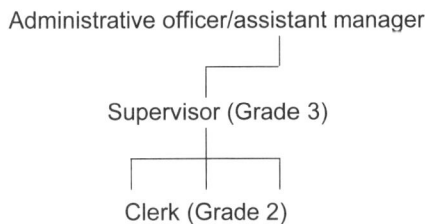

6   *Experience/education:* experience not required, minimum 3 GCSEs or equivalent.

7   *Training to be provided:* initial on-the-job training plus regular formal courses and training.

8   *Hours:* 38 hours per week.

9   *Objectives and appraisal:* Annual appraisal in line with objectives above.

10 *Salary:* refer to separate standard salary structure.

Job description prepared by: Head office personnel department.

Alternatives to job descriptions

5.4 **Detailed** job descriptions are perhaps only suited for jobs where the work is largely repetitive and therefore performed by low-grade employees: once the element of **judgement** comes into a job description it becomes a straitjacket. Many difficulties arise where people adhere strictly to the contents of the job description, rather than responding flexibly to task or organisational requirements.

5.5 Perhaps job descriptions should be written in terms of the **outputs and performance levels** expected. Some firms are moving towards **accountability profiles** in which outputs and performance are identified explicitly.

5.6 Armstrong suggests a crucial difference between:

(a) A job - a group of tasks.

(b) A role. A part played by people in meeting their objectives by working competently and flexibly within the context of the organisation's objectives, structures and processes.

5.7 A **role definition** is wider than a job description. It is less concerned with the details of the job content, but how they interpret the job, and how they perceive them.

Case example

Guinness

According to *People Management*, 11 September 1997, in May 1996 Guinness Brewing Great Britain introduced a new pay system based on competences.

Restrictive job definitions, lengthy job descriptions and a 24-grade structure were replaced by broad role profiles and three pay bands. Roles are now specified in terms of 'need to do' (primary accountabilities), 'need to know' (experience and knowledge requirements) and 'need to be' (levels of competence).

Competences are defined as 'the skill, knowledge and behaviours that need to be applied for effective performance'. There are seven of them, including commitment to results and interpersonal effectiveness. Roles are profiled against each relevant competence and individuals' actual competences are compared with the requirements through the performance management process.

Activity 7.5

Without looking at the real thing, to start with, draw up a job description for your own job and for the job of a personnel officer in your organisation. Now look at the official job descriptions. Are they true, detailed and up-to-date, compared with the actual jobs as you saw them? If not, what does this tell you about (a) job descriptions and (b) perceptions of the personnel function?

---

6 PERSON SPECIFICATION

KEY TERM

'A **person specification**, also known as a job or personnel specification, sets out the education, qualifications, training, experience personal attributes and competences a job holder requires to perform her or his job satisfactorily.' (Armstrong)

6.1 The job description outlines the job: the person specification describes the person needed to do the job. For example, a position of secretary or personal assistant normally requires the holder to have word processing skills.

Traditional approaches to the person specification

6.2 The **Seven Point Plan** put forward by Professor Rodger in 1951 draws the selector's attention to seven points about the candidate.

- **Physical attributes** (such as neat appearance, ability to speak clearly)
- **Attainment** (including educational qualifications)
- **General intelligence**
- **Special aptitudes** (such as neat work, speed and accuracy)
- **Interests** (practical and social)
- **Disposition** (or manner: friendly, helpful and so on)
- Background **circumstances**

Exam alert

In June 2000, a question was set on person specifications and job descriptions. Candidates were asked to **define** each document, to **distinguish** between them, and then to **describe** the structure and content of a person specification. Note that while the content is quite straightforward (if you've read this chapter), you needed to pay close attention to the **instruction words** in the question in order to answer it correctly. This is a very useful lesson to learn!

6.3 **Problems with the Seven Point Plan**.

(a) Physical attributes or disposition might include a person's demeanour. **Eye contact** is considered a sign of honesty and frankness in some cultures, but a sign of disrespect in others.

(b) **General intelligence** is not something that can be measured easily. A criticism of IQ tests is that test scores tell you that you are good at doing IQ tests - and not much else.

(c) **Attainment**: educational qualifications - no attention is paid to the circumstances in which these were obtained.

The plan does not identify a person's **potential**, or suggest how it can be aligned precisely to the organisation's requirements.

Five-Point Pattern

6.4 Munro-Fraser's Five Point Pattern is one alternative.

- **Impact on others**: physical attributes, speech, manner

- **Acquired knowledge** and qualifications

- **Innate abilities**: ability to learn, mental agility

- **Motivation**: What sort of goals does the individual set, how much effort goes into achieving them, how successful.

- **Adjustment**: emotional stability, tolerance of slips.

New approaches: competences

6.5   The two methods described above have been in use for many years. More recruiters are using **competences** (see paragraph 4.15) in designing the person specification.

Preparing the specification

6.6   Each feature in the person specification should be classified as:

(a)   **Essential.** For instance, honesty in a cashier is essential whilst a special aptitude for conceptual thought is not.

(b)   **Desirable.** For instance, a reasonably pleasant manner should ensure satisfactory standards in a person dealing with the public.

(c)   **Contra-indicated**. Some features are actively disadvantageous, such as an inability to work in a team when acting as project leader.

PERSON SPECIFICATION: Customer Accounts Manager			
	ESSENTIAL	DESIRABLE	CONTRA-INDICATED
Physical attributes	Clear speech Well-groomed Good health	Age 25-40	Age under 25 Chronic ill-health and absence
Attainments	2 'A' levels GCSE Maths and English Thorough knowledge of retail environment	Degree (any discipline) Marketing training 2 years' experience in supervisory post	No experience of supervision or retail environment
Intelligence	High verbal intelligence		
Aptitudes	Facility with numbers Attention to detail and accuracy Social skills for customer relations	Analytical abilities (problem solving) Understanding of systems and IT	No mathematical ability Low tolerance of technology
Interests	Social: team activity		Time-consuming hobbies 'Solo' interests only
Disposition	Team player Persuasive Tolerance of pressure and change	Initiative	Anti-social Low tolerance of responsibility
Circumstances	Able to work late, take work home	Located in area of office	

Activity 7.6

Turn your job description for A student into a corresponding Personnel Specification, using the 'essential; desirable; contra-indicated' framework, and either the Seven Point Plan or Five Point Pattern. If you did not do Activity 7.5, do it now! (You might like to consider into which section of your personnel specification 'laziness' would fall....)

7 ADVERTISING THE POSITION

7.1 The object of recruitment advertising is to attract suitable candidates and deter unsuitable candidates.

Content of the advertisement

7.2 It should be:

(a) **Concise,** but comprehensive enough to be an accurate description of the job, its rewards and requirements.

(b) **Attractive** to the maximum number of the right people.

(c) **Positive and honest** about the organisation. Disappointed expectations will be a prime source of dissatisfaction when an applicant actually comes into contact with the organisation.

(d) **Relevant and appropriate to the job and the applicant**. Skills, qualifications and special aptitudes required should be prominently set out, along with special features of the job that might attract - on indeed deter - applicants, such as shiftwork or extensive travel.

7.3 The advertisement, based on information set out in the job description, job and person specifications and recruitment procedures, should contain information about:

(a) The **organisation**: its main business and location, at least.

(b) The **job**: title, main duties and responsibilities and special features.

(c) **Conditions**: special factors affecting the job.

(d) **Qualifications and experience** (required, and preferred); other attributes, aptitudes and/or knowledge required.

(e) **Rewards**: salary, benefits, opportunities for training, career development, and so on.

(f) **Application process**: how to apply, to whom, and by what date.

7.4 It should encourage a degree of **self-selection,** so that the target population begins to narrow itself down. The information contained in the advertisement should deter unsuitable applicants as well as encourage potentially suitable ones.

7.5 **Factors influencing the choice of advertising medium**

(a) **The type of organisation**. A factory is likely to advertise a vacancy for an unskilled worker in a different way to a company advertising for a member of the Institute of Personnel and Development for an HRM position.

(b) **The type of job**. Managerial jobs may merit national advertisement, whereas semi-- skilled jobs may only warrant local coverage, depending on the supply of suitable candidates in the local area. Specific skills may be most appropriately reached through trade, technical or professional journals, such as those for accountants or computer programmers.

(c) **The cost of advertising**. It is more expensive to advertise in a national newspaper than on local radio, and more expensive to advertise on local radio than in a local newspaper etc.

(d) The **readership and circulation** (type and number of readers/listeners) of the medium, and its suitability for the number and type of people the organisation wants to reach.

(e) The **frequency** with which the organisation wants to advertise the job vacancy, and the duration of the recruitment process.

Exam alert

A detailed and practical question was set on the drafting and placement of job advertisements in December 1999. Don't be tempted to rely on 'general knowledge' when you encounter a topic like this that looks familiar or the common-sensical: learn the material!

Activity 7.7

Dealing with individuals demands a certain... ...um...

You've heard the old line...

'You don't have to be mad to work here, but it helps'. It's like that at AOK, but in the nicest possible way. We believe that our Personnel Department should operate for the benefit of our staff, and not that staff should conform to statistical profiles. It doesn't make for an easy life, but dealing with people as individuals, rather than numbers, certainly makes it a rewarding one.

We're committed to an enlightened personnel philosophy. We firmly believe that our staff are our most important asset, and we go a long way both to attract the highest quality of people, and to retain them.

AOK is a company with a difference. We're a highly progressive, international organisation, one of the world's leading manufacturers in the medical electronics field.

...Character

As an expanding company, we now need another experienced Personnel Generalist to join us at our UK headquarters in Reigate, Surrey.

Essentially we're looking for an individual, a chameleon character who will assume an influential role in recruitment, employee relations, salary administration, compensation and benefits, or whatever the situation demands. The flexibility to interchange with various functions is vital. Within your designated area, you'll experience a large degree of independence. You'll be strong in personality, probably already experienced in personnel management in a small company. Whatever your background you'll certainly be someone who likes to help people help themselves and who is happy to get involved with people at all levels within the organisation.

Obviously, in a fast growing company with a positive emphasis on effective personnel work, your prospects for promotion are excellent. Salaries are highly attractive and benefits are, of course, comprehensive.

So if you're the kind of personnel individual who enjoys personal contact, problem solving, and will thrive on the high pace of a progressive, international organisation, such as AOK, get in touch with us by writing or telephoning, quoting ref: 451/BPD, to AOK House, Reigate, Surrey.

What do you think of this advertisement? How can you improve it?

7.6 Media for recruitment advertising

(a) **In-house magazine, notice-boards,** e-mail or its 'intra-net'. An organisation might invite applications from employees who would like a transfer or a promotion to the particular vacancy advertised.

(b) **Professional and specialist newspapers or magazines,** such as *Accountancy Age, Marketing Week* or *Computing.*

(c) **National newspapers** are used for senior management jobs or vacancies for skilled workers, where potential applicants will not necessarily be found through local advertising.

(d) **Local newspapers** would be suitable for jobs where applicants are sought from the local area.

(e) **Local radio, television and cinema.** These are becoming increasingly popular, especially for large-scale campaigns for large numbers of vacancies.

(f) **Job centres.** Vacancies for unskilled work (rather than skilled work or management jobs) are advertised through local job centres, although in theory any type of job can be advertised here.

(g) **School and university careers offices.** Ideally, the manager responsible for recruitment in an area should try to maintain a close liaison with careers officers. Some large organisations organise special meetings or **careers fairs** in universities and colleges (the so-called 'milk round'), as a kind of showcase for the organisation and the careers it offers.

(h) The **Internet**. Any personal computer user may access the network, independently or via an internet service provider such as CompuServe.

Key learning points

- Effective recruitment practices ensure that a firm has enough **people with the right skills**.

- Most recruitment practices aim to **fit the person to the job** by identifying the needs of the job and finding a person who satisfies them.

- The recruitment process involves **personnel specialists** and **'line' managers**, sometimes with the help of recruitment **consultants**.

- First the overall **needs of the organisation** have been identified in the recruitment process.

- The account for each individual position a **job analysis** is prepared, which identifies through various investigative techniques, the content of the job.

- A **job description** is developed from the job analysis. The job description outlines the **tasks** of the job and its place within the organisation.

- A **person specification** identifies the characteristics of a person who will be recruited to do the job identified in the job description.

- The person specification can be used to develop the **job advertisement**. The Seven Point Plan and Five Point Pattern are examples.

- In recent years, recruiters have been using the '**competences**' as a means to select candidates. A **competence** is a person's capacity to behave in a particular way for example to fulfil the requirements of a job, or to motivate people. Work-based competences directly relate to the job (eg the ability to prepare a trial balance); behavioural competences relate to underlying issues of personality.

- *See the Part C mind map summary on page 151.*

BPP PUBLISHING

Quick quiz

1 What is the underlying principle of human resources management?

2 What, in brief, are the stages of the recruitment and selection process?

3 What is the role of line managers in the recruitment process?

4 List the factors determining whether a firm should use recruitment consultants.

5 Briefly summarise:

    (a) job analysis
    (b) job description
    (c) person specification

6 What is a currently fashionable approach to drawing up jobs analysis, job descriptions etc?

7 List the components of the Five Point Pattern.

8 What are the characteristics of a good job advertisement?

Answers to quick quiz

1 People are a scarce resource and need to be managed effectively.

2 Identifying/defining requirements; attracting potential employees; selecting candidates.

3 It depends - making a requisition, identifying departmental needs, interviewing, reviewing the job analysis, job description etc.

4 Cost: expertise; impartiality; organisation structure and politics; time; supply of labour.

5 (a) **Job analysis**. The process of examining a 'job' to identify the component parts and the circumstances in which it is performed.

    (b) **Job description**. A broad statement of the purpose, scope, duties and responsibilities of a particular 'job'.

    (c) **Personnel specification.** The kind of person suitable for the job.

6 The use of competences - work based and behavioural.

7 Impact on others; acquired knowledge and qualifications; innate abilities; motivation; adjustment.

8 Concise; reaches the right people; gives a good impression; relevant to the job, identifying skills required etc.

Answers to activities

Answer 7.1

Large organisations tend to have standard procedures. In order to ensure a standard process, you might have seen a specialist from the personnel department only. Smaller organisations cannot afford such specialists so you might have been interviewed by your immediate boss - but perhaps someone else might also have interviewed you (your boss's boss) to check you out.

Note. There are no formal answers to activities 7.2 to 7.6, as they will depend on your own personal situation and experiences.

Answer 7.7

(a) Goods points about the advertisement and points for improvement

    (i) It is attractively designed in terms of page layout.

    (ii) The tone of the headline and much of the body copy is informal, colloquial and even friendly. It starts with a joke, implying that the company has a sense of humour.

    (iii) The written style is fluent and attractive.

(iv) It appears to offer quite a lot of information about the culture of the company - how it feels about personnel issues, where it's going etc - as well as about the job vacancy.

Improvement that could be made

Job advertisements carry certain 'responsibilities': they are a form of **pre-selection**, and as such should be not be **just** attractive and persuasive, but accurate and complete enough to give a realistic and relevant picture of the post and the organisation.

(i) There is too much copy. Readers may not have the patience to read through so much (rather wordy) prose, particularly since the same phrases are repeated ('progressive international organisation', for example), or look rather familiar in any case ('in the nicest possible ways', 'our staff are our most important asset', 'a company with a difference' etc) and there is very little 'hard' information contained in the ad.

(ii) There are many words and expressions which sound good, and seem to **imply** good things, but are in fact empty of substance, and commit the organisation to nothing. They are usually the 'stock' expressions like 'committed to an enlightened personnel philosophy': what does that actually **mean**?

(iii) There are confusing contradictions, eg between the requirements for flexibility, 'interchange with various functions', do 'whatever the situation demands' etc and the more cautious 'within your designated area …'.

(iv) The copywriters are in places too 'clever' for their own good. The first three lines, for example, could backfire quite badly if a reader failed to catch the next line, or simply didn't appreciate the self-deprecating tone.

(v) The advertisement does not give enough 'hard' information to make effective response likely - and then fails to do its job of facilitating response at all! Despite the invitation to telephone, no number is given. No named corespondent is cited, merely a reference number - despite the claimed emphasis on people as people, not numbers.

(b) **What is learnt about AOK**

The advertisement **claims** to say quite a lot about AOK, its culture, its people-centredness, its expansion and progressive outlook, flexibility, sense of humour etc. Such claims should always be taken with a pinch of salt. We may, however, infer some things about the company.

(i) It has a strong cultural 'flavour', and believes in 'selling' that culture quite hard. It likes, for example, telling people what it is 'committed to', what it 'firmly believes' etc.

(ii) It tends to stress its good points and opportunities: it certainly sees itself (even allowing for advertising hyperbole) as go-ahead, successful and expanding, flexible, people-oriented.

(iii) It is possibly not as deeply people oriented as it tries to project. The areas of involvement for the Personnel Department enumerated, for example, seem rather limited and administrative: there is no suggestion of a wider strategic role for personnel, such as would indicate that 'people issues' really do affect management outlook.

Chapter 8 Selection

Chapter topic list

1   The selection process in outline

2   Application forms

3   Selection methods in outline

4   Interviews

5   Tests

6   Other selection methods

7   Which selection method is best?

8   References

9   Evaluating and improving recruitment and selection practices

---

Learning objectives

On completion of this chapter you will be able to:

	Syllabus reference
• analyse the purpose and effectiveness of the job application form	a
• explain the purpose and usefulness of applicant references	a
• list alternative methods of selection	a
• evaluate the usefulness of selection methods	a
• establish the skills involved in successful selection decision making	a
• explain the importance of good selection decisions to the organisation	a
• outline the purpose of the selection interview	a
• identify who should be involved in selection interviewing	a
• identify the key skills required for selection interviewing	a
• list the most common reasons for ineffective interviewing	a
• explain the importance of the selection interview in the selection process	a
• list the most common reasons for ineffective recruitment and selection	a
• list and describe criteria against which to assess successful recruitment and selection practices.	a

1 THE SELECTION PROCESS IN OUTLINE

1.1 In brief we can outline the main steps.

Step 1. Deal with responses to job advertisements. This might involve sending **application forms** to candidates. Not all firms bother with these, however, preferring to review CVs.

Step 2. Assess each application or CV against **key criteria** in the job advertisement and specification. Critical factors may include age, qualifications, experience or whatever.

Step 3. **Sort applications** into 'possible', 'unsuitable' and 'marginal.

'Possibles' will then be more closely scrutinised, and a shortlist for interview drawn up. Ideally, this should be done by both the personnel specialist and the prospective manager of the successful candidate.

Step 4. **Invite candidates for interviews.**

Step 5. Reinforce interviews with **selection testing,** if suitable.

Step 6. Review un-interviewed 'possibles', and 'marginals', and put potential future candidates on hold, or in reserve.

Step 7. Send standard letters to unsuccessful applicants, and inform them simply that they have not been successful. Reserves will be sent a holding letter: 'We will keep your details on file, and should any suitable vacancy arise in future...'.

Step 8. Make a provisional offer to the recruit.

1.2 Sometimes Steps 4 and 5 will be reversed, so that **testing** comes before **interviewing.** There are good reasons for this, as we shall see.

2 APPLICATION FORMS

2.1 Job advertisements usually ask candidates to fill in a **job application form,** or to send information about themselves and their previous job experience (their CV or **curriculum vitae**), usually with a covering letter briefly explaining why they think they are qualified to do the job.

2.2 Purposes of application forms

- Weeding out unsuitable candidates
- Identifying possible candidates

2.3 Application forms fulfil these jobs in two ways.

Asking specific questions	• The application form will be designed around the personnel specification. So, if a certain number of GCSE's are needed, the applicant will be asked to list educational qualifications.
	• Certain questions **cannot** be asked by law, on account of equal opportunities legislation.
Finding out more	Give candidates the ability to **write about themselves**, their ambitions, why they want the job. Some application forms ask people to write about key successes and failures. This gives information about the candidate's underlying personality as well as matters such as neatness, literacy and the ability to communicate in writing.

AOK PLC

APPLICATION FORM

Post applied for ....

PERSONAL DETAILS

Surname Mr/ Mrs/ Miss/Ms

First name

Address

Post code

Telephone   (Daytime)   (Evenings)

Date of birth

Nationality

Marital status

Dependants

EDUCATION AND TRAINING

- Qualifications

  List academic and/or professional qualifications. (Use initials et GCSE, 'O' levels, BSc, ACCA, MBA etc).

Education (latest first)

Date		Institution	Exams passed/qualifications
From	To		

TRAINING AND OTHER SKILLS

Please give details of any specialised training courses you have attended.

Please note down other skills such as languages (and degree of fluency), driving licence (with endorsements if any), keyboard skills (familiarity with software package).

EMPLOYMENT

Dates		Employer name and address	Title and duties
From	To		

Current salary and benefits …

INTERESTS

Please describe your leisure/hobby/sporting interests

YOUR COMMENTS

Why do you think you are suitable for the job advertised?

ADDITIONAL INFORMATION

Do you have any permanent health problems? If so, please give details.

When would you be able to start work?

REFERENCES

Please give two references. One should be a former employer.

Name	Name
Address	Address
Position	Position
Signed	Date

BPP
PUBLISHING

Activity 8.1

Suggest four possible design faults in job application forms - you may be able to draw on your own personal experience.

Application forms and CVs

2.4 Many firms are either **too small** or cannot be bothered to design a standard application form for all posts. The requirements of a business employing, say, 30 people, are very different from a large employer such as the Civil Service or British Airways. This is why many job advertisements ask for a **curriculum vitae (CV)** and a covering letter.

2.5 How a CV is presented will tell you a great deal about the candidate - not only the information on the CV but the candidate's neatness and ability to structure information.

2.6 Application forms have the merit of being standardised, so that all candidates are asked the same information. Gaps can thus be identified clearly, and essential information can be asked for. CVs on the other hand are easy to mould and manipulate.

Sifting application forms and CVs: biodata

2.7 For some jobs, hundreds or even thousands of people might apply, and so to reduce all this to manageable proportion, recruiters can use structured ways of sifting the data. Some firms even use computers to identify items on CVs or application forms in order to rank the candidates in order to generate a shortlist.

2.8 **Biodata** is the term given to techniques which aim to score and structure biographical information about a candidate in order to predict work performance.

(a) A **biodata questionnaire**, which might even be appended to the application form, asks specific questions about:

- Demographic details (age, sex, family circumstances)
- Education and professional qualifications
- Previous employment history and work experience
- Positions of responsibility outside work
- Leisure interests
- Career and job motivation

(b) **Each item is given a weight**. For example, education and professional qualifications might account for up to 20 marks; leisure interests might account for up to ten marks. Within each weight the candidate is given a score.

(c) The **scores are added up**, to give the candidate a total. A candidate who scores below a certain level will not be accepted.

2.9 Biodata is only really suitable when large numbers of applicants have to be screened. Furthermore, the biodata weights are based on the scores of existing employees, so a large workforce is needed for any meaningful correlation to be made between biodata and work performance.

3 SELECTION METHODS IN OUTLINE

3.1 We will briefly list the main selection methods here. The more important are discussed in the following sections.

Methods	Examples
Interviewing	• Individual (one-to-one) • Interview panels • Selection boards • Assessment centres
Biodata	
Selection tests	• Intelligence • Aptitudes • Personality • Proficiency
Work sampling	
Group selection methods	

4 INTERVIEWS

4.1 Most firms use the selection interview as their main source for decision-making.

4.2 **Purpose of the interview**

(a) Finding the best person for the job, by giving making the organisation a chance to assess applicants (and particularly their interpersonal communication skills) directly.

(b) Making sure that applicants understand what the job, what the career prospects are and have suitable information about the company.

(c) Giving the best possible impression of the organisation - after all, the candidate may have other offers elsewhere.

(d) Making all applicants feel that they have been given **fair treatment** in the interview, whether they get the job or not.

4.3 **Conducting selection interviews: matters to be kept in mind**

(a) The **impression** of the organisation given by the interview arrangements.

(b) The **psychological effects** of the location of the interview and seating arrangements.

(c) The **manner and tone** of the interviewers.

(d) Getting the candidates to talk freely (by asking open questions) and honestly (by asking probing questions), in accordance with the organisation's need for **information.**

(e) The **opportunity for the candidate to learn** about the job and organisation.

(f) The control of **bias** or hasty judgement by the interviewer.

Preparation of the interview

4.4 **Welcoming the candidate.** Candidates should be given:

(a) Clear instructions about the date, time and location - perhaps with a map.
(b) The name of a person to contact.

(c)   A place to wait (with cloakroom facilities), perhaps with tea or coffee.

4.5   **The interview room**

(a)   The interview is where the organisation 'sells' itself and the candidate aims to give a good impression. The layout of the room should be carefully designed. Being 'interrogated' by two people from the other side of a desk may be completely unsuitable.

(b)   Some interviews are **deliberately** tough, to see how a candidate performs under pressure.

4.6   **The agenda.** The agenda and questions will be based on:

(a)   The job description and what abilities are required of the jobholder.

(b)   The personnel specification. The interviewer must be able to judge whether the applicant matches up to the personal qualities required from the jobholder.

(c)   The application form or the applicant's CV: the qualities the applicant claims to possess.

Conduct of the interview

4.7   Questions should be paced and put carefully. The interviewer should not be trying to confuse the candidate, plunging immediately into demanding questions or picking on isolated points; neither, however, should s(he) allow the interviewee to digress or gloss over important points. The interviewer must retain control over the information-gathering process.

Type of question	Comment
Open questions	('Who...? What...? Where...? When...? Why....?') These force candidates to put together their own responses in complete sentences. This encourages them to talk, keeps the interview flowing, and is most revealing ('Why do you want to be an accountant?')
Probing questions	Similar to open questions, these aim to discover the deeper significance of the candidate's answers, especially if they are initially dubious, uninformative, too short, or too vague. ('But what was it about accountancy that **particularly** appealed to you?')
Closed questions	Invite only 'yes' or 'no' answers: ('Did you...?, 'Have you...?'). (a) They elicit an answer **only** to the question asked. This may be useful where there are small points to be established ('Did you pass your exam?')

Type of question	Comment
Multiple questions	Two or more questions are asked at once. ('Tell me about your last job? How did your knowledge of accountancy help you there, and do you think you are up-to-date or will you need to spend time studying?'). This encourages the candidate to talk at some length, without straying too far from the point. It might also test the candidate's ability to listen, and to handle large amount of information.
Problem solving questions	Present the candidate with a situation and ask him/her to explain how he/she would deal with it. ('How would you motivate your staff to do a task that they did not want to do?'). Such questions are used to establish whether the candidate will be able to deal with the sort of problems that are likely to arise in the job.
Leading questions	Encourage the candidate to give a certain reply. ('We are looking for somebody who likes detailed figure work. How much do you enjoy dealing with numbers?' or 'Don't you agree that...?' 'Surely...?). The danger with this type of question is that the candidate will give the answer that he thinks the interviewer wants to hear.

Activity 8.2

Identify the type of question used in the following examples, and discuss the opportunities and constraints they offer the interviewee who must answer them.

(a)   'So, you're interested in a Business Studies degree, are you, Jo?'

(b)   'Surely you're interested in Business Studies, Jo?'

(c)   'How about a really useful qualification like a Business Studies degree, Jo? Would you consider that?'

(d)   'Why are you interested in a Business Studies degree, Jo?

(e)   'Why particularly Business Studies, Jo?'

4.8   **Evaluating the response**

(a)   The interviewer must **listen carefully** to the responses and evaluate them so as to judge what the **candidate** is:

- Wanting to say
- Trying **not** to say
- Saying, but does not mean, or is lying about
- Having difficulty saying

(b)   In addition, the interviewer will have to be aware when he/she is hearing:

- Something he/she needs to know
- Something he/she **doesn't** need to know
- Only what he/she **expects** to hear
- Inadequately - when his or her own attitudes, perhaps prejudices, are getting in the way of an objective response to the candidate

4.9 **Candidates should be given the opportunity to ask questions.** The choice of questions might well have some influence on how the interviewers assess a candidate's interest in and understanding of the job. Moreover, there is information that the candidate will need to know about the organisation, the job, and indeed the interview process.

Types of interview

4.10 **Individual** or **one-to-one interviews.** These are the **most common** selection method.

(a) **Advantages**

(i) **Direct** face-to-face communication.

(ii) **Rapport** between the candidate and the interviewer: each has to give attention solely to the other, and there is potentially a relaxed atmosphere, if the interviewer is willing to establish an informal style.

(b) The **disadvantage** of a one-to-one interview is the scope it allows for a biased or superficial decision.

(i) The **candidate** may be able to **disguise** lack of knowledge in a specialist area of which the interviewer knows little.

(ii) The **interviewer's** perception may be selective or **distorted**, and this lack of objectivity may go unnoticed and unchecked.

(iii) The greater opportunity for personal rapport with the candidate may cause a **weakening of the interviewer's objective judgement**.

4.11 **Panel interviews** are designed to overcome such disadvantages. A panel may consist of two or three people who together interview a single candidate: most commonly, an HR specialist and the departmental manager who will have responsibility for the successful candidate. This saves the firm time and enables better assessment.

4.12 Large formal panels, or **selection boards**, may also be convened where there are a number of individuals or groups with an interest in the selection.

(a) **Advantage**. A number of people see candidates, and share information about them at a single meeting: similarly, they can compare their assessments on the spot, without a subsequent effort at liaison and communication.

(b) **Drawbacks**

(i) Questions tend to be more varied, and more random, since there is **no single guiding force** behind the interview strategy. The candidate may have trouble switching from one topic to another so quickly, especially if questions are not led up to, and not clearly put - as may happen if they are unplanned. Candidate are also seldom allowed to expand their answers and so may not be able to do justice to themselves.

(ii) If there is a **dominating member** of the board, the interview may have greater continuity - but that individual may also influence the judgements of other members.

(iii) Some candidates may not perform well in a formal, artificial situation such as the board interview, and may find such a situation extremely stressful.

(iv) Research shows that **board members rarely agree** with each other in their judgements about candidates.

The limitations of interviews

4.13 Interviews are criticised because **they fail to provide accurate predictions** of how a person will perform in the job, partly because of the nature of interviews, partly because of the errors of judgement by interviewers.

Problem	Comment
Scope	• An interview is **too brief** to 'get to know' candidates in the kind of depth required to make an accurate prediction of work performance. • An interview is an **artificial situation**: candidates may be on their best behaviour or, conversely, so nervous that they do not do themselves justice. Neither situation reflects what the person is really like.
The halo effect	A tendency for people to make an initial **general judgement** about a person based on a **single obvious attribute**, such as being neatly dressed or well-spoken. This single attribute will colour later perceptions, and might make an interviewer mark the person up or down on every other factor in their assessments
Contagious bias	The interviewer changes the behaviour of the applicant by suggestion. The applicant might be led by the wording of questions or non-verbal cues from the interviewer, and change what (s)he is doing or saying in response.
Stereotyping	Stereotyping groups people together who are assumed to share certain characteristics (women, say, or vegetarians), then attributes certain traits to the group as a whole (emotional, socialist etc). It then (illogically) assumes that each individual member of the supposed group will possess that trait.
Incorrect assessment	Qualitative factors such as motivation, honesty or integrity are very difficult assess in an interview.
Logical error	An interviewer might decide that a young candidate who has held two or three jobs in the past for only a short time will be unlikely to last long in any job. (Not necessarily so.)
Inexperienced interviewers	• Inability to evaluate information about a candidate properly • Failure to compare a candidate against the requirements for a job or a personnel specification • Bad planning of the interview • Failure to take control of the direction and length of the interview • A tendency either to act as an inquisitor and make candidates feel uneasy or to let candidates run away with the interview • A reluctance to probe into fact and challenge statements where necessary

4.14 While some interviewers may be experts for the human resources function, it is usually thought desirable to include **line managers** in the interview team. They cannot be full-time interviewers, obviously: they have their other work to do. No matter how much training they are given in the interview techniques, they will lack continuous experience, and probably not give interviewing as much thought or interest as they should.

Activity 8.3

What assumptions might an interviewer make about **you**, based on your:

(a) Accent, or regional/national variations in your spoken English
(b) School
(c) Clothes and hair-style
(d) Stated hobbies, interest, 'philosophies'
(e) Taste in books and TV programmes

For objectivity, you might like to conduct this Activity in class. What assumptions do you make about the person sitting next to you?

Exam alert

Interviews are relevant to many areas of personnel management. The issues described above are relevant to appraisal interviews, disciplinary interviews and so on.

A question set in June 2001 required candidates to explain the *purpose* of selection interviewing, four *disadvantages* of selection interviewing – and the nature, advantages *and* disadvantages of face-to-face and panel interviews. Make sure that you can locate and classify the relevant data in this section of the chapter: how many marks' worth of answer could you give?

5   TESTS

5.1   In some job selection procedures, an interview is supplemented by some form of **selection test**. Tests must be:

(a) **Sensitive** enough to discriminate between different candidates.

(b) **Standardised** on a representative sample of the population, so that a person's results can be interpreted meaningfully.

(c) **Reliable**: in that the test should measure the same thing whenever and to whomever it is applied.

(d) **Valid**: it measures what it is supposed to measure.

5.2   The science of measuring mental capacities and processes is called 'psychometrics'; hence the term **psychometric testing**. Types of test commonly used in practice are:

- Intelligence tests
- Aptitude tests
- Personality tests
- Proficiency tests

5.3   **Intelligence tests.** Tests of **general intellectual ability** typically test memory, ability to think quickly and logically, and problem solving skills.

(a) Most people have experience of IQ tests and the like, and few would dispute their validity as good measure of **general** intellectual capacity.

(b) However, there is **no agreed definition of intelligence**.

5.4   **Aptitude tests.** Aptitude tests are designed to **measure** and predict an individual's potential for performing a job or learning new skills.

- **Reasoning**: verbal, numerical and abstract
- **Spatio-visual ability**: practical intelligence, non-verbal ability and creative ability
- **Perceptual speed and accuracy**: clerical ability
- **'Manual' ability**: mechanical, manual, musical and athletic

5.5 **Personality tests.** Personality tests may measure a variety of characteristics, such as an applicant's skill in dealing with other people, his ambition and motivation or his emotional stability.

Case example

Probably the best known example is the 16PF, originally developed by Cattell in 1950.

The 16PF comprises 16 scales, each of which measure a factor that influences the way a person behaves.

The factors are functionally different underlying personality characteristics, and each is associated with not just one single piece of behaviour but rather is the source of a relatively broad range of behaviours. For this reason the factors themselves are referred to as source traits and the behaviours associated with them are called surface traits.

The advantage of measuring source traits, as the 16PF does, is that you end up with a much richer understanding of the person because you are not just describing what can be seen but also the characteristics underlying what can be seen.

The 16PF analyses how a person is likely to behave generally including, for example, contribution likely to be made to particular work contexts, aspects of the work environment to which the person is likely to more or less suited, and how best to manage the person.

The validity of such tests has been much debated, but is seems that some have been shown by research to be valid predictors of job performance, so long as they are used **properly.**

5.6 **Proficiency tests.** Proficiency tests are perhaps the most closely related to an assessor's objectives, because they **measure ability to do the work involved.** An applicant for an audio typist's job, for example, might be given a dictation tape and asked to type it.

5.7 **Trends in the use of tests**

(a) Continuing **enthusiasm for personality tests**.

(b) The continuing influence of **cognitive ability intelligence** tests.

(c) A focus on certain popular themes - sales ability or aptitude, customer orientation, motivation, teamworking and organisational culture are mentioned.

(d) The growing diversity of test producers and sources (meaning more choice, but also more poor quality measures).

(e) Expanded packages of tests, including tapes, computer disks, workbooks and so on.

(f) A growing focus on **fairness:** the most recent edition of the 16PF test, for example, has been scrutinised by expert psychologists to exclude certain types of content that might lead to bias.

5.8 **Limitations of testing**

(a) There is not always a direct relationship between ability in the test and ability in the job: the job situation is very different from artificial test conditions.

(b) The **interpretation of test results is a skilled task,** for which training and experience is essential. It is also highly subjective (particularly in the case of personality tests), which belies the apparent scientific nature of the approach.

(c) Additional difficulties are experienced with particular kinds of test. For example:

(i) An aptitude test measuring arithmetical ability would need to be constantly revised or its content might become known to later applicants.

    (ii)   Personality tests can often give misleading results because applicants seem able to guess which answers will be looked at most favourably.

    (iii)   It is difficult to design intelligence tests which give a fair chance to people from different cultures and social groups and which test the **kind** of intelligence that the organisation wants from its employees: the ability to **score highly in IQ** tests does not necessarily correlate with desirable traits such as mature **judgement** or **creativity**, merely mental ability.

    (iv)   Most tests are subject to coaching and practice effects.

(d)   **It is difficult to exclude bias from tests.** Many tests (including personality tests) are tackled less successfully by women than by men, or by some candidates born overseas than by indigenous applicants because of the particular aspect chosen for testing.

6   OTHER SELECTION METHODS

Group selection methods

6.1   **Group selection methods** might be used by an organisation as the final stage of a selection process as a more 'natural' and in-depth appraisal of candidates. Group assessments tend to be used for posts requiring leadership, communication or teamworking skills: advertising agencies often use the method for selecting account executives, for example.

6.2   They consist of a series of tests, interviews and group situations over a period of two days, involving a **small number of candidates for a job.** After an introductory session to make the candidates feel at home, they will be given one or two tests, one or two individual interviews, and several group situations in which the candidates are invited to discuss problems together and arrive at solutions as a management team.

6.3   **Techniques in such programmes**

(a)   **Group role-play exercises**, in which they can explore (and hopefully display) interpersonal skills and/or work through simulated managerial tasks.

(b)   **Case studies**, where candidates' analytical and problem-solving abilities are tested in working through described situations/problems, as well as their interpersonal skills, in taking part in (or leading) group discussion of the case study.

6.4   These group sessions might be thought useful because:

(a)   They give the organisation's **selectors a longer opportunity to study the candidates**.

(b)   **They reveal more than application forms, interviews and tests alone** about the ability of candidates to persuade others, negotiate with others, and explain ideas to others and also to investigate problems efficiently. These are typically **management skills**.

(c)   They reveal more about how the **candidate's personalities and attributes will affect the work team** and his own performance.

Work sampling

6.5   Work sampling involves getting the candidate to spend **some time doing the job**, in actual or simulated conditions. A firm wanting to recruit someone to do typesetting work can simply sit that person down in front of a wordprocessor or PC for a few hours to see how they do the job.

7 WHICH SELECTION METHOD IS BEST?

7.1 Smith and Abrahamsen in 1994 referred to a scale that predicts how well a candidate will perform at work if offered that job. This is known as a **predictive validity** scale. The scale ranges from 1 (meaning a method that is right every time) to 0 (meaning a method that is no better than chance). On this basis, they produced the following results.

Method	% use	Predictive validity
Interviews	92	0.17
References	74	0.13
Work sampling	18	0.57
Assessment centres	14	0.40
Personality tests	13	0.40
Cognitive tests	11	0.54
Biodata	4	0.40
Graphology	3	0.00

7.2 The results are most revealing as they show a pattern of employers relying most heavily on the **least** valid selection methods for their recruitment purposes. Interviews, in particular (and for the reasons given earlier) seem not much better than tossing a coin.

8 REFERENCES

8.1 References are a selection tool designed to help the organisation to identify the right person for a vacancy, by:

(a) checking and confirming personal and employment-related data provided by the candidate in a résumé or interview; and

(b) seeking a credible third-party assessment of the candidate's employability.

8.2 References may contain:

(a) Straightforward **factual information** confirming the nature of the applicant's previous job(s), period of employment, pay, and circumstances of leaving; and

(b) **Opinions** about the applicant's personality and other attributes. These should obviously be treated with some caution. Allowances should be made for prejudice (favourable or unfavourable), charity (withholding detrimental remarks), and possibly fear of being actionable for libel (although references are privileged, as long as they are factually correct and devoid of malice).

At least two **employer** references are desirable, providing necessary factual information, and comparison of personal views. **Personal** references tell the prospective employer little more than that the applicant has a friend or two.

8.3 **Written references** save time, especially if a standardised letter or form has been pre-prepared. A simple letter inviting the previous employer to reply with the basic information and judgements required may suffice. A standard form to be completed by the referee may be more acceptable, and might pose a set of simple questions about:

- Job title
- Main duties and responsibilities
- Period of employment
- Pay/salary
- Attendance record

If a judgement of character and suitability is desired, it might be most tellingly formulated as the question: 'Would you re-employ this individual? (If not, why not?)'

8.4 Telephone references may be time-saving if standard reference letters or forms are not available. They may also elicit a more honest opinion than a carefully prepared written statement. For this reason, a telephone call may also be made to check or confirm a poor or grudging reference which the recruiter suspects may be prejudiced.

Problems with references

8.5 References, by themselves, score very low on predictive validity scales such as Smith and Abrahamsen's: they are not a reliable guide to future job performance. While they are useful for confirming factual information provided by candidates, they are of limited value for a number of reasons.

8.6 Opinions about a candidate's character and personal attributes may be unreliable because of:

(a) biased judgement, whether favourable or unfavourable to the candidate;

(b) charity (withholding detrimental remarks in order to avoid prejudicing future employment opportunities);

(c) the withholding of negative opinions for fear of being actionable for libel if opinions prejudice a candidate's standing in the employment market. (In fact, references are legally privileged in this respect, as long as they are factually correct and devoid of malice.);

(d) ill-preparedness to give a specific or factually-confirmed reference (for example, if a reference is sought by telephone without prior warning).

8.7 References from a past employer may also be of limited usefulness because:

(a) they represent a single, potentially biased viewpoint;

(b) the candidate's performance in one job and organisation will not necessarily be transferable to another, with a different work group, environment and management style;

(c) unchecked assumptions may be made about the candidate on the basis of reference facts. For example, the assumption that frequent employment changes are due to lack of focus (rather than circumstance) or that the candidate will want to maintain a previous salary level (whereas he may be motivated by other factors).

8.8 Personal references are of little direct relevance to the job and are inevitably subject to positive bias, being selected by the candidate.

Making best use of references

8.9 Organisations can make best use of references received by:

(a) posing specific job-relevant questions when requesting references (whether in a letter of request or a standard form);

(b) using telephone reference-checking to save time;

(c) using telephone reference-checking in order to pre-empt preparation of guarded or ambiguous statements;

(d) checking dubious written references by telephone, in order to gain a more direct response and ask probing questions;

(e) using personal references only as a back-up to educational/professional references;

(f) making allowances for the potential for bias in the formulation and interpretation of references: avoiding uncritical acceptance of reference claims and identifying unwarranted assumptions;

(g) checking at least two employer references, where available, for greater objectivity;

(h) focusing opinions about the candidate's character and suitability on job-relevant issues, for example by asking: 'Would you (re)employ this individual? If not, why not?'

Exam alert

A detailed question on references and reference-checking was set in the December 2001 exam. This may seem like a 'minor' area of the syllabus, but it is an important tool in human resource management.

Activity 8.4

(a) At the end of a recent selection process one candidate was outstanding, in the view of everyone involved. However, you have just received a very bad reference from her current employer. What do you do?

(b) For fun, rephrase the following comments in the way that you might expect to see them appear in a letter of reference. Mr Smith is:

    (i)   Habitually late
    (ii) Remains immature
    (iii) Socially unskilled with clients

9 EVALUATING AND IMPROVING RECRUITMENT AND SELECTION PRACTICES

9.1 Good recruitment practices might seem like common sense; but common sense, for example that interviews are the best mechanism, can be wrong sometimes.

9.2 To get a clear idea as to how good a firm's recruitment and selection practices are, firms can ask themselves these questions.

- Can we identify human resources requirements from business plans?
- How fast do we respond to demands from line managers for human resources?
- Do we give/receive good advice on labour market trends?
- Do we select the right advertising media to reach the market?
- How effective is our recruitment advertising?
- How long does it take from the initial request for staff to filling the position?
- How do our recruits actually perform - do we end up employing the right people
- Do we retain our new recruits?

9.3 Recruitment and selection practices can be reviewed in these ways.

BPP
PUBLISHING

Review	Comment
Performance indicators	Each stage of the process can be assessed by performance indicators, for example the time it takes to reply to the application. Data can be collected to check any deviation from standard. Delays in replying to applications might encourage candidates to look elsewhere.
Cost-effectiveness	For example, number of responses per advert or, more usefully, number of *relevant* responses. An advert which attracted large numbers of unsuitable candidates might have been badly worded.
Monitoring the workforce	High staff turnover (ie the number and frequency of people leaving) may reflect poor recruitment, if people joined with the wrong expectations
Attitude surveys	The firm can ask its recruits what they thought of the process
Actual performance	A person's actual performance can be compared with what was expected when he/she was recruited

9.4 **Improving the effectiveness of recruitment and selection**

If, as we mentioned in Chapter 1, organisations are seeking to empower their staff and give them more responsibility, then the cost of bad recruitment policies increases.

9.5 Consequently, improving recruitment processes involves:

(a) Specifying much more carefully what is expected of the employee.

(b) Employing a variety of methods, as outlined in section 7, as opposed to relying on interviews alone.

Key learning points

- The process of selection begins when the recruiter receives details of candidates interested in the job, in response, for example, to a job advert, or possibly enquiries made to the recruitment consultant.

- Many firms require candidates to fill out an **application form**. This is standardised and the firm can ask for specific information about **work experience** and **qualifications**, as well as other **personal data**. Some firms do not bother with an application form, being happy to accept CVs with a covering letter.

- Application forms and CVs are then sifted, to weed out unsuitable candidates and to identify others whose applications can be taken further. **Biodata** techniques give weight to the data submitted giving applicants a score.

- Most firms use **interviews**, on a one-to-one basis, using a variety of **open** and **closed questions**. The interviewer should avoid bias in assessing the candidate.

- **Selection tests** can be used before or after interviews. Intelligence tests measures the candidate's general intellectual ability, and personality tests identify the type of person. Other tests are more specific to the job (eg proficiency tests)

- Interviews are unreliable as predictors of actual job performance for many posts, but they are traditional and convenient. A combination of interviews with other methods may be used.

- *See the Part C mind map summary on page 151.*

Quick quiz

1   What should application forms achieve?

2   Why are bio-data techniques useful?

3   What factors should be taken into account in an organisation's interview strategy?

4   Why are open questions useful?

5   Why do interviews fail to predict performance accurately?

6   List the desirable features of selection tests

7   Give examples of group selection methods

8   'Personality and cognitive tests are more reliable predictors of job performance than interviews.' True or False?

9   What should be obtained in a reference?

10   How can firms improve their recruitment and selection practices?

Answers to quick quiz

1   They should give enough information to identify suitable candidates and weed out no-hopers, by asking specific questions and by getting the candidate to volunteer information.

2   Bio-data techniques enable data in application forms/CVs to be weighted and scored, making it easier to sift candidates' applications.

3   In brief, giving the right impression on the organisation and obtaining a rounded, relevant assessment of the candidate.

4   They allow the candidate to volunteer more, and open avenues for further questions.

5   Brevity and artificiality of interview situation combined with the bias and inexperience of interviewers.

6   Sensitive; standardised; reliable; valid

7   Role play exercises; case studies

8   True

9   Facts, corroborating other data supplied by the candidate; opinions about the candidate

10   Clearly identifying what they want from the candidate; not relying on interviews alone.

Answers to activities

Answer 8.1

(a)   Boxes too small to contain the information asked for.

(b)   Forms which are (or look) so lengthy or complicated that a prospective applicant either completes them perfunctorily or gives up (and applies to another employer instead).

(c)   Illegal (eg discriminatory) or offensive questions.

(d)   Lack of clarity as to what (and how much) information is required.

Answer 8.2

(a)   Closed. (The only answer is 'yes' or 'no', unless Jo is prepared to expand on it, at his or her own initiative.)

(b)   Leading. (Even if Jo was interested, (s)he should get the message that 'yes' would not be what the interviewer wanted, or expected, to hear.)

(c)   Leading closed multiple! ('Really useful' leads Jo to think that the 'correct' answer will be 'yes': There is not much opportunity for any other answer, without expanding on it unasked.)

(d)   Open. (Jo has to explain, in his or her own words.)

(e)   Probing. (If Jo's answer has been unconvincing, short or vague, this question forces a more specific answer.)

Answer 8.4

(a)   It is quite possible that her current employer is desperate to retain her. Disregard the reference, or question the referee by telephone, and seek another reference from a previous employer if possible.

(b)   The phrases given are 'translations' by Adrian Furnham (*Financial Times,* December 1991) of the following.

   (i)   'Mr Smith was occasionally a little lax in time keeping'
   (ii)   'Clearly growing out of earlier irresponsibility'

PART C   MIND MAP SUMMARY

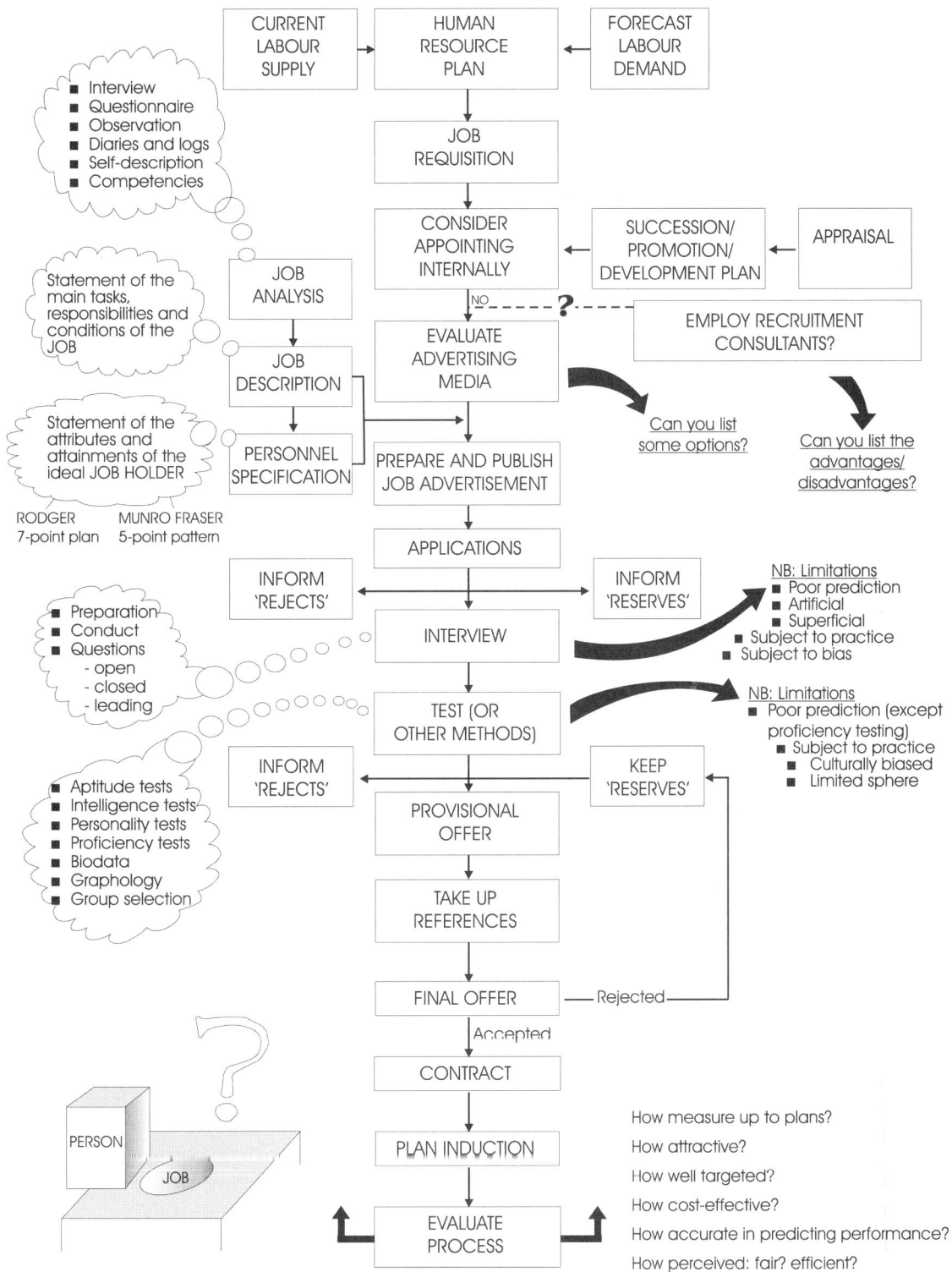

Thought cloud (top left):
- Interview
- Questionnaire
- Observation
- Diaries and logs
- Self-description
- Competencies

CURRENT LABOUR SUPPLY → HUMAN RESOURCE PLAN ← FORECAST LABOUR DEMAND

JOB REQUISITION

CONSIDER APPOINTING INTERNALLY ← SUCCESSION/ PROMOTION/ DEVELOPMENT PLAN ← APPRAISAL

Cloud: Statement of the main tasks, responsibilities and conditions of the JOB

JOB ANALYSIS

NO

EVALUATE ADVERTISING MEDIA

?

EMPLOY RECRUITMENT CONSULTANTS?

JOB DESCRIPTION

Can you list some options?

Can you list the advantages/ disadvantages?

Cloud: Statement of the attributes and attainments of the ideal JOB HOLDER

RODGER 7-point plan   MUNRO FRASER 5-point pattern

PERSONNEL SPECIFICATION

PREPARE AND PUBLISH JOB ADVERTISEMENT

APPLICATIONS

INFORM 'REJECTS'   INFORM 'RESERVES'

NB: Limitations
- Poor prediction
- Artificial
- Superficial
- Subject to practice
- Subject to bias

Cloud:
- Preparation
- Conduct
- Questions
  - open
  - closed
  - leading

INTERVIEW

TEST (OR OTHER METHODS)

NB: Limitations
- Poor prediction (except proficiency testing)
  - Subject to practice
  - Culturally biased
  - Limited sphere

Cloud:
- Aptitude tests
- Intelligence tests
- Personality tests
- Proficiency tests
- Biodata
- Graphology
- Group selection

INFORM 'REJECTS'   KEEP 'RESERVES'

PROVISIONAL OFFER

TAKE UP REFERENCES

FINAL OFFER —— Rejected

Accepted

CONTRACT

PLAN INDUCTION

EVALUATE PROCESS

PERSON / JOB

How measure up to plans?
How attractive?
How well targeted?
How cost-effective?
How accurate in predicting performance?
How perceived: fair? efficient?

BPP PUBLISHING

Part D
Development and performance review

Chapter 9 Employee development and training

Chapter topic list

1 Development and the role of training

2 Identifying training and development needs

3 Methods of development and training

4 The learning process

5 People involved in training and development

6 Evaluating training

Learning objectives

On completion of this chapter you will be able to:

Syllabus reference

- explain and list the benefits and the importance of training and development to the organisation and the individual

  b

- identify the roles and responsibilities of the manager, the supervisor and the training manager in training and development, and the skills needed

  b

- explain the methods used in analysing training and development needs

  b

- suggest ways in which training needs can be met, compare and contrast the methods for developing individuals in the work place and evaluate the effectiveness of internal and external training courses

  b

BPP PUBLISHING

1 DEVELOPMENT AND THE ROLE OF TRAINING

Factors affecting job performance

1.1 There are many factors affecting a person's performance at work, as shown in the diagram below. Training and development are the ways by which organisations seek to improve the performance of their staff and, it is hoped, of the organisation.

What is development?

> ### KEY TERMS
>
> **Development** is 'the growth or realisation of a person's ability and potential through the provision of learning and educational experiences'.
>
> **Training** is 'the planned and systematic modification of behaviour through learning events, programmes and instruction which enable individuals to achieve the level of knowledge, skills and competence to carry out their work effectively'.
>
> (Armstrong, *Handbook of Personnel Management Practice*)

1.2 **Overall purpose of employee and management development**

- **Ensure** the firm meets current and future performance objectives by...
- **Continuous improvement** of the performance of individuals and teams, and...
- **Maximising people's** potential for growth (and promotion).

1.3 **Development activities**
- Training, both on and off the job
- Career planning
- Job rotation
- Appraisal (see next chapter)
- Other learning opportunities

Activity 9.1

Note down key experiences which have developed your capacity and confidence at work, and the skills you are able to bring to your employer (or indeed a new employer!)

1.4 Organisations often have a **training and development strategy**, based on the overall strategy for the business. We can list the following steps.

Step 1. Identify the skills and competences are needed by the **business plan.**

Step 2. Draw up the **development strategy** to show how training and development activities will assist in meeting the targets of the corporate plan.

Step 3. **Implement** the training and development strategy.

The advantage of such an approach is that the training is:

- Relevant
- Problem-based (ie corrects a real lack of skills)
- Action-oriented
- Performance-related

Exam alert

In June 2000, a question was set on the **process of formulating a strategy** for training and development, and on the benefits of training for the individual **and** the organisation. You had to read the question very carefully in order to answer it correctly and fully.

Training and the organisation

1.5 **Benefits for the organisation of training and development programmes**

Benefit	Comment
Minimise the learning costs of obtaining the skills the organisation needs	Training supports the business strategy.
Lower costs and **increased productivity**, thereby improving performance	Some people suggest that higher levels of training explain the higher productivity of German as opposed to many British manufacturers
Fewer accidents, and better health and safety	EU health and safety directives require a certain level of training. Employees can take employers to court if accidents occur or if unhealthy work practices persist.
Less need for detailed supervision	If people are trained they can get on with the job, and managers can concentrate on other things. Training is an aspect of **empowerment**.
Flexibility	Training ensures that people have the **variety** of skills needed – multi-skilling is only possible if people are properly trained.

Benefit	Comment
Recruitment and succession planning	Training and development attracts new recruits and ensures that the organisation has a supply of suitable managerial and technical staff to take over when people retire.
Change management	Training helps organisations manage change by letting people know why the change is happening and giving them the skills to cope with it.
Corporate culture	(1) Training programmes can be used to build the corporate culture or to direct it in certain ways, by indicating that certain values are espoused (2) Training programmes can build relationships between staff and managers in different areas of the business
Motivation	Training programmes can increase commitment to the organisation's goals

1.6 Training cannot do everything. Look at the wheel below paragraph 1.1 again. Training only really covers:

Aspect of performance	Areas covered
Individual	Education; Experience; possibly Personal Circumstances (if successful completion of training is accompanied by a higher salary
Physical and job	Methods of work
Organisational and social	Type of training and supervision

1.7 In other words, **training cannot improve performance problems** arising out of:

- Bad management

- Poor job design

- Poor equipment, factory layout and work organisation

- Other characteristics of the employee (eg intelligence)

- Motivation – training gives a person the ability but not necessarily the willingness to improve

- Poor recruitment

Activity 9.2

Despite all the benefits to the organisation, many are still reluctant to train. What reasons can you give for this?

Training and the individual

1.8 For the individual employee, the benefits of training and development are more clear-cut, and few refuse it if it is offered.

Benefit	Comment
Enhances portfolio of **skills**	Even if not specifically related to the current job, training can be useful in other contexts, and the employee becomes more attractive to employers and more promotable
Psychological benefits	The trainee might feel reassured that he/she is of continuing value to the organisation
Social benefit	People's social needs can be met by training courses – they can also develop networks of contacts
The job	Training can help people do their job better, thereby increasing job satisfaction

2 IDENTIFYING TRAINING AND DEVELOPMENT NEEDS

Exam alert

This topic features in the Pilot Paper, where you are required to draft a report outlining how you would identify staff training and development needs.

The training process in outline

2.1 In order to ensure that training meets the real needs of the organisation, large firms adopt a planned approach to training. This has the following steps.

Step 1. Identify and define the **organisation's training needs**. It may be the case that recruitment might be a better solution to a problem than training

Step 2. **Define the learning required** – in other words, specify the knowledge, skills or competences that have to be acquired. For technical training, this is not difficult: for example all finance department staff will have to become conversant with a new accounting system.

Step 3. **Define training objectives** – what must be learnt and what trainees must be able to do after the training exercise

Step 4. **Plan training programmes** – training and development can be planned in a number of ways, employing a number of techniques, as we shall learn about in Section 3. (Also, people have different approaches to learning, which have to be considered.) This covers:

- Who provides the training
- Where the training takes place
- Divisions of responsibilities between trainers, managers and the individual.

Step 5. **Implement the training**

Step 6. **Evaluate** the training: has it been successful in achieving the learning objectives?

Step 7. Go back to Step 2 if more training is needed.

Activity 9.3

Draw up a training plan for introducing a new employee into your department. Repeat this exercise after you have completed this chapter to see if your chosen approach has changed.

Training needs analysis

2.2 Training needs analysis covers three issues.

Current state	Desired state
Organisation's current results	Desired results, standards
Existing knowledge and skill	Knowledge and skill needed
Individual performance	Required standards

The difference between the two columns is the **training gap**. Training programmes are designed to improve individual performance, thereby improving the performance of the organisation.

Case example

Training for quality

The British Standards for Quality Systems (BS EN ISO 9000: formerly BS 5750) which many UK organisations are working towards (often at the request of customers, who perceive it to be a 'guarantee' that high standards of quality control are being achieved) includes training requirements. As the following extract shows, the Standard identifies training needs for those organisations registering for assessment, and also shows the importance of a systematic approach to ensure adequate control.

The training, both by specific training to perform assigned tasks and general training to heighten quality awareness and t0 mould attitudes of all personnel in an organisation, is central to the achievement of quality.

The comprehensiveness of such training varies with the complexity of the organisation. The following steps should be taken:

1   Identifying the way tasks and operations influence quality in total

2   Identifying individuals; training needs against those required for satisfactory performance of the task

3   Planning and carrying out appropriate specific training

4   Planning and organising general quality awareness programmes

5   Recording training and achievement in an easily retrievable form so that records can be updated and taps in training can be readily identified

BSI, 1990

2.3 **Training surveys** combine information from a variety of sources to discern what the training needs of the organisation actually are. These sources are:

(a) The **business strategy** at corporate level.

(b) **Appraisal and performance reviews** – the purpose of a performance management system (see Chapter 6) is to improve performance, and training maybe recommended as a remedy.

(c) **Attitude surveys** from employees, asking them what training they think they need or would like.

(d) **Evaluation of existing training** programmes.

(e) **Job analysis** (see Chapter 7) can be used. To identify training needs from the job analysis, the job analysis can pay attention to:

(i)   Reported difficulties people have in meeting the skills requirement of the job

(ii) Existing performance weaknesses, of whatever kind, which could be remedied by training

(iii) Future changes in the job

The job analysis can be used to generate a training specification covering the knowledge needed for the job, the skills required to achieve the result, attitudinal changes required.

Setting training objectives

2.4 The **training manager** will have to make an initial investigation into the problem of the gap between job or competence **requirements** and current performance of **competence**.

2.5 If training would improve work performance, training **objectives** can then be defined. They should be clear, specific and related to observable, measurable targets, ideally detailing:

- **Behaviour** - what the trainee should be able to do
- **Standard** - to what level of performance?
- **Environment** - under what conditions (so that the performance level is realistic)?

2.6 EXAMPLE

'At the end of the course the trainee should be able to describe ... or identify ... or distinguish x from y ... or calculate ... or assemble ...' and so on. It is insufficient to define the objectives of training as 'to give trainees a grounding in ...' or 'to encourage trainees in a better appreciation of ...': this offers no target achievement which can be measured.

2.7 Training objectives link the identification of training needs with the content, methods and technology of training. Some examples of translating training needs into learning objectives are given in *Personnel Management, A New Approach* by D Torrington and L Hall.

Training needs	Learning objectives
To know more about the Data Protection Act	The employee will be able to answer four out of every five queries about the Data Protection Act without having to search for details.
To establish a better rapport with customers	The employee will immediately attend to a customer unless already engaged with another customers.
	The employee will greet each customer using the customer's name where known.
	The employee will apologise to every customer who has had to wait to be attended to.
To assemble clocks more quickly	The employee will be able to assemble each clock correctly within thirty minutes.

Having identified training needs and objectives, the manager will have to decide on the best way to approach training: there are a number of types and techniques of training, which we will discuss below.

BPP PUBLISHING

Incorporating training needs into an individual development programme

KEY TERM

A **personal development plan** is a 'clear developmental action plan for an individual which incorporates a wide set of developmental opportunities including formal training.'

2.8 The purpose of a personal development plan will cover:

- Improving performance in the existing job
- Developing skills for future career moves within and outside the organisation.

KEY TERM

Skills: what the individual needs to be able to do if results are to be achieved. Skills are built up progressively by repeated training. They may be manual, intellectual or mental, perceptual or social.

2.9 **Preparing a personal development plan**.

Step 1. **Analyse the current position**. You could do a personal SWOT (strengths, weaknesses, opportunities, threats) analysis. The supervisor can have an input into this by categorising the skills use of the employee on a grid as follows, in a **skills analysis**.

		Performance	
		High	*Low*
Liking of skills	*High*	Like and do well	Like but don't do well
	Low	Dislike but do well	Dislike and don't do well

The aim is to try to incorporate more of the employees' interests into their actual roles.

Step 2. **Set goals to cover performance in the existing job**, future changes in the current role, moving elsewhere in the organisations, developing specialist expertise. Naturally, such goals should have the characteristic, as far as possible of SMART objectives (ie specific, measurable, attainable, realistic and time-bounded).

Step 3. **Draw up action plan** to achieve the goals, covering the developmental activities listed in paragraph 3.1

Activity 9.4

Draw up a personal development plan for yourself over the next month, the next year, and the next five years. You should include your CAT activities.

Exam alert

A detailed question was set on personal development planning in the December 2001 exam: what it is, and what it is for; how a PDP can be prepared and what uses it can be put to. The examiner's report noted that many candidates confused a PDP with a job description, or with job enrichment (covered in Chapter 11). Make sure that you get your basic terms and concepts firmly fixed and distinguished in your mind. Use the Mind Map summaries – or even the Index to this Text – and try to define and distinguish all the terms you see!

3 METHODS OF DEVELOPMENT AND TRAINING

Formal training

3.1 **Formal training**

(a) **Courses** may be run by the organisation's training department or may be provided by external suppliers.

(b) **Types of course**

(i) **Day release**: the employee works in the organisation and on one day per week attends a local college or training centre for theoretical learning.

(ii) **Distance learning, evening classes and correspondence courses,** which make demands on the individual's time outside work.

(iii) **Revision courses** for examinations of professional bodies.

(iv) **Block release** courses which may involve four weeks at a college or training centre followed by a period back at work.

(v) **Sandwich courses,** usually involve six months at college then six months at work, in rotation, for two or three years.

(vi) A **sponsored full-time course** at a university for one or two years.

(c) **Computer-based training** involves interactive training via PC. The typing program, Mavis Beacon, is a good example.

(d) **Techniques** used on the course might include lecturers, seminars, role play and simulation.

3.2 **Disadvantages of formal training**

(a) An individual will not benefit from formal training unless he or she **is motivated to learn**.

(b) If the **subject matter** of the training course does not **relate to an individual's job,** the learning will quickly be forgotten.

On the job training

3.3 **Successful on the job training**

(a) The assignments should have a **specific purpose** from which the trainee can learn and gain experience.

(b) The organisation must **tolerate any mistakes** which the trainee makes. Mistakes are an inevitable part of on the job learning.

(c) The work should **not be too complex**.

3.4 Methods of on the job training

(a) **Demonstration/instruction:** show the trainee how to do the job and let them get on with it. It should combine **telling** a person what to do and **showing** them how, using appropriate media. The trainee imitates the instructor, and asks questions.

(b) **Coaching:** the trainee is put under the guidance of an experienced employee who shows the trainee how to do the job.

  (i) **Establish learning targets**. The areas to be learnt should be identified, and specific, realistic goals (eg completion dates, performance standards) stated by agreement with the trainee.

  (ii) **Plan a systematic learning and development programme.** This will ensure regular progress, appropriate stages for consolidation and practice.

  (iii) **Identify opportunities for broadening the trainee's knowledge and experience:** eg by involvement in new projects, placement on inter-departmental committees, suggesting new contacts, or simply extending the job, adding more tasks, greater responsibility etc.

  (iv) **Take into account the strengths and limitations of the trainee** in learning, and take advantage of learning opportunities that suit the trainee's ability, preferred style and goals.

  (v) **Exchange feedback**. The coach will want to know how the trainee sees his or her progress and future. He or she will also need performance information in order to monitor the trainee's progress, adjust the learning programme if necessary, identify further needs which may emerge and plan future development for the trainee.

(c) **Job rotation:** the trainee is given several jobs in succession, to gain experience of a wide range of activities. (Even experienced managers may rotate their jobs, to gain wider experience; this philosophy of job education is commonly applied in the Civil Service, where an employee may expect to move on to another job after a few years.)

(d) **Temporary promotion:** an individual is promoted into his/her superior's position whilst the superior is absent due to illness. This gives the individual a chance to experience the demands of a more senior position.

(e) **'Assistant to' positions:** a junior manager with good potential may be appointed as assistant to the managing director or another executive director. In this way, the individual gains experience of how the organisation is managed 'at the top'.

(f) **Action learning:** a group of managers are brought together to solve a real problem with the help of an 'advisor' who exposes the management process that actually happens.

(g) **Committees:** trainees might be included in the membership of committees, in order to obtain an understanding of inter-departmental relationships.

(h) **Project work**. work on a project with other people can expose the trainee to other parts of the organisation.

Activity 9.5

Suggest a suitable training method for each of the following situations.

(a) A worker is transferred onto a new machine and needs to learn its operation.

(b) An accounts clerk wishes to work towards becoming qualified with the relevant professional body.

(c) An organisation decides that its supervisors would benefit from ideas on participative management and democratic leadership.

(d) A new member of staff is about to join the organisation.

Exam alert

Again, you needed to distinguish clearly between terms in the June 2001 exam, where you were asked to explain 'coaching', 'mentoring' and 'on the job training' for 5 marks each.

Induction training

3.5   On the first day, a manager or personnel officer should welcome the new recruit. He/she should then introduce the new recruit to the person who will be their **immediate supervisor.**

3.6   The immediate supervisor should commence the **on-going process of induction**.

Step 1.   Pinpoint the areas that the recruit will have to learn about in order to **start the job**. Some things (such as detailed technical knowledge) may be identified as areas for later study or training.

Step 2.   Explain first of all the nature of the job, and the goals of each task, both of the recruit's job and of the department as a whole.

Step 3.   Explain about hours of work, and stress the importance of time-keeping. If flexitime is operated, the supervisor should explain how it works.

Step 4.   Explain the structure of the department: to whom the recruit will report, to whom he/she can go with complaints or queries and so on.

Step 5.   Introduce the recruit to the people in the office. One particular colleague may be assigned to the recruit as a **mentor**, to keep an eye on them, answer routine queries, 'show them the ropes'.

Step 6.   Plan and implement an appropriate **training programmes** for whatever technical or practical knowledge is required. Again, the programme should have a clear schedule and set of goals so that the recruit has a sense of purpose, and so that the programme can be efficiently organised to fit in with the activities of the department.

Step 7.   Coach and/or train the recruit; and check regularly on their progress, as demonstrated by performance, as reported by the recruit's mentor, and as perceived by the recruit him or herself.

3.7   Note that induction is an **on-going process**, embracing mentoring, coaching, training, monitoring and so on. It is not just a first day affair! After three months, six months or one year the performance of a new recruit should be formally appraised and discussed with them. Indeed, when the process of induction has been finished, a recruit should continue to receive periodic appraisals, just like every other employee in the organisation.

Activity 9.6

'Joining an organisation with around 8,500 staff, based on two sites over a mile apart and in the throes of major restructuring, can be confusing for any recruit. This is the situation facing the 20 to 30 new employees recruited each month by the Guy's and St Thomas' Hospital Trust, which was formed by the merger of the two hospitals in April.

'In a climate of change, new employees joining the NHS can be influenced by the negative attitudes of other staff who may oppose the current changes. So it has become increasingly important for the trust's management executive to get across their view of the future and to understand the feelings of confusion new staff may be experiencing.'

Personnel Management Plus, August 1993

See if you can design a **one day** induction programme for these new recruits, in the light of the above. The programme is to be available to **all** new recruits, from doctors and radiographers to accountants, catering and cleaning staff and secretaries.

Development

3.8 In Section 1, we defined development, and stressed the role of training in providing 'learning and educational experiences' for development. However, you should be aware that development is a 'wider' concept than training and education. This is what it covers.

(a) **Development** of job-relevant knowledge, skills and competence (through off-the-job and on-the-job training)

(b) **Career development**: the planned progression of competent individuals through the organisation, both 'upwards' through promotion and management succession, and 'laterally' through the acquisition of wide-ranging experience

(c) **Personal development**: taking account of people's wider needs and aspirations

3.9 Career development requires attention to three key issues.

(a) The types of **experience** employees – and particularly potential managers – will have to acquire. For example, opportunities might be given to learn about both line and staff/specialist management, different functions, different geographical areas of the business and so on.

(b) The individual's **guides and role models** in the organisation. At any stage in a career, a mentor will be an important source of challenge, guidance, feedback and support.

(c) The level of **opportunities and challenges** offered to the developing employee, in order to 'stretch' him or her without risk or stress.

3.10 Personal development may seem like a luxury in organisational terms, but businesses are increasingly offering employees more wide-ranging development opportunities, not necessarily related to the job, because of the following advantages.

(a) Personal development creates **more rounded, competent employees**, who may contribute more innovatively and flexibly to the organisation's future needs.

(b) Personal development **encourages employees to take responsibility for their development and future careers**. Organisations are no longer able to guarantee long-term employment, and it is socially responsible to recognise this fact. The concept of 'employability' training is based on the idea that employees should develop a portfolio of competence and experience that will enhance their value in the labour market in general – not just in the job or the current organisation.

(c) Personal development **fulfils the wider needs and aspirations of employees** for self-actualisation, and as such may be a powerful source of job satisfaction, commitment and loyalty.

(d) Personal development helps to create a **culture in which learning is valued**: a learning organisation.

3.11 Many organisations are using Personal Development Plans (PDPs), formulated during performance management and appraisal, to encourage employees to seek and organise training and experience for their own self-development. The advantage of a self-development orientation is that employees are more fully involved in and committed to their learning goals.

4 THE LEARNING PROCESS

4.1 There are different schools of learning theory which explain and describe how people learn.

(a) **Behaviourist psychology** concentrated on the relationship between **stimuli** (input through the senses) and **responses** to those stimuli. 'Learning' is the formation of **new** connections between stimulus and response, on the basis of **conditioning**. We modify our responses in future according to whether the results of our behaviour in the past have been good or bad.

(b) The **cognitive approach** argues that the human mind takes sensory information and imposes organisation and meaning on it: we interpret and rationalise. We use feedback information on the results of past behaviour to make **rational decisions** about whether to maintain successful behaviours or modify unsuccessful behaviours in future, according to our goals and our plans for reaching them.

4.2 Whichever approach it is based on, learning theory offers certain useful propositions for the design of **effective training programmes**.

Proposition	Comment
The individual should be **motivated** to learn	The advantages of training should be made clear, according to the individual's motives - money, opportunity, valued skills or whatever.
There should be clear **objectives and standards** set, so that each task has some meaning	Each stage of learning should present a challenge, without overloading the trainee or making them lose confidence. Specific objectives and performance standards for each will help the trainee in the planning and control process that leads to learning, and providing targets against which performance will constantly be measured.
There should be timely, relevant **feedback** on performance and progress	This will usually be provided by the trainer, and should be concurrent - or certainly not long delayed. If progress reports or performance appraisals are given only at the year end, for example, there will be no opportunity for behaviour adjustment or learning in the meantime.
Positive and negative **reinforcement** should be judiciously used	Recognition and encouragement enhance an individuals confidence in their competence and progress: punishment for poor performance - especially without explanation and correction - discourages the learner and creates feelings of guilt, failure and hostility
Active **participation** is more telling than passive reception (because of its effect on the motivation to learn, concentration and recollection).	If a high degree of participation is impossible, practice and repetition can be used to reinforce receptivity. However, participation has the effect of encouraging 'ownership' of the process of learning and changing - committing the individual to it as their **own** goal, not just an imposed process.

BPP
PUBLISHING

Learning styles

4.3 The way in which people learn best will differ according to the type of person. That is, there are **learning styles** which suit different individuals. Peter Honey and Alan Mumford have drawn up a popular classification of four learning styles.

(a) **Theorists**

- Seek to understand basic principles and to take an intellectual, 'hands-off' approach based on logical argument. They prefer training to be:
  - Programmed and structured
  - Designed to allow time for analysis
  - Provided by teachers who share his/her preference for concepts and analysis

(b) **Reflectors**

- Observe phenomena, think about them and then choose how to act
- Need to work at their own pace
- Find learning difficult if forced into a hurried programme
- Produce carefully thought-out conclusions after research and reflection
- Tend to be fairly slow, non-participative (unless to ask questions) and cautious

(c) **Activists**

- Deal with practical, active problems and do not have patience with theory
- Require training based on hands-on experience
- Excited by participation and pressure, such as new projects
- Flexible and optimistic, but tend to rush at something without due preparation

(d) **Pragmatists**

- Only like to study if they can see its direct link to practical problems
- Good at learning new techniques in on-the-job training
- Aim is to implement action plans and/or do the task better
- May discard good ideas which only require some development

Training programmes should ideally be designed to accommodate the preferences of all four styles. This can often be overlooked especially as the majority of training staff are activitists.

Activity 9.7

With reference to the four learning styles drawn up by Honey and Mumford, which of these styles do you think most closely resembles your own? What implications has this got for the way you learn?

Exam alert

A detailed question was set on learning theory in December 1998. The examiner was exasperated to find candidates confusing the four learning styles, or getting the sequence of the learning cycle wrong. Make sure that when you cite or describe a theory, you get it right!

The learning cycle

4.4 Another useful model is the **experiential learning cycle** devised by David Kolb. Experiential learning involves **doing**, however, and puts the learners in an active problem-solving role: a form of **self-learning** which encourages the learners to formulate and commit themselves to their own learning objectives.

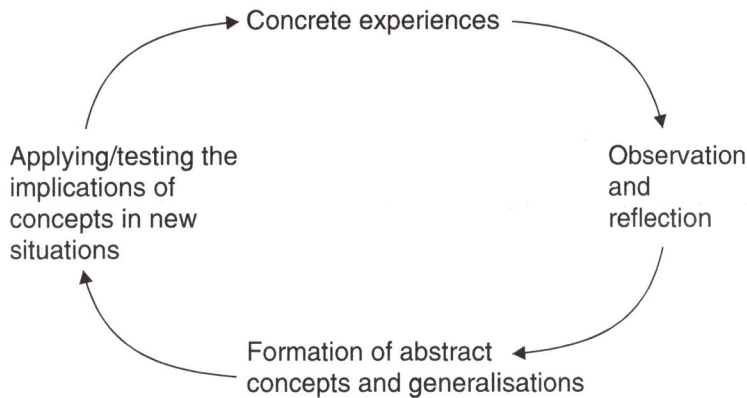

Concrete experiences

Observation and reflection

Formation of abstract concepts and generalisations

Applying/testing the implications of concepts in new situations

4.5 EXAMPLE

An employee interviews a customer for the first time (concrete experience). He observes his own performance and the dynamics of the situation (observation) and afterwards, having failed to convince the customer to buy his product, the employee analyses what he did right and wrong (reflection). He comes to the conclusion that he failed to listen to what the customer really wanted and feared, underneath his general reluctance: he realises that the key to communication is listening (abstraction/ generalisation). In his next interview he applies his strategy to the new set of circumstances (application/testing). This provides him with a new experience with which to start the cycle over again.

4.6   Simplified, this learning by doing approach involves:

Act: Analyse action: Understand principles: Apply principles:

Activity 9.8

With reference to Kolb's learning cycle, think of a situation on your present course where you have been involved in a practical exercise or 'experiential learning'. Illustrate the stages of the learning cycle using your chosen example.

Barriers to learning

4.7   According to Peter Senge, there are seven sources of **learning disability** in organisations which prevent them from attaining their potential - which trap them into 'mediocrity', for example, when they could be achieving 'excellence'.

   (a) **'I am my position'**. When asked what they do for a living, most people describe the tasks they perform, not the **purposes** they fulfil; thus they tend to see their responsibilities as limited to the boundaries of their position.

   (b) **'The enemy is out there'**. If things go wrong it is all too easy to imagine that somebody else 'out there' was at fault.

   (c) **The illusion of taking charge.** The individual decides to be more active in fighting the enemy out there, trying to destroy rather than to build.

   (d) **The fixation on events.** Conversations in organisations are dominated by concern about events (last month's sales, who's just been promoted, the new product from our competitor), and this focus inevitably distracts us from seeing the longer-term patterns of change.

(e) **The parable of the boiled frog.** Failure to adapt to gradually building threats is pervasive. (If you place a frog in a pot of boiling water, it will immediately try to scramble out; but if you place the frog in room temperature water, he will stay put. If you heat the water gradually, the frog will do nothing until he boils: this is because 'the frog's internal apparatus for sensing threats to survival is geared to sudden changes in his environment, not to slow, gradual changes'.)

(f) **The delusion of learning from experience.** We learn best from experience, but we never experience the results of our most important and significant decisions. Indeed, we never know what the outcomes would have been had we done something else.

(g) **The myth of the management team.** All too often, the management 'team' is not a team at all, but is a collection of individuals competing for power and resources.

Activity 9.9

How far do Senge's seven learning disabilities apply to your own organisation, or to some other significant organisation with which you may be familiar?

4.8   For individuals, the barriers may be:

*   'A waste of time': people see no personal benefit from training
*   Training programmes employ the wrong techniques for people's learning styles
*   Unwillingness to change

Encouraging learning: what managers can do

4.9   Managers can try to **develop the learning organisation**.

*   Encourages continuous learning and knowledge generation at all levels
*   Has the processes to move knowledge around the organisation
*   Can transform knowledge into actual behaviour

4.10   Let's start with a definition.

KEY TERM

Learning organisation is 'An organisation that facilitates the learning of all its members and continuously transforms itself'.

4.11   **The building of the learning organisation**

Characteristics	Comments
Systematic problem solving	Problems should be tackled in a scientific way.
Experimentation	Experimentation can generate new insights.
Learn from experience	Knowledge from past failures can help avoid them in future.
Learn from others	Customers and other firms can be a good source of ideas. Learning opportunities should be sought out.
Knowledge transfer	Knowledge should be transferred throughout the organisation.

Exam alert

In December 2000, a question was set on the learning organisation: what it is, what it is like, and what the barriers to learning (Senge) are. You needed a firm grasp on **all** the content of Paragraphs 4.7-4.11 to get good marks.

5 PEOPLE INVOLVED IN TRAINING AND DEVELOPMENT

The trainee

5.1 Many people now believe that the ultimate responsibility for training and development lies, not with the employer, but with the **individual**. People should seek to develop their own skills, to improve their own careers rather than wait for the organisation to impose training upon them. Why? The current conventional wisdom is that:

(a) **Delayering** means there are fewer automatic promotion pathways; promotion was once a source of development but there might not be further promotions available.

(b) Technological change means that new skills are always needed, and people who can find new work will be learning new skills.

Activity 9.10

You are currently studying for the ACCA Technician qualification. Was this your own decision, or were you encouraged to do so by your employer?

The human resources department or training department

5.2 The human resources department is ideally concerned with developing people. Some organisations have extensive development and career planning programmes. These shape the progression of individuals through the organisation, in accordance with the performance and potential of the individual and the needs of the organisation. Of course, only large organisations can afford or use this sort of approach.

5.3 The HR department also performs an **administrative** role by recording what training and development opportunities and individual might be given – in some firms, going on a training programme is an entitlement that the personnel department might have to enforce.

The supervisor and manager

5.4 Line managers and supervisors bear some of the responsibility for training and development within the organisation by identifying:

- The training needs of the department or section
- The current competences of the individuals within the department
- Opportunities for learning and development on the job
- When feedback is necessary.

5.5 The **supervisor** may be required to organise training programmes for staff.

Mentoring

5.6 A mentor is a guide, ideally both more experienced and more powerful in the organisation, whose concern is the trainee's long-term personal development. (S)he may occupy a role as the trainee's teacher/coach, counsellor, role model, organisational champion, encourager, constructive critic and so on, as appropriate to the situation over time.

The process of mentoring involves:

(a) helping the trainee to greater self-awareness;

(b) helping the trainee to formulate and clarify his or her work and non-work needs and ambitions;

(c) helping the trainee to identify opportunities for development at work;

(d) encouraging the trainee to take responsibility for his or her development, while offering support where required; and

(e) collaborating with the trainee to plan specific development directions.

The training manager

5.7 The training manager is a member of staff appointed to arrange and sometimes run training. The training manager generally reports to the **human resources** or **personnel director**, but also needs a good relationship with line managers in the production and other departments where the training takes place.

5.8 **Responsibilities of the training manager**

Responsibility	Comment
Liaison	With HRM department and operating departments
Scheduling	Arranging training programmes at convenient times
Skills identifying	Discerning existing and future skills shortages
Programme design	Develop tailored training programmes
Feedback	The trainee, the department and the HR department

6 EVALUATING TRAINING

Exam alert

This topic was covered in the Pilot Paper and again in the June 2001 exam, when you had to discuss how training could be evaluated from the point of view of the *individual* and the *organisation*.

KEY TERM

Validation of training means observing the results of the course and measuring whether the training objectives have been achieved.

Evaluation of training means comparing the actual costs of the scheme against the assessed benefits which are being obtained. If the costs exceed the benefits, the scheme will need to be redesigned or withdrawn.

6.1 From the point of view of the **organisation**, training may be evaluated by:

(a) measuring what the trainees have learned on the course, by means of a test or assessment of competence linked to training needs and objectives;

(b) measuring changes in job behaviour following training: studying the subsequent behaviour of the trainees in their jobs, to assess how the training scheme has altered the way they do their work in line with training needs and objectives;

(c) measuring the correlation between training and other indicators (error/wastage rates, accident rates, absenteeism, labour turnover, disciplinary actions and so on), to assess how training may have impacted on areas such as quality and employee morale;

(d) measuring the correlation between training and the achievement of organisational goals and objectives, to assess bottom-line effectiveness;

(e) measuring all the above in relation to the costs of training.

6.2 From the point of view of the **individual**, training may be evaluated by:

(a) measuring what trainees have learned on the course, by means of a test or assessment of competence linked to departmental training needs and objectives. (This is an element in individual trainee motivation and learning, as well as organisational effectiveness);

(b) measuring what trainees have learned and the qualifications they have obtained against their personal aspirations, goals and personal development plans;

(c) measuring trainee reactions to and perceptions of training: using Feedback Forms and Attitude Surveys, for example, to ask the trainees whether they thought the training programme was relevant to their work, effectively implemented, suitable for their learning style, generally worthwhile and so on;

(d) measuring individual post-training attainment and trainee satisfaction against the costs of training.

Activity 9.11

Outline why it is important to evaluate and validate a training programme and describe possible methods for achieving this.

Key learning points

- In order to achieve its goals, an organisation requires a **skilled workforce**. This is partly achieved by training.

- The main purpose of training and development is to **raise competence and therefore performance standards**. It is also concerned with **personal development**, helping and motivating employees to fulfil their potential.

- A thorough analysis of **training needs** should be carried out as part of a systematic approach to training, to ensure that training programmes meet organisational and individual requirements. Once training needs have been identified, they should be translated into **training objectives**.

- Individuals can incorporate training and development objectives into a personal development plan.

- There are different schools of thought as to how people learn. Different people have different learning styles.

- There are a variety of training methods. These include:

  o   Formal education and training

  o   On-the-job training

  o   Awareness-oriented training

- Managers can design and manager the organisation to encourage learning.

- *See Part D mind map summary on page 195.*

Quick quiz

1   List examples of development opportunities within organisations.

2   List how training can contribute to:

(a)   Organisational effectiveness
(b)   Individual effectiveness and motivation

3   According to ISO 9000, what are the main steps to be adopted in a systematic approach to training?

4   Define the term 'training need'.

5   How should training objectives be expressed?

6   What does learning theory tell us about the design of training programmes?

7   List the four learning styles put forward by Honey and Mumford.

8   List the four stages in Kolb's experiential learning cycle.

9   List the available methods of on-the-job training.

10   What are the levels of training validation/evaluation?

11   What is the supervisor's role in training?

Answers to quick quiz

1   Career planning, job rotation, deputising, on-the-job training, counselling, guidance, education and training.

2   (a)   Increased efficiency and productivity; reduced costs, supervisory problems and accidents; improved quality, motivation and morale.

(b)   Demonstrates individual value, enhances security, enhances skills portfolio, motivates, helps develop networks and contacts.

3   Identify how operations influence quality; identify individual training needs against performance requirements; plan and conduct training; plan and organise quality awareness programmes; record training and achievement.

4   The required level of competence minus the present level of competence.

5   Actively - 'after completing this chapter you should understand how to design and evaluate training programmes'.

6   The trainee should be motivated to learn, there should be clear objectives and timely feedback. Positive and negative reinforcement should be used carefully, to encourage active participation where possible.

7   Theorist, reflector, activist and pragmatist.

8   Concrete experience, observation/reflection, abstraction/generalisation, application/testing.

9   Induction, job rotation, temporary promotion, 'assistant to ' positions, project or committee work

10   Reactions, learning, job behaviour, organisational change, ultimate impact.

11   Identifying training needs of the department or section. identifying the skills of the individual employee, and deficiencies in performance. Providing or supervising on-the-job training (eg coaching). Providing feedback on an individuals performance.

Answers to activities

Answer 9.1

Few employers throw you in at the deep end – it is far too risky for them! Instead, you might have been given induction training to get acclimatised to the organisation, and you might have been introduced slowly to the job. Ideally, your employer would have planned a programme of tasks of steadily greater complexity and responsibility to allow you to grow into your role(s).

Answer 9.2

Cost: training can be costly. Ideally, it should be seen as an investment in the future or as something the firm has to do to maintain its position. In practice, many firms are reluctant to train because of poaching by other employers – their newly trained staff have skills which can be sold for more elsewhere. This got so bad that staff at one computer services firm were required to pay the firm £4,000 if they left (to go to another employer) within two years of a major training programme.

Answer 9.5

Training methods for the various workers indicated are as follows.

(a)   Worker on a new machine: on-the-job training, coaching.

(b)   Accounts clerk working for professional qualification: external course - evening class or day-release.

(o)   Supervisors wishing to benefit from participative management and democratic leadership: internal or external course. However, it is important that monitoring and evaluation takes place to ensure that the results of the course are subsequently applied in practice.

(d)   New staff: induction training.

Answer 9.6

Here is the actual programme for new recruits (of all types) at Guy's and St Thomas' Hospital Trust, as published in *Personnel Management Plus*.

9.00	Welcome	
9.05	Introduction	*Ground rules and objectives for the day*
9.25	Presentation	*The history of Guy's and St Thomas' hospitals*
10.25	Presentation	*Talk on structure of the management team, trust board and executive*
10.45	Group exercise	*With chief executive Tim Matthews on patient care, funding, hospital processes and measuring the care provided*
12.20	Lunch	
1.15	Tour of Guy's	
2.30	Presentation	*Looking at trust with new eyes - suggestions for change*
2.20	Presentation	*Information on staff organisations*
3.10	Presentation	*Security issues, fire drills, health and safety (including handouts)*
3.30	Presentation	*Session on occupational health*
3.40	Presentation	*Local areas and staff benefits*
3.45	Tour of St Thomas'	
4.30	Presentation	*Facilities management and patient care*
4.45	Closing session	*Evaluation and finish*

Particularly important is the focus on patient care and the group exercises. 'Feedback from the participants shows that they enjoy the discussions and learn a lot more about their colleagues and the trust by participating rather than being talked at.'

Answer 9.7

Depending on your answer you will learn most effectively in particular given situations. For example, the theorist will learn best from lectures and books, whereas the activist will get most from practical activities.

Answer 9.8

Which part of Kolb's cycle you have experienced will be individual to you. for example, you may have been involved in a group project where you contributed less than other group members. Here the cycle is as follows:

- Concrete experience (make a poor contribution to group project)

- Observation/reflection (note that you felt unsure about the subject matter of the group project from the outset)

- Abstraction/generalisation (conclude that your style is to keep quiet when unsure in order to avoid showing your ignorance)

- Application/testing (at the next available opportunity speak out if you don't understand something - you will probably not be alone!)

Answer 9.11

Validation of a new course is important to ensure that objectives have been achieved. Evaluation of it is more difficult, but at least as important because it identifies the value of the training programme to the organisation.

Taking the example of a one-day customer-service training programme for all staff, you could use the following methods of validation and evaluation.

Chapter 10 Appraisal and competence assessment

Chapter topic list

1   Appraisal and performance management

2   The purpose of appraisal

3   The process of appraisal

4   The appraisal report

5   The appraisal interview

6   Follow-up

7   Barriers to effective appraisal

8   New approaches to appraisal

9   How effective is the appraisal scheme?

Learning objectives

On completion of this chapter you will be able to:

Syllabus reference

- outline the purposes and benefits of staff appraisal — b

- explain the process of competence assessment — b

- explain the link between the appraisal process and employee development — b

- describe the role of the appraisee in the appraisal process — b

- describe the process of preparing an appraisal interview (including location, pre-interview correspondence — b

- identify the management and communication skills involved in appraisal interviews — b

- explain the importance of feedback and follow through — b

- describe the barriers to effective staff appraisal — b

- suggest ways of measuring the effectiveness of an appraisal scheme — b

BPP PUBLISHING

1 APPRAISAL AND PERFORMANCE MANAGEMENT

Performance management: set objectives for the future

1.1 Performance management is an approach which aims 'to get better results from the organisations, teams and individuals by measuring and managing performance within agreed frameworks of objectives and competence requirements, assessing and improving performance'. Performance management is part of the control system of the organisation.

Appraisal: review past performance to establish the current position.

1.2 The process of appraisal is part of this system of performance management.

> **KEY TERM**
>
> Whilst performance management as a whole is forward looking, the process of **appraisal** is designed to review performance over the past period, with a view to identifying any deficiencies, and improving it in the future.

2 THE PURPOSE OF APPRAISAL

2.1 The general purpose of any appraisal system is to improve the efficiency of the organisation by ensuring that the individuals within it are performing to the best of their ability and developing their potential for improvement.

   (a) **Reward review**. Measuring the extent to which an employee is deserving of a bonus or pay increase as compared with his or her peers.

   (b) **Performance review**, for planning and following-up training and development programmes, ie identifying training needs, validating training methods and so on.

   (c) **Potential review**, as an aid to planning career development and succession, by attempting to predict the level and type of work the individual will be capable of in the future.

2.2 **Objectives of appraisals**

   (a) Establishing what **the individual has to do** in a job in order that the objectives for the section or department are realised.

   (b) Establishing the **key or main results** which the individual will be expected to achieve in the course of his or her work over a period of time.

   (c) **Comparing the individual's level of performance against a standard**, to provide a basis for remuneration above the basic pay rate.

   (d) Identifying the individual's training and development **needs** in the light of actual **performance**.

   (e) Identifying **potential candidates for promotion**.

   (f) Identifying **areas of improvement**.

   (g) Establishing an **inventory of actual and potential performance** within the undertaking to provide a basis for manpower planning.

   (h) Monitoring the undertaking's **initial selection procedures** against the subsequent performance of recruits, relative to the organisation's expectations.

(i) **Improving communication** about work tasks between different levels in the hierarchy.

2.3 **The need for formal appraisal systems**

(a) Managers and supervisors may obtain **random impressions** of subordinates' performance (perhaps from their more noticeable successes and failures), but rarely form a coherent, complete and objective picture.

(b) They may have a fair idea of their subordinates' shortcomings - but may not have devoted **time and attention** to the matter of improvement and development.

(c) Judgements are **easy to make**, but **less easy to justify** in detail, in writing, or to the subject's face.

(d) **Different assessors** may be applying a **different set of criteria**, and varying standards of objectivity and judgement. This undermines the value of appraisal for comparison, as well as its credibility in the eyes of the appraisees.

(e) Unless stimulated to do so, managers rarely give their subordinates adequate **feedback** on their performance.

Exam alert

A June 1999 question asked you to discuss the objectives of appraisal from the point of view both of the organisation **and** the individual. Look out for such detailed instructions in exam questions – and be sure to obey them precisely! (In this case, make sure you attempt Activity 10.1.)

Activity 10.1

List four disadvantages to the individual of not having a formal appraisal system.

2.4 **Three basic problems**

(a) The **formulation and appreciation of desired traits and standards** against which individuals can be consistently and objectively assessed.

(b) **Recording assessments.** Managers should be encouraged to utilise a standard and understood framework, but still allowed to express what they consider important, and without too much form-filling.

(c) **Getting the appraiser and appraisee together,** so that both contribute to the assessment and plans for improvement and/or development.

3 THE PROCESS OF APPRAISAL

3.1 **A typical appraisal system**

Step 1. Identification of criteria for assessment, perhaps based on job analysis, performance standards, person specifications and so on.

Step 2. The preparation by the subordinate's manager of an **appraisal report**. In some systems both the appraisee and appraiser prepare a report. These reports are then compared.

Step 3. An **appraisal interview,** for an exchange of views about the appraisal report, targets for improvement, solutions to problems and so on.

BPP PUBLISHING

> *Step 4.* **Review of the assessment** by the assessor's own superior, so that the appraisee does not feel subject to one person's prejudices. Formal appeals may be allowed, if necessary to establish the fairness of the procedure.

> *Step 5.* The preparation and implementation of **action plans** to achieve improvements and changes agreed.

> *Step 6.* **Follow-up:** monitoring the progress of the action plan.

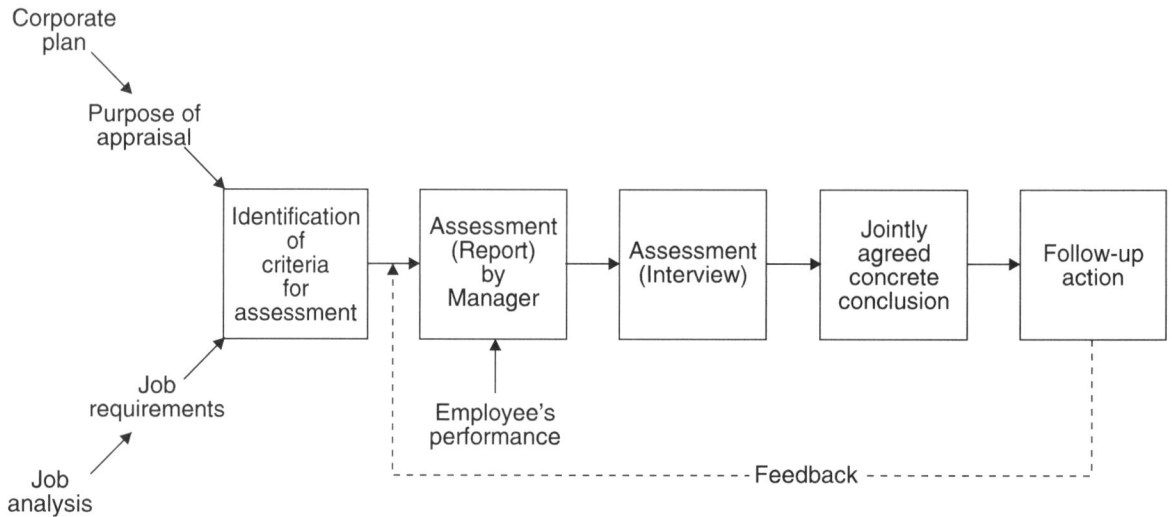

4 THE APPRAISAL REPORT

What is appraised?

4.1   Assessments must be related to a **common standard**, in order for comparisons to be made between individuals: on the other hand, they should be related to **meaningful performance criteria**, which take account of the **critical variables in each different job.**

4.2   An **appraisal report** is written before the interview. An example of a report is given on the next page.

(a)   Key issues relate to the **job description**.

(b)   **Personality**: not relevant unless specifically related to performance.

(c)   A **competence** is an observable skill or ability to complete a particular task successfully. It can include the ability to transfer skills and knowledge to new situations. Some competences for **managers and supervisors** might be adapted for appraisal as follows.

APPRAISAL REPORT

Name:	Time in position
Position:	Period of review:
Company:	Age:

	A	B	C	D	E	Comment
Overall assessment						
Job knowledge						
Effective output						
Co-operation						
Initiative						
Time-keeping						
Other relevant facts (specify)						

A= Outstanding   A = above standard   C = To required standard
D = Shot of standard in some respects   E= Not up to required standard

Potential	A	B	C	D	E	Comment

A = Overdue for promotion   B = Ready for promotion   C = Potential for promotion
D = No evidence of promotion potential at present
E = Has not worked long enough with me for judgement

Training, if any, required

Assessment discussed with employee?	Yes	No

Signed	Date

Confirmed	Date

Management competence	Comment	
Intellectual	(1)	Ability to see 'the wood for the trees'.
	(2)	Analysis and judgement (eg seeks relevant information, due attention to detail).
	(3)	Planning and organising (eg scheduling and delegating).
Interpersonal	(1)	Managing staff (eg leadership style, developing people).
	(2)	Persuasiveness (good in negotiation).
	(3)	Assertiveness and decisiveness.
	(4)	Interpersonal sensitivity (is flexible in dealing with others).
	(5)	Oral communication.
Adaptability and resilience	Can operate under pressure and adversity	
Results-orientation	(1)	Energy and initiative (is a 'self starter', maintains a high level of activity).
	(2)	Achievement motivation (sets demanding goals).
	(3)	Business sense.

Many competences are obviously **more detailed and technical**. It is possible to assess competences in the appraisal process by judging the individual's performance against the competences he or she is *supposed* to have.

Activity 10.2

Identify specific competences which may be relevant to some jobs of your choice.

4.3 Appraisal techniques

(a) **Overall assessment**. The manager writes in narrative form his judgements about the appraisee. There will be no guaranteed consistency of the criteria and areas of assessment, however, and managers may not be able to convey clear, effective judgements in writing.

(b) **Guided assessment**. Assessors are required to comment on a number of specified characteristics and performance elements, with guidelines as to how terms such as 'application', 'integrity' and 'adaptability' are to be interpreted in the work context. This is more precise, but still rather vague.

(c) **Grading**. Grading adds a comparative frame of reference to the general guidelines, whereby managers are asked to select one of a number of levels or degrees to which the individual in question displays the given characteristic. These are also known as **rating scales**.

Numerical values may be added to ratings to give rating scores. Alternatively a less precise **graphic scale** may be used to indicate general position on a plus/minus scale.

Factor: job knowledge

High _____√_____ Average _____ Low

(d) **Behavioural incident methods**. These concentrate on **employee behaviour**, which is measured against typical behaviour in each job, as defined by common **critical incidents** of successful and unsuccessful job behaviour reported by managers.

(e) **Results-orientated schemes**. This reviews performance against specific targets and standards of performance **agreed in advance by manager and subordinate together.**

   (i)   The subordinate is more involved in appraisal because he/she is able to evaluate his/her progress in achieving, jointly-agreed targets.

   (ii) The manager is relieved of a critic's role, and becomes a counsellor.

   (iii) Clear and known targets help modify behaviour.

   The effectiveness of the scheme will depend on the **targets set** (are they clearly defined? realistic?) and the **commitment** of both parties to make it work.

Activity 10.3

What sort of appraisal systems are suggested by the following examples?

(a) The Head Teacher of Dotheboys Hall sends a brief report at the end of each term to the parents of the school's pupils. Typical phrases include 'a satisfactory term's work', and 'could do better'.

(b) A firm of auditors assess the performance of their staff in four categories: technical ability, relationships with clients, relationships with other members of the audit team, and professional attitude. On each of these criteria staff are marked from A (= excellent) to E (= poor).

(c) A firm of insurance brokers assesses the performance of its staff by the number of clients they have visited and the number of policies sold.

Self-appraisals

4.4 Self-appraisals occur when individuals carry out their own self-evaluation as a major input into the appraisal process.

(a) **Advantages** of self appraisal

   (i)   It **saves the manager time** as the employee identifies the areas of competence which are relevant to the job and his/her relative strengths.

   (ii) It offers **increased responsibility** to the individual which may improve motivation.

   (iii) This reconciles the goals of the individual and the organisation.

   (iv) It may overcome the problem of needing skilled appraisers, thus cutting training costs and reducing the managerial role in appraisal.

   (v)   In giving the responsibility to an individual, the scheme may offer more **flexibility** in terms of timing, with individuals undertaking ongoing self-evaluation.

(b) **Disadvantage**

   People are often not the best judges of their own performance.

4.5 Many schemes combine the two - manager and subordinate fill out a report and compare notes.

BPP PUBLISHING

5 THE APPRAISAL INTERVIEW

5.1 The process of the interview is given below.

Step 1. Prepare

- Plan and place, time and environment
- Review employee's history
- Consult other managers - let employee prepare
- Prepare report. Review employee's self-appraisal

Step 2. Interview

- Listen to employee. Discuss, don't argue
- Encourage employee to talk, identify problems and solutions
- Be fair

Step 3.
- Gain employee commitment
- Agree plan of action
- Summarise to check understanding

Step 4.
- Complete appraisal report, if not already prepared

Step 5.
- Take action as agreed
- Monitor progress
- Keep employee informed

Interview and counselling

5.2 The extent to which any interview is based on the written report varies in practice.

(a) The report may be distributed to the appraisee in advance of the interview, so that he has a chance to make an independent assessment for discussion with his manager. The appraisee may complete the self-appraisal form.

(b) Maier *(The Appraisal Interview)* identifies three types of approach to appraisal interviews. Most appraisees prefer the third (option 5.5, below) of the alternatives suggested.

5.3 **The tell and sell method**. The manager tells the subordinate how he/she has been assessed, and then tries to 'sell' (gain acceptance of) the evaluation and the improvement plan. This requires unusual human relations skills in order to convey constructive criticism in an acceptable manner, and to motivate the appraisee to alter his/her behaviour.

5.4 **The tell and listen method**. The manager tells the subordinate how he/she has been assessed, and then invites the appraisee to respond. The manager therefore no longer dominates the interview throughout, and there is greater opportunity for **counselling** as opposed to pure **direction**.

(a) The employee is **encouraged to participate** in the assessment and the working out of improvement targets and methods: it is an accepted tenet of behavioural theory that participation in problem definition and goal setting increases the individual's commitment to behaviour and attitude modification.

(b) This method does not assume that a change in the employee will be the sole key to improvement: the manager may receive helpful feedback about how job design, methods, environment or supervision might be improved.

5.5   **The problem-solving approach**. The manager abandons the role of critic altogether, and becomes a helper. The discussion is centred not on the assessment, but on the employee's **work problems**. The employee is encouraged to think solutions through, and to commit himself to the recognised need for personal improvement. This approach encourages intrinsic motivation through the element of self-direction, and the perception of the job itself as a problem-solving activity. It may also stimulate creative thinking on the part of employee and manager alike, to the benefit of the organisation's adaptability and methods.

Activity 10.4

What approach was taken at your last appraisal interview? Could it have been better?

---

6   FOLLOW-UP

6.1   After the appraisal interview, the manager may complete the report, with an overall assessment, assessment of potential and/or the jointly-reached conclusion of the interview, with **recommendations for follow-up action**. The manager should then discuss the report with the counter-signing manager (usually his or her own superior), resolving any problems that have arisen in making the appraisal or report, and agreeing on action to be taken. The report form may then go to the management development adviser, training officer or other relevant people as appropriate for follow-up.

6.2   **Follow-up procedures**

(a)   **Informing appraisees of the results** of the appraisal, if this has not been central to the review interview.

(b)   **Carrying out agreed actions** on training, promotion and so on.

(c)   **Monitoring the appraisee's progress** and checking that he/she has carried out agreed actions or improvements.

(d)   Taking necessary steps to **help the appraisee to attain improvement objectives**, by guidance, providing feedback, upgrading equipment, altering work methods or whatever.

Activity 10.5

What would happen without follow-up?

---

7   BARRIERS TO EFFECTIVE APPRAISAL

Problems in practice

7.1   In theory, such appraisal schemes may seem very fair to the individual and very worthwhile for the organisation, but in practice the **appraisal system often goes wrong**. L Lockett (in *Effective Performance Management*) suggests that these appraisal barriers can be identified as follows.

Appraisal barriers	Comment
Appraisal as confrontation	Many people dread appraisals, or use them 'as a sort of show down, a good sorting out or a clearing of the air.' • There is a lack of agreement on performance levels. • The feedback is subjective - in other words the manager is biased, allows personality differences to get in the way of actual performance etc. • The feedback is badly delivered. • Appraisals are 'based on yesterday's performance not on the whole year'. • Disagreement on long-term prospects.
Appraisal as judgement	The appraisal 'is seen as a one-sided process in which the manager acts as judge, jury and counsel for the prosecution'. The subordinate is defensive. However, the process of performance management 'needs to be jointly operated in order to retain the commitment and develop the self-awareness of the individual.'
Appraisal as chat	The superior is defensive. The appraisal is a friendly chat 'without ... purpose or outcome ... Many managers, embarrassed by the need to give feedback and set stretching targets, reduce the appraisal to a few mumbled "well dones!" and leave the interview with a briefcase of unresolved issues.'
Appraisal as bureaucracy	Appraisal is a form-filling exercise, to satisfy the personnel department. Its underlying purpose, improving individual and organisational performance, is forgotten.
Appraisal as unfinished business	Appraisal should be part of a continuing process of performance management.
Appraisal as annual event	Many targets set at annual appraisal meetings become irrelevant or out-of-date.

Appraisal and pay

7.2   Another problem is the extent to which the appraisal system is related to the **pay and reward system**. Many employees consider that the appraisal system should be definitely linked with the reward system, on the ground that extra effort should be rewarded. Although this appears, superficially, a 'common sense' and fair view, there are major drawbacks to it.

   (a) **Funds available** for pay rises rarely depend on one individual's performance alone - the whole company has to do well.

   (b) **Continuous improvement** is always necessary - many firms have 'to run to stand still'. Continuous improvement should perhaps be expected of employees as part of their work, not rewarded as extra.

   (c) In low-inflation environments, **cash pay rises are fairly small**.

   (d) **Comparisons between individuals** are hard to make, as many smaller firms cannot afford the rigour of a job evaluation scheme.

(e) Performance management is about a lot more than pay for *past* performance - it is often **forward looking** with regard to future performance.

Appraisal, management expertise and empowerment

7.3 In 7.1 above, we suggested that appraisals could be subverted by managers who were biased, badly briefed or who only looked at yesterday's performance.

7.4 In organisations where **empowerment** is practised and employees are given more responsibility:

(a) Many **managers may not have the time** to keep a sufficiently close eye on individual workers to make a fair judgement.

(b) In some jobs, **managers do not have the technical expertise** to judge an employee's output.

(c) Employees depend on **other people** in the workplace/organisation to be effective - in other words, an individual's results may not be entirely under his/her control. A person's performance is often indirectly or directly influenced by the **management style** of the person doing the appraisal.

Activity 10.6

This activity shows some of the problems of operating appraisal schemes in practice.

It is time for Pauline Radway's annual performance appraisal and Steve Taylor, her manager, has sought your advice on two problem areas which he has identified as 'motivation' and 'the organisation's systems'.

The appraisal system has a six point rating scale:

1	Excellent	4	Acceptable
2	Outstanding	5	Room for improvement
3	Competent	6	Unacceptable

The annual pay increase is determined, in part, by the overall rating of the employee.

Pauline was recruited into Steve's section 18 months ago. She took about five months to learn the job and achieve competence. Accordingly, at last year's appraisal she and Steve agreed that an overall rating of '4' was appropriate.

Over the next six months Pauline worked hard and well and in effect developed her job so she was able to accept more responsibility and expand her range of activities into areas which were both interesting and demanding.

During the last six months the section has been 'rationalised' and the workforce has been reduced (although the workload has increased). Steve is under pressure to contain costs - particularly in the area of salary increases.

Steve now has to rely on Pauline performing her enriched job which, taking the past six months as a whole and given the increased pressure, she performs 'satisfactorily' rather than 'outstandingly'; there are aspects of her performance in this enriched job which she could improve.

When Steve met Pauline to agree the time for the appraisal interview she said - only half jokingly - 'I warn you, I'm looking forward to a respectable pay rise this year.'

Task

(a) Outline the problems for Steve that arise from the above scenario:

    (i)   in relation to Pauline's feelings;
    (ii) in relation to the organisation's systems.

(b)   Suggest how Steve should proceed.

8   NEW APPROACHES TO APPRAISAL

Improving the system

8.1   The appraisal scheme should itself be assessed (and regularly re-assessed) according to the following general criteria for evaluating appraisal schemes.

Criteria	Comment
Relevance	• Does the system have a useful purpose, relevant to the needs of the organisation and the individual? • Is the purpose clearly expressed and widely understood by all concerned, both appraisers and appraisees? • Are the appraisal criteria relevant to the purposes of the system?
Fairness	• Is there reasonable standardisation of criteria and objectivity throughout the organisation? • Is it reasonably objective?
Serious intent	• Are the managers concerned committed to the system - or is it just something the personnel department thrusts upon them? • Who does the interviewing, and are they properly trained in interviewing and assessment techniques? • Is reasonable time and attention given to the interviews - or is it a question of 'getting them over with'? • Is there a genuine demonstrable link between performance and reward or opportunity for development?
Co-operation	• Is the appraisal a participative, problem-solving activity - or a tool of management control? • Is the appraisee given time and encouragement to prepare for the appraisal, so that he can make a constructive contribution? • Does a jointly-agreed, concrete conclusion emerge from the process? • Are appraisals held regularly?
Efficiency	• Does the system seem overly time-consuming compared to the value of its outcome? • Is it difficult and costly to administer?

Upward appraisal

8.2   A notable modern trend, adopted in the UK by companies such as BP and British Airways, is **upward appraisal**, whereby employees are not rated by their superiors but by their subordinates. The followers appraise the leader.

8.3   The **advantages of upward appraisal**

(a)   Subordinates tend to know their superior better than superiors know their subordinates.

(b) As all subordinates rate their managers statistically, these ratings tend to be more reliable - the more subordinates the better. Instead of the biases of individual managers' ratings, the various ratings of the employees can be converted into a representative view.

(c) Subordinates' ratings have more impact because it is more unusual to receive ratings from subordinates. It is also surprising to bosses because, despite protestations to the contrary, information often flows down organisations more smoothly and comfortably than it flows up. When it flows up it is qualitatively and quantitatively different. It is this difference that makes it valuable.

8.4 **Problems** with the method include fear of reprisals, vindictiveness, and extra form processing. Some bosses in strong positions might refuse to act, even if a consensus of staff suggested that they should change their ways.

Activity 10.7

Look up the procedures manual of your organisation, and read through your appraisal procedures. Also get hold of any documentation related to them; the appraisal report form and notes, in particular.

How effective do you think your appraisal procedures are? Measure them against the criteria given above. How do you *feel* about appraisal interviews?

If you can get hold of an appraisal report form, have a go at filling one out for yourself - a good exercise in self-awareness!

Customer appraisal

8.5 In some companies part of the employee's appraisal process must take the form of **feedback from 'customers' (whether internal or external).** This may be taken further into an influence on remuneration (at Rank-Xerox, 30% of a manager's annual bonus is conditional upon satisfactory levels of 'customer' feedback). This is a valuable development in that customers are the best judges of customer service, which the appraisee's boss may not see.

360 degree appraisal

8.6 Taking downwards, upwards and customer appraisals together, some firms have instituted **360 degree appraisal** (or multi-source appraisal) by collecting feedback on an individual's performance from the following sources.

(a) The person's immediate boss.

(b) People who report to the appraisee, perhaps divided into groups

(c) Peers co-workers: most people interact with others within an organisation, either as members of a team or as the receivers or providers of services. They can offer useful feedback.

(d) Customers: if sales people know what customers thought of them, they might be able to improve their technique.

(e) The manager personally: all forms of 360 degree appraisal require people to rate themselves. Those 'who see themselves as others see them will get fewer surprises.'

8.7 Sometimes the appraisal results in a counselling session, especially when the result of the appraisals are conflicting. For example, an appraisee's boss may have a quite different view of the appraisee's skills than subordinates.

Case example

W H Smith

W H Smith (reported by Mike Thatcher, *People Management*, 21 March 1996), decided to supplement their existing upwards appraisal system (introduced 1990), covering 1,200 managers, with 360 degree appraisal. The personnel function was chosen.

'Between eight and fifteen people filled in forms covering each manager's competences and personal objectives. The appraisers were asked to rate them on a scale of one to five and give anecdotal examples to support the marks. The forms were sent to an independent third party for collating.

Ainley is pleased with the results, which have sharpened the developmental aspects of W H Smiths standard appraisal meetings. But there have been problems: a minimum of eight people commenting on 15 managers means at least 120 forms - a significant increase in administration; many appraisers found it difficult to comment on the individual manager's objectives; and there was a reluctance to back up ratings with anecdotal comments.

The second trial involving senior IT managers has just finished and the results are currently being evaluated. This time, the processing has been done in house to save costs, whilst a computerised system is being developed to cut down on the bureaucracy.

Ainley is now considering extending 360 degree appraisal to the rest of the organisation.'

9 HOW EFFECTIVE IS THE APPRAISAL SCHEME?

9.1 A survey by Saville and Holdsworth (cited by Mike Thatcher in *People Management*, 21 March 1996) indicated the mixed success of appraisal schemes in meeting objectives.

%	*Very good/good*	*Adequate*	*Poor/very poor*
Review past performance	84	12	3
Set individual objectives	76	19	5
Improve current performance	64	32	4
Determine one-off bonus	63	26	10
Identify training and development needs	64	32	4
Motivate staff	52	25	23
Set group goals	46	46	8
Assist career or succession	38	28	34
Determine salary rise	36	27	36
Assess potential	33	37	30

9.2 Evaluating the appraisal scheme can involve the following.

Measurement	Evaluating what?
Asking appraisers and appraisees how they felt about the process.	Is the appraisal system taken seriously?
	Is the system perceived to be fair and useful?
	Are appraisers able to be honest/constructive?
	Do appraisees feel threatened/judged or supported and involved in performance improvement?
Monitoring performance results	Has appraisal resulted in problem-solving and development with the effect of enhanced performance by individual employees/groups and the organisation as a whole?
Monitoring training provision and results	Has appraisal resulted in identification and take-up of training/development opportunities

Measurement	Evaluating what?
Monitoring other human resource indicators, such as attitudes, staff turnover and absenteeism, disciplinary actions and so on.	Has appraisal resulted in employee motivation and a culture of continuous improvement?
Monitoring succession and promotion processes	Has appraisal identified promotable individuals and resulted in development for smooth promotion from within the organisation?
Measuring the time and costs spent on appraisal against perceived benefits in performance improvement	Is the system efficiently organised and cost-efficient?

9.3   However, firms should not expect too much of the appraisal scheme. Appraisal systems, because they target the individual's performance, concentrate on the **lowest level of performance feedback**. They ignore the organisational and systems context of that performance. (For example, if an army is badly led, no matter how brave the troops, it will be defeated.) Appraisal schemes would seem to regard most **organisation problems** as a function of the **personal characteristics** of its members, rather than the **problem** of its overall design.

Key learning points

- **Appraisal** is part of the system of **performance management**.

- The main difference in emphasis is that appraisals are **backward** looking, whereas performance management as a whole looks to the **future**.

- Appraisal can be used to **reward** but also to identify **potential**.

- Three **basic problems** are defining what is to be appraised, recording assessments, and getting the appraiser and appraisee together.

- A variety of appraisal **techniques** can be used.

- Normally a **report** is written - but both manager and appraisee can contribute to the process, hence the value of self-appraisal.

- **Problems** with appraisal are its implementation in practice and the fact that it ignores, by and large, the context of performance.

- **New techniques** of appraisal aim to monitor the appraisee's effectiveness from a number of perspectives.

- *See Part D mind map summary on page 196.*

Quick quiz

1   What are the purposes of appraisal?

2   What bases or criteria of assessment might an appraisal system use?

3   Outline a results-oriented approach to appraisal, and its advantages.

4   What is a 360-degree feedback, and who might be involved?

5   What is upward appraisal?

6   What follow-up should there be after an appraisal?

7   How can appraisals be made more positive and empowering to employees?

8   What kinds of criticism might be levelled at appraisal schemes by a manager who thought they were a waste of time?

9   What is the difference between performance appraisal and performance management?

10   What techniques might be used to measure an employee's potential to become a successful senior manager?

Answers to quick quiz

1   Identifying performance levels, improvements needed and promotion prospects; deciding on rewards; assessing team work and encouraging communication between manager and employee.

2   Job analysis, job description, plans, targets and standards.

3   Performance against specific mutually agreed targets and standards.

4   Refer to paragraph 8.6

5   Subordinates appraise superiors.

6   Appraisees should be informed of the results, agreed activity should be taken, progress should be monitored and whatever resources or changes are needed should be provided or implemented.

7   Ensure the scheme is relevant, fair, taken seriously, and co-operative.

8   The manager may say that he has better things to do with his time, that appraisals have no relevance to the job and there is no reliable follow-up action, and that they involve too much paperwork.

9   Appraisal *on its own* is a backward-looking performance review. But it is a vital input into performance management, which is forward-looking.

10   Key indicators of performance should be determined and the employee should be assessed against them. The employee could be placed in positions simulating the responsibilities of senior management.

Answers to activities

Answer 10.1

Disadvantages to the individual of not having an appraisal system include: the individual is not aware of progress or shortcomings, is unable to judge whether s/he would be considered for promotion, is unable to identify or correct weaknesses by training and there is a lack of communication with the manager.

Answer 10.2

You might have identified such things as:

(a)   Numerical ability applicable to accounts staff, say, more than to customer contact staff.
(b)   Ability to drive safely, essential for transport workers - not for desk-bound ones.
(c)   Report-writing (not applicable to manual labour, say).

Answer 10.3

(a)   Overall assessment of the blandest kind.
(b)   This is a grading system, based on a guided assessment.
(c)   Results orientated scheme.

Answer 10.5

The appraisal would merely be seen as a pleasant chat with little effect on future performance, as circumstances change. Moreover the individual might feel cheated.

Answer 10.6

(a) *Steve's problems*

(i) *Pauline's feelings*

Pauline, not unreasonably, makes a connection between performance and reward. She feels she has worked hard and that this should be recognised in financial terms. Steve, on the other hand, is under pressure to keep costs under control. In fact, one of the reasons for Pauline's increased responsibility is the rationalisation of the department.

Pauline, however, does make a crude assumption that effort equals performance. She is highly motivated at the moment, but her performance is not outstanding. Her performance is only satisfactory in her changed job, and therefore it would not be appropriate to tell her otherwise. However, using expectancy theory, we can assert that a pay increase for her is an important motivating factor to get her to work hard.

Steve is thus faced with a dilemma. If she is not rewarded, it is likely that she will make less effort to perform well, and this would be suggested by expectancy theory. Steve will suffer, as the rationalised department depends on her continual hard work. In short, this is a hygiene factor.

Another factor is fairness. Pauline cannot expect special treatment, when compared to other workers, who may have made an equal effort. Over-rewarding average performance, despite the effort, might demotivate other staff who will accuse Steve of favouritism.

(ii) *The organisation's systems*

It is clear that Steve is having to negotiate the requirements and failings of four different systems here.

(1) The budgetary control system, restricting pay rises.

(2) The appraisal system, which conflates effort and performance.

(3) The remuneration system, by which pay rises are awarded.

Finally, Pauline's job is very different from what it was when she first started.

The source of the problem is the failure to recognise that Pauline is now doing a different job. Her job should have been re-evaluated. If this were the case, Steve could assess her reward on the basis of the performance in this re-evaluated job. She would have higher pay, commensurate with her enhanced responsibilities, but not an unfairly favourable grading.

However, Steve realises that the appraisal system is the one over which he has most direct control. He is in a position to reward her effort, but this would be anomalous as her performance in the new job is not exceptional. Her rating would not be appropriate to her performance. Yet her enhanced responsibilities need to be recognised somehow, although Steve, under pressure from the budgetary control system, may not be able to reward it financially.

There is little Steve can do about the budgetary factors, apart from stating to Pauline that everybody is in the same boat. There might be non-financial rewards that he can offer her. Pauline might like to have her own separate office space, for example, if it were available, or Steve might be able to offer her increased annual leave or a unique job title.

Pauline might also resent waiting for the outcome of a job re-evaluation exercise, as, from her point of view, that is the organisation's problem, not hers.

(b) *What Steve should do*

Steve has a choice either to overrate Pauline, according to the appraisal system, in recognition of her efforts rather than her performance in the changed job, or, alternatively, to try and negotiate a job re-evaluation first, with the risk that Pauline will become demotivated.

Steve needs to consider the effects of an unfairly favourable appraisal grading on the other staff. There are good reasons to believe that, while it might let him off the hook immediately, it would have bad long term repercussions, as it would send the wrong signals to Pauline about her current performance. Next year, for example, if her performance had not improved, he would have to downgrade her.

He will have to try and persuade Pauline of the complexities of the situation.

Pauline is obviously strongly motivated by money. Steve has to give some guarantee that her efforts will be recognised. While a low pay rise may be a negative hygiene factor, Steve should try and invoke motivator factors to counterbalance this effect.

Steve can promise Pauline that the job will be re-evaluated. This might be a long term objective. He can promise Pauline that he will be supportive in the re-evaluation exercise, and involve her in any input to it.

Steve can also suggest new targets for Pauline to achieve in her changed job, to give her something to aim for. This might still motivate her, providing Steve can explain to her the slightly difficult situation he is in.

He might give her formal recognition of her status, and allow her more autonomy in planning her work, if she is sufficiently competent.

Obviously he cannot guarantee the result of the job evaluation system, but he can make some effort to solve the problem.

PART D MIND MAP SUMMARY

Chapter 9

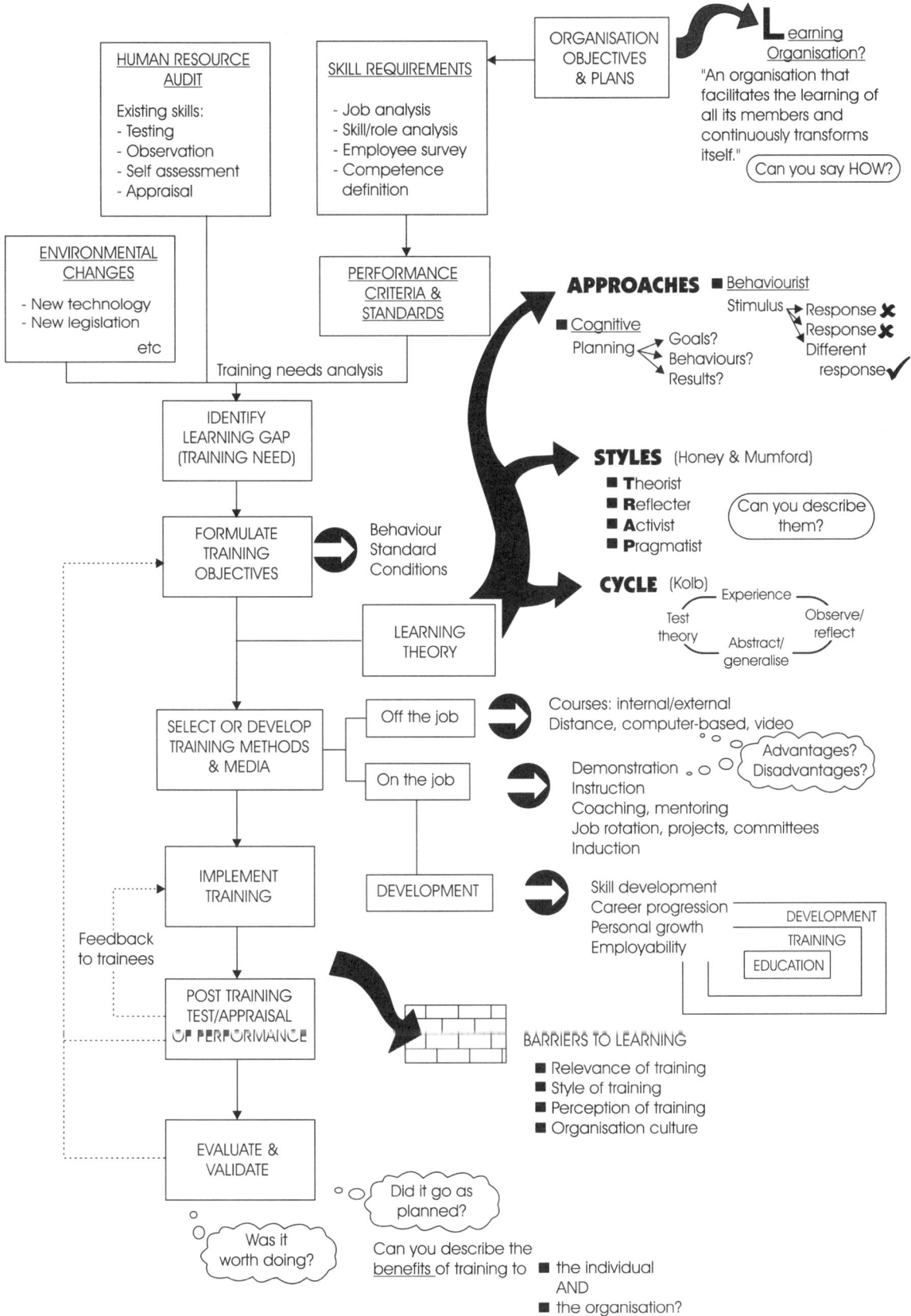

ORGANISATION OBJECTIVES & PLANS

Learning Organisation?
"An organisation that facilitates the learning of all its members and continuously transforms itself."
Can you say HOW?

HUMAN RESOURCE AUDIT

Existing skills:
- Testing
- Observation
- Self assessment
- Appraisal

SKILL REQUIREMENTS
- Job analysis
- Skill/role analysis
- Employee survey
- Competence definition

ENVIRONMENTAL CHANGES
- New technology
- New legislation
            etc

PERFORMANCE CRITERIA & STANDARDS

Training needs analysis

APPROACHES ■ Behaviourist
Stimulus → Response ✗
          → Response ✗
          Different response ✓
■ Cognitive
Planning → Goals?
          → Behaviours?
          → Results?

IDENTIFY LEARNING GAP (TRAINING NEED)

FORMULATE TRAINING OBJECTIVES

Behaviour Standard Conditions

STYLES (Honey & Mumford)
■ **T**heorist
■ **R**eflecter
■ **A**ctivist
■ **P**ragmatist
Can you describe them?

LEARNING THEORY

CYCLE (Kolb)
Experience — Observe/reflect — Abstract/generalise — Test theory

SELECT OR DEVELOP TRAINING METHODS & MEDIA

Off the job

Courses: internal/external
Distance, computer-based, video

On the job

Advantages? Disadvantages?

Demonstration
Instruction
Coaching, mentoring
Job rotation, projects, committees
Induction

IMPLEMENT TRAINING

DEVELOPMENT

Skill development
Career progression
Personal growth
Employability

DEVELOPMENT
TRAINING
EDUCATION

Feedback to trainees

POST TRAINING TEST/APPRAISAL OF PERFORMANCE

BARRIERS TO LEARNING
■ Relevance of training
■ Style of training
■ Perception of training
■ Organisation culture

EVALUATE & VALIDATE

Did it go as planned?

Was it worth doing?

Can you describe the benefits of training to ■ the individual
AND
■ the organisation?

PART D   MIND MAP SUMMARY

Chapter 10 (see also Chapter 6)

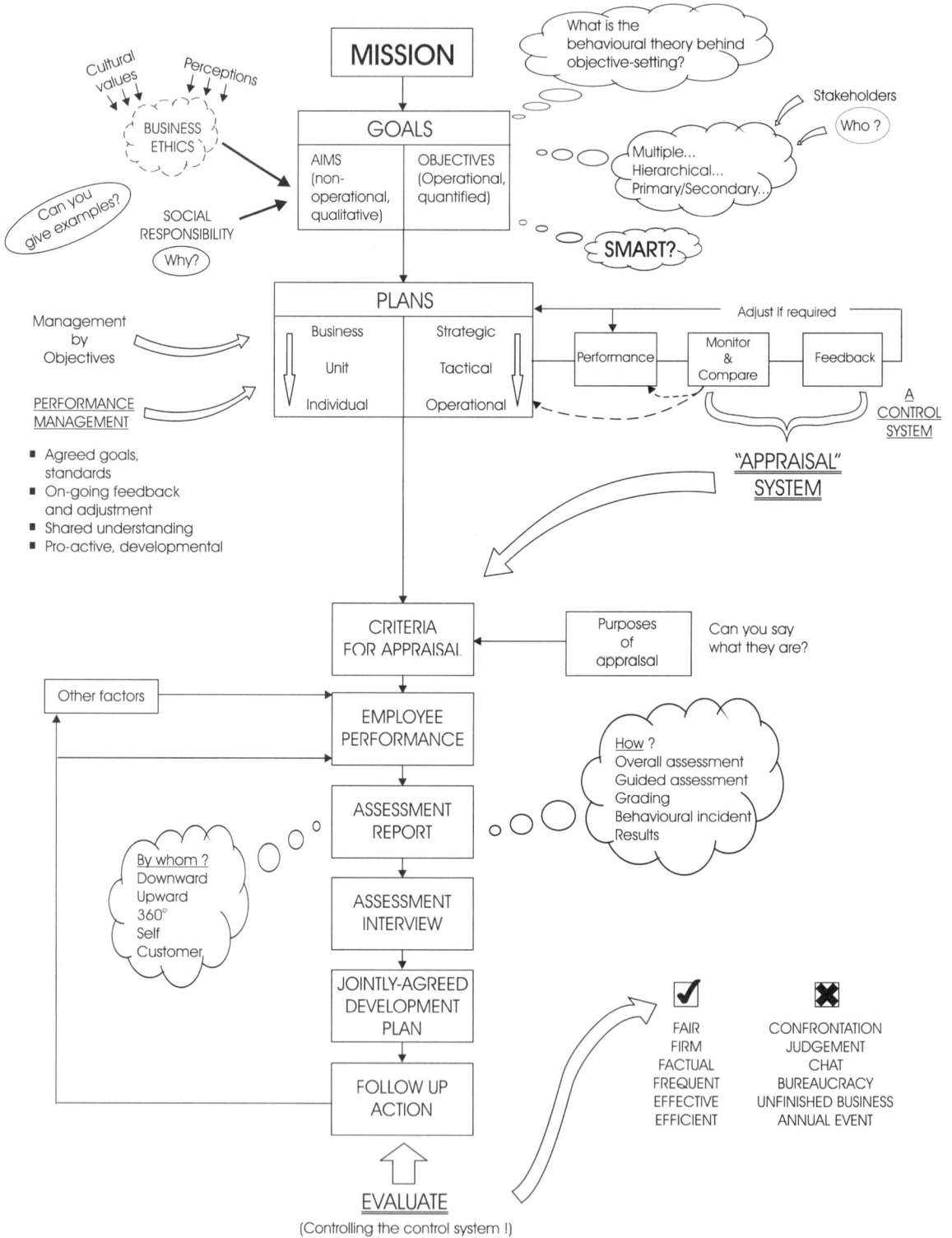

MISSION

What is the behavioural theory behind objective-setting?

Cultural values

Perceptions

BUSINESS ETHICS

Can you give examples?

SOCIAL RESPONSIBILITY

Why?

GOALS

AIMS (non-operational, qualitative)

OBJECTIVES (Operational, quantified)

Stakeholders — Who?

Multiple... Hierarchical... Primary/Secondary...

SMART?

PLANS

Management by Objectives

PERFORMANCE MANAGEMENT

- Agreed goals, standards
- On-going feedback and adjustment
- Shared understanding
- Pro-active, developmental

Business   Strategic

Unit   Tactical

Individual   Operational

Adjust if required

Performance   Monitor & Compare   Feedback

A CONTROL SYSTEM

"APPRAISAL" SYSTEM

CRITERIA FOR APPRAISAL

Purposes of appraisal

Can you say what they are?

Other factors

EMPLOYEE PERFORMANCE

How? Overall assessment, Guided assessment, Grading, Behavioural incident, Results

ASSESSMENT REPORT

By whom? Downward, Upward, 360°, Self, Customer

ASSESSMENT INTERVIEW

JOINTLY-AGREED DEVELOPMENT PLAN

FOLLOW UP ACTION

✓ FAIR, FIRM, FACTUAL, FREQUENT, EFFECTIVE, EFFICIENT

✗ CONFRONTATION, JUDGEMENT, CHAT, BUREAUCRACY, UNFINISHED BUSINESS, ANNUAL EVENT

EVALUATE
(Controlling the control system !)

Part E
Motivation

Chapter 11   Behaviour and motivation at work

Chapter topic list

1   Individual behaviour at work

2   Needs and goals

3   Theories of motivation

4   Rewards and incentives

5   Pay as a motivator

Learning objectives

On completion of this chapter you will be able to:

Syllabus reference

- outline key theories of motivation   d

- outline the difference between content and process theories of motivation   d

- describe how managers can motivate staff   d

- explain the importance of the reward system in the process of motivation   d

- explain performance related pay   c

- compare and contrast negative and positive behaviour   d

- examine ways of rewarding a team   c

BPP
PUBLISHING

1 INDIVIDUAL BEHAVIOUR AT WORK

Personality

1.1 In order to identify, describe and explain the differences between people, psychologists use the concept of personality.

> **KEY TERM**
>
> **Personality** is the total pattern of characteristic ways of thinking, feeling and behaving that constitute the individual's distinctive method of relating to the environment.

1.2 Self and self-image

Personality develops from dynamic process whereby the individual interacts with his or her environment and other people, through experience.

(a) **Self-image.** If people regularly praise your hard work for example, you may have an image of yourself as a successful worker. People tend to behave, and expect to be treated, in accordance with their self-image.

(b) **Personality development.** People tend, as they mature, to become more actively independent, to take on more equal or superior relationships (moving from child-adult, to adult-adult and adult-child relationships) and to develop self control and self awareness.

1.3 Personality and work behaviour

An individual should be 'compatible' with ' work' in three ways.

Compatibility	Comments
With the task	Different personality types suit different types of work. A person who appears unsociable and inhibited will find sales work, involving a lot of social interactions, intensely stressful - and will probably not be very good at it.
With the systems and management culture of the organisation	Some people hate to be controlled, for example, but others (or an 'authoritarian' personality type) want to be controlled and dependent in a work situation, because they find responsibility threatening.
With other personalities in the team	Personality clashes are a prime source of conflict at work. An achievement-oriented personality, for example, tends to be a perfectionist, is impatient and unable to relax, and will be unsociable if people seem to be getting in the way of performance: such a person will clearly be frustrated and annoyed by laid-back sociable types working (or not working) around him.

1.4 Where incompatibilities occur the manager or supervisor will have to:

(a) **Restore compatibility**: this may be achieved by reassigning an individual to tasks more suited to his personality type, for example, or changing management style to suit the personalities of the team.

(b) **Achieve a compromise**: individuals should be encouraged to:

   (i)   **Understand the nature** of their differences. Others have the right to be themselves (within the demands of the team); personal differences should not be 'taken personally', as if they were adopted deliberately to annoy.

   (ii) **Modify their behaviour** if necessary.

(c) **Remove the incompatible personality**. In the last resort, obstinately difficult or disruptive people may simply have to be weeded out of the team.

Activity 11.1

Look at the following list and number the qualities in priority order. 1 is very important, 2 is quite important, 3 is unimportant.

(a)	Good appearance	(f)	A pleasant personality
(b)	Ability to do the job	(g)	The ability to reason
(c)	Ability to answer questions clearly	(h)	Being interested in further training
(d)	A pleasant speaking voice	(i)	Being used to working in a team
(e)	Being objective	(j)	Being a good listener

Perception

1.5   Different people 'see' things differently and human beings behave in (and in response to) the world, not 'as it really is', but as they see it.

> **KEY TERM**
>
> **Perception** is the psychological process by which stimuli or in-coming sensory data are selected and organised into patterns which are meaningful to the individual.

1.6   Perception may be determined by any or all of the following.

(a) **The context**. People 'see what they want to see': whatever is necessary or relevant in the situation in which they find themselves. You might notice articles on management in the newspapers while studying this module which normally you would not notice.

(b) **The nature of the stimuli**. Our attention tends to be drawn to large, bright, loud, unfamiliar, moving and repeated (not repetitive) stimuli. Advertisers know it.

(c) **Internal factors**. Our attention is drawn to stimuli that match our personality, needs, interests, expectations and so on If you are hungry, for example, you will pick the smell of food out of a mix of aromas.

(d) **Fear or trauma**. People are able to avoid seeing things that they don't want to see: things that are threatening to their security of self-image, or things that are too painful for them.

1.7   A complementary process of **perceptual organisation** deals with the **interpretation** of the data which has been gathered and filtered.

Perception and work behaviour

1.8   People do not respond to the world 'as it really is', but as they **perceive it to be**. If people act in ways that seem illogical or contrary to you, it is probably not because of stupidity or defiance, but because they simply do not see things in the same way you do.

(a) Consider whether **you** might be misinterpreting the situation.

(b) Consider whether **others** might be misinterpreting the situation or interpreting it differently from you.

(c) When tackling a task or a problem get the people involved to **define the situation** as they see it.

(d) Be aware of the most common clashes of perception at work.

(i) **Managers and staff.** The experience of work can be very different for managerial and non-managerial personnel. Efforts to bridge the gap may be viewed with suspicion.

(ii) **Work cultures.** Different functions in organisations may have very different time-scales and cultures of work, and will therefore perceive the work, and each other, in different ways.

(iii) **Race and gender.** A joke, comment or gesture that one person may see as a 'bit of a laugh' may be offensive - and construed as harassment under the law - to another.

Activity 11.2

Identify the perceptual problem(s) in the following cases.

(a) An autocratic manager tries to adopt a more participative style of management, in order to improve the morale of his staff. He tells them they will be given more responsibility, and will be 'judged and rewarded accordingly'. For some reason, morale seems to worsen, and several people ask to transfer to other departments.

(b) A woman has just be promoted to the management team. At the first management meeting, the chairman introduces her to her new colleagues - all male - and says: 'At least we'll get some decent tea in these meetings from now on, eh?' Almost everyone laughs. For some reason, the woman does not contribute much in the meeting, and the chairman later tells one of his colleagues: 'I hope we haven't made a mistake. She doesn't seem to be a team player at all.'

(c) A new employee wanders into the office canteen, and is offered a cup of coffee by a youngster in jeans and an T-shirt, who has been chatting to the canteen supervisor. The youngster joins the man at his table (to his surprise) and asks how he likes working there so far. After a while, glancing uneasily at the man behind the serving counter, the new employee asks: 'Is it OK for you to be sitting here talking to me? I mean, won't the boss mind?' The youngster replies: 'I am the boss. Actually, I'm the boss of the whole company. Biscuit?'

Attitudes

1.9 Attitudes are our general standpoint on things: the positions we have adopted in regard to particular issues, things and people, as we perceive them.

KEY TERM

An **attitude** is 'a mental state ... exerting a directive or dynamic influence upon the individual's response to all objects and situations with which it is related.'

1.10 Attitudes are thought to contain three basic components.

- Knowledge, beliefs or disbeliefs, perceptions
- Feelings and desires (positive or negative)
- Volition, will or the intention to perform an action

Attitudes and work

1.11 Behaviour in a work context will be influenced by:

(a) **Attitudes to work:** the individual's standpoint on working, work conditions, colleagues, the task, the organisation and management.

(b) **Attitudes at work:** all sorts of attitudes which individuals may have about other people, politics, education, religion among other things, and which they bring with them into the work place - to act on, agree, disagree or discuss.

1.12 Positive, negative or neutral attitudes to other workers, or groups of workers, to the various systems and operations of the organisation, to learning - or particular training initiatives - to communication or to the task itself will obviously influence performance at work. In particular, they may result in varying degrees of:

- Co-operation or conflict between individuals and groups, or between departments
- Co-operation with or resistance to management
- Success in communication - interpersonal and organisation wide
- Commitment and contribution to the work

Activity 11.3

Suggest four elements which would make up a positive attitude to work. (An example might be the belief that you get a fair day's pay for a fair day's work.)

1.13 **Non-work factors that might influence attitudes to work, or affecting work:**

(a) **Class and class consciousness:** attitudes about the superiority or inferiority of others, according to birth, wealth and education; attitudes to money and work (necessity or career?).

(b) **Age**. Attitudes to sexual equality, family and morality can vary widely from one generation to the next.

(c) **Race, culture or religion**. These will affect the way people regard each other and their willingness to co-operate in work situations. Culture and religion are also strong influences on attitudes to work.

(d) **Lifestyle and interests.** Attitudes to these areas affect interpersonal relations and self-image, as well as the relative importance of work and leisure to the individual.

(e) **Sex**. Attitudes to the equality of the sexes and their various roles at work and in society may be influential in:

(i) **Interpersonal relations at work**: sexist attitudes and language

(ii) **The self concept of the individual:** women at work may be made to feel inferior, incompetent or simply unwelcome, while men working for female managers might feel threatened

(iii) **Attitudes to work.** Stereotypical role profiles ('a women's place is in the home', 'the man has to support the family') may be held by both sexes and may create feelings of guilt, resentment or resignation about wanting or having to work.

BPP PUBLISHING

1.14 **Intelligence** is a wide and complex concept. Intelligence/ability takes many forms.

(a) **Analytic intelligence**: measured by IQ test.

(b) **Spatial intelligence**: the ability to see patterns and connections, most obvious in the creative artist or scientist.

(c) **Musical intelligence**: 'the good ear' that musicians, mimics and linguists have.

(d) **Physical intelligence**: obvious in athletes and dancers.

(e) **Practical intelligence**: some people can make and fix things without theoretical knowledge.

(f) **Intra-personal intelligence**: the ability to know, be sensitive to and express oneself, observable in poets, artists and mystics.

(g) **Inter-personal intelligence**. The ability to relate to the work through others; essential in leaders.

2 NEEDS AND GOALS

Needs

2.1 Individual behaviour is partly influenced by human biology, which requires certain basics for life. When the body is deprived of these essentials, biological forces called **needs** or **drives** are activated (eg hunger), and dictate the behaviour required to end the deprivation: each, drink, flee and so on. However, we retain freedom of choice about **how** we satisfy our drives: they do not dictate specific or highly predictable behaviour. (Say you are hungry: how many specific ways of satisfying your hunger can you think of?)

Goals

2.2 Each individual has a different set of goals. The relative importance of those goals to the individual may vary with time, circumstances and other factors including the following.

Influence	Comment
Childhood environment and education	Aspiration levels, family and career models and so on are formed at early stages of development
Experience	This teaches us what to expect from life: we will either strive to repeat positive experiences, or to avoid or make up for negative ones.
Age and position	There is usually a gradual process of 'goal shift' with age. Relationships and exploration may preoccupy young employees. Career and family goals tend to conflict in the 20-40 age group: career launch and 'take-off' may have to yield to the priorities associated with forming permanent relationships and having children.
Culture	Some studies suggest that Japanese goals show a greater concern than in Europe for relationships at work and a lesser preoccupation with power and autonomy.
Self-concept	All the above factors are bound up with the individual's own self-image. The individual's assessments of his own abilities and place in society will affect the relative strength and nature of his needs and goals.

2.3 You should now be able to identify some of the needs and goals that people might have, where they might come from and why the might change. So why are they relevant to a manager?

2.4 **The significance of personal goals**

(a) People behave in such a way as to **satisfy their needs and fulfil their goals**.

(b) An **organisation is in a position to offer some of the satisfactions** people might seek: relationships and belonging, challenge and achievement, progress on the way to self-actualisation, security and structure and so on.

(c) The **organisation can therefore influence people** to behave in ways it desires (to secure work performance) by **offering them the means to satisfy their needs** and fulfil their goals **in return for** that behaviour. This process of influence is called **motivation.**

(d) If people's needs are being met, and goals being fulfilled, at work, they are more likely to have a positive attitude to their work and to the organisation.

3 THEORIES OF MOTIVATION

3.1 Managers might have certain **basic assumptions** about subordinates. Such assumptions were usefully summarised by Douglas MacGregor, who suggested that managers in the USA usually behaved as though they subscribed to one of two opposing philosophies about people's attitudes to work.

He identified two extreme sets of assumptions (Theory X and Theory Y) and explored how management style differs according to which set of assumptions is adopted.

(a) **Theory X** holds that human beings have an inherent dislike of work and will avoid it if they can. People prefer to be directed, wishing to avoid responsibility. They have relatively little ambition and want security above all, resisting change. They are self-interested, and make little effort to identify with the organisation's goals. They must be coerced, controlled, directed, offered rewards or threatened with punishments in order to get them to put adequate effort into the achievement of organisation objectives: this is management's responsibility.

(b) According to **Theory Y**, however, the expenditure of physical and mental effort in work is as natural as play or rest. The ordinary person does not inherently dislike work: according to the conditions, it may be a source of satisfaction or deprivation. A person will exercise self-direction and self-control in the service of objectives to which they are committed: they are not naturally passive or resistant to organisational objectives, but may have been made so by bad experience. The most significant reward that can be offered in order to obtain commitment is the satisfaction of the individual's personal growth and development needs. The average human being learns, under proper conditions, not only to accept but to seek responsibility. Management's responsibility is to create conditions and methods that will enable individuals to integrate their own and the organisation's goals.

You will have your own viewpoints on the validity of Theory X and Theory Y. In fact, McGregor intentionally polarised his theories as the extremes of a continuum along which most managers' attitudes fall at some point. However, he also recognised that the assumptions are self-perpetuating, even where the 'types' of employee described did not really exist. If people are treated according to Theory X (or Theory Y) assumptions, they will begin to act accordingly – thus confirming management in its beliefs and practices. Essentially, Theory X embodies the 'hard-tight' **control theory of management**, while Theory Y embodies the 'soft-loose' **commitment theory of management.**

3.2 A number of theories of '**leadership style**' were developed to reflect the continuum between Theory X and Theory Y. Some that you may have encountered in your studies include:

(a) The 'tells-sells-consults-joins' model of leadership developed by the Ashridge Management College

(b) The dictatorial – laissez-faire continuum of Tannenbaum and Schmidt

(c) The managerial grid developed by Blake and Mouton, in which one axis represents concern for people and the other concern for production

Charles Handy developed a contingency approach to leadership which suggests that there is a 'loose-tight' continuum of managerial control, and that a more or less loose or tight style will be appropriate depending on situational factors including: the leader's abilities, attitudes, preferred style and power; the team's abilities, attitudes and cultural values; and the extent to which the task requires close supervision, or initiative, flexibility and innovation.

Activity 11.4

What factors in yourself or your organisation motivate you to:

(a) Turn up to work at all?
(b) Do an average day's work?
(c) 'Bust a gut' on a task or for a boss?

Go on - be honest!

KEY TERMS

Motivation is 'a decision-making process through which the individual chooses the desired outcomes and sets in motion the behaviour appropriate to acquiring them'. (Buchanan and Huczynski).

Motives: 'learned influences on human behaviour that lead us to pursue particular goals because they are socially valued'. (Buchanan and Huczynski).

3.3 In practice the words **motives** and **motivation** are commonly used in different contexts to mean the following.

(a) **Goals or outcomes** that have become desirable for a particular individual. We say that money, power or friendship are motives for doing something.

(b) The **mental process of choosing desired outcomes,** deciding how to go about them (and whether the likelihood of success warrants the amount of effort that will be necessary) and **setting in motion** the required behaviours.

(c) The **social process** by which **other people motivate us** to behave in the ways they wish. Motivation in this sense usually applies to the attempts of organisations to get workers to put in more effort.

3.4 Many theories try to explain motivation and why and how people can be motivated. One classification is between content and process theories.

(a) **Content theories** ask the question: '**what** are the things that motivate people?'

They assume that human beings have a *set* of needs or desired outcomes. Maslow's hierarchy theory and Herzberg's two-factor theory, both discussed shortly, are two of the most important approaches of this type.

(b) **Process theories** ask the question: '**how** can people be motivated?'

They explore the process through which outcomes **become** desirable and are pursued by individuals. This approach assumes that people are able to select their goals and choose the paths towards them, by a conscious or unconscious process of calculation. Expectancy theory and Handy's 'motivation calculus', discussed soon, are theories of this type.

Exam alert

A detailed question on content and process theories was set in June 2000 and again in December 2001. Make sure you have grasped the difference between them **and** can cite specific theories and their authors. (The other halves of these questions were an explanation of Theory X and Theory Y, and Maslow and Vroom, respectively.) Motivation is a *major* area in people management, and you *must* get to grips with it in detail.

Content theories

Maslow's hierarchy of needs

3.5 Maslow outlined seven needs, as in the diagram below, and put forward certain propositions about the motivating power of each need.

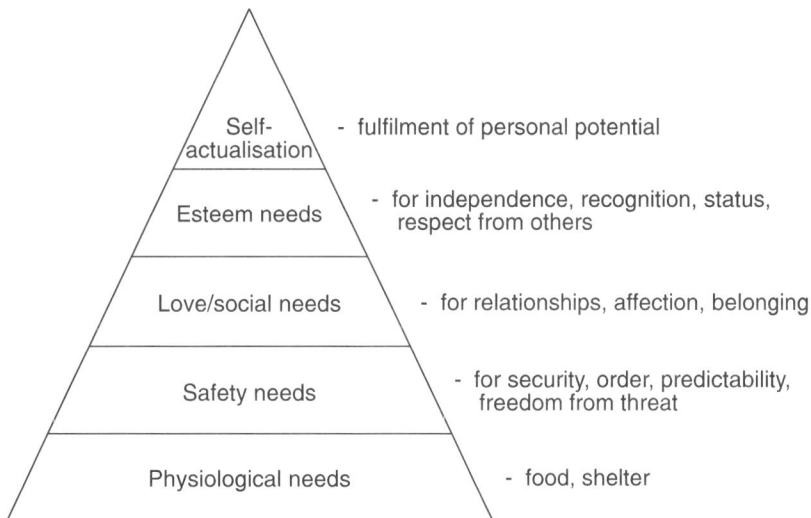

(a) Any individual's needs can be arranged in a '**hierarchy** of relative pre-potency'.

(b) Each level of need is **dominant until satisfied**; only then does the next level of need become a motivating factor.

(c) A need which has been satisfied no longer motivates an individual's behaviour. The need for self-actualisation can rarely be satisfied.

(d) In addition, Maslow described:

    (i) Freedom of enquiry and expression needs (for social conditions permitting free speech, and encouraging justice, fairness and honesty)

    (ii) Knowledge and understanding needs (to gain knowledge of the environment, to explore, learn).

Activity 11.5

Decide which of Maslow's categories the following fit into.

(a) Receiving praise from your manager

(b) A family party

(c) An artist forgetting to eat

(d) A man washed up on a desert island

(e) A pay increase

(f) Joining a local drama group

(g) Being awarded the OBE

(h) Buying a house

3.6 **Problems with Maslow's hierarchy**

(a) An individual's behaviour may be in response to **several needs**. Work, after all, can either satisfy or thwart the satisfaction of a number of needs.

(b) The **same need may cause different behaviour** in different individuals.

(c) It ignores the concept of **deferred gratification** by which people are prepared to ignore current suffering for the promise of future benefits.

(d) **Empirical verification is hard to come by**. In particular tests revealed it had a bias towards US and UK cultures.

Herzberg's two-factor theory

3.7 **Herzberg's** two-factor theory identified **hygiene factors** and **motivator factors**.

(a) **Hygiene factors** are based on a **need to avoid unpleasantness.**

If inadequate, they cause **dissatisfaction** with work. They work analogously to sanitation, which minimises threats to health rather than actively promoting 'good health'. Unpleasantness demotivates: pleasantness is a steady state. Hygiene factors (the conditions of work) include:

- Company policy and administration
- Salary
- The quality of supervision
- Interpersonal relations
- Working conditions
- Job security

(b) **Motivator factors** are based on a **need for personal growth.**

They actively create job satisfaction and are effective in motivating an individual to superior performance and effort. These factors are:

- Status (this may be a hygiene factor too)
- Advancement
- Gaining recognition
- Responsibility
- Challenging work
- Achievement
- Growth in the job

3.8 A lack of motivators at work will encourage employees to concentrate on bad hygiene factors such as to demand more pay. Stemming from his fundamental division of motivator and hygiene factors, Herzberg encouraged managers to **change the job** itself (the type of work done, the nature of tasks, levels of responsibility) rather than conditions of work. (We discuss this in Section 6 below.)

Process theories

Expectancy theory

3.9 Expectancy theory (Victor Vroom) states that people will decide how much they are going to put into their work, according to two factors.

(a) **Valence:** the value that they place on this outcome (whether the positive value of a reward, or the negative value of a punishment)

(b) **Expectancy:** the strength of their expectation that behaving in a certain way will in fact bring out the desired outcome.

Expectancy x *Valence* = *Force of motivation.*

Case example

Expectancy theory in action

This example illustrates the complexity of expectancy theory when applied to, say, the case of an insurance company sales representative who is male and in his 50s. For a given level of effort (E), he may perceive the possible outcomes as follows.

(a) A 75% chance of selling 17 policies in a week
(b) a 15% chance of selling 13 policies in a week
(c) A 10% chance of selling 30 policies in a week

There is 100% probability that this given level of effort (E) will produce the following effects.

(a) Exhaustion
(b) Sarcastic comments from his colleagues
(c) Aggravation to his sciatica

If he succeeds in selling 17 policies a week, the perceived outcomes will be as follows.

(a) Praise from his manager
(b) Accusations from colleagues about setting impossibly high standards
(c) Sufficient earnings (from commission) to buy a present for his wife

If he only sells 13 policies in the week, the perceived outcomes will be as follows.

(a) Criticism from his manager
(b) Tacit approval from colleagues
(c) A poor level of commission on earnings and income, leading to disapproval from his wife.

Selling 20 policies in a week will generate these perceived outcomes:

(a) Loud praise from his manager
(b) Extreme hostility from his colleagues
(c) Family expectations that income on this level will be sustained

The sales representative must assign a probability to each of these outcomes, eg a 75% probability that selling 17 policies will produce accusations from colleagues, and a 60% probability that selling 17 policies will produce praise from his manager.

Finally, the sales representative must attach a **valence** to each of the expected outcomes. Earning enough money to buy a present for his wife may have **high valence** for him; attracting the disapproval of colleagues may have **low valance.**

It can be seen from this (much simplified) example that trying to predict which choice will be made, in any given situation, becomes impossibly arduous.

Handy's motivation calculus

3.10 Charles Handy suggests that for any individual decision, there is a conscious or unconscious **motivation calculus** which is an assessment of three factors.

(a) The **individual's own set of needs.**

(b) The **desired results** - what the individual is expected to do in his job.

(c) **'E' factors** (effort, energy, excitement in achieving desired results, enthusiasm, emotion, and expenditure).

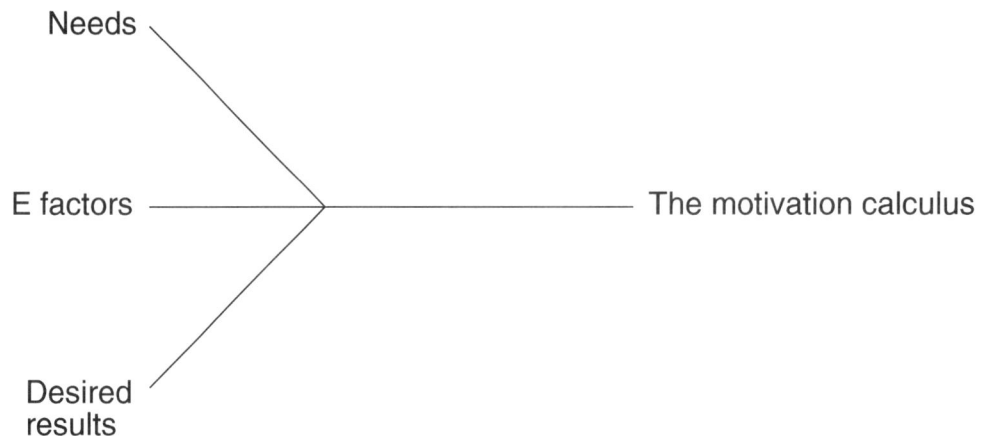

Needs

E factors ⟩ The motivation calculus

Desired results

3.11 The **motivation decision** will depend on:

- The **strength of the individual's needs**
- The **expectancy** that expending 'E' will lead to a desired result
- How far the result will be **instrumental** in satisfying the individual's needs

3.12 **Consequences for management**

(a) **Intended results should be made clear**, so that the individual can complete the calculation by knowing **what is expected**, the **reward**, and **how much 'E'** it will take.

(b) Individuals are more committed to **specific goals** which they **have helped to set themselves**.

(c) **Feedback.** Without knowledge of **actual results**, there is no check that the 'E' expenditure was justified (and will be justified in future).

(d) If an individual is **rewarded** according to performance tied to standards (management by objectives), however, he or she may well set lower standards: the instrumentality part of the calculus (likelihood of success and reward) is greater if the standard is lower, so less expense of 'E' is indicated.

Motivation and performance

3.13 Motivation, from the manager's view, is the controlling of the work environment and the offering of rewards in such a way as to encourage extra performance from employees.

3.14 You may be wondering whether motivation is really so important. It could be argued that if a person is employed to do a job, he will do that job and no question of motivation arises. If the person doesn't want to do the work, he can resign. So why try to motivate people?

(a) Motivation is about getting *extra* levels of commitment and performance from employees, over and above mere compliance with rules and procedures. If individuals can be motivated, by one means or another, they might work more efficiently (and productivity will rise) or they will produce a better quality of work.

(b) The case for **job satisfaction** as a factor in improved performance is not proven.

(c) The key is to work 'smarter'.

3.15 Motivation can be a negative process (appealing to an individual's need to **avoid** unpleasantness, pain, fear etc) as well as a positive one (appealing to the individual's need to attain certain goals).

(a) **Negative motivation** is wielding the big stick: threatening dismissal or demotion, reprimand etc - it is negative reinforcement.

(b) **Positive motivation** is dangling the carrot, and may be achieved by:

  (i) The offer of extrinsic rewards, such as pay incentives, promotion, better working conditions etc

  (ii) Internal or psychological satisfaction for the individual ('virtue is its own reward'), a sense of achievement, a sense of responsibility and value etc.

Morale

KEY TERM

'**Morale**' is a term drawn primarily from a military context, to denote the state of mind or spirit of a group, particularly regarding discipline and confidence. It can be related to 'satisfaction', since 'low morale' implies a state of dissatisfaction.

Morale relates to how a group feels.

3.16 The 'signs' by which morale is often gauged are by no means clear cut.

(a) **Low productivity** is not invariably a sign of low morale. In fact there may be **little correlation between morale and output**.

(b) **High labour turnover** is not a reliable indicator of low morale: the age structure of the workforce and other factors in natural wastage will need to be taken into account. Low turnover, likewise, is no evidence of high morale: people may be staying because of lack of other opportunities in the local job market, for example.

(c) There is some evidence that satisfaction correlates with mental health - so that symptoms of **stress or psychological failure** may be a signal to management that all is not well, although again, a range of non-work factors may be contributing.

(d) **Attitude surveys** may indicate workers' perception of their job satisfaction, by way of interview or questionnaire.

4 REWARDS AND INCENTIVES

KEY TERMS

A **reward** is a token (monetary or otherwise) given to an individual or team in recognition of some contribution or success.

An **incentive** is the offer or promise of a reward for contribution or success, designed to motivate the individual or team to behave in such a way as to earn it. (In other words, the 'carrot' dangled in front of the donkey!)

4.1 Not all the incentives that an organisation can offer its employees are directly related to **monetary** rewards. The satisfaction of **any** of the employee's wants or needs maybe seen as a reward for past of incentive for future performance.

4.2 **Different individuals have different goals,** and get different things out of their working life: in other words they have different **orientations** to work. There are any number of reasons why a person works, or is motivated to work well.

(a) The 'human relations' school of management theorists regarded **work relationships** as the main source of satisfaction and reward offered to the worker.

(b) Later writers suggested a range of 'higher' motivations, notably:

- **Job satisfaction**, interest and challenge in the job itself - rewarding work
- **Participation** in decision-making - responsibility and involvement

(c) **Pay** has always occupied a rather ambiguous position, but since people need money to live, it well certainly be part of the reward 'package' an individual gets from his work.

Intrinsic and extrinsic factors

4.3 The **rewards offered to the individual** at work may be these.

(a) **Extrinsic rewards**

These are external to the individual, and are given to him by others, such as wage or salary, bonuses and prizes, working conditions, a car, training opportunities.

(b) **Intrinsic rewards**

There are within individual himself: feelings of companionship, comfort, sense of achievement, enjoyment of status and recognition, interest in the job, responsibility, pride in the organisation's success etc.

4.4 The system of rewards used in an organisation or in the department will largely depend on:

- The **assumptions the managers make** about their subordinates' working life
- The **employees' goals**

4.5 Child has outlined six management **criteria for a reward system**. It should:

(a) Encourage people to **fill job vacancies** and to stay in their job (ie not leave).

(b) Increase the **predictability of employees' behaviour,** so that employees can be depended on to carry out their duties consistently and to a reasonable standard.

(c) Increase **willingness to accept change** and flexibility. (Changes in work practices are often 'bought' from trade unions with higher pay.)

(d) Foster and **encourage innovative behaviour.**

(e) **Reflect the nature of jobs** in the organisation and the skills or experience required. The reward system should therefore be consistent with seniority of position in the organisation structure, and should be thought fair by all employees.

(f) **Motivate** (increase commitment and effort).

Exam alert

Questions on motivation may be practical/contextual, as in the Pilot Paper, where it was set in a firm which had recently instituted voluntary redundancies. They may, however, cover detailed theoretical knowledge: a June 1999 question focused on the difference between extrinsic and intrinsic rewards. Any candidates who did not know the terms (or got them the wrong way round), were immediately in difficulty.

The job as a motivator

4.6   The job itself can be used as a motivator, or it can be a cause of dissatisfaction.

KEY TERM

Job design is the incorporation of the tasks the organisation needs to be done into a job for one person.

4.7   One of the consequences of mass production was what might be called a micro-division of labour, or **job simplification**.

   (a) **Little training**. A job is divided up into the smallest number of sequential tasks possible. Each task is so simple and straightforward that it can be learned with very little training.

   (b) **Replacement**. If labour turnover is high, this does not matter because unskilled replacements can be found and trained to do the work in a very short time.

   (c) **Flexibility**. Since the skill required is low, workers can be shifted from one task to another very easily. The production flow will therefore be unaffected by absenteeism.

   (d) **Control**. If tasks are closely defined and standard times set for their completion, production is easier to predict and control.

   (e) **Quality**. Standardisation of work into simple tasks means that quality is easier to predict. There is less scope for doing a task badly, in theory.

4.8   **Disadvantages**

   (a) The work is **monotonous** and makes employees tired, bored and dissatisfied. The consequences will be high labour turnover, absenteeism, spoilage, unrest.

   (b) **People work better** when their work is **variable**, unlike machines.

   (c) An individual doing a simple task feels like a small cog in a large machine, and has no **sense of contributing to the organisation's end product** or service.

   (d) Excessive specialisation **isolates** the individual in his or her work and inhibits not only social contacts with 'work mates', but knowledge generation.

   (e) In practice, excessive job simplification leads to **lower quality, through inattention**.

4.9   Herzberg suggest three ways of improving job design, to make jobs more interesting to the employee, and hopefully to improve performance: job enrichment, job enlargement and job rotation.

Job enrichment

> ### KEY TERM
>
> **Job enrichment** is planned, deliberate action to build greater responsibility, breadth and challenge of work into a job. Job enrichment is similar to **empowerment** although the emphasis of job enrichment is on the individual rather than on the team.

4.10 A job may be enriched by:

 (a) Giving the job holder **decision-making capabilities of a 'higher' order**. What is, mundane detail at a high level can represent significant job interest at a lower level.

 (b) Giving the **employee greater freedom** to decide how the job should be done.

 (c) Encouraging employees **to participate** in the planning decisions of their superiors.

 (d) Giving the employee regular **feedback**.

4.11 Job enrichment alone will not **automatically** make employees more productive. 'Even those who want their jobs enriched will expect to be rewarded with more than job satisfaction. Job enrichment is not a cheaper way to greater productivity. Its pay-off will come in the less visible costs of morale, climate and working relationships'. (Handy).

Job enlargement

> ### KEY TERM
>
> **Job enlargement** is the attempt to widen jobs by increasing the number of operations in which a job holder is involved.

4.12 By reducing the number of repetitions of the same work, the dullness of the job should also be reduced. Job enlargement is therefore a '**horizontal' extension** of an individual's work, whereas job enrichment is a 'vertical' extension.

 (a) Just by giving an employee tasks which span a larger part of the total production work should **reduce boredom**.

 (b) Enlarged jobs can provide a **challenge and incentive**. For example, a trusted employee might be given added responsibilities, for example:

 - **Checking the quality of output**
 - **On the job training** of new recruits

 (c) Enlarged jobs might also be regarded as 'status' jobs within the department, and as stepping stones towards promotion.

Job rotation

4.13 **Job rotation** might take two forms.

 (a) An employee might be **transferred to another job** after a period of, say, two to four years in an existing job, in order to give him or her a new interest and challenge, and to bring a fresh person to the job being vacated.

(b) **Job rotation might be regarded as a form of training**. Trainees might be expected to learn a bit about a number of different jobs, by spending six months or one year in each job before being moved on. The employee is regarded as a 'trainee' rather than as an experienced person holding down a demanding job.

Job optimisation

4.14 A **well designed job** should therefore provide the individual with:

- **Scope** for setting his own work standards and targets
- **Control** over the pace and methods of working
- **Variety** by allowing for inter-locking tasks to be done by the same person
- **Voice**: A chance to add his comments about the design of the product, or his job
- **Feedback** of information to the individual about his performance

Participation as a motivator

4.15 People want more interesting work and to have a say in decision-making. These expectations are a basic part of the movement towards greater **participation** at work.

4.16 The methods of achieving increased involvement have largely crystallised into two main streams.

(a) **Immediate participation** is used to refer to the involvement of employees in the **day-to-day** decisions of their work group.

(b) **Distant participation** refers to the process of including company employees at the top levels of the organisation which deal with long-term policy issues including investment and employment. Typical examples of this type of participation would be found in any major German company with the **two-tier** board structure. although firms in the EU are to have **works councils**.

4.17 Participation can involve employees and make them feel committed to their task, given the following conditions (5 Cs).

- **Certainty**. Participation should be genuine.

- **Consistency**. Efforts to establish participation should be made consistently over a long period.

- **Clarity**. The purpose of participation is made quite clear.

- **Capacity**. The individual has the ability and information to participate effectively.

- **Commitment**. The manager believes in participation.

4.18 Motivation through **employee satisfaction** is not a useful concept because employee satisfaction is such a **vague idea**. Drucker suggested that employee satisfaction comes about through encouraging - if need be, by pushing - employees to accept responsibility. There are four ingredients to this.

(a) **Careful placement of people in jobs** so that an individual is suited to the role.

(b) **High standards of performance in the job,** so that the employee should know what to aim for.

(c) **Providing the worker with feedback control information.** The employee should receive routine information about how well or badly he or she is doing without having to be told by his boss.

(d) **Opportunities for participation** in decisions that will give the employee managerial vision.

5   PAY AS A MOTIVATOR

5.1   Extrinsic rewards include:

- Basic pay and overtime
- Bonuses
- Performance-related pay
- Share-ownership schemes
- Benefit car or allowance
- Holiday entitlement
- Sick pay and maternity pay over the legal minimum
- Contributions to a pension scheme
- Private health care
- Sickness and disability insurance
- Crèches
- Season ticket loans

You may be able to think of some more.

5.2   Pay is important because:

- It is an important cost
- People feel strongly about it
- It is a legal issue (minimum wage, equal opportunities legislation)

How is pay determined?

5.3   As pay is such a **complex** issue, there are a number of ways by which organisations determine pay.

(a) **'Job evaluation'**. This is a systematic process for establishing the relative worth of jobs within an organisation. Its purpose is to:

(i)   Provide a rational basis for the design and maintenance of an equitable and defensible pay structure

(ii)   Help manage differences existing between jobs within the organisation

(iii)   Enable consistent decisions to be made on grading and rates of pay

(iv)   Establish the extent to which there is comparable worth between jobs so that equal pay can be provided for work of equal value.'

The salary structure is based on **job content**, and **not on the personal merit** of the job-holder. (The individual job-holder can be paid extra personal bonuses in reward for performance.)

(b) **Fairness.** Pay must be **perceived** and felt to match the level of work, and the capacity of the individual to do it.

(c) **Negotiated pay scales**. Pay scales, differentials and minimum rates may have been negotiated at plant, local or national level, according factors such as legislation, government policy, the economy, trade unions, the labour market.

(d) **Market rates.** Market rates of pay will have most influence on pay structures where there is a standard pattern of supply and demand in the open labour market. If an organisation's rates fall below the benchmark rates in the local or national labour market from which it recruits, it will have trouble attracting and holding employees.

(e) **Individual performance in the job.**

What do people want from pay?

5.4 **Pay has a central - but ambiguous - role in motivation theory**. It is not mentioned explicitly in any need list, but it **offers the satisfaction of many of the various needs**

(a) Physiological - pay for food, shelter

(b) Security

(c) Esteem needs - pay might be a mark of status, but also a level of pay may be a sign of fairness

(d) Self-actualisation - pay gives people resources to pursue self-actualisation outside the working environment

5.5 Individuals may also have needs unrelated to money, however, which money cannot satisfy, or which the pay system of the organisation actively denies. So to what extent is pay an inducement to better performance: a motivator or incentive?

5.6 Although the size of their income will affect their standard of living, most people tend not to be concerned to **maximise** their earnings. They may like to earn more but are probably more concerned to:

(a) Earn **enough**

(b) Know that their pay is **fair** in comparison with the pay of others both inside and outside the organisation

5.7 Pay is more of a 'hygiene' factor than a motivator factor. It gets taken for granted, and so is more usually a source of dissatisfaction than satisfaction. However, pay is the **most important of the hygiene factors**, according to Herzberg. It is valuable not only in its power to be converted into a wide range of other satisfactions but also as a consistent measure of worth or value, allowing employees to compare themselves and be compared with other individuals or occupational groups inside and outside the organisation. But this clearly **conflicts with performance-related pay**.

Case example

The Affluent Worker research of Goldthorpe, Lockwood et all (1968) illustrated an **instrumental** orientation to work (the attitude that work is not an end in itself but a means to other ends). The highly-paid Luton car assembly workers experienced their work as routine and dead-end. The researchers concluded that they had made a rational decision to enter employment offering high monetary reward **rather** than intrinsic interest: they were getting out of their jobs what they most wanted from them.

The Luton researchers did not claim that all workers have an instrumental orientation to work, however, but suggested that a person will seek a suitable balance of:

- The rewards which are important to him
- The deprivations he feels able to put up with

Even those with an instrumental orientation to work have limits to their purely financial aspirations, and will cease to be motivated by money if the deprivations - in terms of long working hours poor conditions, social isolation or whatever- become too great. In other words, if the 'price' of pay is too high.

High taxation rates may also weigh the deprivation side of the calculation; workers may perceive that a great deal of extra effort will in fact earn them little extra reward

---

5.8 Unlike other 'hygiene' or 'motivator' factors at work, pay is the only factor which is impossible to 'leave behind' at the office.

BPP
PUBLISHING

(a) Furthermore, if pay is a dominant motivator, then you would expect **difficulties in recruiting** for certain lower paid jobs. Academic research is not particularly well paid, but the job has other satisfactions, such as interest, status or esteem.

(b) Pay is thus only one of several **intrinsic or extrinsic rewards** offered by work. If pay is used to motivate, it can only do so in a **wider context of the job** and the other rewards. **Thanks, praise and recognition** are also relevant.

Activity 11.6

Hertzberg says that money is a **hygiene** factor in the motivation process. if this is true, it means that lack of money can demotivate, but the presence of money will not in itself be a motivator.

How far do you agree with this proposition? Can individual be motivated by a pay rise? What are the arguments against trying to motivate people purely by means of monetary incentives?

Performance related pay (PRP)

> **KEY TERM**
>
> **Performance related pay (PRP)** is related to output (in terms of the number of items produced or time taken to produce a unit or work), or results achieved (performance to defined standards in key tasks, according to plan).

5.9 The most common individual PRP scheme for wage earners is straight **piecework**: payment of a fixed amount per unit produced, or operation completed.

5.10 For managerial and other salaried jobs, however, a form of **management by objectives** will probably be applied. PRP is often awarded at the discretion of the line manager, subject to the budget overall. Guidelines may suggest, for example, that those rated exceptional get a rise of 10% whereas those who have performed less well only get, say, 3%.

(a) Key results can be identified and specified, for which merit awards will be paid.

(b) There will be a clear model for evaluating performance and knowing when, or if, targets have been reached and payments earned.

(c) The exact conditions and amounts of awards can be made clear to the employee, to avoid uncertainty and later resentment.

5.11 For service and other departments, a PRP scheme may involve **bonuses** for achievement of key results, or **points schemes**, where points are awarded for performance of various criteria (efficiency, cost savings, quality of service and so on). Certain points totals (or the highest points total in the unit, if a competitive system is used) then win cash or other awards.

5.12 Here are the supposed benefits and problems of performance related pay.

(a) **Benefits of PRP cited**

- Improves **commitment** and capability
- **Complements other HR initiatives**
- Improves focus on the business's performance objectives
- Better **two-way communications**
- Greater **supervisory responsibility**
- It **recognises achievement** when other means are not available

(b) **Potential problems cited**

- Subjectivity
- Supervisors' commitment and ability
- Translating appraisals into pay
- Divisive/against team working
- Union acceptance/employee attitudes

Case example

People Management (September 1996) reported several local authorities who had withdrawn from their PRP schemes. PRP was adopted by around 70 councils between 1988 and 1991: the figure is now in decline. The London Borough of Brent dropped PRP because of the difficulty in measuring performance and a general unease about its position in local government. Cambridgeshire Country Council axed its PRP scheme as part of an overhaul of salary policy, while the London Borough Lewisham abandoned PRP in favour of other programmes such as Investors in People, and ISO 9000, claiming that it demotivated more people than it inspired.

Activity 11.7

Why might PRP fail to motivate?

Rewarding the team

Group bonus schemes

5.13 **Group incentive schemes** typically offer a bonus for a which achieves or exceeds specified targets. Offering bonuses to a **whole team** may be appropriate for tasks where individual contributions cannot be isolated, workers have little control over their individual output because tasks depend on each other, or where team-building is particularly required. It may enhance team-spirit and co-operation as well as provide performance incentives, but it may also create pressures within the group if some individuals are seen to be 'not pulling their weight'.

Profit-sharing schemes

5.14 Profit-sharing schemes offer employees (or selected groups of them) bonuses, directly on profits or 'value added'. Profit sharing is based on the belief that all employees can contribute to profitability, and that that contribution should be recognised. The effects may include profit-consciousness and motivation in employees, commitment to the future prosperity of the organisation etc.

5.15 The actual incentive value and effect on productivity may be wasted, however, if the scheme is badly designed.

(a) The sum should be **significant**.

(b) There should be a **clear and timely link** between effort/performance and reward. Profit shares should be distributed as frequently as possible with the need for reliable information on profit forecasts, targets etc and the need to amass significant amounts for distribution.

(c) The scheme should only be introduced if profit forecasts indicate a **reasonable chance of achieving** the above: profit sharing is welcome when profits are high, but the potential for disappointment is great.

(d) The greatest effect on productivity arising from the scheme may in fact arise from its use as a focal point for discussion with employees, about the relationship between their performance and results, areas and targets for improvement etc. Management must be seen to be **committed** to the principle.

Share schemes

5.16 Some firms choose to reward employees and managers by way of shares, again allowing them to participate in the success of the company as measured by the share price. In effect, the employee is allowed to purchase, at a future date, shares in the firm at the current price or perhaps at a discount. If the share price has risen the employee can sell the shares and make a profit.

(a) This is used often in the remuneration of chief executives; there has been some criticism especially with regard to rewarding executives of privatised utilities.

(b) Many firms have introduced such schemes for all their staff. There have been some tax incentives also.

Key learning points

- Personality is the total pattern of an individual's thoughts, feelings and behaviours. It is shaped by a variety of factors, both inherited and environmental.

- Perception is the process by which the brain selects and organises information in order to make sense of it. People behave according to what they perceive - not according to what 'really is'.

- People develop attitudes about things, based on what they think, what they feel and what they want to do about it. Attitudes are formed by perception, experience and personality which in turn are shaped by wider social influences.

- Ability is the capacity to do something. It is often equated with intelligence. It is now recognised that there are many types of ability/intelligence, not all of which are based on mental dexterity or verbal fluency.

- People have certain innate needs. Maslow has categorised needs as physiological, security, love/social, esteem and self-actualisation. People also have goals, through which they expect their needs to be satisfied.

- Content theories of motivation suggest that each person has a package of needs: the best way to motivate an employee is to find out what his/her needs are and offer him/her rewards that will satisfy those needs.

  ° Abraham Maslow identified a hierarchy of needs which an individual will be motivated to satisfy, progressing towards higher order satisfactions, such as self-actualisation.

  ° Frederick Herzberg identified two basic need systems: the need to avoid unpleasantness and the need for personal growth. He suggested factors which could be offered by organisations to satisfy both types of need: 'hygiene' and 'motivator' factors respectively.

- Process theories of motivation do not tell managers what to offer employees in order to motivate them but help managers to understand the dynamics of employees' decisions about what rewards are worth going for. They are generally variations on the expectancy model: $F = V \times E$

- Various means have been suggested or improving job satisfaction but there is little evidence that a satisfied worker actually works harder.

- Pay is the most important of the hygiene factors, but it is ambiguous in its effect on motivation.

- Ways in which managers can improve employees' motivation range from encouraging employees to accept responsibility to careful design of jobs (including job enrichment, job enlargement and job rotation) to increasingly sophisticated and performance-related pay and incentive schemes.

- *See Part E mind map summary on page 235.*

Quick quiz

1   What is a trait cluster, and why might it be useful in everyday social interaction?

2   List three factors for a manager to consider in managing 'personality' at work.

3   Give three examples of areas where people's perceptions commonly conflict.

4   What are the three components of an 'attitude'?

5   Give three examples of non-work factors that might influence attitudes to work.

6   What is (a) 'positive reinforcement' and (b) self actualisation?

7   List the five categories in Maslow's Hierarchy of Needs.

8   How do an individual's goals change with age?

9   List three ways in which an organisation can offer motivational satisfaction.

10   What is the difference between a reward and an incentive?

11   List five motivator and five hygiene factors.

12   Explain the formula 'F = V × E'.

13   Distinguish between job enrichment and job enlargement.

14   'People will work harder and harder to earn more and more pay.' Do you agree? Why (or why not)?

Answers to quick quiz

1   A number of related or compatible traits which form a personality type.

2   The compatibility of an individual's personality with the task, with the systems and culture of the organisation and with other members of the team.

3   Managers and staff, work culture, race and gender.

4   Knowledge, feelings and desires, volition.

5   Class, age, race, culture or religion, interests and sex,

6   (a)   Encouraging a certain type of behaviour by rewarding it.
    (b)   Personal growth and fulfilment of potential.

7   Physiological, safety, love/social, esteem, self-actualisation.

8   Increasingly they include forming permanent relationships, having children, power and autonomy.

9   Relationships, belonging, challenge, achievement, progress, security, money.

10   A reward is given for some contribution or success. An incentive is a promise or offer of reward.

11   Motivator - status, advancement, recognition, responsibility, challenging work, achievement, growth. Hygiene - company policy and administration, salary, quality of supervision, relationships, job security, working conditions.

12   Force of motivation - Valence × Expectation

13   See Paragraphs 4.10-4.12.

14   People work to earn enough pay which can then be converted into other satisfactions. If they enjoy a good income, they may become more concerned with increasing leisure time.

BPP PUBLISHING

Answers to activities

Answer 11.1

You probably felt as we did that none of the qualities listed were unimportant. You probably had similar priorities to ours, as follows.

1 = b, c, e, g, j.   2 = a, d, f, h, i.

Answer 11.2

The perceptual problems in the situations given are as follows.

(a)   The manager perceives himself as 'enlightened', and his style as an opportunity and gift to his staff. he clearly thinks that assessment and reward on the basis of more responsibility is a positive thing, probably offering greater rewards to staff. He does not perceive his use of the work 'judged' as potentially threatening: he uses it as another word for 'assessed'. His staff obviously see things differently. 'More responsibility' means their competence - maybe their jobs - are on the line. Feeling this way, and with the expectations they have of their boss (based on past experience of his autocratic style), they are bound to perceive the work 'judged' as threatening.

(b)   The chairman thinks he is being funny. Maybe he is only joking about the woman making the tea - but he may really perceive her role that way. He lacks the perception that his new colleague may find his remark offensive. From the woman's point of view, she is bound to be sensitive and insecure in her first meeting and with all male colleague: small wonder that, joke or not, she perceives the chairman's comment as a slap in the face. The chairman later fails to perceive the effect his joke has had on her, assuming that her silence is a sign of poor co-operation or inability to communicate.

(c)   This is a case of closure leading to misinterpretation. The new employee sees the informal dress, the position behind the counter, and the offer of coffee: his brain fills in the gaps, and offers the perception that the youngster must be the tea-boy. Perceptual selectivity also plays a part filtering out awkward information that does not fit his expectations (like the fact that the 'tea-boy' comes to chat with him).

Answer 11.3

Elements of a positive attitude to work may include a willingness to:

(a)   Commit oneself to the objectives of the organisation, or adopt personal objectives that are compatible with those of the organisation.

(b)   Accept the right of the organisation to set standards of acceptable behaviour for its members.

(c)   Contribute to the development and improvement of work practices and performance.

(d)   Take advantages of opportunities for personal development at work.

Answer 11.5

Maslow's categories for the listed circumstances are as follows.

(a)   Esteem needs
(b)   Social needs
(c)   Self-actualisation needs
(d)   He will have physiological needs
(e)   Safety needs initially; esteem needs above in a certain income level
(f)   social needs or self-actualisation needs
(g)   Esteem needs
(h)   Safety needs or esteem needs

Answer 11.7

(a) The rewards from PRP are often too small to motivate effectively. Anyhow, some employees may not expect to receive the rewards and hence will not put in the extra effort.

(b) It is often unfair, especially in jobs where success is determined by uncontrollable factors.

(c) As people are rewarded individually, they are less willing to work as a team. Consequently 'teamwork' might be included as a factor to be rewarded - but this is hard to measure.

(d) People concentrate on performance indicators rather than on longer-term issues such as innovation or quality. In other words, people put all their energy into hitting the target rather than doing their job better.

(e) PRP schemes have to be well designed to ensure performance is measured properly, people consider them to be fair and there is consent to the scheme.

(f) Performance is often hard to measure.

(g) If too many factors have to be taken into account, the whole process becomes subjective and unfair.

Chapter 12 Effective leadership

Chapter topic list

1   What is leadership?

2   Trait theories of leadership

3   Style theories of leadership

4   Task, team and people

Learning objectives

On completion of this chapter you will be able to:

	Syllabus reference
• define the term 'leadership'	d
• compare and contrast the terms 'leadership' and 'supervision'	d
• identify the skills of a leader	d
• illustrate the role of the supervisor in achieving tasks	d
• explain the role of the supervisor in building the team and developing individuals	d

1 WHAT IS LEADERSHIP?

> **KEY TERM**
>
> **Leadership** is the 'influential increment over and above mechanical compliance with the routine directives of the organisation' (Katz and Kahn, *The Social Psychology of Organisations*).

1.1 In this chapter, we explore various theories and aspects of leadership. Let's distinguish clearly between **leadership** and **management**.

1.2 Leadership is the process of **influencing** others to work **willingly** towards goals.

    (a) Leadership is an **interpersonal** process: it depends on relationships, communication and influence – not organisational authority.

    (b) 'The essence of leadership is **followership**.' (Koontz, O'Donnell, Weihrich) The leader's power depends on the perceptions of others: it is conferred from below, not delegated from above.

    (c) Leadership is the '**influential increment** over and above mechanical compliance with the routine directives of the organisation' (Katz and Kahn). Compliance – or obedience – may be sufficient for routine work, but the modern flexible organisation increasingly requires extra input from employees: co-operation, effort, creativity and so on.

1.3 **Management** can be exercised over resources and activities: **leadership** can only be exercised over people. **Management** involves planning and budgeting, organising and staffing, controlling and problem-solving: activities concerned with structure, analysis and control, aimed at producing predictable outputs from planned inputs. **Leadership**, on the other hand, requires a completely different set of activities.

    (a) Creating a **sense of direction** (often, something different to the current status quo)

    (b) Communicating a **vision** (particularly powerful if it meets the needs of others, or if the leader gives it credibility)

    (c) **Energising, inspiring and motivating others** to translate the vision into achievement

    (d) **Creating the culture** that will support the achievement

1.4 All of these activities involve dealing with people rather than things. But remember that leadership is a conscious activity. If you yawn and others around you do the same, it is more properly called '**behavioural contagion**' than leadership.

Activity 12.1

Suppose you were in a cinema and smelt smoke. How would you categorise the following possible actions on your part? Your options are behavioural contagion, management and leadership.

(a) You rush to the door screaming 'Fire!' and every one follows you.

(b) You rush to the door, switch on the lights, hit the fire alarm, and, grabbing a fire extinguisher, start looking for the source of the fire. People start moving towards the exist when they hear the fire alarm.

(c) You rush to the door, switch on the lights, shout for people not to panic but to move towards the exits (which they do) and ask for help to locate the fire and get the fire extinguishers (which you get).

(d)   You do any or all of the above, but nobody takes any notice.

2   TRAIT THEORIES OF LEADERSHIP

2.1   Early theories suggested that there are certain qualities, personality characteristics or 'traits' which make a good leader. These might be aggressiveness, self-assurance, intelligence, initiative, a drive for achievement or power, appearance, interpersonal skills, administrative ability, imagination, a certain upbringing and education, the 'helicopter factor' (ie the ability to rise above a situation and analyse it objectively) etc.

2.2   Trait theory, although superficially attractive, is now largely discredited, in favour of other theories which we now discuss.

3   STYLE THEORIES OF LEADERSHIP

3.1   Leaders accept responsibility for the outcomes of the groups they lead. While leaders have to exercise authority, the way in which this is done (the *style* of leadership) might vary. It is generally accepted that a leader's style of leading can affect the motivation, efficiency and effectiveness of the leader's followers.

The Ashridge model

3.2   The Research Unit at Ashridge Management College distinguished four different management styles. They are outlined, with their strengths and weaknesses, in the table on the next page. Note that the Ashridge model has not included any real equivalent of the laissez-faire style. The Ashridge studies found:

(a)   In an ideal world, subordinates preferred the **consults** style of leadership. Those managed in that way had the most favourable attitude to work, but managers were most commonly thought to be exercising the **tells** or **sells** style.

(b)   In practice, consistency was far more important. The least favourable attitudes were found amongst subordinates who were **unable to perceive a consistent style** of leadership in their boss.

Activity 12.2

Suggest an appropriate style of management for each of the following situations. Think about your reasons for choosing each style in terms of the results you are trying to achieve, the need to secure commitment from others, and potential difficulties with both.

(a)   Due to outside factors, the personnel budget has been reduced for your department and one-quarter of your staff must be made redundant. Records of each employee's performance are available.

(b)   There is a recurring administrative problem which is minor, but irritating to every one in your department. Several solutions have been tried in the past, but without success. You think you have a remedy which will work, but unknown problems may arise, depending on the decisions made.

(c)   A decision needs to be made about working hours. The organisation wishes to stagger arrival and departure times in order to relieve traffic congestion. Each department can make its own decisions. It doesn't really matter what the times are, so long as department members conform to them.

(d)   Even though they are experienced, members in your department don't seem to want to take on responsibility. Their attitude seems to be: 'You are paid to manage, we are paid to work: you make the decisions'. Now a decision has come up which will personally affect every person in your department.

Style	Characteristics	Strengths	Weaknesses
Tells (autocratic)	The manager makes all the decisions, and issues instructions which must be obeyed without question.	(1) Quick decisions can be made when speed is required. (2) It is the most efficient type of leadership for highly-programmed routine work.	(1) It does not encourage the subordinates to give their opinions when these might be useful. (2) Communications between the manager and subordinate will be one-way and the manager will not know until afterwards whether the orders have been properly understood. (3) It does not encourage initiative and commitment from subordinates.
Sells (persuasive)	The manager still makes all the decisions, but believes that subordinates have to be motivated to accept them in order to carry them out properly.	(1) Employees are made aware of the reasons for decisions. (2) Selling decisions to staff might make them more committed. (3) Staff will have a better idea of what to do when unforeseen events arise in their work because the manager will have explained his intentions.	(1) Communications are still largely one-way. Sub-ordinates might not accept the decisions. (2) It does not encourage initiative and commitment from subordinates.
Consults	The manager confers with subordinates and takes their views into account, but has the final say.	(1) Employees are involved in decisions before they are made. This encourages motivation through greater interest and involvement. (2) An agreed consensus of opinion can be reached and for some decisions consensus can be an advantage rather than a weak compromise. (3) Employees can contribute their knowledge and experience to help in solving more complex problems.	(1) It might take much longer to reach decisions. (2) Subordinates might be too inexperienced to formulate mature opinions and give practical advice. (3) Consultation can too easily turn into a façade concealing, basically, a sells style.
Joins (democratic)	Leader and followers make the decision on the basis of consensus.	(1) It can provide high motivation and commitment from employees. (2) It shares the other advantages of the consultative style (especially where subordinates have expert power).	(1) The authority of the manager might be undermined. (2) Decision-making might become a very long process, and clear decisions might be difficult to reach. (3) Subordinates might lack enough experience.

Style and effectiveness

3.3   Rensis Likert's research showed that **effective managers** display each of the four characteristics below, in relation to leadership skills. Such managers:

(a)   **Expect high levels of performance** from subordinates, other departments and themselves.

(b)   **Are employee-centred**. They spend time getting to know their workers and develop a situation of trust whereby their employees feel able to bring their problems to them. Such managers face unpleasant facts in a constructive manner and help their staff to do the same.

(c)   **Do not practise close supervision**. The truly effective manager knows performance levels that can be expected from each individual and has helped them to define their own targets. The manager judges results and does not closely supervise the actions of subordinates.

(d)   **Operate the participative style of management as a natural style**. If a job problem arises they do not impose a favoured solution. Instead, they pose the problem and ask the staff member involved to find the best solution. Having then agreed their solution the participative manager would assist his staff in implementing it.

4   TASK, TEAM AND PEOPLE

Blake and Mouton's managerial grid

4.1   Robert Blake and Jane Mouton carried out research (The Ohio State Leadership Studies) into managerial behaviour and observed two basic dimensions of leadership: **concern for production** (or task performance) and **concern for people.**

4.2   Along each of these two dimensions, managers could be located at any point on a **continuum** from very low to very high concern. Black and Mouton observed that the two concerns did not seem to correlate, positively or negatively: a high concern in one dimension, for example, did not seem to imply a high or low concern in the other dimension. Individual managers could therefore reflect various permutations of task/people concern.

4.3   Blake and Mouton modelled these permutations as a grid, which became known as 'The Managerial Grid'. One axis represented concern for people, and the other concern for production. Black and Mouton allotted nine points on each axis, from 1 (low) to 9 (high).

4.4   A questionnaire was designed to enable users to analyse and plot the positions of individual respondents on the grid. This was to be used as a means of analysing individuals' **managerial styles** and areas of weakness or 'unbalance', for the purposes of management development.

Blake's Grid

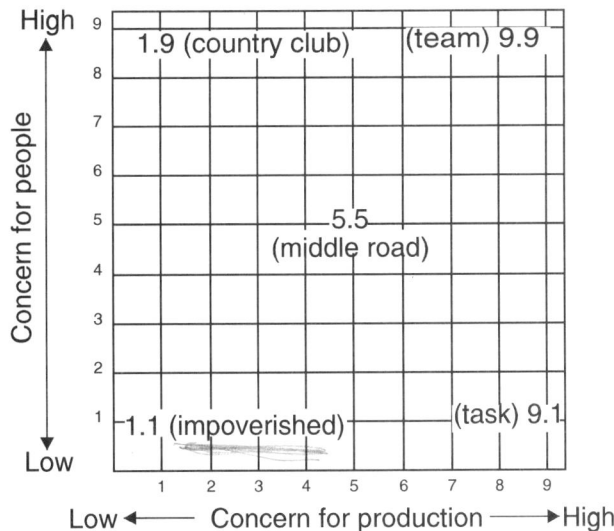

4.5   The extreme cases shown on the grid are:

(a)   1.1 **impoverished:** the manager is lazy, showing little interest in either staff or work.

(b)   1.9 **country club:** the manager is attentive to staff needs and has developed satisfying relationships. However, there is little attention paid to achieving results.

(c)   9.1 **task management:** almost total concentration on achieving results. People's needs are virtually ignored.

(d)   5.5 **middle of the road** or the **dampened pendulum:** adequate performance through balancing the necessity to get out work while maintaining morale of people at a satisfactory level.

(e)   9.9 **team:** high performance manager who achieves high work accomplishment through 'leading' committed people who identify themselves with the organisational aims.

The usefulness of the Managerial Grid

4.6   The managerial Grid was intended as an **appraisal and management development tool.** It recognises that a balance is required between concern for task and concern for people, and that a high degree of both is possible (and highly effective) at the same time.

4.7   The Grid thus offers a number of useful insights for the identification of management **training and development** needs. It shows in an easily assimilated form where the behaviour and assumptions of a manager may exhibit a lack of balance between the dimensions and/or a low degree of concern in either dimension or both. It may also be used in team member selection, so that a 1.9 team leader is balance by a 9.1 co-leader, for example.

4.8   However, the grid is a **simplified** model, and as such has **practical limitations.**

(a)   It assumes that 9.9 is the desirable model for effective leadership. In some managerial contexts, this may not be so. Concern for people, for example, would not be necessary in a context of comprehensive automation: compliance is all that would be required.

(b)   It is open to oversimplification. Scores can appear polarised, with judgements attached about individual managers' suitability or performance. The Grid is intended as a simplified 'snapshot' of a manager's preferred style, not a comprehensive description of his or her performance.

(c) Organisational context and culture, technology and other 'givens' (Handy) influence the manager's style of leadership, not just the two dimensions described by the Grid.

(d) Any managerial theory is only useful in so far as it is useable in practice by managers: if the grid is used only to inform managers that they 'must acquire greater concern for people', it may result in stress, uncertainty and inconsistent behaviour.

Exam alert

A very detailed question was set in the June 1999 paper, asking you to 'describe the Managerial Grid' (10 marks available), as well as identifying its extreme scores and discussing its usefulness. This is a reminder to **critically appraise** major theories as well as to learn their key points.

Activity 12.3

Here are some statements about a manager's approach to meetings. Which position on Blake's Grid do you think each might represent?

(a) I attend because it is expected. I either go along with the majority position or avoid expressing my views.

(b) I try to come up with good ideas and push for a decision as soon as I can get a majority behind me. I don't mind stepping on people if it helps a sound decision.

(c) I like to be able to support what my boss wants and to recognise the merits of individual effort. When conflict rises, I do a good job or restoring harmony.

Adair's action-centred leadership

4.9 The **action-centred** or **functional** model of leadership was developed by John Adair. Like other contingency thinkers, Adair argued that the common perception of leadership as 'decision-making' was inadequate to describe the range of action required by the complex situation in which managers find themselves. He described a context made up of three main interrelated variables: task needs, group needs and individual needs. The **overall leadership situation dictates the relative priority** that must be given to each of the **three sets of needs**. Effective leadership is identifying and acting on those priorities to create a balance between the needs.

4.10 The meeting of the various needs can be expressed as specific management roles:

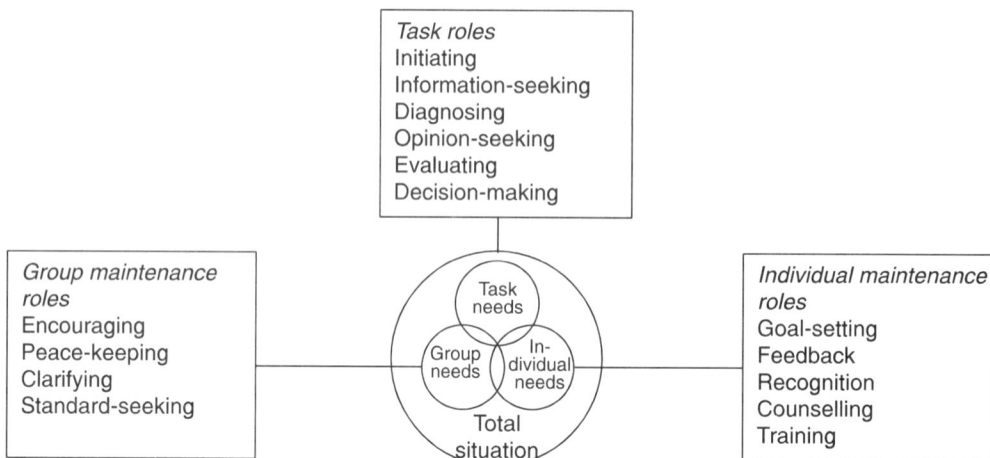

Task roles
Initiating
Information-seeking
Diagnosing
Opinion-seeking
Evaluating
Decision-making

Group maintenance roles
Encouraging
Peace-keeping
Clarifying
Standard-seeking

Task needs
Group needs
In-dividual needs
Total situation

Individual maintenance roles
Goal-setting
Feedback
Recognition
Counselling
Training

4.11 Around this framework, Adair developed a scheme of leadership training based on precept and practice in each of eight leadership activities – as applied to the task, team and individual.

- Defining the task
- Planning
- Briefing
- Controlling

- Evaluating
- Motivating
- Organising
- Setting an example

Exam alert

Another detailed question was set in December 2000 on action-centred leadership. You needed to identify the term with John Adair's model and to outline that model.

Activity 12.4

In your career so far, you might have worked for a number of managers. Jot down the following features of each situation on a scale of 1-5 for comparative purposes.

(a) The degree to which you had autonomy over your own work.
(b) The degree to which you were consulted on decisions which affected you.
(c) The degree to which your advice was sought about decisions affecting your section.

If you worked for managers who had different approaches to these issues, do you think these approaches influenced **your** effectiveness? What score to questions (a), (b) and (c) would you give your **ideal boss**? and your **current boss**?

A contingency approach to leadership

4.12 A contingency approach to leadership is one which argues that the ability of a manager to lead and to influence his work group will vary according to:

(a) The **leader's** personality, character and preferred style of operating.

(b) The **subordinates**: their individual and collective personalities, and their preference for a particular style of leadership.

(c) The **task**: If the tasks of a work group are simple, few in number and repetitive, the best style of leadership will be different from a situation in which tasks are varied and difficult.

(d) The **context**.

   (i)   The position of **power** held by the leader in the organisation and the group. A person with power is better able to choose a personal style and leadership, select subordinates and re-define the task of the work group.

   (ii) Organisational **norms** and the structure and technology of the organisation. No manager can act in a manner which is contrary to the customs and standards of the organisation.

4.13 For each of the three factors, a spectrum can be drawn ranging from 'tight' to 'flexible'. Handy argues that the most effective style of leadership in any particular situation is one which brings the first three factors - a leader, subordinates and task - into a 'best fit'.

	The leader	*The subordinates*	*The task*
Tight	Preference for autocratic style, high estimation of his own capabilities and a low estimation of his subordinates. Dislikes uncertainty.	Low opinion of own abilities, do not like uncertainty in their work and like to be ordered. They regard their work as trivial; past experience in work leads to acceptance of orders, cultural factors lean them towards autocratic/dictatorial leaders.	Job requires no initiative, is routine and repetitive or has a certain outcome; short time scale for completion. Trivial tasks.
The Spectrum	Preference for democratic style, confidence in his subordinates, dislikes stress, accepts reasonable risk and uncertainty.	High opinion of own abilities; likes challenging important work; prepared to accept uncertainty and longer time scales for results; cultural factors favour independence.	Important tasks with a longer timescale; problem-solving or decision-making involved, complex work.
Flexible			

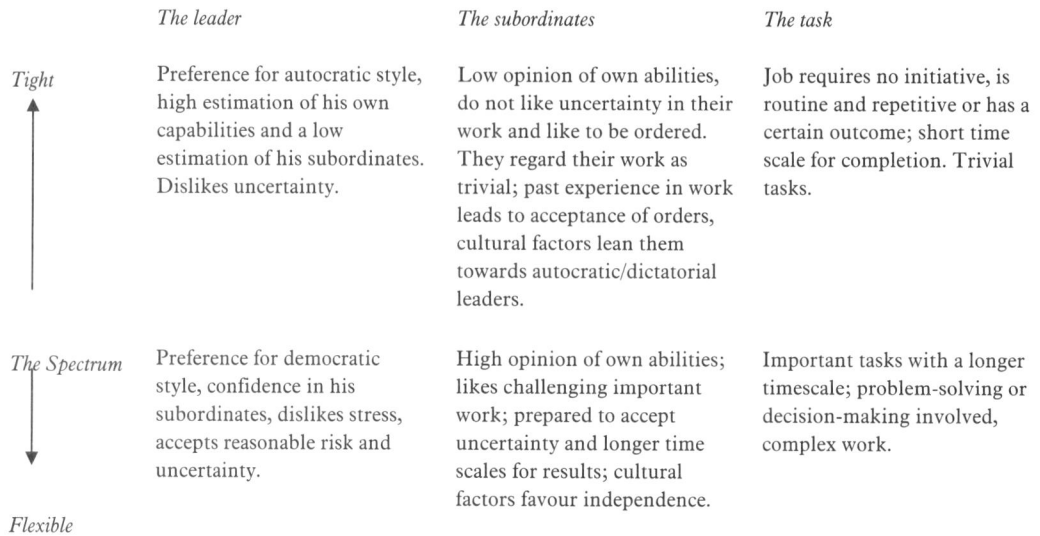

4.14 (a) A **best fit** occurs when all factors are on the same level in the spectrum.

(b) In practice, there is likely to be a misfit. Confronted with a lack of fit, **the leader must decide which factor(s) should be changed** to bring all three into line. In the short-term, the **easiest is to change the leadership style**. There are often long-term benefits to be achieved from re-defining the task (eg job enlargement) or from developing the work group.

Activity 12.5

List four ways in which an organisation, by dealing with 'environmental constraints' can help its managers to adopt an appropriate management style.

Liking or respect?

4.15 This is a tough question. It relates to managerial effectiveness: will the team give more to a manager they like, or to one they respect - or even fear? It also touches on the needs of the manager as a person.

- A manager has needs for belonging, relationship and approval
- A manager needs to be in control, in order to achieve objectives

4.16 Managers who are responsible for task performance will inevitably have to make decisions that will be unpopular with all or some of their team members. Individuals have different **needs and expectations,** only some of which will be in harmony with those of others and with organisational goals. **Resources** are limited, and individuals are in competition for them. So **consensus** decisions will not always be possible, and unpleasant decisions (such as disciplinary action or redundancies) may be required.

Key learning points

- **Leadership** is the proves of influencing others to work willingly towards the achievement of organisational goals.

- **Theories of leadership** have been based on the following aspects.

  (a) Traits which appear to be common to successful leaders.

  (b) Styles which can be adopted. These are often expressed as a range or continuum, reflecting either the manager's approach to control or the manager's priorities.

  Tells ←——————— sells ——————— consults ———————→ joins

  Tight ←——————————————————————————→ loose

  Wholly task oriented ←——————————————→Wholly people oriented

- A **contingency approach** to leadership suggests that a style may be appropriate or inappropriate (and therefore effective or ineffective) depending on variables including:

  (a) The structure and demands of the task
  (b) The characteristics and needs of the team and its individual members
  (c) The characteristics and needs of the leader
  (d) The organisational development

- *See the Part E mind map summary on page 236.*

Quick quiz

1. How do people become leaders in a group or situation?

2. What is the difference between a 'sells' and 'consults' style of management?

3. What might be the disadvantages of a 'tells' style of management?

4. What type of task makes tight control a suitable style?

5. What factors in the environment influence the choice of a tight or loose style?

6. What is the most effective style suggested by Blake's managerial grid and why is it so effective in theory? Why might it not be effective in practice?

7. Do teams need to have a leader? Would they be as effective without one?

8. Why is consistency of management style important - and why might this be a problem?

Answers to quick quiz

1. Through different forms of influence such a vision, inspiration and motivation.

2. 'Sells' - the manager still makes all decisions but explains them to subordinates to get them to carry them out willingly. 'Consults' - the manager confers with subordinates, takes their views and feelings into account, but retains the right to make the final decision.

3. 'Telling' is one-way, there is no feedback. It does not encourage contributions or initiative.

4. Those which lack initiative, are routine, trivial or have a short time scale.

5. The position of power held by the leader, organisational norms, structure and technology, the variety of tasks and subordinates.

6. 9.9. It is effective if there is sufficient time and resources to attend fully to people needs, if the manager is good at dealing with people and if the people respond. It is ineffective when a task **has** to be completed in a certain way or by a certain deadline even if people don't like it.

7. Someone has to ensure the objective is achieved, make decisions and share out resources. If everyone on the team is equally able and willing to do these things (unlikely in practice) a good information system is probably all that is needed, not a leader.

8. Inconsistency results in subordinate feeling unsure and distrusting the manager.

Answers to activities_____

Answer 12.1

Categorisation of different behaviour on smelling smoke in a cinema is as follows.

(a) Behavioural contagion: people are simply copying you, with no conscious intention to lead on your part.

(b) Management. You are dealing with logistics: planning and organising. You are not, however, concerned with influencing the people: they simply respond to the situation.

(c) Leadership. You intend to mobilise others in pursuit of your aims, and you succeed in doing so.

(d) Whatever it is, it isn't leadership - because you have gained no followers.

Answer 12.2_____

Styles of management suggested in the situations described, using the tells-sells-consults-joins model.

(a) You may have to 'tell' here: nobody is gong to like the idea and, since each person will have his or her own interests at heart, you are unlikely to reach consensus. You could attempt to 'sell', if you can see a positive side to the change in particular cases: opportunities for retraining, say.

(b) You could 'consult' here: explain your remedy to staff and see whether they can suggest potential problems. They may be in a position to offer solutions - and since the problem effects them too, the should be committed to solving it.

(c) We prefer a 'joins' style here, since the team's acceptance of the decision is more important than the details of the decision itself.

(d) We would go for 'consult' despite the staff's apparent reluctance to participate. They may prefer you to 'tell' - but may resist decisions they disagree with anyway. Perhaps their reluctance is to do with lack of confidence - or lack of trust that you will take their input seriously, in which case, persistent use of a 'consults' style may encourage them. You could use a 'sells' approach initially, to get them used to a less authoritarian style than they seem to expect.

Answer 12.3_____

Blake's Grid positioning of the given managerial approaches are:

(a) 1.1: low task, low people
(b) 9.1: High task, low people
(c) 1.9: high people, low task

Answer 12.5_____

The 'environment' can be improved for leaders if senior management ensure that:

(a) Managers are given a clear role and the power (over resources and information) to back it up.

(b) Organisational 'norms' can be broken without fear of punishment - ie the organisation culture is adaptive, and managers can change things if required.

(c) The organisational structure is not inflexible: managers can redesign task and team arrangements.

(d) Team members are selected or developed so that they are, as far as possible, of the same 'type' in terms of their attitudes to work and supervision.

(e) Labour turnover is reduced as far as possible (by having acceptable work conditions and terms, for example), so that the team does not constantly have to adjust to new members, or leaders

PART E   MIND MAP SUMMARY

Chapter 11

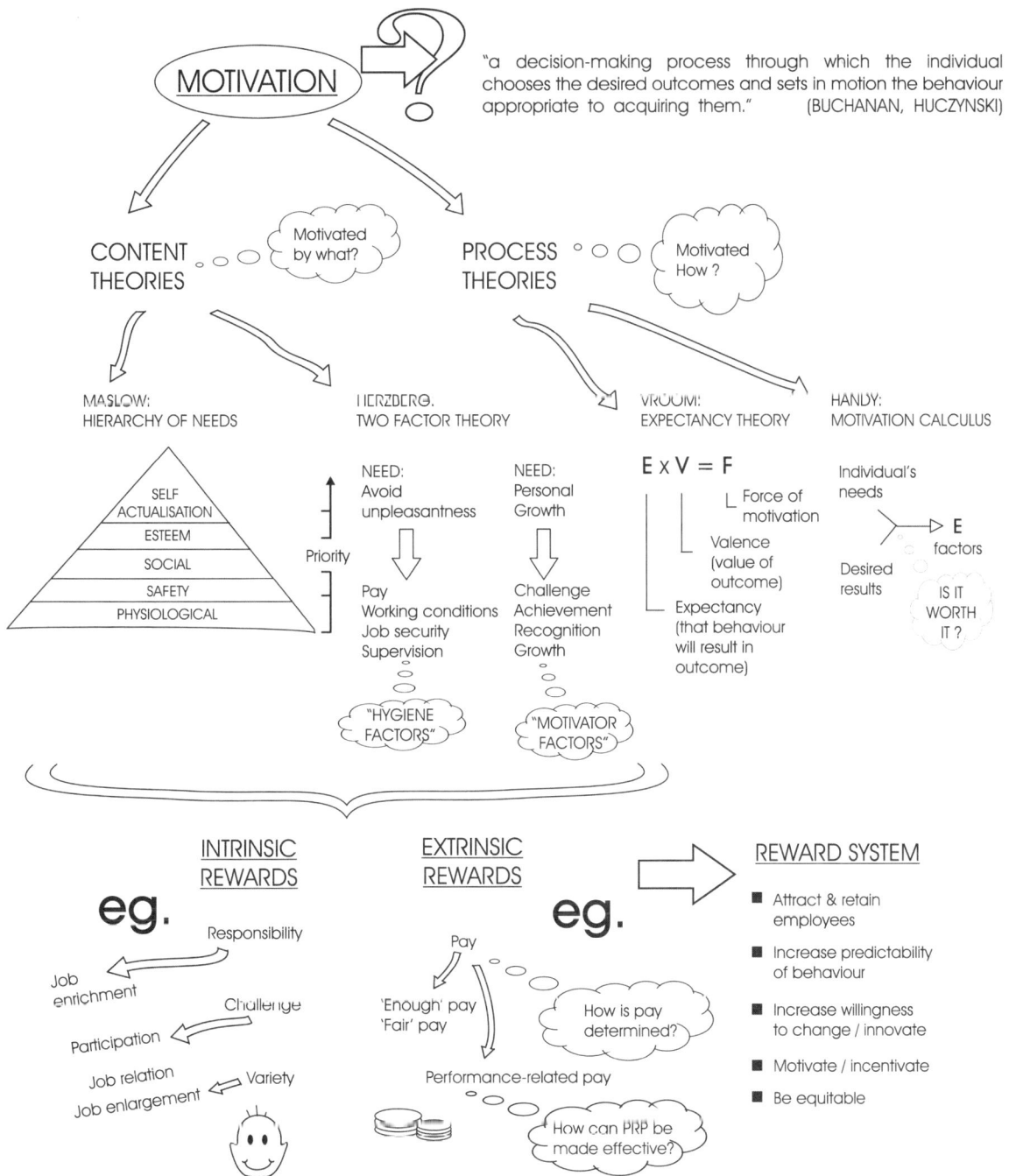

MOTIVATION

"a decision-making process through which the individual chooses the desired outcomes and sets in motion the behaviour appropriate to acquiring them."   (BUCHANAN, HUCZYNSKI)

CONTENT THEORIES

Motivated by what?

PROCESS THEORIES

Motivated How ?

MASLOW: HIERARCHY OF NEEDS

HERZBERG: TWO FACTOR THEORY

VROOM: EXPECTANCY THEORY

HANDY: MOTIVATION CALCULUS

SELF ACTUALISATION
ESTEEM
SOCIAL
SAFETY
PHYSIOLOGICAL

Priority

NEED:
Avoid unpleasantness

NEED:
Personal Growth

$E \times V = F$

└ Force of motivation
Valence (value of outcome)
Expectancy (that behaviour will result in outcome)

Individual's needs

E factors

Desired results

IS IT WORTH IT ?

Pay
Working conditions
Job security
Supervision

Challenge
Achievement
Recognition
Growth

"HYGIENE FACTORS"

"MOTIVATOR FACTORS"

INTRINSIC REWARDS

eg.

Responsibility

Job enrichment

Challenge

Participation

Job relation

Job enlargement

Variety

EXTRINSIC REWARDS

eg.

Pay

'Enough' pay 'Fair' pay

How is pay determined?

Performance-related pay

How can PRP be made effective?

REWARD SYSTEM

- Attract & retain employees
- Increase predictability of behaviour
- Increase willingness to change / innovate
- Motivate / incentivate
- Be equitable

BPP PUBLISHING

PART E   MIND MAP SUMMARY

Chapter 12

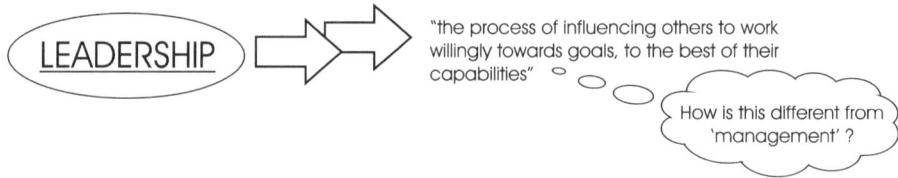

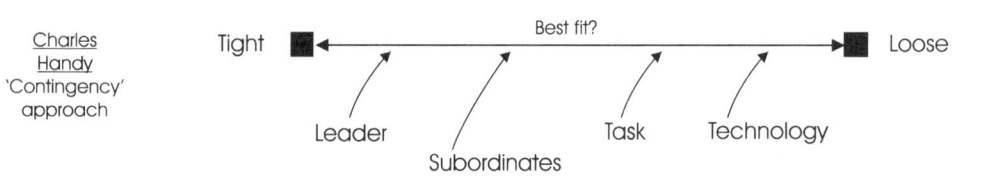

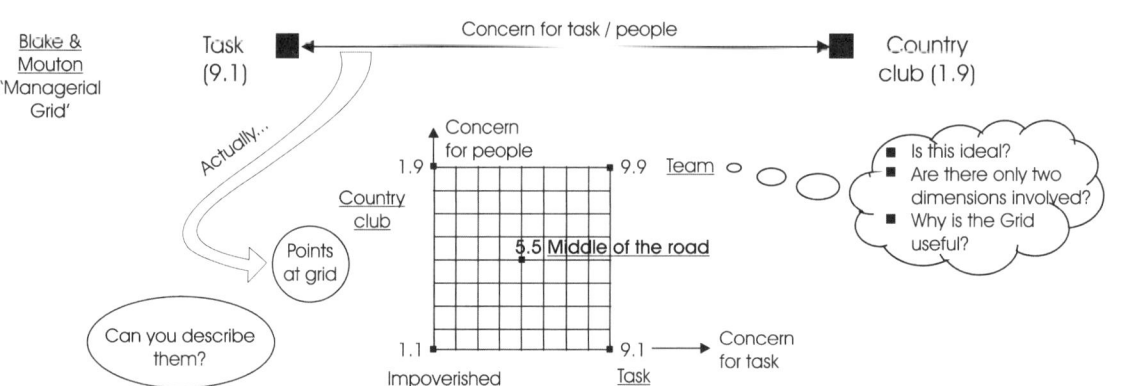

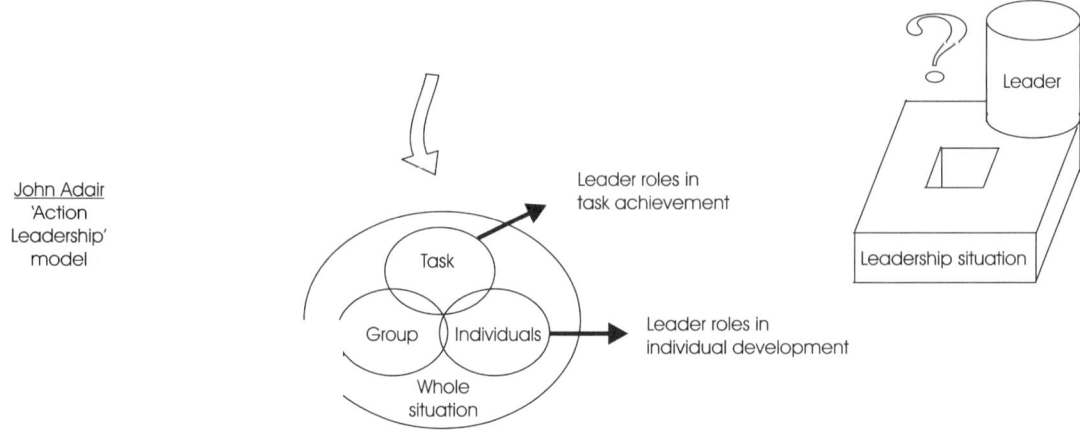

Part F
Working with people

Chapter 13 Interpersonal and communication skills

Chapter topic list

1 Interpersonal skills and working relationships

2 Assertiveness

3 Communication in the organisation

4 Face-to-face and oral communication

5 Textual communications

6 Counselling

Learning objectives

On completion of this chapter you will be able to:

Syllabus reference

- define the term 'interpersonal skills'   e
- explain the importance of developing effective working relationships   e
- distinguish between verbal and non-verbal forms of communication   e
- outline ways of gaining commitment from staff   e
- compare and contrast the difference between aggressive and assertive behaviour   e
- illustrate the link between interpersonal skills and effective management practice   e
- explain the importance of good communication, both formal and informal, in the work place   e
- explain how the process of communication can be modelled   e
- outline the importance of effective communication to the supervisor   e
- list and describe the attributes of effective communication   e
- list the main methods of communication   e
- describe the effects of poor communication   e
- outline the importance of effective communication to managing staff   e
- describe the benefits of disseminating information to others   e
- explain the importance of the process of consultation   e
- explain the importance of effective counselling   e
- identify the key skills used in the process of effective counselling   e
- suggest reasons why the need to counsel a member of staff may arise   e
- outline the role of the manager when counselling staff   e

BPP
PUBLISHING

1   INTERPERSONAL SKILLS AND WORKING RELATIONSHIPS

> **KEY TERM**
>
> **Interpersonal behaviour** is behaviour between people. It includes:
>
> (a)   Interaction between people, a two way process such as communication, delegating, negotiating, resolving conflict, persuading, selling, using and responding to authority.
>
> (b)   An individual's behaviour in relationship to other people.

1.1   The way you behave in response to other people includes:

(a)   How you **perceive** other people

(b)   **Listening to** and **understanding** other people

(c)   **Behaving** in a way which builds on this understanding

(d)   Being **sensitive** to the impression you give, in the light of the roles you are expected to play.

Role theory

1.2   Many people behave in any situation according to the roles they are expected to perform, and the role tends to influence the type of interpersonal relationships that people have.

(a)   A **role set** is a group of people who respond to a person in a particular way. As a supervisor or manager, your subordinates and superiors are likely to respond to you as a supervisor or manager rather than according to the other roles that you play.

(b)   **Role signs** indicate what role people are in at any particular time. A good example is office dress. Some firms are very strict about this.

(c)   **Role ambiguity**. There is confusion about the roles a person plays.

(d)   People select role models on which to base themselves throughout life. An individual's attraction as role model may come from their:

- Charisma, or personality
- Expertise or talent
- Success
- Dominance

Activity 13.1

Choose one role in which your regularly interact with other people. (The role of 'student', say?)

(a)   Identify your role set and role signs.

(b)   Identify any areas of ambiguity, compatibility or conflict the role presents. What could be done about each (if anything)? Could the other members of your role set help?

Activity 13.2

Managers could exert a powerful influence over team members if they could establish themselves as role models. What kind of example could they set that might be helpful for the team members and for the organisation?

Interpersonal skills

1.3 **Interpersonal skills** are needed by an individual in order to:

(a) Understand and 'manage' the roles, relationships, attitudes and perceptions operating in any situation in which two or more people are involved.

(b) Communicate clearly and effectively.

(c) Achieve his or her aims from an interpersonal encounter (ideally, allowing the other parties to emerge satisfied too).

1.4 Issues to consider in interpersonal communication and work relationships

Issue	Comment
Goal	What does the other person want from the process? What do you want from the process? What will both parties need and be trying to do to achieve their aims? Can both parties emerge satisfied?
Perceptions	What, if any, are likely to be the factors causing 'distortion' of the way both parties see the issues and each other? (Attitudes, personal feelings, expectations?)
Roles	What 'roles' are the parties playing? (Superior/subordinate, customer/server, complainer/soother?) What expectations does this create of the way they will behave?
Resistances	What may the other person be 'afraid' of? What may he or she be trying to protect? (His or her ego/self-image, attitudes?) Sensitivity will be needed in this area.
Attitudes	What sources of difference, conflict or lack of understanding might there be, arising from attitudes and other factors which shape them (sex, race, specialism, hierarchy)?
Relationships	What are the relative positions of the parties and the nature of the relationship between them? (Superior/subordinate? Formal/informal? Work/non-work)? What 'style' is appropriate to it?
Environment	What factors in the immediate and situational environment might affect the issues and the people? (eg competitive environment customer care; pressures of disciplinary situation nervousness; physical surroundings formality/ informality)

1.5 In addition, a range of **communication skills** will be deployed.

1.6 **Skills in the selected medium of communication.** (Use this as a checklist.)

Oral	Written	Visual/non verbal
Clear pronunciation	Correct spelling	Understanding of control
Suitable vocabulary	Suitable vocabulary	over 'body language' and
Correct grammar/syntax	Correct grammar/syntax	facial expressions
Fluency	Good writing or typing	Drawing ability
Expressive delivery	Suitable style	

1.7 **General skills in sending messages**

(a) **Selecting and organising your material:** marshalling your thoughts and constructing your sentences, arguments and so on.

(b) **Judging the effect of your message** on the particular recipient in the particular situation.

(c) **Choosing language and media** accordingly.

(d) **Adapting your communication style** accordingly: putting people at their ease, smoothing over difficulties (tact), or being comforting/challenging/informal/formal as the situation and relationship demand.

(e) **Using non-verbal signals** to reinforce (or at least not to undermine) your spoken message.

(f) **Seeking and interpreting feedback.**

1.8 **Skills in receiving messages**

(a) **Reading** attentively and actively: making sure you understand the content, looking up unfamiliar words and doubtful facts if necessary; evaluating the information given: is it logical? correct? objective?

(b) **Extracting relevant information** from the message, and filtering out inessentials.

(c) **Listening** attentively and actively; concentrating on the message - not on what you are going to say next, or other matters; questioning and evaluating what you are hearing.

(d) **Interpreting the message's underlying meaning,** if any, and evaluating your own reactions: are your reading into the message more or less than what is really there?

(e) **Asking questions** in a way that will elicit the information you wish to obtain. This will usually involve **open** questions

(f) **Interpreting non-verbal signals,** and how they confirm or contradict the spoken message.

(g) **Giving helpful feedback,** if the medium is inappropriate (eg a bad telephone line) or the message is unclear, insufficient or whatever.

> ### Exam alert
>
> In June 2000, a question was set on the importance of interpersonal skills in general, and why they are needed in certain specific areas of management. In December 2000, you were also required to list receiving and feedback skills. Learn to think **critically** and **practically** – even with 'soft' topics like communication.

The importance of good working relationships and good interpersonal skills

1.9 Good interpersonal relationships assist in the following areas of the supervisor's position.

Area	Comment
Motivation	Work can satisfy people's social needs, according to Maslow, because it provides relationships.
Communication	Bad interpersonal relationships can form a barrier to communicating effectively - messages will be misinterpreted

Area	Comment
Teamworking and team building	In Chapter 4 we discussed team building and the importance of developing a climate in which people can communicate openly and honestly.
Customer care	Good interpersonal skills are recognised as being increasingly important when dealing with customers.
Career development	Good interpersonal skills are increasingly necessary to get promotion
Managerial roles	Chapter 3 listed some management roles. Many of these -such as the liaison role - require interpersonal skills
Power: persuade, not command	Interpersonal skills can be a source of personal power in an organisation. The supervisor may not be in a position to command or coerce individuals for information or favours – interpersonal skills may help make the supervisor more effective.
Team management	The manager's tasks of appraisal, interviewing etc require good interpersonal skills if they are to be performed effectively.

2   ASSERTIVENESS

KEY TERM

Assertive behaviour is a considered response to frustration, conflict or threat which seeks to satisfy the needs and wants of all parties involved in the situation.

Aggressive behaviour is a 'fight' reaction to frustration, conflict or threat. It usually takes the form of a verbal or physical attack on another person or object.

Assertive beliefs

2.1   The psychologist and assertiveness trainer Anne Dickson identifies eleven 'human rights' which form the basis of any approach to assertiveness.

> 1   'I have the right to state my own needs and set my own priorities as a person; independent of any roles that I may assume in my life.' (eg as employee, or wife and mother).

BPP PUBLISHING

Assertive behaviour

2.2 According to Back & Back (*Assertiveness at Work*) assertive behaviour involves:

(a) standing up for your own rights in such a way that you do not violate another person's rights;

(b) expressing your needs, wants, opinions, feelings and beliefs in direct, honest and appropriate ways.

2.3 EXAMPLE

Say your boss asked you, at short notice, to undertake an immediate task, when you were in the middle of another project which you really wanted to finish before tomorrow.

An **assertive response** might be: 'I appreciate that you would like this task done immediately. But when I have to leave work in mid-task, it really sets me back. I'd prefer to complete the project I'm currently working on: then I could start your task fresh, tomorrow morning. Will that work for you?'

2.4 The **observed characteristics of assertive behaviour** are as follows.

(a) Verbal behaviours which stand up for one's own rights without violating those of others. For example: simple 'I' statements ('I think ...', 'I prefer ....'); distinctions between opinion and fact, avoiding black and white statements; giving constructive criticism without blaming or point-scoring (attacking the problem, not the person); offering genuine suggestions without 'shoulds' and 'oughts'; asking honest, unloaded questions to ascertain the needs, wants and viewpoints of others.

(b) Verbal behaviours which express a collaborative, 'win win' approach and a desire to maintain the relationship: for example, 'How can we do that?', 'What would make it would make it work for you?'.

(c) Non-verbal behaviours expressing openness, honesty and calm confidence. For example: steady, firm, mid-volume vocal tone; sincere and appropriate use of facial expressions; firm but relaxed posture, facial muscles and so on; 'open' body language inviting contribution from others (open hands, steady eye contact).

Aggressive behaviour

2.5 Aggression is *not* to be confused with assertion.

2.6 According to Back & Back aggression implies:

(a) standing up for your rights in such a way that you violate the rights of others;

(b) ignoring or dismissing the needs, wants, feelings or viewpoints of others;

(c) expressing your own needs, wants and opinions in inappropriate ways.

2.7 EXAMPLE

An example of an **aggressive response** in the scenario in paragraph 2.3 above might be: 'Just because you've left the job late and now it's urgent? I'm not going to disrupt my work to bail you out. Get someone else to do it: I'm busy.'

2.8 The **observed characteristics of aggressive behaviour** may be as follows (allowing for the fact that verbal and non-verbal signals vary according to context and cultural differences).

(a) Physically violent behaviour: for example pushing, prodding, hitting, throwing or damaging things.

(b) Physically intimidating non-verbal behaviours: for example, 'exploding' or using threatening or dismissive proximity, posture or gestures: standing over someone, finger pointing, 'fighting' stance, glaring or staring someone down, scowling, exaggerated expressions of disbelief, sarcastic (or 'wry') smile, impatient movements.

(c) Overriding or intimidating vocal behaviour: for example, shouting; talking over or interrupting another person; using a strident, overly firm or coldly sarcastic tone of voice.

(d) Verbally denying other people's right to their own feelings and viewpoint, in various ways: for example by insisting you are right and expressing opinions as facts; blaming or insulting; sarcasm and put-downs; issuing orders, threats or ultimatums ('Do it, or else').

(e) Involuntary physiological signs of 'a fight' reaction: flush or pallor, wide eyes, muscle rigidity or twitch, bared teeth.

Exam alert

A detailed question on this area was set in the December 2001 exam. Reference to Back's work would have been highly regarded, since 'Assertiveness at Work' is a key text in this area. Make sure you can distinguish accurately between assertion and aggression.

Techniques of assertion

2.9 **Asking for what you want: essential skills**

(a) **Decide what it is you want or feel, and express it directly and specifically.** Don't assume that others will know, or work out from hints, what it is that you really want.

(b) **Stick to your statement.** If you are ignored, refused or responded to in some other negative way, don't back down, 'fly off the handle', or enter into arguments designed to deflect you from your purpose. Stick to your position, and repeat it calmly, as often as necessary: repetition projects an image of determination and reinforces your own confidence and conviction.

(c) **Deflect responses from the other person.** Show that you have heard and understood the other person's response, but are not going to be side-tracked.

2.10 **Saying no without upsetting yourself or your colleagues**

Saying 'no' can be very difficult for people: they feel it is selfish, or will cause offence.

(a) **Don't be pushed.** If you are at all hesitant about whether to say 'yes' or 'no' try asking for time to decide, to think or obtain more information. Why should you make an instant decision? Acknowledge your doubts: ask your questions. Feel free to change your mind.

(b) **Say 'no' clearly and calmly, if that is your answer.** Explain why, if you think it appropriate - not because you are anxious to excuse yourself, as if it were not your right to say 'no'. Don't express regret unless you feel regretful. Remember that when you say 'no', you are refusing a request, not rejecting a person.

(c) **Acknowledge your feelings**. If you feel awkward about refusing, or under pressure to accept, say so: the other person will be reassured that you are giving him or her due consideration.

(d) **Watch your body language.** If you have said 'yes' when you wanted to say 'no', don't start giving 'no' signals by sulking. If you are saying 'no', don't give contradictory signals by smiling ingratiatingly, lingering as if waiting to be talked out of it etc.

2.11 Receiving criticism and feedback

Distinguish between **valid criticism** (which you know to be legitimate), **invalid criticism** (which you now to be untrue) and a **put down** (intended to be hurtful or humiliating).

(a) **Invalid criticism and put-downs** should be handled simply and assertively with a straightforward denial: 'I don't accept that at all'.

(b) **Valid criticism** should be regarded positively as a potentially helpful experience.

    (i) **Negative assertions:** learning how to agree with a criticism if it does in fact apply to you, without growing defensive or abjectly apologetic. You simply acknowledge the truth in what the critic is saying, together with your response to the situation.

    (ii) **Negative enquiry:** learning how to take the initiative, to **prompt** specific criticism, in order to use the information if it is constructive **or** expose an attempt to put you down or be negative.

2.12 Giving criticism

Expressing negative feelings to others so that they hear what you are saying but do not feel personally attacked or rejected is not easy. Effective communication will be impossible if you make the other person defensive or aggressive, or if you let your own feelings get in the way. Guidelines are as follows.

(a) **Describe the behaviour and express your feelings about the behaviour - to the individual personally.**

(b) **Ask for a specific change of behaviour**. Being specified separates constructive criticism (which involves give and take) from attack or complaint.

(c) **End on a positive note.** This does not mean backing off your criticism ('it's not that important, really: I just thought I'd mention it'), but stating something positive that you feel. For example: 'I'm glad I've had a chance to say this', or 'In all other areas, you're doing fine, so I hope we can get this sorted out'.

Activity 13.3

Look at 'right' number 3 in paragraph 2.1: 'I have the right to express my feelings'. Why do you need to be assertive about this: in what sort of situations is this right denied you (even by yourself)? For example: suppose a colleague - or even your boss - asks you to come in to work early to discuss something. You turn up - but he or she does not. You are reluctant to say how angry and aggrieved you feel, because you might appear to be petty or irrational - or you fear that the other person was prevented by some genuine problems and you might offend or upset him/her - or you want the other person to like and approve of you because you are so understanding and forgiving. You are denying yourself the right to say what you felt. The appropriate assertive response would be: 'I was annoyed that you didn't turn up, especially after I had come in early at your request. [I would like you to show more consideration in future.]'

For each of the other 'rights' listed:

(a) Think of the way or situation in which you would tend to deny yourself that right.

(b) Give the appropriate assertive response for that situation - including some of the techniques discussed in this section.

3 COMMUNICATION IN THE ORGANISATION

3.1 In any organisation, the communication of information is necessary for:

(a) **Management decision-making**

(b) **Interdepartmental co-ordination**. All the interdependent systems for purchasing, production, marketing and administration can be synchronised to perform the right actions at the right times to co-operate in accomplishing the organisation's aims.

(c) **Individual motivation and effectiveness,** so people know what they have to do and why.

3.2 Communication in the organisation may take the following forms.

- Giving instructions
- Giving or receiving information
- Exchanging ideas
- Announcing plans or strategies
- Comparing actual results against a plan
- Rules or procedures
- Communication about the organisation structure and job descriptions

The communication process

3.3 The process of communication can be shown as follows.

The communication process

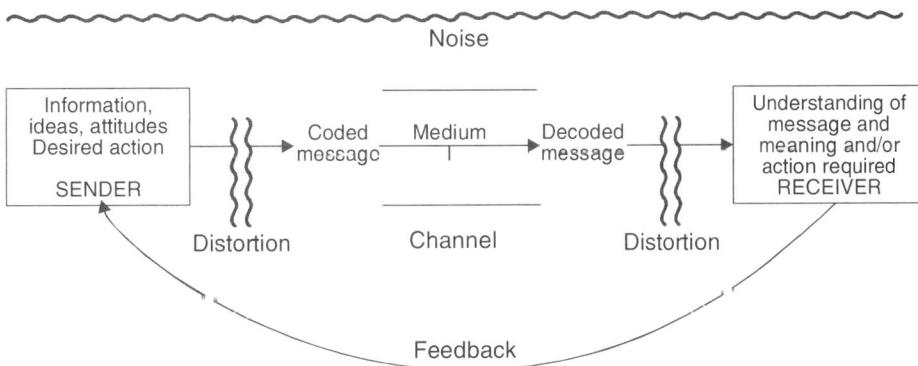

Process	Comment
Coding of a message	The code or 'language' of a message may be verbal (spoken or written) or it may be non-verbal, in pictures, diagrams, numbers or body language.
Medium for the message	There are a number of channels for communication, such as a conversation, a letter, a notice board or via computer. The choice of medium used in communication depends on a number of factors such as urgency, permanency, complexity, sensitivity and cost.

Process	Comment
Feedback	The sender of a message needs feedback on the receiver's reaction. This is partly to test the receiver's understanding of it and partly to gauge the receiver's reaction.
Distortion	The meaning of a message can be lost in coding and decoding stages. Usually the problem is one of language and the medium used; it is easier to 'get the wrong end of the stick' in a telephone call than from a letter.
Noise	Distractions and interference in the environment in which communication is taking place may be physical noise (passing traffic), technical noise (a bad telephone line), social noise (differences in the personalities of the parties) or psychological noise (anger, frustration, tiredness).

Direction of communication flows

3.4 Communication flows can be:

(a) **Vertical** ie up and down the scalar chain (from superior to subordinate and back). This is mainly used for reporting and feedback, and sometimes also suggestions and problem-solving input.

(b) **Horizontal or lateral:** between people of the same rank, in the same section or department, or in different sections or departments. Horizontal communication between 'peer groups' is usually easier and more direct then vertical communication, being less inhibited by considerations of rank.

 (i) **Formally:** to co-ordinate the work of several people, and perhaps departments, who have to co-operate to carry out a certain operation.

 (ii) **Informally:** to furnish emotional and social support to an individual.

(c) **Diagonal**. This is interdepartmental communication by people of different ranks. Departments in the technostructure which serve the organisation in general, such as Human Resources or Information Systems, have no clear 'line authority' linking them to managers in other departments who need their involvement. Diagonal communication aids co-ordination, and also innovation and problem-solving, since it puts together the ideas and information of people in different functions and levels. It also helps to by-pass longer, less direct channels, avoiding blockages and speeding up decision-making.

> **Exam alert**
>
> A December 1999 question was set on the **purposes** of 'communication flows', meaning the **direction** of communication discussed above. Some candidates instead discussed 'patterns' of communication, and others discussed 'processes' instead of purposes. Make sure you read questions carefully!

Barriers to communication

3.5 **Desirable qualities of a communication system in an organisation**

(a) **Clarity.** The coder of a message must bear in mind the potential recipient. **Jargon can be used** - and will even be most appropriate - **where the recipient shares the same expertise**. It should be avoided for those who do not.

(b) **Recipient.** The recipient should be clearly identified, and the right medium should be chosen, to minimise distortion and noise.

(c) **Medium.** The channel or medium should be chosen to ensure it reaches the target audience. Messages of general application (eg Health and Safety signs) should be displayed prominently.

(d) **Timing.** Information has to be timely to be useful.

3.6 **General faults in the communication process**

- **Distortion** or omission of information by the sender
- **Misunderstanding** due to lack of clarity or technical jargon
- **Non-verbal signs** (gesture, facial expression) contradicting the verbal message
- **'Overload'** - a person being given too much information to digest in the time available
- **People** hearing **only what they want** to hear in a message
- **Differences** in social, racial or educational **background**

3.7 **Communication difficulties at work**

(a) **Status** (of the sender and receiver of information).

(i) A senior manager's words are listened to closely and a colleague's perhaps discounted.

(ii) A subordinate might mistrust his or her superior and might look for 'hidden meanings' in a message.

(b) **Jargon.** People from different job or specialist backgrounds (eg accountants, personnel managers, IT experts) can have difficulty in talking on a non-specialist's wavelength.

(c) **Suspicion.** People discount information from those not recognised as having expert power.

(d) **Priorities.** People or departments have different priorities or perspectives so that one person places more or less emphasis on a situation than another.

(e) **Selective reporting.** Subordinates giving superiors incorrect or incomplete information (eg to protect a colleague, to avoid 'bothering' the superior); also a senior manager may only be able to handle edited information because he does not have time to sift through details.

(f) **Use.** Managers who are prepared to make decisions on a 'hunch' without proper regard to the communications they may or may not have received.

(g) **Timing.** Information which has **no immediate** use tending to be forgotten.

(h) **Opportunity.** No opportunity, formal or informal, for people to say what they think may be lacking.

(i) **Conflict.** Where there is conflict between individuals or departments, communications will be withdrawn and information withheld.

(j) **Personal differences,** such as age, educational/social background or personality mean that people have different views as to what is important or different ways of expressing. sometimes views may be discounted because of who they are, not what they say.

(k) **Culture**

    (i) **Secrecy.** Information might be given on a need-to-know basis, rather than be considered as a potential resource for everyone to use.

    (ii) **Can't handle bad news.** The culture of some organisations may prevent the communication of certain messages. Organisations with a 'can-do' philosophy may not want to hear that certain tasks are impossible.

Activity 13.4

Before reading on, what problems are suggested by the following?

(a) [On the noticeboard] 'P Brown. Your complaint about the behaviour of your colleague S Simms is being looked into. Manager.'

(b) 'Prima facie, I would postulate statutory negligence, as per para 22 Sec three et seq. Nil desperandum.' 'Eh?'

(c) 'Smith - you've been scratching your head and frowning like mad ever since I started the briefing half an hour ago. I've tried to ignore it but - have you got fleas or something?'

(d) 'Sorry, this line's terrible - *how* many? *how* much? - what was that? NO, it's OK: I'll remember it all. We'll deliver on Monday - no, MONDAY: no, MONday ...'

(e) Date: 11 March. Report on communication for staff meeting 12 March. 463 pages.

(f) 'Look. Nobody pays you to think: leave that to us professionals. Just do your job.'

Improving the communications system

3.8   Depending on the problem, the solution may be as follows.

(a) **Establish better communication links** in all 'directions'.

    (i) **Standing instructions** should be recorded in easily accessible manuals which are kept fully up-to-date.

    (ii) Management **decisions** should be sent to all people affected by them, preferably in writing.

    (iii) Regular **staff meetings,** or formal consultation with trade union representatives should be held.

    (iv) **A house journal** should be issued regularly.

    (v) **'Appraisal' interviews** between a manager and his subordinates, to discuss the job performance and career prospects of the subordinates.

    (vi) Use **new technology** such as e-mail - but not so as to overload everybody in the financial messages of no importance.

(b) Use the **informal organisation** to supplement this increased freedom of communication.

3.9   Clearing up misunderstandings about message content.

(a) **Redundancy** - issuing a message in more than one form (eg by word of mouth at a meeting, confirmed later in minutes)

(b) **Reporting by exception** should operate to prevent **information overload** on managers.

(c) **Train** managers who do not express themselves clearly and concisely. Necessary jargon should be taught in some degree to people new to the organisation or unfamiliar with the terminology of the specialists.

Case example

Procter and Gamble have a rule that no memo should be longer than one side of paper.

3.10 Communication between superiors and subordinates will be improved when **interpersonal trust** exists. Exactly how this is achieved will depend on the management style of the manager, the attitudes and personality of the individuals involved, and other environmental variables. Peters and Waterman advocate 'management by walking around' (MBWA), and **informality in superior/subordinate relationships** as a means of establishing closer links.

Exam alert

In December 2000, 15 marks were available for drafting **guidelines** for improving organisational communication: that is, recommending an efficient and effective standard approach to communication issues. Don't let familiarity of a topic keyword (like 'communication') blind you to the specifics of the question being asked!

4 FACE-TO-FACE AND ORAL COMMUNICATION

Oral communication

4.1 Face-to-face communication (meetings etc) plays an important part in the life of any organisation, whether it is required by government legislation or the Articles of a company, or is held informally for information exchange, problem-solving and decision-making.

4.2 Face-to-face communication is good for:

- **Generating new ideas**
- **'On the spot' feedback,** constructive criticism and exchange of views
- **Co-operation** and sensitivity to personal factors
- **Spreading information quickly** through a group of people

4.3 However, such communication can be non or counter productive unless:

(a) People **know the reason** for the group discussion.

(b) Participants are **willing and effective communicators** and are concise and clear in what they have to say.

(c) There is sufficient **guidance** or leadership to control proceedings.

(d) People maintain standards of **courtesy**.

Listening

4.4 Listening is about **decoding and receiving** information and carries much of the burden of communication. Listening is more than just a natural instinct, and listening skills can be taught and developed. Effective listening helps:

- The **sender** to listen effectively in return to the receiver 's reply
- **Reduce** the effect of '**noise**'
- **Resolve problems by encouraging understanding** from someone else's viewpoint

4.5 **Good listening checklist**

(a) **Be prepared to listen**. Put yourself in the right frame of mind (ie a readiness to maintain attention). In meetings, be prepared to grasp the main concepts.

(b) **Try to be interested.** Make an effort to analyse the message for its relevance.

(c) **Keep an open mind.** Your own beliefs and prejudices can get in the way of what the other person is actually saying.

(d) **Keep an ear open for the main ideas.** Learn to distinguish between the 'gist' of the argument and supporting evidence.

(e) **Listen critically.** Assess what the other person is saying by identifying any **assumptions, omissions and biases.**

(f) **Avoid distraction.** People have a natural attention curve, high at the beginning and end of an oral message, but sloping off in the middle.

(g) **Take notes,** although note taking can be distracting at times.

(h) **Wait** before interrupting.

Non-verbal communication

4.6 Non-verbal communication (often called '**body language**') consists of facial expression, posture, proximity, gestures and non-verbal noises (grunts, yawns ctc).

(a) Consciously or unconsciously, we send messages through body language during every face to face encounter.

(b) We can use it deliberately to confirm our verbal message - for example, by nodding and smiling as we tell someone we are happy to help them - or to contradict it, if we want to be sarcastic (saying 'How interesting!' with a yawn, for example).

(c) More often, however, our body language **contradicts** our verbal message without our being aware of it, giving a 'mixed message' like your saying you understand an instruction while looking extremely perplexed.

(d) Body language can also 'give away' messages that we would - for social or business reasons - rather not send, such as lack of interest, hostility or whatever.

4.7 **Control and use of body language** is needed to:

- Provide an appropriate 'physical' **feedback** to the sender of a message
- Create a desired **impression**
- Establish a desired **atmosphere** or conditions (friendly smile)
- **Reinforce our spoken messages** with appropriate indications

4.8 **Reading other people's body language** helps you to:

- Receive **feedback** from a listener and modify the message accordingly.
- Recognise people's **real feelings** when their words are constrained by formalities.
- Recognise **existing or potential personal problems**.
- '**Read**' **situations** in order to modify our own communication and response strategy.

4.9 **Improved performance.** This can be achieved in the following ways.

(a) Become more aware of what your body language is 'saying' to people.

(b) **Control your body language**. If you are bored or irritated when talking to a customer, in particular, suppress the signals. On the other hand, you can use positive body language to reinforce the message you want to give - of professionalism, confidence etc.

(c) **Seek feedback** when communicating: you will then discover when a recipient is getting a 'mixed message' from you.

(d) Ask colleagues and friends to be honest with you about when your body language is confusing or off-putting, to help you become more aware.

Committees

4.10 A committee is a group of people who meet for a particular purpose, often on a permanent basis. Uses of committees are these.

(a) **Making decisions**

(b) **Delaying** decisions (for more information)

(c) The **relaying of decisions** and instructions (eg briefings)

(d) The **dissemination of information** and the collection of feedback.

(e) **Problem solving**, by consultation with people in different departments or fields (eg a task force or working party).

(f) **Brainstorming**: free exchanges with a view to generating new approaches and ideas.

(g) **Co-ordination** of the efforts of a large number of people representing department or interest groups.

(h) Formal **recommendations** that others follow a course of action.

(i) **Representation** of a number of people from divergent disciplines.

Exam alert

This may seem like a small area of the syllabus, but a 10-mark question was set on it in December 1999. Revise as thoroughly as you can.

4.11 **Disadvantages of committees**

(a) **Size.** They are apt to be too large for constructive action, since the time taken by a committee to resolve a problem tends to be in direct proportion to its size.

(b) **Time-consuming and expensive**. In addition to the cost of highly paid executives' time, secretarial costs will be incurred in the preparation of agendas, recording of proceedings and the production and distribution of minutes.

(c) **Delays** may occur in the production cycle if matters of a routine nature are entrusted to committees.

(d) **Distraction.** Operations of the enterprise may be jeopardised by the frequent attendance of executives at meetings, and by distracting them from their real duties.

BPP PUBLISHING

(e) **Superficiality.** Incorrect or ineffective decisions may be made, owing to the fact that members of a committee are unfamiliar with the deeper aspects of issues under discussion.

(f) **Weakened individual responsibility** throughout the organisation.

(g) **Dominance.** Proceedings may be dominated by outspoken or aggressive members, thus unduly influencing decisions and subsequent action, perhaps adversely; there may be 'tyranny' by a minority.

4.12 **Potential misuses of committees**

(a) **Replace managers**. A committee cannot do all the tasks of management (eg leadership) and therefore cannot replace managers entirely.

(b) **Carry out research work**. A committee may be used to create new ideas, but work on those ideas cannot be done effectively by a committee itself.

(c) **Make unimportant decisions**. This would be expensive and time-consuming.

(d) **Discuss decisions beyond the authority of its participants**. This might occur, for example, when an international committee of government ministers is created, but ministers send deputies in their place to meetings, without giving the deputy sufficient authority to enable the committee to make important decisions.

(e) Committees **'paper over the cracks'** in a badly designed organisation structure.

Using committees successfully

4.13 Here are some guidelines.

(a) **Well defined areas** of authority, time scales of operations and purpose must be specified in writing.

(b) The **chairman must have the qualities** of leadership to co-ordinate and motivate the other committee members.

(c) **Size.** The committee should not be so large as to be unmanageable.

(d) **Membership.** The members of the committee must have the necessary skills and experience to do the committee's work. Where the committee is expected to liaise with functional departments, the members must also have sufficient status and influence with those departments.

(e) **Minutes.** Minutes of the meetings should be taken and circulated, with any action points arising out of the meetings notified to the members responsible for doing the work (see below).

Other group communication methods

4.14 **Brainstorming sessions** are problem-solving conferences of six to twelve people who produce spontaneous 'free-wheeling' ideas to solve a particular problem. Ideas are produced but not evaluated at these meetings, so that originality is not stifled in fear of criticism. Brainstorming sessions rely on the ability of conference members to feed off each other's ideas. They have been used in many organisations and might typically occur, for example, in advertising agencies to produce ideas for a forthcoming campaign.

4.15 **Quality circles** emerged first in the United States, but it was in Japan that they were adopted most enthusiastically. They are still used, but some commentators suggest they are outmoded and are being superseded by other team-based working methods.

> **KEY TERM** *quality & quality control*
>
> A **quality circle** consists of a group of employees which meets regularly to discuss problems of quality and quality control in their area of work, and perhaps to suggest ways of improving quality. The quality circle has a leader or supervisor who directs discussions and possibly also helps to train other members of the circle.

4.16 A **team briefing** is a means of communicating at team level, not in the more impersonal or abstract level of the house journal or noticeboard. It is given by a **team leader**, who should have been thoroughly trained and briefed, or, occasionally, a more senior member of management.

> **KEY TERM**
>
> **Team briefings** are a form of face-to-face communication mechanism which are designed to increase the commitment and understanding of the workforce.

4.17 The **purpose of a team briefing** is to communicate and explain management decisions in the hope that this will reduce any disruption, dispel any rumours, and enhance employees' commitment. Subjects include:

- Policies (new or changed, and why)
- Plans
- Progress
- Personnel issues

4.18 **Reasons for failure**
- Lack of senior management commitment
- Interference
- A lack of enthusiasm shown by middle managers
- The reluctance of management to allow the discussion of matters of real importance.

4.19 Team briefings can be seen as a tool which tries to **motivate** by **communicating**. However, it is **not** clear whether, using Herzberg's model, information has a role in motivation.

(a) If lack of information (as a result of management secrecy) is a **hygiene** factor, you would expect little **long-term** change in the level of motivation from a more open management approach.

(b) If providing more information and being more open is a **motivator** factor, you would expect greater enthusiasm.

Interviews

4.20 The interview informal or otherwise is an excellent internal system for handling the problems or queries of individuals, allowing **confidentiality** and flexible response to personal factors. Interviews are, however, costly in terms of managerial time. Some interviews are built into the **formal** communication system.

(a) **Grievance** interviews are where employees voice their complaints.

(b) **Disciplinary** interviews are where the organisation can air its complaints.

(c) **Appraisal** interviews are used to discuss the employee's performance, progress and possible need for improvement.

(d) **Counselling** interviews will be discussed below.

Telephone calls and voice mail

4.21 The **telephone** provides all the interactive and feedback advantages of face to face communication, while saving the travel time. It is, however, more 'distant' and impersonal than an interview for the discussion of sensitive personal matters, and it does not **by itself** provide the concreteness of written media.

4.22 **Voice mail** is a means of leaving spoken memos, for someone to listen to later. It can be useful as an extension of **paging**, so that a person can leave detailed messages for someone who is absent without the inconvenience of having to write a memorandum or the hazard of leaving a message.

4.23 **Video conferencing** has grown in popularity since the Gulf War and with the decreasing cost of technology compared to the cost and inconvenience of flying. It is a meeting conducted over long distance. Each participant shares a room, and interacts with a video broadcast image of the other participants.

5 TEXTUAL COMMUNICATIONS

Forms

5.1 Routine information flow is largely achieved through the use of **forms**. A well designed form can be filled quickly and easily with brief, relevant and specifically identified details of a request or instruction. They are simple to file, and information is quickly retrieved and confirmed. Examples include: expense forms, timesheets, insurance forms, stock request forms etc.

Notice board

5.2 **A notice board** is a channel through which various written media can be cheaply transmitted to a large number of people. It allows the organisation to present a variety of information to any or all employees: items may have a limited time span of relevance but will at least be available for verification and recollection for a while. The drawbacks to notice boards are that:

(a) They can easily fall into **neglect**, and become untidy or irrelevant (or be sabotaged by graffiti).

(b) They are wholly **dependent** on the intended recipient's **curiosity** or desire to receive information.

House journal

5.3 Larger companies frequently run an **internal magazine** or newspaper to inform employees about:

* Staff appointments and retirements
* Meetings, sports and social events

- Results and successes; customer feedback
- New products or machinery
- Motivating competitions eg for suggestions, office maintenance, safety

Organisation manual or handbook

5.4 An organisation (or office) manual is useful for drawing together and **keeping up to date** all relevant information for the guidance of individuals and groups as to:

- The structure of the organisation (perhaps an organisation chart)
- Background: the organisation's history and geography
- The organisation's products, services and customers
- Rules and regulations
- Conditions of employment: pay structure, hours, holidays, notice etc
- Standards and procedures for health and safety
- Procedures for grievance, discipline, salary review
- Policy on trade union membership
- Facilities for employees

Letters and faxes

5.5 **The letter** is flexible in a wide variety of situations, and useful in providing a written record and confirmation of the matters discussed.

(a) It is widely used for external communication, via the **external mailing system** (Post Office) or taxi or courier.

(b) A direct letter may be used internally in certain situations where a confidential written record is necessary or personal handling required.

5.6 **Fax** achieves the same object as a letter, but is more immediate. Most faxes are followed up with a letter.

Memoranda

5.7 **A memorandum** is the equivalent of the letter in internal communication. It is sent via the **internal mail system** (eg in special envelopes) of an organisation. Memoranda are useful for exchanging many sorts of message and particularly for confirming telephone conversations: sometimes, however, they are used instead of telephone conversations, where the call would have been quicker, cheaper and just as effective. Many memoranda are unnecessarily typed where a short hand-written note would be adequate.

E-mail

5.8 As an alternative to paper-based media such as letters and memos, people are increasingly using **e-mail**, especially in firms with a high penetration of **networked PCs**.

(a) Each PC on the network is connected to a **central server**.

(b) Messages are sent to the central server. At regular intervals (eg every 30 minutes) these are distributed to each PC on the network.

5.9 E-mail addresses are accessible to those **inside** the organisation and to **outsiders**, if they too have e-mail facilities and are signed up with a service provider (such as Compuserve or

Demon). The facilities of e-mail can also be supplemented by promotional media such as **internet web-sites**. Many firms have **intra-nets.**

5.10 **Problems with e-mail**

(a) Information overload - it is easier to send an e-mail than to distribute a memo, so people perhaps send unnecessary messages.

(b) E-mails, unlike other forms of communication, are **not private**.

Report writing

5.11 A formal **report** enables a number of people to review the complex facts and arguments relating to an issue on which they have to base a plan or make a decision. This is primarily an **internal medium** used by management, but can be used externally for the information of shareholders, the general public, government agencies etc (eg the company's Annual Report).

5.12 The written report does not allow for effective discussion or immediate feedback, as does a meeting, and can be a time-consuming and expensive document to produce. However, as a medium for putting across a body of ideas to a group of people, it has several **advantages.**

(a) People can **study the material in their own time**, rather than arranging to be present at one place and time

(b) **No time need be wasted on irrelevancies** and the formulation of arguments, such as may occur in meetings

(c) The report should be **presented objectively and impartially**, in a formal and impersonal style: emotional reactions or conflicts will be avoided.

5.13 **Stylistic requirements in the writing of reports**

(a) A report must first **identify** the recipient, the preparer, the date and subject matter.

(b) **Bias and over-emotive language** can undermine the credibility of the report and its recommendations.

(c) Avoid **colloquialisms** and abbreviated forms.

(d) **Ease of understanding.**

  (i) Write for the **user:** jargon is perfectly suitable for some readers, but intimidating to others.

  (ii) Organise material logically, especially if it is leading up to a conclusion or recommendation. Aim for clarity.

  (iii) Signal relevant themes by appropriate headings or highlighting.

  (iv) The **layout** of the report should display data clearly and attractively. Figures and diagrams should be used with discretion, and it might be helpful to highlight key figures which appear within large tables of numbers.

5.14   Here is an example of a report.

To: [Name(s)/position(s) of recipient(s)]
From: [Sender]
Date:
Subject: [Title of report, such as *Communication Media in A Ltd*]

Contents:

1   Terms of reference and work undertaken
2   Executive summary
3   Organisational problems
4   Operational issues
5   Conclusion and recommendation

1   **Terms of reference and work undertaken**

1.1   [Here is laid out the scope and purpose of the report: what is to be investigated, what information is required, whether recommendations should be made.

1.2   The scope of work done, how data was collected etc

2   **Executive summary** [Many reports have a brief description of their key points at the top.]

3   **Organisation issues**

3.1   [Reports could use numbered paragraphs like this. This makes it easier for the user to refer to them.]

3.2   [The content in this and the following sections should be complete but concise and clearly structured in chronological order, order of importance or any other logical relationship.]

4   **Operational problems**

5   **Conclusion and recommendations**

5.1   [This section allows for a summary of main findings and their implications. Recommendations could come here, referenced, if necessary, to the findings of the earlier section. The recommendations will allow the recipient to make a decision if necessary.]

Exam alert

You may well be asked to use report format in an answer to an exam question, although it is not clear from the pilot paper how many marks are available for this.

Activity 13.5

Indicate the most effective way in which the following situations should be communicated.

(a)   Spare parts needed urgently.

(b)   A message from the managing director to all staff.

(c)   Fred Bloggs has been absent five times in the past month and his managers intends taking action.

(d)   You need information quickly from another department.

(e)   You have to explain a complicated operation to a group.

6   COUNSELLING

KEY TERM

'**Counselling** can be defined as 'a purposeful relationship in which one person helps another to help himself. It is a way of relating and responding to another person so that that person is helped to explore his thoughts, feelings and behaviour with the aim of reaching a clearer understanding. The clearer understanding may be of himself or of a problem, or of the one in relation to the other.'   (Rees)

6.1   The need for workplace counselling can arise in many different situations.
- During appraisal
- In grievance or disciplinary situations
- Following change, such as promotion or relocation
- On redundancy or dismissal
- As a result of domestic or personal difficulties
- In cases of sexual harassment or violence at work

6.2   Effective counselling is not merely a matter of pastoral care for individuals, but is very much in the **organisation's** interests. Counselling:

(a)   **Prevents underperformance**, reduces labour turnover and absenteeism and increase commitment from employees.

(b)   Demonstrates an organisation's **commitment** to and concern for its employees.

(c)   Give employees the confidence and encouragement necessary to take responsibility for self and career development.

(d)   Recognises that the organisation may be contributing to the **employees' problems** and therefore it provides an opportunity to reassess organisational policy and practice.

6.3   Most of what follows is derived from the IPD's 1992 *Statement on Counselling in the Workplace*.

The counselling process

6.4   The counselling process has three stages.

Step 1.   **Recognition and understanding**. Often it is the employee who takes the initiative, but managers should be aware that the problem raised initially may be just the tip of the iceberg. (*Personnel Management Plus*, February 1993, cites a case where an employee came forward with a problem about pension contributions, and mentioned, as he was about to leave 'By the way - my wife wants a divorce'.)

Step 2.   **Empowering**. This means enabling the employee to recognise their own problem or situation and encouraging them to express it.

Step 3.   **Resourcing**. The problem must then be managed, and this includes the decision as to who is best able to act as counsellor. A specialist or outside resource may be better than the employee's manager.

Counselling skills

6.5 Remember that the aim of counselling is to help the employee to help himself. Counsellors need to be **observant** enough to note behaviour which may be symptomatic of a problem, be **sensitive** to beliefs and values which may be different from their own (for example religious beliefs), be **empathetic** to the extent that they appreciate that the problem may seem overwhelming to the individual, and yet remain **impartial** and refrain from giving advice. Counsellors must have the belief that the individual has the resources to solve their own problems, albeit with passive or active help.

6.6 Interviewing skills are particularly relevant. Open questioning, listening actively (probing, evaluating, interpreting and supporting), seeing the problem from the individual's point of view, and above all being genuinely and sincerely interested are skills identified in the IPD Statement.

Confidentiality

6.7 There will be situations when an employee cannot be completely open unless he is sure that his comments will be treated confidentially. However, certain information, once obtained by the organisation (for example about fraud or sexual harassment) calls for action. In spite of the drawbacks, therefore, the IPD statement is clear that employees must be made aware when their comments will be passed on to the relevant authority, and when they will be treated completely confidentially.

The interview

6.8 The checklist below contains much useful advice for meeting and interviewing people generally, not merely in counselling situations.

Counselling checklist

Preparation

- Choose a place to talk which is quiet, free from interruption and not open to view

- Research as much as you can before the meeting and have any necessary papers readily available

- Make sure you know whether the need for counselling has been properly identified or whether you will have to carefully probe to establish if a problem exists

- Allow sufficient time for the session. (If you know you must end at a particular time, inform the individual of this)

- Decide if it is necessary for the individual's department head to be aware of the counselling and its purpose

- Give the individual the option of being accompanied by a supportive colleague

- If you are approaching the individual following information received from a colleague, decide in advance the extent to which you can reveal your source

- Consider how you are going to introduce and discuss your perceptions of the situation

- Be prepared for the individual to have different expectations of the discussion, eg the individual may expect you to solve the problem - rather than come to terms with it himself/herself

- Understand that the individual's view of the facts of the situation will be more important than the facts themselves and that their behaviour may not reflect their true feelings

---

BPP
PUBLISHING

Format of discussion

- Welcome the individual and clarify the general purpose of the meeting

- Assure the individual that matters of confidentiality will be treated as such

- The individual may be reticent through fear of being considered somewhat of a risk in future and you will need to give appropriate reassurances in this regard

- Be ready to prompt or encourage the individual to move into areas he/she might be hesitant about

- Encourage the individual to look more deeply into statements

- Ask the individual to clarify statements you do not quite understand the individual and which you both might prefer to avoid

- Recognise that some issues may be so important to the individual that they will have to be discussed over and over again, even though this may seem repetitious to you

- If you sense that the individual is becoming defensive, try to identify the reason and relax the pressure by changing your approach

- Occasionally summarise the conversation as it goes along, reflecting back in your own words (not parrot phrasing) what you understand the individual to say

- Try to take the initiative in probing important areas which may be embarrassing/emotional to the interviewee

- Sometimes emotions may be more important than the words being spoken, so it may be necessary to reflect back what you see the individual feeling

- At the close of the meeting, clarify any decisions reached and agree what follow-up support would be helpful

Overcoming dangers

- If you take notes at an inappropriate moment, you may set up a barrier between yourself and the individual

- Realise you may not like the individual and be on guard against this

- Recognise that repeating problems does not solve them

- Be careful to avoid taking sides

- Overcome internal and external distractions. Concentrate on the individual and try to understand the situation with him/her

- The greater the perceived level of listening, the more likely the individual will be to accept comments and contributions from you

- Resist the temptation to talk about your own problems, even though these may seem similar to those of the individual

Source: IPD Statement on Counselling in the Workplace

Key learning points

- **Interpersonal behaviour** is behaviour between one or more individuals and the behaviour of one individual in relation to others.

- Individuals assume **roles** in relation to each other and to the situation: these are the 'hats' that people wear.

- **Communication** is a two-way process involving the transmission or exchange of information, and the provision of feedback. Individual differences, poor communication skills and situational factors may create barriers to effective communication which must be overcome.

- The way in which the communication **process** is structured can influence the effectiveness with which tasks are handled.

- Any communication can be mapped on a simple model. The sender codes the message and transmits it through a medium to the receiver who decodes it into information.

- **Barriers to communication** are 'noise' (from the environment), poorly constructed or coded/decoded messages (distortion) and failures in understanding caused by the relative positions of senders and receivers.

- A variety of communication **media** exist, written and oral. **Electronic communication** has some of the features of both written and oral communication. Electronic communications facilitate homeworking.

- **Informal communication** supplements the formal system. The grapevine can act very fast in spreading rumours. Networking is a technique whereby an 'informal' communications network is created. It can be recognised as such by the management hierarchy.

- **Counselling** is an interpersonal interview, the aim of which is to facilitate another person's identification and working through a problem.

- *See the Part F mind map summary on page 286.*

Quick quiz

1   What are (a) role signs and (b) role ambiguity?

2   Draw a simple diagram of the communication process using dotted or broken lines where 'distortion' may be a problem.

3   Give five examples of non-verbal communication, and suggest what they might be used to indicate.

4   What is the difference between aggression and assertiveness?

5   What is meant by communication which is:

   (a)   Upward?
   (b)   Downward?
   (c)   Horizontal?

6   What are the advantages and disadvantages of giving orders or briefings by telephone?

7   What might be covered in regular 'team briefings'?

8   What are the main purposes of upward communication in organisations?

9   What are the stages of the counselling process?

Answers to quick quiz

1   (a)   How someone dresses and behaves to match the role.
    (b)   If an individual is unsure of what his/her role is in a certain situation.

2   Refer to Section 4.9. The dotted lines would run alongside all the arrows.

3   A nod of agreement, a smile to encourage, a frown to disapprove, a yawn to show boredom, turning away to discourage.

4   Aggressive behaviour is competitive; assertion means that every individual has certain rights, and is entitled to stand by them.

5   (a)   From subordinate to superior
     (b)   From superior to subordinate
     (c)   Between individuals, teams, departments on the same level of the organisation chart

6   Advantages are that it cuts down on time and physical movement. Disadvantages are that only one person is reached at a time, there are no non-verbal signals and it is more difficult to persuade and to respond to physical factors.

7   Organisational policy and changes, plans, progress, results.

8   To give feedback, to inform and to make suggestions.

9   Recognition and understanding; empowerment; resourcing.

Answers to activities

Answer 13.1

Your answer might be along the following lines.

(a)   If you chose 'student' your role set would consist of fellow students, lecturers, library and administrative staff. Your role signs may include dressing and acting informally with your colleagues, but being rather more formal with others.

(b)   Lecturers who dress and act informally with their students may cause problems. Mature students with partners and children may find role incompatible when study interferes with personal life.

Answer 13.2

You may have your own views on examples managers could set. Basically, successful managers provide an aspirational model: showing junior staff that it is possible for them to achieve organisational success and the lifestyle that may go with it. A manager may also model the roles of popular leaders, a person who combines work and home/leisure life, a person who does not panic in a crises, a person who is developing their skills and so on. Models are, after all, in the eye of the beholder!

Answer 13.4

Problems suggested by the statements made may be summed up as follows.

(a)   A complete lack of tact and diplomacy. it may be that the manager is deliberately alerting 'S Simms' to the complaint by 'P Brown' but, of course, by putting the information on the notice board the whole department will be aware of it too.

(b)   Here is someone from a specialist background talking in a jargon which will mean virtually nothing to the average recipient.

(c)   At least the speaker has noticed Smith's body language! Even if the suggestion about fleas is an attempt to be facetious, the speaker appears to have misunderstood the nature of feedback: Smith is giving clear signals that (s)he is perplexed by the briefing.

(d)   Technical 'noise', plus a further problem, which you may have spotted: the speaker has chosen an inappropriate medium, since he is not writing down the details which are clearly important and will require reference and confirmation later.

(e)   A 463 page report to be read for the following day sounds like overload; (and since it's on 'communication', it sounds like a contradiction in terms!).

(f)   Status differentials (real or imagined) are the principal source of difficulty here, the speaker evidently wishing to 'put down' the listeners and 'keep them in their place'. S(he) is potentially losing valuable contributions.

Answer 13.5

Communicating the situations given might best be done as follows.

(a)   Telephone, confirmed in writing (order form, letter)

(b)   Noticeboard, general meeting or email.

(c)   Face-to-face conversation. It would be a good idea to confirm the outcome of the meeting in writing so that records can be maintained.

(d)   Either telephone or face to face.

(e)   Team briefing

Chapter 14   Conflict, grievance and discipline

Chapter topic list

1   Conflict in organisations

2   Causes, symptoms and tactics of conflict

3   Managerial response to conflict

4   Discipline

5   Grievance

6   Appeals procedures

Learning objectives

On completion of this chapter you will be able to:

<table>
<tr><td></td><td>Syllabus reference</td></tr>
<tr><td>• identify the main cause of conflict within an organisation</td><td>e</td></tr>
<tr><td>• outline procedures for managing conflict</td><td>e</td></tr>
<tr><td>• outline a suitable framework (both internal and external to the organisation) for dealing with grievance and disciplinary matters</td><td>e</td></tr>
<tr><td>• explain the need for effective organisational procedures</td><td>e</td></tr>
<tr><td>• explain the role of management in respect of disciplinary matters</td><td>e</td></tr>
<tr><td>• suggest ways in which the outcome of the disciplinary process should be communicated to the individual concerned</td><td>e</td></tr>
</table>

1   CONFLICT IN ORGANISATIONS

1.1   The existence of **conflict** in organisations might be considered inevitable or unnatural, depending on your viewpoint.

The 'happy family' view: conflict is unnatural

1.2   The happy family view presents organisations as:

(a)   **Co-operative structures**, designed to achieve agreed common objectives, with no systematic conflict of interest.

(b)   **Harmonious environments**, where conflicts are **exceptional** and arise from:

- Misunderstandings
- Personality factors
- The expectations of inflexible employees
- Factors outside the organisation and its control

1.3   Conflict is thus **blamed** on bad management, lack of leadership, poor communication, or 'bloody-mindedness' on the part of individuals or interest groups that impinge on the organisation. The theory is that a strong culture, good two-way communication, co-operation and motivational leadership will 'eliminate' conflict.

Activity 14.1

How accurate is the 'happy family' perspective when applied to your own organisation, or to any organisation with which you are sufficiently familiar?

To what extent would you subscribe to the claim that the 'happy family' view is publicised by managers within their own organisations, not so much as an accurate description of reality, but rather because adoption of the 'happy family' perspective itself helps to reduce the level of articulated conflict?

The conflict view

1.4   In contrast, some see organisations as **arenas** for conflict on individual and group levels.

(a)   Members battle for limited resources, status, rewards and professional values.

(b)   **Organisational politics** involve constant struggles for control, and choices of structure, technology and organisational goals are part of this process. Individual and organisational interests will not always coincide.

The 'evolutionary' view

1.5   This view regards conflict as a means of **maintaining the status quo,** as a useful basis for **evolutionary change**.

- **Conflict** keeps the organisation **sensitive to the need to change**, while reinforcing its essential framework of control.

- The **legitimate pursuit of competing interests** can balance and preserve social and organisational arrangements.

BPP PUBLISHING

1.6 This '**constructive conflict**' view may perhaps be the most useful for managers and administrators of organisations, as it neither:

(a) Attempts to dodge the issues of conflict, which is an observable fact of life in most organisations; nor

(b) Seeks to pull down existing organisational structures altogether.

1.7 Conflict can be highly desirable. Conflict is constructive, when its effect is to:

- Introduce different **solutions** to problems
- **Define power relationships** more clearly
- Encourage **creativity**, the testing of ideas
- **Focus attention** on individual contributions
- **Bring emotions** out into the open
- **Release of hostile feelings** that have been, or may be, repressed otherwise

1.8 **Conflict can also be destructive**. It may:

- **Distract attention** from the task
- **Polarise** views and 'dislocate' the group
- Subvert **objectives** in favour of secondary goals
- Encourage **defensive** or 'spoiling' behaviour
- Force the group to **disintegrate**
- Stimulate emotional, **win-lose conflicts,** ie hostility

Case example

Tjosvold and Deerner researched conflict in different contexts. They allocated to 66 student volunteers the roles of foremen and workers at an assembly plant, with a scenario of conflict over job rotation schemes. Foremen were against, workers for.

One group was told that the organisational norm was to 'avoid controversy'; another was told that the norm was 'co-operative controversy', *trying* to agree; a third was told that groups were out to win any arguments that arose, 'competitive controversy'. The students were offered rewards for complying with their given norms. Their decisions, and attitudes to the discussions, were then monitored.

(a) Where controversy was avoided, the foremen's views dominated.

(b) Competitive controversy brought no agreement - but brought out feelings of hostility and suspicion.

(c) Co-operative controversy brought out differences in an atmosphere of curiosity, trust and openness: the decisions reached seemed to integrate the views of both parties.

But can real managers and workers be motivated to comply with useful organisational 'norms' in this way?

Conflict between groups

1.9 **Conflicts of interest** may exist throughout the organisation - or even for a single individual. There may be conflicts of interest between local management of a branch or subsidiary and the organisation as a whole.

- Sales and production departments in a manufacturing firm (over scheduling, product variation)

- Trade unions and management.

1.10 **Interest groups** such as trade unions tend to wield greater power in conflict situations than their members as individuals. Trade Unions are organisations whose purpose it is to promote their members' interests. (Strike action has to be preceded by a ballot.)

Activity 14.2

What other examples of 'conflicts of interest' can you identify within an organisation? Having selected some instances, can you detect any common patterns in such conflicts?

Case example

Conflict can also operate **within** groups.

In an experiment reported by Deutsch (1949), psychology students were given puzzles and human relation problems to work at in discussion groups. Some groups ('co-operative' ones) were told that the grade each individual got at the end of the course would depend on the performance of his group. Other groups ('competitive' ones) were told that each student would receive a grade according to his own contributions.

No significant differences were found between the two kinds of group in the amount of interest and involvement in the tasks, or in the amount of learning. But the co-operative groups, compared with the competitive ones, had greater productivity per unit time, better quality of product and discussion, greater co-ordination of effort and sub-division of activity, more diversity in amount of contribution per member, more attentiveness to fellow members and more friendliness during discussion.

Conflict and competition

1.11 Sherif and Sherif conducted a number of experiments into groups and competing groups.

(a) People tend to identify with a group.

(b) New members of a group quickly learn the norms and attitudes of the others, no matter whether these are 'positive' or 'negative', friendly or hostile.

(c) When a group competes, this is what happens to it **within the group**.

    (i) Members close ranks, and submerge their differences; loyalty and conformity are demanded.

    (ii) The 'climate' changes from informal and sociable to work and task-oriented; individual needs are subordinated to achievement.

    (iii) Leadership moves from democratic to autocratic, with the group's acceptance.

    (iv) The group tends to become more structured and organised.

    (v) The opposing group begins to be perceived as 'the enemy'.

    (vi) Perception is distorted, presenting an idealised picture of 'us' and a negative stereotype of 'them'.

    (vii) Communication between groups decreases.

1.12 In a 'win-lose' situation, where competition is not perceived to result in benefits for both sides.

(a) The **winning** group will:

    • Retain its cohesion

    • Relax into a complacent, playful state

- Return to group maintenance and concern for members' needs
- Be confirmed in its group 'self-concept' with little re-evaluation

(b) The **losing** group might behave as follows.

(i) Deny defeat if possible, or place the blame on the arbitrator, or the system

(ii) Lose its cohesion and splinter into conflict, as 'blame' is apportioned.

(iii) Be keyed-up, fighting mad.

(iv) Turn towards work-orientation to regroup, rather than members' needs or group maintenance.

(v) Tend to learn by re-evaluating its perceptions of itself and the other group. It is more likely to become a cohesive and effective unit once the 'defeat' has been accepted.

1.13 Members of a group will act in unison if the group's existence or patterns of behaviour are threatened from outside. Cohesion is naturally assumed to be the result of positive factors such as communication, agreement and mutual trust - but in the face of a 'common enemy' (competition, crisis or emergency) cohesion and productivity benefit.

Activity 14.3

How applicable are Sherif's 1965 research findings to the cause, symptoms and treatment of conflict in a modern organisation? In what ways, if at all, could Sherif's findings be used as a means of improving employee performance within an organisation?

Exam alert

A detailed question set in June 2001 required you to identify *causes* of conflict, conflict *control* strategies and (perhaps more challenging) circumstances in which conflict may be constructive and destructive. Make sure that you attend to this material in sufficient detail. It may also help to highlight some of the writers and researchers associated with the topic, to support your knowledge and avoid the risk of vague, 'common sense' answers.

2   CAUSES, SYMPTOMS AND TACTICS OF CONFLICT

2.1   **Causes of conflict**

(a) **Differences in the objectives** of different groups or individuals.

(b) **Scarcity of resources**.

(c) **Interdependence of two departments** on a task. They have to work together but may do so ineffectively.

(d) **Disputes about the boundaries of authority.**

(i) The technostructure may attempt to encroach on the roles or 'territory' of line managers and usurp some of their authority.

(ii) One department might start '**empire building**' and try to take over the work previously done by another department.

(e) **Personal differences,** as regards goals, attitudes and feelings, are also bound to crop up. This is especially true in **differentiated organisations**, where people employed in the different sub-units are very different.

2.2 Symptoms of conflict

- Poor communications, in all 'directions'
- Interpersonal friction
- Inter-group rivalry and jealousy
- Low morale and frustration
- Widespread use of arbitration, appeals to higher authority, and inflexible attitudes

2.3 The tactics of conflict

(a) **Withholding information** from one another

(b) **Distorting information**. This will enable the group or manager presenting the information to get their own way more easily.

(c) **Empire building**. A group (especially a specialist group such as accounting) which considers its influence to be neglected might seek to **impose rules, procedures,** restrictions or official requirements on other groups, in order to bolster up their own importance.

(d) **Informal organisation**. A manager might seek to by-pass formal channels of communication and decision-making by establishing informal contacts and friendships with people in a position of importance.

(e) **Fault-finding** in the work of other departments: department X might duplicate the work of department Y - hoping to prove department Y 'wrong' - and then report the fact to senior management.

3 MANAGERIAL RESPONSE TO CONFLICT

3.1 Management responses to the handling of conflict (not all of which are effective).

Response	Comment
Denial/withdrawal	'Sweeping it under the carpet'. If the conflict is very trivial, it may indeed blow over without an issue being made of it, but if the causes are not identified, the conflict may grow to unmanageable proportions.
Suppression	'Smoothing over', to preserve working relationships despite minor conflicts. As Hunt remarks, however: 'Some cracks cannot be papered over'.
Dominance	The application of power or influence to settle the conflict. The disadvantage of this is that it creates all the lingering resentment and hostility of 'win-lose' situations.
Compromise	Bargaining, negotiating, conciliating. To some extent, this will be inevitable in any organisation made up of different individuals. However, individuals tend to exaggerate their positions to allow for compromise, and compromise itself is seen to weaken the value of the decision, perhaps reducing commitment. **Negotiation** is: 'a process of interaction by which two or more parties who consider they need to be jointly involved in an outcome, but who initially have different objectives seek by the use of argument and persuasion to resolve their differences in order to achieve a mutually acceptable solution'.

Response	Comment
Integration/ collaboration	Emphasis must be put on the task, individuals must accept the need to modify their views for its sake, and group effort must be seen to be superior to individual effort.
Encourage co-operative behaviour	Joint problem-solving team, goals set for all teams/departments to follow.

Activity 14.4

In the light of the above consider how conflict could arise, what form it would take and how it might be resolved in the following situations.

(a) Two managers who share a secretary have documents to be typed.

(b) One worker finds out that another worker who does the same job as he does is paid a higher wage.

(c) A company's electricians find out that a group of engineers have been receiving training in electrical work.

(d) Department A stops for lunch at 12.30 while Department B stops at 1 o'clock. Occasionally the canteen runs out of puddings for Department B workers.

(e) The Northern Region and Southern Region sales teams are continually trying to better each others results, and the capacity of production to cope with the increase in sales is becoming overstretched.

The win-win model

3.2 One useful model of conflict resolution is the **win-win model**. This states that there are three basic ways in which a conflict or disagreement can be worked out.

Method	Frequency	Explanation
Win-lose	This is quite common.	**One party gets what (s)he wants at the expense of the other party**: for example, Department A gets the new photocopier, while Department B keeps the old one (since there were insufficient resources to buy two new ones). However well-justified such a solution is (Department A needed the facilities on the new photocopier more than Department B), there is often lingering resentment on the part of the 'losing' party, which may begin to damage work relations.
Lose-lose	This sounds like a senseless outcome, but actually **compromise** comes into this category. It is thus very common.	**Neither party gets what (s)he really wanted**: for example, since Department A and B cannot both have a new photocopier, it is decided that neither department should have one. However 'logical' such a solution is, there is often resentment and dissatisfaction on *both* sides. (Personal arguments where neither party gives ground and both end up storming off or not talking are also lose-lose: the parties may not have lost the argument, but they lose the relationship ...) Even positive compromises only result in half-satisfied needs.

Method	Frequency	Explanation
Win-win	This may not be common, but working towards it often brings out the best solution.	**Both parties get as close as possible to what they really want.** How can this be achieved?

3.3 It is critical to the **win-win approach** to discover **what both parties really want** - as opposed to:

- What they think they want (because they have not considered any other options)
- What they think they can get away with
- What they think they need in order to avoid an outcome they fear

For example, Department B may want the new photocopier because they have never found out how to use all the features (which do the same things) on the old photocopier; because they just want to have the same equipment as Department A; or because they fear that if they do not have the new photocopier, their work will be slower and less professionally presented, and they may be reprimanded (or worse) by management.

3.4 The important questions in working towards win-win are:

- What do you want this for?
- What do you think will happen if you don't get it?

These questions get to the heart of what people really need and want.

3.5 In our photocopier example, Department A says it needs the new photocopier to make colour copies (which the old copier does not do), while Department B says it needs the new copier to make clearer copies (because the copies on the old machine are a bit blurred). Now there are **options to explore**. It may be that the old copier just needs fixing, in order for Department B to get what it really wants. Department A will still end up getting the new copier - but Department B has in the process been consulted and had its needs met.

3.6 EXAMPLE: THE WIN-WIN APPROACH

Two men are fighting over an orange. There is only one orange, and both men want it.

(a) If one man gets the orange and the other does not, this is a **win-lose** solution.

(b) If they cut the orange in half and share it (or agree that neither will have the orange), this is a **lose-lose** solution - despite the compromise.

(c) If they talk about what they each need the orange for, and one says 'I want to make orange juice' and the other says 'I want the skin of the orange to make candied peel', there are further options to explore (like peeling the orange) and the potential for both men to get exactly what they wanted. This is a **win-win** approach.

3.7 **Win-win** is not always possible: It is **working towards it** that counts. The result can be mutual respect and co-operation, enhanced communication, more creative problem-solving and - at best - **satisfied needs all round**.

Activity 14.5

Suggest a (i) win-lose, (ii) compromise and (iii) win-win solution in the following scenarios.

(a) Two of your team members are arguing over who gets the desk by the window: they both want it.

(b) You and a colleague both need access to the same file at the same time. You both need it to compile reports for your managers, for the following morning. It is now 3.00pm, and each of you will need it for two hours to do the work.

(c) Manager A is insisting on buying new computers for her department before the budgetary period ends. Manager B cannot understand why - since the old computers are quite adequate - and will moreover be severely inconvenienced by such a move, since her own systems will have to be upgraded as well, in order to remain compatible with department A. (The two departments constantly share data files.) Manager B protests, and conflict erupts.

4 DISCIPLINE

KEY TERM

Discipline can be considered as: 'a condition in an enterprise in which there is orderliness in which the members of the enterprise behave sensibly and conduct themselves according to the standards of acceptable behaviour as related to the goals of the organisation'.

4.1 Another definition of 'positive' and 'negative' discipline makes the distinction between methods of maintaining sensible conduct and orderliness which are technically co-operative, and those based on warnings, threats and punishments.

(a) Positive (or constructive) discipline relates to procedures, systems and equipment in the work place which have been designed specifically so that the employee has **no option** but to act in the desired manner to complete a task safely and successfully. A machine may, for example, shut off automatically if its safety guard is not in place.

(b) **Negative discipline** is then the promise of **sanctions** designed to make people choose to behave in a desirable way. Disciplinary action may be punitive (punishing an offence), deterrent (warning people not to behave in that way) or reformative (calling attention to the nature of the offence, so that it will not happen again).

4.2 The best discipline is **self discipline**. Even before they start to work, most mature people accept the idea that following instructions and fair rules of conduct are normal responsibilities that are part of any job. Most team members can therefore be counted on to exercise self discipline.

Exam alert

In the June 1999 paper, you were asked to explain the term 'discipline': Bear in mind that it is not just 'punishment'. You were also asked to give examples of situations where discipline may be required (see below) and to outline a formal disciplinary procedure (see below). The examiner complained that candidates failed to distinguish between the 'process' of discipline and the 'procedure' to be followed: make sure you know the difference.

A major article on 'disciplinary and grievance procedures' appeared in *Student Accountant* in February 2001, especially targeted at Paper C6. (We refer to some of its main points in this chapter.) Clearly, a 'hot' topic.

Types of disciplinary situations

4.3 There are many types of disciplinary situations which require attention by the manager. S R Das Gupta (*Student Accountant*, February 2001) suggests the following handy mnemonic.

STRICT DISCPLINE

Sleeping while on duty
Threatening co-workers
Refusing to perform assigned duties
Intoxication
Conviction of criminal offence
Tarnishing of company image

Disobedience
Infraction of company policies
Safety procedures ignored
Carrying out illegal/immoral activities in company premises
Irregular attendance
Poor performance
Lying
Improper behaviour
Negative attitude
Embezzlement

4.4 Managers might be confronted with disciplinary problems stemming from employee behaviour *off* the job. These may be an excessive drinking problem, the use of drugs or some form of narcotics, or involvement in some form of law breaking activity. In such circumstances, whenever an employee's off-the-job conduct has an impact upon performance on the job, the manager must be prepared to deal with such a problem within the scope of the disciplinary process.

Disciplinary action

4.5 The purpose of discipline is not punishment or retribution. Disciplinary action must have as its goal the improvement of the future behaviour of the employee and other members of the organisation. The purpose obviously is the avoidance of similar occurrences in the future.

4.6 **Principles for any disciplinary action,** Gupta (*Student Accountant*, February 2001).

   (a) Disciplinary proceedings should be based on **facts** and not hearsay.

   (b) Affected employees must be given all **reasonable opportunity to explain and defend** (if necessary) their action. Final action can only be taken after such explanation/defence has been given due consideration by the management.

   (c) No employee should be punished more than the infraction warrants.

   (d) Personal bias against an employee should not be used to influence disciplinary action.

4.7 The suggested steps of progressive disciplinary action follow ACAS guidelines, in the UK. (Other countries may have other legal or voluntary guidelines.)

   Step 1. **The informal talk**

   If the infraction is of a relatively minor nature and if the employee's record has no previous marks of disciplinary action, an informal, friendly talk will clear up the situation in many cases. Here the manager discusses with the employee his or her behaviour in relation to standards which prevail within the enterprise.

Step 2. **Oral warning or reprimand**

In this type of interview between employee and manager, the latter emphasises the undesirability of the subordinate's repeated violation, and that ultimately it could lead to serious disciplinary action.

Step 3. **Written or official warning**

These are part of the ACAS code of practice. A written warning is of a formal nature insofar as it becomes a permanent part of the employee's record. Written warnings, not surprisingly, are particularly necessary in unionised situations, so that the document can serve as evidence in case of grievance procedures.

Step 4. **Disciplinary layoffs, or suspension**

This course of action would be next in order if the employee has committed repeated offences and previous steps were of no avail. Disciplinary lay-offs usually extend over several days or weeks. Some employees may not be very impressed with oral or written warnings, but they will find a disciplinary layoff without pay a rude awakening.

Step 5. **Demotion**

This course of action is likely to bring about dissatisfaction and discouragement, since losing pay and status over an extended period of time is a form of constant punishment. This dissatisfaction of the demoted employee may easily spread to co-workers, so most enterprises avoid downgrading as a disciplinary measure.

Step 6. **Discharge**

Discharge is a drastic form of disciplinary action, and should be reserved for the most serious offences. For the organisation, it involves waste of a labour resource, the expense of training a new employee, and disruption caused by changing the make-up of the work team. There also may be damage to the morale of the group.

Activity 14.6

How (a) accessible and (b) clear are the rules and policies of your organisation/office: do people really know what they are and are not supposed to do? Have a look at the rule book or procedures manual in your office. How easy is it to see - or did you get referred elsewhere? is the rule book well-indexed and cross-referenced, and in language that all employees will understand?

How (a) accessible and (b) clear are the disciplinary procedures in your office? Are the employees' rights of investigation and appeal clearly set out, with ACAS guidelines? Who is responsible for discipline?

Relationship management in disciplinary situations

4.8 Even if the manager uses sensitivity and judgement, imposing disciplinary action tends to generate **resentment** because it is an unpleasant experience. The challenge is to apply the necessary disciplinary action so that it will be least resented.

(a) **Immediacy**

Immediacy means that after noticing the offence, the manager proceeds to take disciplinary action as *speedily* as possible, subject to investigations while at the same time avoiding haste and on-the-spot emotions which might lead to unwarranted actions.

(b) **Advance warning**

Employees should know in advance (eg in a Staff Handbook) what is expected of them and what the rules and regulations are.

(c) **Consistency**

Consistency of discipline means that each time an infraction occurs appropriate disciplinary action is taken. Inconsistency in application of discipline lowers the morale of employees and diminishes their respect for the manager.

(d) **Impersonality**

Penalties should be connected with the act and not based upon the personality involved, and once disciplinary action has been taken, no grudges should be borne.

(e) **Privacy**

As a general rule (unless the manager's authority is challenged directly and in public) disciplinary action should be taken in private, to avoid the spread of conflict and the humiliation or martyrdom of the employee concerned.

Disciplinary interviews

4.9 **Preparation for the disciplinary interview**

(a) **Gathering the facts** about the alleged infringement

(b) **Determination of the organisation's position:** how valuable is the employee, potentially? How serious are his offences/lack of progress? How far is the organisation prepared to go to help him improve or discipline him further?

(c) **Identification of the aims of the interview**: punishment? deterrent to others? improvement? Specific standards of future behaviour/performance required need to be determined.

(d) **Ensure that the organisation's disciplinary procedures have been followed**

(i) Informal oral warnings (at least) have been given.

(ii) The employee has been given adequate notice of the interview for his own preparation.

(iii) The employee has been informed of the complaint against his right to be accompanied by a colleague or representative and so on.

4.10 **The content of the disciplinary interview**

Step 1. The manager will explain the purpose of the interview.

Step 2. The charges against the employee will be delivered, clearly, unambiguously and without personal emotion.

Step 3. The manager will explain the organisation's position with regard to the issues involved: disappointment, concern, need for improvement, impact on others. This can be done frankly - but tactfully, with as positive an emphasis as possible on the employee's capacity and responsibility to improve.

Step 4. The organisation's expectations with regard to future behaviour/performance should be made clear.

Step 5. The employee should be given the opportunity to comment, explain, justify or deny. If he is to approach the following stage of the interview in a positive way, he must not be made to feel 'hounded' or hard done by.

Step 6. The organisation's expectations should be reiterated, or new standards of behaviour set for the employee.

(i) They should be specific and quantifiable, performance related and realistic.

(ii) They should be related to a practical but reasonably short time period. A date should be set to review his progress.

(iii) The manager agrees on measures to help the employee should that be necessary. It would demonstrate a positive approach if, for example, a mentor were appointed from his work group to help him check his work. If his poor performance is genuinely the result of some difficulty or distress outside work, other help (temporary leave, counselling or financial aid) may be appropriate.

Step 7. The manager should explain the reasons behind any penalties imposed on the employee, including the entry in his personnel record of the formal warning. He should also explain how the warning can be removed from the record, and what standards must be achieved within a specified timescale. There should be a clear warning of the consequences of failure to meet improvement targets.

Step 8. The manager should explain the organisation's appeals procedures: if the employee feels he has been unfairly treated, there should be a right of appeal to a higher manager.

Step 9. Once it has been established that the employee understands all the above, the manager should summarise the proceedings briefly.

Records of the interview will be kept for the employee's personnel file, and for the formal follow-up review and any further action necessary.

Activity 14.7

Outline the steps involved in a formal disciplinary procedure (for an organisation with unionised employees) and show how the procedure would operate in a case of:

(a) Persistent absenteeism
(b) Theft of envelopes from the organisation's offices

4.11 The ACAS code of practice (September 2000) highlights the features of a good disciplinary system.

ACAS Code of Practice

Disciplinary and grievance procedures should:

- be in written form*

- specify to whom they apply (all, or only some of the employees?)

- be capable of dealing speedily with disciplinary matters

- indicate the forms of disciplinary action which may be taken (such as dismissal, suspension or warning)

- specify the appropriate levels of authority for the exercise of disciplinary actions

- provide for individuals to be informed of the nature of their alleged misconduct

---

- allow individuals to state their case, and to be accompanied by a fellow employee (or union representative)

- ensure that every case is properly investigated before any disciplinary action is taken

- ensure that employees are informed of the reasons for any penalty they receive

- state that no employee will be dismissed for a first offence, except in cases of gross misconduct

- provide for a right of appeal against any disciplinary action, and specify the appeals procedure

* The ACAS code of practice does not extend to informal 'first warnings', but these are an important part of the organisation's policy: don't forget them!

5 GRIEVANCE

KEY TERM

A **grievance** occurs when an individual thinks that he is being wrongly treated by his colleagues or supervisor: perhaps he or she is being picked on, unfairly appraised in his annual report, unfairly blocked for promotion or discriminated against on grounds of race or sex; rules may be inappropriately interpreted and applied; recognition for work performance may be withheld unfairly; and so on.

5.1 When an individual has a grievance he should be able to pursue it and ask to have the problem resolved. Gupta (*Student Accountant*, February 2001) notes that:

> 'unless the employee's grievance is addressed from the very beginning, it can be a constant source of worry and anger for the employee which in turn may impact on his work performance. Disgruntled employees may be a source of danger not only to the organisation but also to the other employees in the organisation. Such an employee can also cause nuisance value to the company. Therefore grievance should be addressed and resolved at the earliest opportunity.'

Some grievances should be capable of solution informally by the individual's manager. However, if an informal solution is not possible, there should be a formal grievance procedure.

5.2 **Issues to consider when developing a grievance policy**

(a) Employees must be accorded at all times an **open-door policy without any fear**.

(b) Reasonable opportunity must be provided for the employees to **adequately express** their grievances.

(c) If desired by the employees, permission should be given to be **accompanied** by a labour union or other representative.

(d) Every employee must be given **adequate opportunity** to pursue his case until a satisfactory resolution is reached

(e) A specific **time limit** must be set for a fair and equitable resolution.

5.3 Formal grievance procedures, like disciplinary procedures, should be set out in **writing** and made available to all staff. These procedures should do the following things.

(a) State what **grades of employee** are entitled to pursue a particular type of grievance.

    (b) State the **rights of the employee** for each type of grievance, including what the individual would be entitled to claim.

    (c) State what the **procedures for pursuing a grievance** should be.

        Step 1. The individual should discuss the grievance with a staff/union representative (or a colleague). If his case seems a good one, he should take the grievance to his immediate boss.

        Step 2. The first interview will be between the immediate boss (unless he is the subject of the complaint, in which case it will be the next level up) and the employee, who has the right to be accompanied by a colleague or representative.

        Step 3. If the immediate boss cannot resolve the matter, or the employee is otherwise dissatisfied with the first interview, the case should be referred to his own superior (and if necessary in some cases, to an even higher authority).

        Step 4. Cases referred to a higher manager should also be reported to the personnel department. Line management might decide at some stage to ask for the assistance/advice of a personnel manager in resolving the problem.

    (d) **Distinguish between individual grievances and collective grievances,** such as claims for better pay or working conditions.

    (e) Allow for the **involvement of an individual's or group's trade union** or staff association representative.

    (f) **State time limits** for initiating certain grievance procedures and subsequent stages of them.

    (g) **Require written records** of all meetings concerned with the case to be made and distributed to all the participants.

Grievance interviews

5.4   The dynamics of a grievance interview are broadly similar to a disciplinary interview, except that it is the subordinate who primarily wants a positive result from it. Prior to the interview, the manager should have some idea of the complaint and its possible source. The meeting itself can then proceed through three phases.

        Step 1. **Exploration.** What is the problem: the background, the facts, the causes (manifest and hidden)? At this stage, the manager should simply try to gather as much information as possible, without attempting to suggest solutions or interpretations: the situation must be seen to be open.

        Step 2. **Consideration.** The manager should:

            (i) Check the facts. No action should be taken on the basis of hearsay or unconfirmed reports

            (ii) Analyse the causes - the problem of which the complaint may be only a symptom

            (iii) Evaluate options for responding to the complaint, and the implication of any response made

        It may be that information can be given to clear up a misunderstanding, or the employee will - having 'got it off his chest' - withdraw his complaint. However, the meeting may have to be adjourned (say, for 48 hours) while the manager gets extra information and considers extra options.

Step 3. **Response/resolution**. The manager, having reached and reviewed his conclusions, reconvenes the meeting to convey (and justify, if required) his decision, hear counter-arguments and appeals. The outcome (agreed or disagreed) should be recorded in writing.

5.5 Grievance procedures should be seen as an employee's right. To this end, managers should be given formal training in the grievance procedures of their organisation, and the reasons for having them. Management should be persuaded that the grievance procedures are beneficial for the organisation and are not a threat to themselves (since many grievances arise out of disputes between subordinates and their boss). According to Gupta: 'Every case of grievance must be treated as an opportunity to improve the working environment and not as a nuisance created by an employee.'

Activity 14.8

Find your organisation's grievance procedures in the office manual, or ask your union or staff association representative. Study the procedures carefully. Think of a complaint or grievance you have (or have had) at work. Have you taken it to grievance procedures? If so, what happened: were you satisfied with the process and outcome? If not, why not?

Exam alert

A substantial and specific question was set on grievance in December 1999, asking you to outline a grievance procedure and to describe stages in the grievance interview. Don't be tempted to dismiss any area of the syllabus, however small a part it may play in your current experience, as irrelevant to this paper.

5.6 The Student Accountant article offered a handy mnemonic for the dangers – or potential problems – of allowing grievances to go unresolved.

Divulge sensitive information to competitors and external business associates/destroy company records/damage company properties

Instigate fellow workers to engage in undesirable activities

Spread damaging and/or false rumours against the company

Resort to inappropriate behaviour and/or unacceptable attitude

Use company assets for personal benefits

Purposely slow down business activities

Tamper with safety/security equipment

6 APPEALS PROCEDURES

6.1 The ACAS Code of Practice discussed in section 4.11 above) states that there should be a right of appeal by the employee against any disciplinary action and the written disciplinary and grievance procedures should specify the appeals procedure.

6.2 In many organisations, the appeals procedure is set out in the employment or staff handbook. There is no formal guidance as to the precise format the appeals procedure must take, but it could be something like this:

1.   Employee's manager decides there has been a breach of discipline and issues a formal written warning to be kept on the employee's file.

2.   Within a specified time (eg 14 days) the employee invokes in writing the organisation's appeals procedure. This might provide for the employee to appeal to the Board of Directors (or the head of the human resources department in a very large company).

3.   The Chairman of the Board appoints any two directors to hear the appeal.

4.   The employee may be allowed to be accompanied to the appeal by a friend or colleague to provide support. Such a person would not be expected to take an active part in proceedings.

5.   The nominated directors would hear the appeal as soon as possible and communicate their decision in writing to the employee within (say) seven days.

6.3   In a very large organisation, where an initial appeal is heard by the head of the human resource department, it may then be possible for a further appeal to be made against that person's decision.

Key learning points

- **Conflict** can be viewed as:

    ○   Inevitable owing to the class system
    ○   A continuation of organisation politics by other means
    ○   Something to be welcomed as it avoids complacency
    ○   Something resulting from poor management
    ○   Something which should be avoided at all costs

- Conflict is possible owing to the different degrees of **power**, **influence** and **authority** that different groups have. Negative power, for example, is the power to disrupt.

- Conflict can be **constructive**, if it introduced new information into a problem, if it denies a problem or if it encourages creativity. It can be destructive if it distracts attention from the task or inhibits communication.

- One constructive response to conflict is the **'win-win'** model.

- **Discipline** has the same end as **motivation** - ie to secure a range of desired behaviour from members of the organisation.

    ○   Motivation may even be called a kind of **self discipline** - because motivated individuals exercise choice to behave in the way that the organisation wishes.

    ○   Discipline however, is more often related to **negative motivation**, an appeal to the individual's need to avoid punishment, sanctions or unpleasantness.

- Progressive **discipline** includes the following **stages**.

    ○   Informal talk
    ○   Oral warning
    ○   Written/official warning
    ○   Lay-off or suspension
    ○   Dismissal

- **Grievance procedures** embody the employee's right to appeal against unfair or otherwise prejudicial conduct or conditions that affect him and his work.

- **Grievance interviews** follow: exploration, consideration, reply.

- *See the Part F mind map summary on page 286.*

Quick quiz

1   What are the features of the 'happy family view' of the organisation?

2   Give an alternative to the happy family view.

3   When can conflict be constructive?

4   What happens when two groups are put in competition with each other?

5   What are the possible outcomes of conflict, according to the 'win-win' model?

6   What causes conflict?

7   What is discipline?

8   What is progressive discipline?

9   What factors should a manager bear in mind in trying to control the disciplinary situation?

10   Outline typical grievance procedures, or the grievance procedures of your own firm.

Answers to quick quiz

1   Organisations are co-operative and harmonious. Conflict arises when something goes wrong.

2   Conflict is inevitable, being in the very nature of the organisation. Conflict can be constructive.

3   It can introduce solutions, define power relations, bring emotions, hostile or otherwise, out into the open.

4   They become more cohesive internally and more achievement-orientated.

5   Win-lose, lose-lose, win-win.

6   Different objectives, scarcity of responses, personal differences, interdependence of departments.

7   People behave according to the standard the organisation has set.

8   A system whereby the disciplinary action gets more severe with repeated 'offence'.

9   Immediacy, advance warning, consistency, impersonality, privacy.

10   Grievance procedures should state employees' rights, the procedures distinguish between individual and collective grievances state time limits. The interview should explore the facts, consider the issues and provide a resolution.

Answers to activities

Answer 14.1

The 'happy family' perspective rarely fits most organisations, even those pursuing a common ideological goal, like a political party. Such organisations regularly face conflict (eg the Conservatives' divisions over Europe), if only about **how** to attain their goals. Cynics argue that managers promote the 'happy family' view to suppress conflict. Asda at one time referred to all its staff as 'colleagues'.

Answer 14.2

Conflicts occur anywhere in an organisation. Individuals, groups, departments or subsidiaries compete for scarce (financial/human/physical) resources.

Answer 14.3

Sherif's work applies to conflict in organisations. To improve employee performance, win-lose conflict can be turned towards competitors, who become 'the enemy'.

Answer 14.4

(a) Both might need work done at the same time. Compromise and co-ordinated planning can help them manage their secretary's time.

(b) Differential pay might result in conflict with management - even an accusation of discrimination. There may be good reasons for the difference (eg length of service). To prevent conflict such information should be kept confidential. Where it is public, it should be seen to be **not arbitrary.**

(c) The electricians are worried about their jobs, and may take industrial action. Yet if the engineers' training is unrelated to the electricians' work, management can allay fears by giving information. The electricians cannot be given a veto over management decisions: a 'win-lose' situation is inevitable, but both sides can negotiate.

(d) The kitchen should plan its meals better - or people from both departments can be asked in advance whether they want puddings.

(e) Competition **between** sales regions is healthy as it increases sales. the conflict lies between sales regions and the production department. In the long-term, an increase in production capacity is the only solution. Where this is to possible, proper co-ordination methods should be instituted.

Answer 14.5

(a) (i) **Win-lose**: one team member gets the window desk, and the other does not. (Result: broken relationships within the team.)

   (ii) **Compromise**: the team members get the window desk on alternate days or weeks. (Result: half satisfied needs.)

   (iii) **Win-win**: what do they want the window desk for? One may want the view, the other better lighting conditions. This offers options to be explored: how else could the lighting be improved, so that both team members get what they really want? (Result: at least, the positive intention to respect everyone's wishes equally, with benefits for team communication and creative problem-solving.)

(b) (i) **Win-lose**: one of you gets the file and the other doesn't.

   (ii) **Compromise**: one of you gets the file now, and the other gets it later (although this has an element of win-lose, since the other has to work late or take it home).

   (iii) **Win-win**: you photocopy the file and **both** take it, or one of your consults his or her boss and gets an extension of the deadline (since getting the job done in time is the real aim - not just getting the file). These kind of solutions are more likely to emerge if the parties believe they **can** both get what they want.

(c) (i) **Win-lose**: Manager A gets the computers, and Manager B has to upgrade her systems.

   (ii) **Compromise**: Manager A will get some new computers, but keep the same old ones for continued data-sharing with Department B. Department B will also need to get some new computers, as a back-up measure.

   (iii) **Win-win**: what does Manager A want the computers for, or to avoid? Quite possibly, she needs to use up her budget allocation for buying equipment before the end of the budgetary period: if not, she fears she will lose that budget allocation. Now, that may not be the case, or there may be other equipment that could be more usefully purchased - in which case, there is no losing party.

Answer 14.7

Apart from the outline of the steps involved - which can be drawn from the chapter, this question raises an interesting point about the nature of different offences, and the flexibility required in the handling of complex disciplinary matters.

- There is clearly a difference in kind and scale between

   o unsatisfactory conduct (eg absenteeism)
   o misconduct (eg insulting behaviour, persistent absenteeism, insubordination) and
   o 'gross misconduct' (eg theft or assault).

- The attitude of the organisation towards the purpose of disciplinary action will to a large extent dictate the severity of the punishment.
  - If it is punitive it will 'fit the crime'.
  - If it is reformative, it may be a warning only, and less severe than the offence warrants.
  - If it is deterrent, it may be more severe than is warranted (ie to 'make an example').

The absenteeism question assumes that counselling etc. has failed, and that some sanction has to be applied, to preserve credibility. The theft technically deserves summary dismissal (as gross misconduct), but it depends on the scale and value of the theft, the attitude of the organisation to use of stationery for personal purposes (ie is it theft?) etc. Communicating the situations given might best be done as follows.

(a) Telephone, confirmed in writing (order form, letter)

(b) Noticeboard or general meeting

(c) Fact-to-face conversation. it would be a good idea to confirm the outcome of the meeting in writing so that records can be maintained.

(d) Either telephone or face-to-face.

PART F   MIND MAP SUMMARY

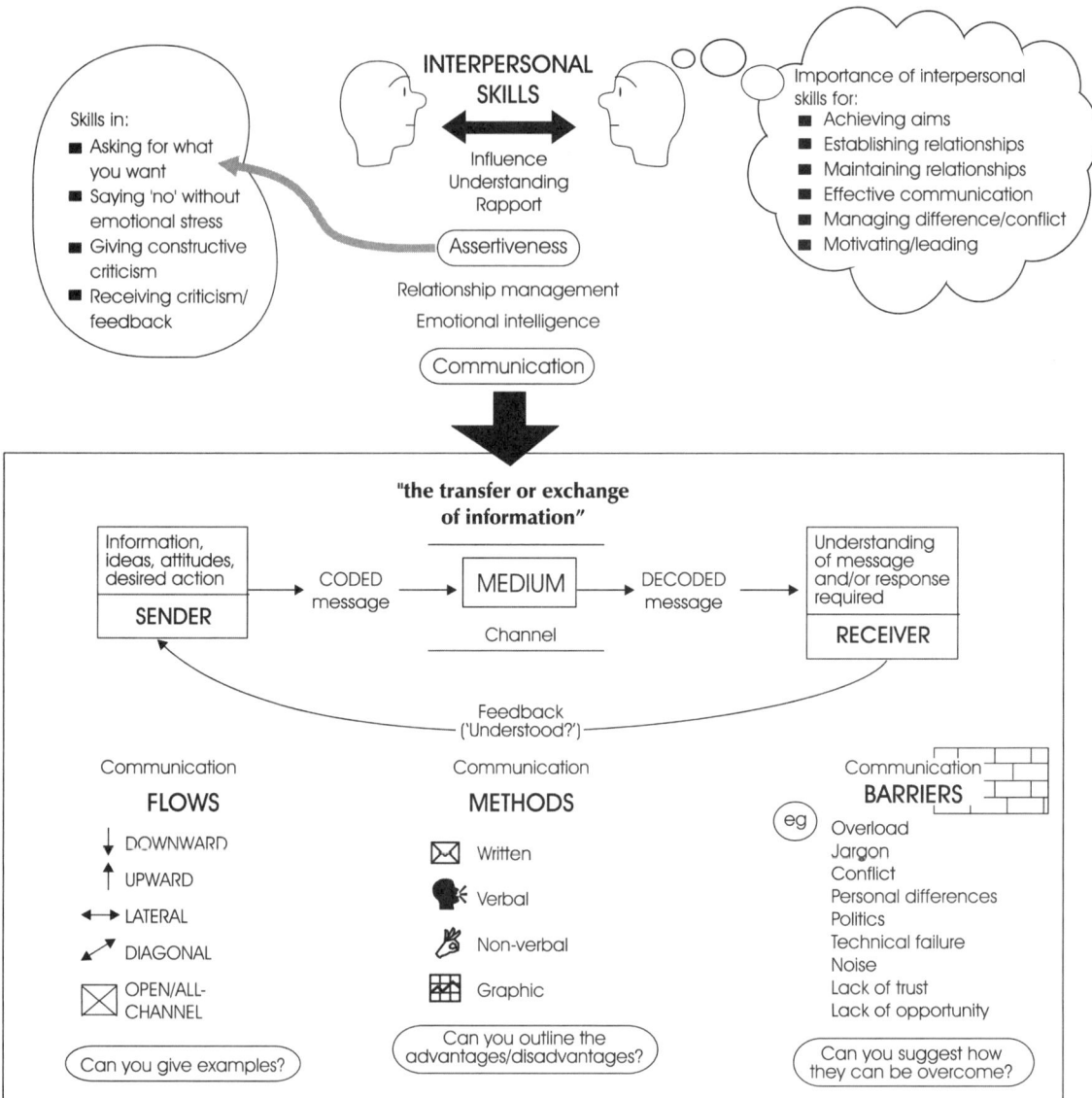

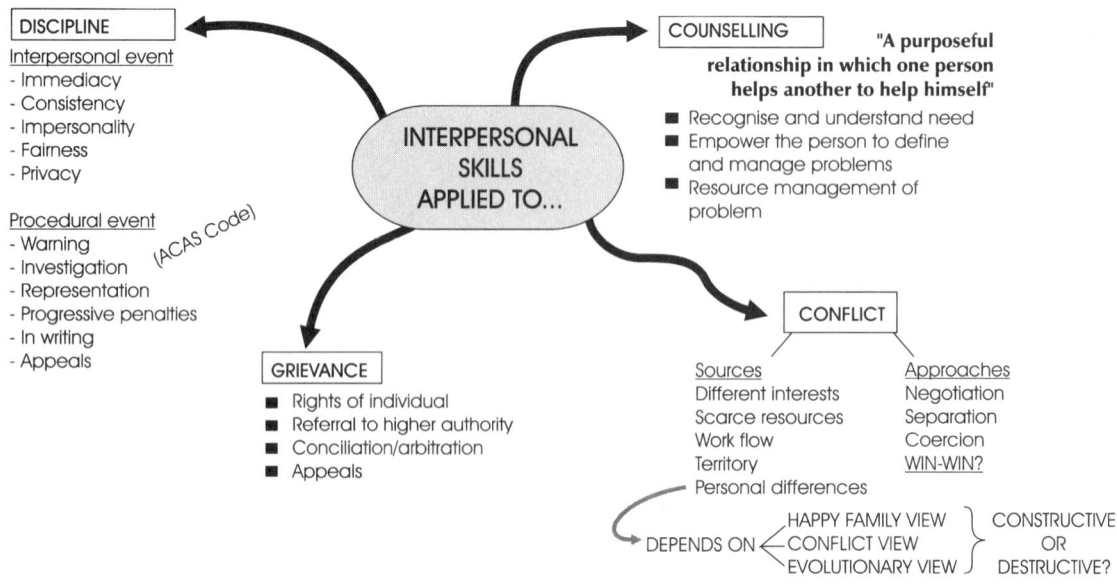

INTERPERSONAL SKILLS

Influence
Understanding
Rapport

Skills in:
- Asking for what you want
- Saying 'no' without emotional stress
- Giving constructive criticism
- Receiving criticism/feedback

Assertiveness

Importance of interpersonal skills for:
- Achieving aims
- Establishing relationships
- Maintaining relationships
- Effective communication
- Managing difference/conflict
- Motivating/leading

Relationship management
Emotional intelligence

Communication

"the transfer or exchange of information"

Information, ideas, attitudes, desired action	→ CODED message	→ MEDIUM	→ DECODED message	→ Understanding of message and/or response required
SENDER		Channel		RECEIVER

Feedback ('Understood?')

Communication
FLOWS
- ↓ DOWNWARD
- ↑ UPWARD
- ↔ LATERAL
- ↗ DIAGONAL
- ⊠ OPEN/ALL-CHANNEL

Can you give examples?

Communication
METHODS
- ✉ Written
- 🗣 Verbal
- ✋ Non-verbal
- ▦ Graphic

Can you outline the advantages/disadvantages?

Communication
BARRIERS
eg
- Overload
- Jargon
- Conflict
- Personal differences
- Politics
- Technical failure
- Noise
- Lack of trust
- Lack of opportunity

Can you suggest how they can be overcome?

DISCIPLINE

Interpersonal event
- Immediacy
- Consistency
- Impersonality
- Fairness
- Privacy

Procedural event   (ACAS Code)
- Warning
- Investigation
- Representation
- Progressive penalties
- In writing
- Appeals

INTERPERSONAL SKILLS APPLIED TO...

COUNSELLING   **"A purposeful relationship in which one person helps another to help himself"**
- Recognise and understand need
- Empower the person to define and manage problems
- Resource management of problem

GRIEVANCE
- Rights of individual
- Referral to higher authority
- Conciliation/arbitration
- Appeals

CONFLICT

Sources
Different interests
Scarce resources
Work flow
Territory
Personal differences

Approaches
Negotiation
Separation
Coercion
WIN-WIN?

DEPENDS ON ← HAPPY FAMILY VIEW / CONFLICT VIEW / EVOLUTIONARY VIEW → CONSTRUCTIVE OR DESTRUCTIVE?

Managing People

Essay Question Paper:	
Time allowed	**3 hours**
Answer FOUR questions	

Level C
Paper 6

DO NOT OPEN THIS PAPER UNTIL YOU ARE READY TO START
UNDER EXAMINATION CONDITIONS

Answer FOUR questions

1   The management board of your organisation has just released a report to shareholders which contains the following statement.

> 'Our continued downsizing programme was again successful, and this year saw the departure of a further 300 of our people on entirely voluntary redundancy terms. Since 1990, we have reduced the workforce by more than 1,800 (20%).'

At a recent meeting the managing director has said the organisation needs 'highly motivated people to ensure our customers get the best possible service'. You are a section leader in the accounts department of the organisation and have ten clerical and junior accounts staff reporting to you.

Required

Explain how you would ensure your staff remain highly motivated despite the continued presence of a staff reduction programme.   **(25 marks)**

2   You have attended recently a week long course to improve and develop your communication skills. Part of the course emphasised the importance of 'questioning and listening' as key skills for managers. You are about to conduct an appraisal interview with one of your staff.

Required

Suggest how the development of these skills will help you to more effectively carry out the appraisal interview.   **(25 marks)**

3   Your organisation is expanding its activities which requires the setting up of a number of regional distribution depots. Each depot will employ two bookkeeping staff to deal with local routine accounting matters. Depot accounting staff will report to the central accounts department at your head office. In the recent past your organisation has found it difficult to recruit good quality staff.

Required

Write a short report to the finance director suggesting how the key stages of the recruitment and selection process should be organised so as to ensure effective and efficient recruitment of the new staff.   **(25 marks)**

4   You have been placed in charge of a cross-functional project team. It comprises half a dozen members who are unknown to each other and to you. The team will not only have to work together co-operatively but also deliver high quality results.

Required

Using your concepts from team building and group behaviour outline how you would ensure the team welded together to become an effective unit.   **(25 marks)**

5   You have been asked by your manager to plan the training and development of your section for the next year.

Required

Draft a report outlining the following.

(a)   How you would identify the staff training and development needs.   (10 marks)

(b)   What methods you would choose to satisfy the training and development needs.

(5 marks)

(c)   The way in which you would evaluate whether the training and development has been effective.
(10 marks)

(25 marks)

Answer bank

WARNING! APPLYING THE ACCA MARKING SCHEME

If you decide to mark your paper using the ACCA marking scheme (reproduced at the end of each BPP suggested solution), you should bear in mind the following points.

1   Our answers are not definitive: we have applied our own interpretation of the marking scheme to our solutions to show how good answers should gain marks, but there may be more than one way to answer the question. You must try to judge fairly whether different points made in your answers are correct and relevant and therefore worth marks.

2   If you have a friend or colleague who is studying or has studied this paper, you might ask him or her to mark your paper for you, thus gaining a more objective assessment. Remember you and your friend are not trained or objective markers, so try to avoid complacency or pessimism if you appear to have done very well or very badly.

Before marking your exam, you should read the guidance given by the examiner to markers of this paper, which is reproduced below. This should aid your own marking process. It is most important that you analyse your solutions in detail and that you attempt to be as objective as possible.

ACCA note to marking scheme

The marking scheme is used as a guide only to markers in the context of the suggested answer. Given the practical nature of the paper, scope is given to markers to award marks for alternative approaches to a question, including relevant comment, and where well reasoned conclusions are provided.

---

1   MOTIVATION AND DOWNSIZING

> *Tutorial note.* This question describes a practical real-life situation, probably relevant to many companies, and many accounts sections. As a section leader, you cannot control the downsizing exercise, but you must consider its effect on your staff.

The context

Downsizing and staff reduction programmes are becoming increasingly common. They result from new technology, and increased pressures to improve financial performance in the light of a business environment characterised by change. Many employees feel 'insecure' - although these feelings may not be entirely related to the reality of the labour market.

Downsizing and motivation

The consequences of downsizing on motivation will vary depending on the *individual* and on the manner in which the downsizing programme is *implemented*. A section leader has no control over these two key variables.

Some people will welcome the prospect of voluntary redundancy and early retirement, and so for them downsizing will be relatively painless. Those not taking voluntary redundancy may see it as an opportunity - a clearing out of 'deadwood', with opportunities for more interesting work and promotion.

Many will feel unhappy about the downsizing. It might mean more work, and they might worry that they, themselves, will be affected eventually. Even so, the fact that redundancies are voluntary has helped matters.

Downsizing programmes can adversely affect motivation: people may ask why they should be committed to an organisation which is not committed to them? A number of theories of motivation can be used to help the supervisor maintain motivation. They indicate the variety of factors to be considered.

Motivation and different individuals

Different people might be motivated by different things or in different ways. For example, people have different goals at different stages in their life. The goals of a person fresh from college and new firm are likely to be very different to those of someone who has been there for some time

(a)   Maslow identified a hierarchy of needs. Each need is satisfied in turn; the needs are physiological, security, social esteem and self-actualisation.

(b)   Work and pay satisfies many of these needs, by providing the wherewithal for food and security needs. Work also satisfies social needs (for relationships) and esteem needs for praise and promotion.

   Maslow's model of motivation does not only apply to work, it can apply elsewhere and there are difficulties in this particular case in applying it. For example, downsizing means that people's security needs are not met.

   Herzberg suggested that in a work situation, needs could be analysed into two types of need.

(a)   The need to avoid unpleasantness are satisfied by 'hygiene' factors. They are essentially negative and will not inspire people to greater effort, but they can de-motivate if not dealt with. Pay and conditions of work are, according to Herzberg, hygiene factors.

(b)   The need for personal growth is satisfied by 'motivator' factors, which include interest in the job, praise, recognition, career advancement and the opportunity to learn.

   McLelland identified other needs (eg for achievement, power and for affiliation) which can also be used.

Applying motivation theories

Hygiene factors. The section leader cannot deal with most hygiene factors.

Pay and job security. For example, if the supervisor tried to reassure a member of staff that his/her job was safe this would, in most cases, be completely dishonest, as it is outside the section leader's power. A section leader with ten staff cannot decide to increase everybody's pay, as this also will be outside his/her power.

Motivator factors. The section leader in the case can deal with some of the motivator factors.

(a)   Choosing a suitable management and leadership style which relates to them.

(b)   Offer opportunities for job enrichment - members of staff can be delegated extra responsibility.

(c)   Job enrichment also encourages learning - any opportunities for learning the organisation provides should be grasped. The section leader can encourage staff to go on training courses.

(d)   Attend to the individual needs of team members. (According to Adair, the effective team leader attends to individual, group and task needs.) The manager can act as a coach.

(e)   Provide constructive feedback on how team members are performing, the appraisals.

(f)   To enhance the satisfaction of social needs, encourage an open and friendly atmosphere within the team (eg going out for a drink after work).

(g)   The supervisor can recommend promotion, but opportunities might be rare.

(h)   Give people recognition and praise.

(i)   Empower people to take control over what they might do.

Practical constraints on what the section leader can do

(a)   Maslow and Herzberg deal with people's needs, but expectancy theory suggests that motivation is more complex than merely satisfying needs. It involves a calculus: people weigh up the effort needed, the rewards available and the likelihood of getting the reward. In a firm that is perpetually downsizing, people might be worried about losing their jobs, and so work harder - but they might assume that nothing they do will make any difference. The supervisor may not be able to offer any 'rewards'.

(b)   The section leader is in charge of ten staff - but they are not insulated from the wider culture, structure and reward system of the organisation. The section leader only has limited influence.

ACCA official marking scheme

The question requires a practical approach with clear identification of 'how' a section leader might motivate his/her staff. Use of examples which provide evidence of knowledge and understanding is likely to strengthen answers. The relevant application of theory to a practical situation should be evident.

	Marks
Broad reference to issues in the operating environment	1-2
Comment on the effects of organisational downsizing on staff motivation	2-3
Making use of relevant motivation theory	1-2
Maslow's hierarchy	2-3
Herzberg's two-factor theory	1-2
Other relevant references	
Individual differences and the relevance for management and staff motivation	3-4
Motivation and hygiene factors	
Establishing a link between theory and the practical issues of staff motivation	1-2
Identification of the main influences on staff motivation	
Organisational culture/management style	2-3
Communication and feedback	2-3
Staff appraisal/performance review	1-3
Training and development	1-3
Coaching and mentoring	2-3
Promotion and career development	1-2
Pay, profit sharing, bonuses, etc	1-2
Outlining practical issues for management involved in staff motivation	3-4
Any other relevant points	1-2
	25 marks

2   COMMUNICATION SKILLS IN APPRAISAL INTERVIEWS

Tutorial note. The question appears to cover two areas of the syllabus: communication skills and appraisal, but it actually covers three topics: communication skills in general, questioning and listening skills in particular and their relationship to appraisal.

Communication skills in general

Communication skills are an essential part of the manager's or supervisor's repertoire:

(a) They ensure that information is transmitted throughout the organisation with a minimum of distortion and noise - in other words that the right message gets to the right person in time.

(b) They are part of day to day management. Mintzberg's list of management roles (informational, decisional, interpersonal) suggests many of the communication skills a manager needs. Even in the tasks of planning and co-ordinating, interpersonal skills are needed.

Types of communication employed by managers

Managers use both oral and written communications in different circumstances. Written communication maintains a record, and can be used to transmit information that would be too time consuming or inconvenient to read at one go.

Oral communication is used for an immediate response or request, and is less formal. Oral communication can be more private and informal and has the benefit of being interactive. Also, it is better at conveying information about feelings - there is a rich repertoire of body language which can be used.

Communication is an essential feature of interpersonal behaviour which involves relating to other people, often with an objective in mind. Successful interpersonal behaviour is based on acting and responding to how other people behave and what they say, being aware of one's own presence on the situation.

A model of communication suggests it is a two way process - sending a message and understanding the response via feedback. Listening skills are essential in the process of understanding the response and accepting feedback. Questioning skills are essential to elicit information.

Appraisal interviews

An interview is a discussion between two or more people with some end in mind. It is structured in that the interviewer and interviewee have different roles and expectations about the interview, related to their wider role in the organisation.

The appraisal system is part of the system of *performance management*. Appraisal is the review of the past performance of an individual with a view to improving it in future. In many organisations it is part of the vexed issue of salary and reward - this might be the result of the interview but the content of the interview is primarily about performance. Any serious discussion requires good questioning and listening skills on the part of both participants.

Appraisal is part of the control system of the organisation, by setting standards, monitoring performance and taking corrective action to see that people meet them.

The stages of appraisal interview

Preparation: decide what is going to be discussed. As mentioned above, it may deal with pay. If not, the interviewer may have to have answers ready as to why not. In some appraisal systems, both appraise and appraiser have to fill in forms - employing their skills of clear, concise written communication, in order to describe key challenges in the year and how both view the appraisee's performance.

Performance review. Appraisals are often one-off exercises, on an annual basis. A problem with them is managers rarely look at performance over the whole year. The appraisal interview should take the whole year into account - the manager should have kept records if necessary to gather the right information, to ensure objectivity.

Form-filling

At the interview

Unlike a recruitment interview, the appraiser is not so much seeking to ask questions to gain factual information - he/she should after all be aware of the key issues in the performance.

However, the interviewer may wish to delve deeper as the appraisee may have reasons for particular performance issues. Some cite a 70/30 rule, where at any interview, the interviewee should be speaking for 70% of the time. Whether this is relevant to appraisal depends on the type of appraisal interview chosen. If it follows the 'tell and listen' style where the appraiser simply gives comments then the appraisee will say little. In a discussion you might expect a more equal balance - after all the purpose is to give and respond to feedback.

When information is required, two types of questions might be used.

Open questions ('What do you think went well during the year) allow the appraisee to discuss his or her triumphs, and can be elaborated on, prompting further questions. *Closed questions* require a definite response (eg 'Do you intend to finish your CAT studies in the next six months?')

In fact both appraiser and appraisee can use open questions, given that the appraisal can be a wide ranging discussion of various performance issues.

Appraiser and appraisee have different levels of power in the interview, even though many try to pretend otherwise, and there are appraisal systems such as upwards appraisal and 360 degrees appraisal in which this applies differently.

The appraiser is trying to concentrate on performance, not on personality, and so a relaxed and open atmosphere will encourage open and honest communication between both sides. The appraiser must also be aware of his/her tendency to bias and stereotype. the interview must be succeeded by *follow-up action.*

Clear communication skills are needed because:

- People can read different meanings into a message

- The interview will have to be summed up and signed by both parties

- Both parties will have to agree on various performance issues and objectives for the future. Listening skills - on both participants in the interview - are essential in this context.

ACCA official marking scheme

Good answers will make a link between questioning and listening skills and the part they play in conducting a successful appraisal interview A sound knowledge and understanding of the communication process and its importance to the management's supervisory role is expected. Generally, answers will indicate a satisfactory knowledge of the process of appraisal and, specifically, the value of the appraisal interview in the process.

	Marks
Importance of communication skills	2-3
Methods of communication	
Formal/informal	1-2
Verbal and written	1-2
Link with motivation and feedback	2-3
Purpose of appraisal process	2-3
Importance of the appraisal interview	2-3
The part listening and questioning skills play	2-3
Key stages in the appraisal interview	
Preparation	2-3
Information gathering	1-2
Structure	1-2
Interviewing skills	
The importance of questioning and listening	
Establish rapport/relaxed atmosphere	1-2
70/30 rule	1-2
Use of closed/open questions	2-3
Avoiding stereotyping	1-2
Avoid subjectivity/emotional responses	1-2
Review/action plan/future review	1-2
Any other points	2-3
	25 marks

---

3 RECRUITMENT AND SELECTION PROCESS

Tutorial note. This question asked specifically for report formal -testing your skills of written communication. Otherwise the question tests your basic knowledge of recruitment and selection.

To: Finance director

From: Accounting Technician

Date: 31 March 1998

Re: Recruitment and selection procedures

1 Introduction

(a) Recruitment and selection involves determining the needs of the company for people, identifying the work that needs to be done and the types of jobs to be created to do the work, developing job descriptions, advertising the post, selecting candidates and via interviews and tests supplemented by references, choosing the new staff.

(b) Effective recruitment is necessary so that the organisation has the right level of skills. It may be the case that recruitment from outside the organisation is not necessary if there are members of staff internally available.

(c) The aim of recruitment should be to attract people to work for the firm, and so remuneration policies have to be designed accordingly. This is outside the scope of the process of recruitment and selection process as such but will be relevant.

(d) People involved include the human resources department, responsible for advertising and much of the initial selection work, as part of their wider role of developing the human resources of the organisation. Line managers are also responsible for some interviewing although earlier on, they will be responsible for job requisition.

2   The business plan

The need for new recruits has already been identified in the business plan, hence the need for accounts staff in depots. The problems in the past have perhaps been in *implementing* the recruitment process.

3   Job analysis

Most recruitment processes start with *job analysis*. This is an exercise indicating the type of work required in any particular job. For bookkeeping, the job analysis will reveal the level of skill required (eg taking the bookkeeping to trial balance; use of software packages).

4   Job description

From the job analysis, the next step is to draw up the *job description*. A job description contains the key tasks of the job, and details about the job holder's role in the organisation, and the person to whom the job holder is reporting. The nature of the routine accounting matters dealt with will be specified, and the people to whom the recruits must report.

5   Person specification

The person specification translates the needs outline in the job description into a specification of the type of person who swill be a suitable recruit for the position. For example, the bookkeepers may need to have a certain degree of experience already - unless the firm intends to train its staff from scratch. The person specification determines the desired attributes of new staff needed. The firm therefore has a good idea of the sort of 'quality' of staff needed.

6   Job advertisement

Advertising the job involves two distinct processes.

(a) *Researching the local labour markets* to find the most appropriate 'catchment area' of new recruits and finding out the right channels to reach them. The firm may choose to advertise directly although it could go through local recruitment consultancies or job centres.

(b) *Designing an advertisement* that will attract such recruits. The advertisement will give the broad outlines of the job, other details of the post (such as pay) and perhaps a description of the organisation. The advertisement, reach the right people, must find the right media.

7   Application forms and CVs

Those replying to the ad may be sent a standard application form, or they may simply be asked to provide a CV. Whichever method is used, the firm wants details of the candidate's qualification, employment history, experiences and other relevant skills and aspirations.

Application forms can be reviewed, and it should be a relatively easy matter to draw up a shortlist of those suitable. Application forms can be scored (using bio-data techniques) if a scientific approach is needed.

8   Selection tests

Selection tests can be used to gain more information about the candidates. In this case, the whole gamut of personality and psychometric testing will not be cost effective but some type of aptitude or competence testing, if only to confirm the application forms, may be helpful. Selection tests are probably the most reliable predictor of ultimate success in the job.

Assessment centres involve a variety of tests with general interviewees.

9   **Interviews**

(a)   The selection tests should have narrowed the list of desirable candidates, and the remainder will be interviewed, after which the final shortlist will be made. The interview should be designed to get information about the candidate. Candidates may have to go to two or more interviews, one with a member of the human resources department and one perhaps with the financial controller or the person to whom they will report.

(b)   In practice, many firms interview first and then apply selection tests later.

10   **The job offer and references**

The desired candidate is offered a job, and is asked to respond within a specific deadline. This job is always subject to obtaining references, to check out the candidate's employment history.

11   **Evaluation**

The recruitment and selection process should ensure that the firm attracts the right sort of applicants, but key issues of salary, for example, have to be taken into account. If the process is done systematically, with attention to the most appropriate source of recruits, and with the right procedures, the firm should attract candidates of the right quality. However, reliance on interviews alone will probably not predict good performers.

ACCA official marking scheme

The main focus of the answer should be to analyse the recruitment and selection process and to suggest ways in which it might be more effective. Reference to the scenario of the question is expected. Knowledge of the key stages of recruitment and selection will be evident with critical comment and relevant suggestions on how to improve each stage of the process should be made.

	Marks
Overview of the recruitment and selection process	1-2
Need for effective research and development	2-3
Identification of those involved in the process and responsibilities	2-3
Key stages explained	
Job analysis	2-3
Job description	1-2
Person specification	1-2
Recruitment sources	1-2
Application forms	1-2
Use of references	1-2
Methods of selection	
Assessment centres	2-3
The use of tests	1-2
The selection interview	
Value of the selection interview	1-2
The process of information gathering	1-2
Skills of interviewing	2-3
Those involved and why	1-2
Evaluating the process	
Justifying the process of evaluation	2-3
Possible methods of evaluation	1-2
Any other relevant points	1-2
	25 marks

4   CROSS FUNCTIONAL PROJECT TEAM

> *Tutorial note.* A practical situation - but you are specifically asked to use 'concepts' and 'theory' in your answer. Key issues are that the team members do not know each other personally, and that they work in different disciplines in the organisation.

Cross-functional project teams

Team working has become more prevalent, partly because organisations are supposed to be more flexible, and partly because teams are an effective medium of empowerment.

Whilst team working can satisfy people's *social* needs for companionship, organisations are adopting team based structures because they produce *effective work results*.

Cross functional teams contain members from different departments in the business. For example, a cross-functional team in charge of implementing a new sales order processing system should ideally contain team members from the sales function, the finance function, and any specialist IT employees.

Effective teams

A group is a collection of people who perceive themselves to be a group, and who can distinguish between members and outsiders. Groups can be formal or informal. A *team* is a special type of group. A team is formed of people who have to pursue a particular objective (eg install a new IT system, win the cup final). It thus has a purpose. This purpose is, for teams working within organisations, imposed from the outside, as is the case in this question.

Other differences between teams and groups relate to the following.

- The interpersonal relationships - in an effective team, people can be open about work issues and trusting of the others within the team

- People have to learn explicitly how to work as a team. Issues related to the processes of the team have to be worked out overtly rather than covertly.

- Finally teams are formed not in practice to satisfy social needs, although team member satisfaction is an important outcome of teamwork, but to get a task completed. A focus on the task is a characteristic of teams.

Team members

A feature of effective teams is that people can play a number of roles in the dynamics of the team. Belbin identified nine roles.

- Co-ordinator
- Shaper
- Plant
- Monitor/evaluator
- Resource investigator

- Implementer
- Finisher
- Team worker
  and, from outside, the specialist

According to Belbin, most people have preference for one of these roles, but team members may find they have to play a different role, to maintain a balance between the roles. In the situation described, this issue is complicated by the fact that the team is a cross-functional project team drawn from different departments. So the roles they play may be determined by their expertise at any one time. For example, the accountant in a cross functional project team might have the job of ensuring the project keeps within financial targets, more of a monitor-evaluator role than say a finisher.

Team development

According to Tuckman, teams are formed in four stages

Forming. This is when the members of the team are brought together, and the purpose and identity of the team are first defined. The cross functional project team in the question is in this stage of team development. People are still individuals and the prime allegiance of members of the cross functional project team are likely to be the individual department.

Storming involves open conflict, perhaps against the decisions reached in the forming stage. At the forming stage people toe the line, but at the storming stage they begin to assert themselves individually. This stage has the advantage of bringing key issues into the open. However, some teams may get stuck in this stage, and so the successful team builder has to resolve the issues raised.

Norming. The team settles down and establishes a procedures for getting the task done. Decisions are hopefully reached by consensus. In this stage, people might adopt one or more of the roles identified by Belbin.

Performing. The team gets on with the job it is brought together to do.

Building the team

The manager will want to speed up the process of team development to the performing stage - after all time is a scarce resource, and organisations cannot indulge the team too much.

Leadership. The *leader* of a team must, to be successful, give appropriate attention to the needs of the task, the needs of the team and the needs of the individuals.

Team building involves:

- Building team identity: the team can be given a defined name or role in the confines of the organisation

- Encouraging group loyalty/solidarity, by encouraging interpersonal relationships, controlling conflict and expressing solidarity. The team leader has to build support and trust

- Encouraging commitment to shared objectives. This can be achieved by clearly setting out the team's objectives, involving the team in target setting, giving regular clear feedback, giving positive reinforcement and championing the team within the organisation.

These team building methods must be used against time-wasting blockages to building the team. These blockages include confusion as to roles, excessive competition between group members who are unwilling to share anything.

Action plan

The team leader of the project under consideration should set up an action plan for building the team. The aim of the plan is to get the *forming, storming and norming stages over in two meetings*, and also to build the team identity and its commitment to the objective.

(a)   Clearly identify the task (eg install a new computer system).

(b)   Define membership and get the agreement of the participants (and their bosses)

(c)   Get resources for the team - eg an office, where necessary, admin backup

(d)   At the first team meeting:

   (i)   Get the agreement of team members on a timetable for the project (eg the sales system will be set up within six months). This should be realistic - nothing will be gained by underplaying the work involved, and expectations should not be too high.

   (ii)   Explain to them the importance of the project, what the firm expects, and why they have been chosen: this is a key opportunity to build team identity.

   (iii)   Have a brainstorming or 'get-to-know you' session, perhaps to get early difficulties out of the way (eg sales personnel may not appreciate the cost implications of the project; accounts staff may not appreciate the need for the system to assist the sales unction as well as generate management accounts).

   (iv)   Team members should leave the meeting with a task (eg ask them to come up with various ideas).

(e)   Second team meeting

   (i)   Define and agree objectives in order to achieve the objectives of the team.

   (ii)   Define methodology - what approaches should be taken

   (iii)   Agree how the project will be monitored

(f)   Subsequent meetings should deal with the actual work of the team.

ACCA official marking scheme

The answer should be based on a sound knowledge of the basis for team building with reference to relevant concepts. These concept should provide a sound framework for the practical nature of the question. Demonstration of a systematic approach to an action plan for practical team building is called for and reflected in the marking scheme.

	Marks
Broad references to the increased awareness of the current need for team building initiatives linked to changes in organisational structures	2-3
Identification of the need to relate team building to required outcomes	1-2
Effective task achievement	
Team member satisfaction	
Differentiation between groups and teams	2-3
List of differences	
Greater demands of team building in terms of time and effort	
Features of effective teamwork - drawn from following list	4-5
Balance of roles and skills, honesty and openness, mistakes openly faced, helpful competition support and trust, good relations, pride in success high level of task achievement	
Impact of *Belbin's* team roles on effectiveness	
	2-3
Identification of the roles	1-2
Need for balance in roles	
Identification of how stage of team development affects practical team building	2-3
Tuckman's stages indicated	
Forming, storming, norming, performing	
Importance of norming stage	
Blockages to, and building blocks for, team building, drawing on *Woodcock* list	4-5
How the awareness of problems in these areas can waste time and money and lower morale	
Factors to be aware of in practical approach a plan	4-5
Including clear aims start modestly, relate to work of organisation, realistic Timetables consult openly, do not raise false expectations	
Need for action plan and indication of major stages of such a plan	3-4
	25 marks

5 TRAINING AND DEVELOPMENT PLAN

> *Tutorial note.* Although this report covers training, it also examines your skills at written communication - it has to be in report format.

To: Manager

From: Technician

Date: 4/11/19X8

Re: Training

1 Role of training

(a) Training develops the attitudes, skills and knowledge and individual is required to have in order to do a job properly. Training will enable the section (and the organisation) to develop the skills needed to do the job, to enhance organisational learning and to respond flexibility to the demands of the organisation and its environment. The training plan is part of the wider human resources plan, covering the entire range of the organisation's skills and management needs.

(b) Training is important for individuals in the section. It maintains their 'employability' in an environment where new technologies are being adopted. It also provides an avenue for promotion and can enhance interest in the job.

2 Identifying training and development needs

(a) Training needs can be identified from two different perspectives: from the perspective of the organisation as a whole, and from the perspective of the individual trainee.

(b) Training needs from the organisation's perspective can be identified, ultimately, from the *business plan* and strategy. This determines what the organisation intends to do, what products and services it chooses to offer to the customer and so on. The implications of this for the organisation's skills bases are implemented in the human resources plan: this outlines recruitment and training issues.

(c) Training needs analysis forms part of the process of human resource planning. Clearly, if the organisation has certain expectations of the section, the training needs can be identified from this. For example, if the section is to be required to provide new types of management information, then training will be needed so that people know what they have to do, and whether they need any new skills.

(d) From the individual's perspective, training needs analysis can be identified as follows:

    (i) From the individual's performance in the job, as observed in the normal course of events by the manager of the employee.

    (ii) From the *appraisal system*. The annual review encourages section leaders and team members to review their performance with a view to improving it, and to set objectives for the forthcoming period. Training may thus be remedial (to bring performance up to standard) or forward looking (with the future in mind).

3 Training methods

A variety of training methods can be used. They needs not be used in isolation, and the individual's training programme may contain a mix of training methods.

(a) *On the job training* is provided at the work place. The trainee is given real work to do, as instructed by a supervisor or colleague. The trainee's progress is monitored until the trainee becomes proficient in the task. Effectively, the trainee is *coached* in the job.

(b) *Mentoring* is less related to detailed training issues than overall development. A mentor is not the trainee's boss, but someone else in the organisation who can give advice.

(c) The firm can run its own *internal courses*, on subjects specific to the needs of the firm. Induction training is often run internally. A number of *external training options* exist as well.

    (i) Trainees can do distance learning courses .These are suitable for studying for professional qualifications. Candidates study in their own time, and sit exams set by a college or course provider (such as BPP).

    (ii) Some training courses require study leave. Again, these are often used for professional qualifications. The firm may well support those employees who choose this particular route.

(d) In practice these can be combined in a development programme. Many firms are adopting NVQs (National Vocational Qualifications) at various levels. These combined work-based skills assessment and experience with underpinning knowledge and understanding.

4 Evaluating training

Training is often an expensive exercise, but successful training can be a key element in the success of a firm's human resources strategy. As in any use of resources its success must be evaluated.

(a) *Improved performance of the individual.* This is the ultimate test of a success of a training programme, and will be assessed by line managers. Many courses, however, take place too early in the trainee's job and the trainee must be given the opportunity to exercise those skills.

(b) *Improved performance of the section.* The value of training will be seen in the improved performance of the section. For example, a sales section might be given training in dealing with customers over the telephone.

(c) *Tests.* Trainees can be given tests to see if the training has in fact worked.

(d) *End of course questionnaires.* Trainees can be asked what they feel about the course. The problem with this approach is that the feedback comes too soon. It covers the delivery of the training, but the how useful the training is in real life. Of course, trainees can respond later to other questionnaires.

(e) Finally, training should satisfy the development needs of individuals and the organisation. If the firm has to recruit outside for key skills, this might indicate that the training is not of the right type or quality.

ACCA official marking scheme

The answer should be based o the systematic approach to training and development. Answers should reflect a managerial/section leader responsibility

		Marks
Training and development		
importance to organisation and individual		2-3
management responsibility		2-3
(a)	*Training needs analysis*	
	Part it plays in the process	1-2
	The usefulness of process	1-2
	Link to business plan	1-2
	Review of past performance	1-2
	Appraisal interview	1-2
	Observation	1-2
		(10 marks)
(b)	*Methods*	
	Internal v external	2-3
	Distance learning	1-2
	Computer based training	1-2
	Mentoring and coaching	1-2
		(10 marks)
(c)	*Evaluation*	
	Importance of evaluation	2-3
	Questionnaires	2-3
	Testing	1-2
	Job performance levels	1-2
	Career development	1-2
	Business/section results	1-2
Any other relevant points		2-3
		(10 marks)
		25 marks

List of
key terms
and index

BPP
PUBLISHING

BPP PUBLISHING

See overleaf for information on other
BPP products and how to order

CAT Order

To BPP Publishing Ltd, Aldine Place, London W12 8AA
Tel: 020 8740 2211. Fax: 020 8740 1184
email: publishing@bpp.com
online: www.bpp.com

Mr/Mrs/Ms (Full name) _____
Daytime delivery address _____

Postcode _____
Daytime Tel _____
Email _____ Date of exam (month/year) _____

	6/02 Texts	1/02 Kits	i-Learn CD	i-Pass CD	i-Learn Workbook	Virtual Campus enrolment
LEVEL A						
Paper A1 Transaction Accounting	£16.95 ☐		£29.95 ☐		£9.95 ☐	£80 ☐
Paper A2 Office Practice and Procedure	£16.95 ☐	£8.95 ☐	£29.95 ☐	£19.95 ☐	£9.95 ☐	£80 ☐
LEVEL B						
Paper B1 Maintaining Financial Records and Accounts (UK)	£16.95 ☐	£8.95 ☐	£30.95 ☐	£19.95 ☐	£9.95 ☐	£80 ☐
(International)	£16.95 ☐	£8.95 ☐				
Paper B2 Cost Accounting Systems	£16.95 ☐	£8.95 ☐	£30.95 ☐	£19.95 ☐	£9.95 ☐	£80 ☐
Paper B3 Information Technology Processes	£16.95 ☐	£8.95 ☐	£30.95 ☐	£19.95 ☐	£9.95 ☐	£80 ☐
LEVEL C						
Paper C1 Drafting Financial Statements (Industry and Commerce) (UK)	£16.95 ☐	£8.95 ☐	£30.95 ☐	£21.95 ☐	£9.95 ☐	£80 ☐
(International)	£16.95 ☐	£8.95 ☐				
Paper C2 Information for Management	£16.95 ☐	£8.95 ☐	£30.95 ☐	£21.95 ☐	£9.95 ☐	£80 ☐
Paper C3 Auditing Practice and Procedure (UK)	£16.95 ☐	£8.95 ☐	£30.95 ☐	£21.95 ☐	£9.95 ☐	£80 ☐
(International)	£16.95 ☐	£8.95 ☐				
Paper C4 Preparing Taxation Computations and Returns FA2002 (10/02 Text)	£16.95 ☐	£8.95 ☐				
Paper C5 Managing Finances	£16.95 ☐	£8.95 ☐	£30.95 ☐	£21.95 ☐	£9.95 ☐	£80 ☐
Paper C6 Managing People	£16.95 ☐	£8.95 ☐	£30.95 ☐	£21.95 ☐	£9.95 ☐	£80 ☐

SUBTOTAL £ _____

Register via our website, and pay on-line
www.bpp.com/virtualcampus/cat

POSTAGE & PACKING

Study Texts and Workbooks

	First	Each extra	
UK	£3.00	£2.00	£ ___
Europe*	£5.00	£4.00	£ ___
Rest of world	£20.00	£10.00	£ ___

Kits

	First	Each extra	
UK	£2.00	£1.00	£ ___
Europe*	£2.50	£1.00	£ ___
Rest of world	£15.00	£8.00	£ ___

CDs

	First	Each extra	
UK	£2.00	£2.00	£ ___
Europe*	£2.00	£2.00	£ ___
Rest of world	£20.00	£10.00	£ ___

Grand Total (Cheques to *BPP Publishing*) I enclose a cheque for (incl. Postage) £ ☐

Or charge to Access/Visa/Switch

Card Number ☐☐☐☐☐☐☐☐☐☐☐☐☐☐

Expiry date _____ Start Date _____

Issue Number (Switch Only) ☐☐☐

Signature _____

We aim to deliver to all UK addresses inside 5 working days; a signature will be required. Orders to all EU addresses should be delivered within 6 working days. All other orders to overseas addresses should be delivered within 10 working days. * Europe includes the Republic of Ireland and the Channel Islands.

REVIEW FORM & FREE PRIZE DRAW

All original review forms from the entire BPP range, completed with genuine comments, will be entered into one of two draws on 31 January 2003 and 31 July 2003. The names on the first four forms picked out on each occasion will be sent a cheque for £50.

Name: _____   Address: _____

_____

Date:_____   _____

How have you used this Interactive Text?
(Tick one box only)

☐ Home study (book only)

☐ On a course: college _____

☐ With 'correspondence' package

☐ Other _____

Why did you decide to purchase this Interactive Text? *(Tick one box only)*

☐ Have used complementary Practice & Revision Kit

☐ Have used BPP Texts in the past

☐ Recommendation by friend/colleague

☐ Recommendation by a lecturer at college

☐ Saw advertising

☐ Other _____

During the past six months do you recall seeing/receiving any of the following?
(Tick as many boxes as are relevant)

☐ Our advertisement in *ACCA Student Accountant*

☐ Other advertisement _____

☐ Our brochure with a letter through the post

Which (if any) aspects of our advertising do you find useful?
(Tick as many boxes as are relevant)

☐ Prices and publication dates of new editions

☐ Information on Interactive Text content

☐ Facility to order books off-the-page

☐ None of the above

Your ratings, comments and suggestions would be appreciated on the following areas

	Very useful	Useful	Not useful
Introductory section (How to use this Interactive Text)	☐	☐	☐
Chapter learning objectives	☐	☐	☐
Key terms	☐	☐	☐
Examples	☐	☐	☐
Activities and answers	☐	☐	☐
Key learning points	☐	☐	☐
Exam alerts	☐	☐	☐
List of key terms and index	☐	☐	☐
Structure & presentation	☐	☐	☐
Icons	☐	☐	☐

	Excellent	Good	Adequate	Poor
Overall opinion of this Interactive Text	☐	☐	☐	☐

Do you intend to continue using BPP Interactive Texts/Kits?   ☐ Yes ☐ No

Please note any further comments and suggestions/errors on the reverse of this page.

Please return to: Lynn Watkins, BPP Publishing Ltd, FREEPOST, London, W12 8BR

REVIEW FORM & FREE PRIZE DRAW (continued)

Please note any further comments and suggestions/errors below

FREE PRIZE DRAW RULES

1   Closing date for 31 January 2003 draw is 31 December 2002. Closing date for 31 July 2003 draw is 30 June 2003.

2   Restricted to entries with UK and Eire addresses only. BPP employees, their families and business associates are excluded.

3   No purchase necessary. Entry forms are available upon request from BPP Publishing. No more than one entry per title, per person. Draw restricted to persons aged 16 and over.

4   Winners will be notified by post and receive their cheques not later than 6 weeks after the relevant draw date. Lists of winners will be published in BPP's *focus* newsletter following the relevant draw.

5   The decision of the promoter in all matters is final and binding. No correspondence will be entered into.